Knowledge and Entrepreneurship in Public Policy

Economy, Polity, and Society

Series Editors: Virgil Storr and Jayme Lemke, Mercatus Center

The foundations of political economy—from Adam Smith to the Austrian school of economics, to contemporary research in public choice and institutional analysis—are sturdy and well established, but far from calcified. On the contrary, the boundaries of the research built on this foundation are ever expanding. One approach to political economy that has gained considerable traction in recent years combines the insights and methods of three distinct but related subfields within economics and political science: the Austrian, Virginia and Bloomington schools of political economy. The vision of this book series is to capitalize on the intellectual gains from the interactions between these approaches in order to both feed the growing interest in this approach and advance social scientists' understanding of economy, polity, and society.

This series seeks to publish works that combine the Austrian school's insights on knowledge, the Virginia school's insights into incentives in non-market contexts, and the Bloomington school's multiple methods, real-world approach to institutional design as a powerful tool for understanding social behaviour in a diversity of contexts.

Titles in the series

Toward a Hayekian Theory of Social Change, edited by Peter J. Boettke, Erwin Dekker, and Chad Van Schoelandt

Knowledge and Entrepreneurship in Public Policy, edited by Christopher J. Coyne, Abigail R. Hall, and Eileen Norcross

Social Coordination and Public Policy: Explorations in Theory and Practice, edited by Roberta Herzberg, Gavin Roberts, and Brianne Wolf

Market Process and Market Order: From Human Action, But Not of Human Design, edited by Rosolino A. Candela, Kristen R. Collins, and Christopher J. Coyne

Institutions and Incentives in Public Policy: An Analytical Assessment of Non-Market Decision-Making, edited by Rosolino Candela, Rosemarie Fike, and Roberta Herzberg

Economics and the Public Good: The End of Desire in Aristotle's Politics and Ethics, by John Antonio Pascarella

Culture, Sociality, and Morality: New Applications of Mainline Political Economy, edited by Paul Dragos Aligica, Ginny Seung Choi, And Virgil Henry Storr

Nudging Public Policy: Examining the Benefits and Limitations of Paternalistic Public Policies, edited by Rosemarie Fike, Stefanie Haeffele, And Arielle John

Informing Public Policy: Analyzing Contemporary Us and International Policy Issues through the Lens of Market Process Economics, edited by Stefanie Haeffele, Abigail R. Hall, and Adam Millsap

Exploring the Political Economy and Social Philosophy of Vincent and Elinor Ostrom, edited by Peter J. Boettke, Bobbi Herzberg, and Brian Kogelmann

Knowledge and Entrepreneurship in Public Policy

Edited by
Christopher J. Coyne, Abigail R. Hall, and
Eileen Norcross

LEXINGTON BOOKS
Lanham • Boulder • New York • London

Published by Lexington Books
An imprint of The Rowman & Littlefield Publishing Group, Inc.
4501 Forbes Boulevard, Suite 200, Lanham, Maryland 20706
www.rowman.com

86-90 Paul Street, London EC2A 4NE

British Library Cataloguing in Publication Information Available

Library of Congress Cataloging-in-Publication Data

Names: Coyne, Christopher J., editor. | Hall, Abigail R., editor. | Norcross, Eileen, editor.
Title: Knowledge and entrepreneurship in public policy / edited by Christopher J. Coyne, Abigail R. Hall, and Eileen Norcross.
Description: Lanham : Lexington Books, [2024] | Series: Economy, polity, and society | Includes bibliographical references and index. | Summary: "The chapters in this volume analyze the interplay between knowledge, public policy, and entrepreneurship in both theory and practice. In particular, they examine how policymakers often struggle with limited economic knowledge, which hinders their ability to intervene in the market process to achieve their desired ends" —Provided by publisher.
Identifiers: LCCN 2023038982 (print) | LCCN 2023038983 (ebook) | ISBN 9781666934137 (cloth) | ISBN 9781666934144 (epub)
Subjects: LCSH: Entrepreneurship—Government policy. | Knowledge Economy—Government policy.
Classification: LCC HB615 .K6248 2024 (print) | LCC HB615 (ebook) | DDC 658.4/21—dc23/eng/20231031
LC record available at https://lccn.loc.gov/2023038982
LC ebook record available at https://lccn.loc.gov/2023038983

Contents

List of Figures and Tables

FIGURES

TABLES

Introduction

Christopher J. Coyne, Abigail R. Hall, and Eileen Norcross

What is the relationship between knowledge, entrepreneurship, and public policy? To begin to answer this question we need to clarify how these concepts fit together. Entrepreneurship is an omnipresent part of human action—innate to human creativity. It is evident throughout history and across cultural and geographic borders. Matt Ridley (2020, 12) notes that "By the middle of the [twenty-first] century the human race will have expanded in ten thousand years from less than ten million to nearly ten billion people." Despite this significant population growth, "the vast majority of people are much better fed, much better sheltered, much better entertained, much better protected against disease and much more likely to live to old age than their ancestors have ever been" (Ridley 2020, 12). The reason is human creativity and innovation as manifested through entrepreneurship.

The view of entrepreneurship as reflecting the human drive to create, to act rationally, with purpose and insight is a major contribution of the Austrian school of economics. Ludwig von Mises (1949), Friedrich Hayek (1948), and Israel Kirzner (1973; 1979; 1992) deepened and enriched an overly rigid neoclassical concept of economic activity, grounded in a "mechanical and passive" act of optimization in the service of profits to a dynamic feature of the market process in which alert individuals transform dispersed knowledge—not known to anyone in full—to meet their goals and aims thereby bettering their condition and improving society (Boettke 2014). As Kirzner (1973, 35) noted, it is an appreciation of entrepreneurship "that is responsible for our understanding of human action as active, creative and human rather than as passive, automatic, and mechanical."

The knowledge needed for entrepreneurs to act is not mere data or scientific or technical know-how. It is tacit. "The idiosyncratic, dispersed bits of understanding of 'circumstances of time and place'" (Hayek 1948, 77) that are communicated in the form of relative prices and profit and loss. For that information to be unearthed, the rules or institutions that frame economic life must enable individuals to seek profit, allow for prices to adjust freely, and to let adjustments be made based on losses. The protection of private property and enforcement of contract under the rule of law are essential for market entrepreneurship and development to occur (Boettke and Coyne 2003). The extent to which entrepreneurship is beneficial, or even possible, is thus contingent on a web of institutions, or what Douglass North (1990; 2005) described as "the rules of the game," which include the cultural norms, constitutions, statutes, laws, and regulations that prevail in any given time and place. This complex and ever-changing ecology of rules includes a vast array of public policies: governmental spending and regulatory programs, the tax regime, and the economic and regulatory interventions, that are designed, enacted, and enforced by regulatory and legislative bodies. These policies may act as inducements or barriers thereby incentivizing or discouraging productive entrepreneurship (Boettke and Coyne 2009). This network of rules makes up an entangled political economy (Wagner 2016) of market, governmental and civil society in which individuals pursue their economic and social goals in private and public settings (Boettke and Storr 2002).

Entrepreneurship is not only a market phenomenon but occurs whenever social dilemmas are present, both in a free economy and in a free society—within administrative and public settings as well as in civil society, though it is of a different type (Aligica, 2018; Boettke 2018; Aligica, Boettke, and Tarko 2019). Entrepreneurship within the administrative state, or bureaucratic free enterprise (Mises 1944, Tullock 1965), is rational and purposive but operates on the fiscal commons absent the information contained in prices, profit, and loss. How to conceptualize and evaluate entrepreneurship in these settings presents a challenge for scholars to "find mechanisms that are functionally equivalent to the roles played by property, prices, and profit/loss within the market economy in order to come to an understanding of the self-regulating social order in realism outside the market context" (Boettke 2014, 245).

The work of Elinor Ostrom demonstrates that competition also occurs in public settings as citizens attempt to improve services based on tacit knowledge of local needs (Cole and McGinnis 2014; Tarko 2016; Aligica 2018). As such, public entrepreneurship is aimed at providing public goods and solving both collective action and common-pool resource problems. As with private sector entrepreneurship, the efficacy of public entrepreneurship is institutionally contingent. The rules must allow individuals the freedom to communicate, coordinate, and engage in entrepreneurial discovery. In democratic societies these institutions include freedom of exchange, choice, and association (Aligica 2018, 20). In addition to the rules and policies that influence entrepreneurial action and strategies, Ostrom stresses the cultural, social, and natural environment as essential context for understanding how public entrepreneurship emerges to solve social dilemmas (Aligica 2018, 39).

The eleven chapters in this book consider how entrepreneurial discovery occurs in the entangled political economy of market, government, and civil society under different rules and incentive structures. How does public policy hamper or encourage innovation, discovery, and creativity in solving social dilemmas? The chapters in this book tackle this question in three different settings: (1) within the market where private sector innovation occurs under legal and regulatory rules and public policies, (2) in civil society during times of crisis where governmental institutions and policy responses are weak or ineffectual in meeting the needs of a community, thereby spurring private or local action, and (3) within the administrative state in judicial, regulatory, and legislative settings where individuals craft public policies in order to achieve their stated goals more effectively and market information is muted or absent, and political incentives prevail.

The first section of the book, "How Public Policy Shapes Entrepreneurship in the Private Sector," consists of four chapters. In chapter 1, "Framing Our Thinking About Entrepreneurship and Public Policy," Abigail R. Hall delves into the fundamental concepts necessary for the study of entrepreneurship, offering suggestions for veins of inquiry as well as positing distinct differences between the study of entrepreneurship within markets and outside of market contexts, utilizing historical examples to illustrate.

In chapter 2, "Moral Entrepreneurship: Integrating Equity within Antimicrobial Resistance Innovation," Ximena Benavides examines the incentive structure around pharmaceutical R&D and the extent to which it discourages the development of high risk but less profitable novel antibiotics in response to the global rise in antimicrobial resistant infections. This dilemma points to the need to consider what solutions might emerge in a "sustainable innovation" policy framework that increases access to lifesaving interventions while encouraging private sector innovation.

Some of the most consequential public policies to shape economic decision-making come in the form of regulations that are intended to protect consumers and employees. In chapter 3, "Successful Evasive Entrepreneurship: Nature or Circumstance? Three Case Studies in the Area of Health and Safety Regulation," Alexander Köhler hypothesizes that innovators may choose to evade some regulations and adhere to others—a behavior that contributes to a regulation's "stickiness" over time. He discusses different elements which may contribute to regulatory stickiness, focusing on health and safety regulations across industries.

In addition to the formal rules, laws, and regulations that influence entrepreneurial action, culture plays a part in how and whether formal laws are enforced or ignored. The post–Civil War legacy of cultural discrimination against African Americans contributed to an environment of reduced entrepreneurial opportunity for those moving from the legally segregated South to the North during the Great Migration. In chapter 4, "Exploring the Persistent Effects of Racial Discrimination on Economic Growth," Olivia Gonzalez demonstrates how "sundown towns" in Northern states prevented African Americans from locating and working in certain neighborhoods. Operating in a gray area between legal discrimination and cultural racism, sundown towns functioned as an exclusionary barrier for African Americans to participation in economic life, thereby undermining two of the essential institutions for entrepreneurship to occur: the rule of law and property rights.

The volume's second section, "Entrepreneurship in Civil Society and in Response to Crisis," consists of two chapters that explore how public policies and governmental institutions designed to provide certainty and stability to economic and social life may fail due to poor design, weak enforcement, or an inherent inability to respond to crisis and shocks. Such failures provide an opportunity for alert entrepreneurial actors to propose alternatives solutions, often at a smaller scale based on tacit knowledge and local circumstances and needs.

Economic crisis may also provide a catalyst for entrepreneurial action when governmental institutions fail. In chapter 5, "'Hot Money': A Hayekian Process of Polycentric Public Entrepreneurship in Currency Formation in Great Depression North Carolina," Thomas Storrs documents a case of public entrepreneurship that helped the town of Greensboro, North Carolina, continue conducting commerce after a crisis in the national currency. A coalition of governments and private sector interests promoted the issuance of scrip money after the collapse in the local supply of U.S. dollars, allowing local businesses to continue operating.

The failure of government to adequately provide public goods and services such as maintaining public safety may provide the impetus for creative solutions to emerge in the private sector. In chapter 6, "Sub-Innovation: The Case of *Fraccionamiento* in Mexico," Carlos Noyola offers a case study of how local citizens responded to the lack of public safety in Mexico by establishing enclosed neighborhoods under specific rules, limiting access, and providing enhanced security for residents. The design and implementation of the rules governing the enclosure are essential to whether individuals opt to live within these communities.

The final section, "Public Policy Entrepreneurship Within the Administrative State," consists of five chapters which recognize that politics is a peculiar type of business commerce (Wagner 2016). While rational actors in governmental settings are not informed by market prices, profit, and loss, they are guided by different types of information and political incentives that may produce inefficient outcomes for society. How might the incentives within bureaucracies be better aligned with the public interest?

In chapter 7, "Exploring the Interplay of Taxation and Regulation in Institutional Arrangements," Dallin Overstreet presents a model for improving efficiency within the bureaucracy by better aligning the incentives of bureaucrats and the public interest. Bureaucracies are incentivized to overproduce public goods, wasting tax revenues, while also creating excessive regulations. By assigning both the taxation and regulatory functions to agencies, bureaucrats would be presented with a tradeoff between maximizing budgets to produce goods and creating excessive regulations.

In chapter 8, "Representation, Taxation, and Policy Entrepreneurship," Natalia Pushkareva considers the incentives at play in how tax policies are established in international bodies and if it is possible to develop a more robust framework that "closes the influence gap" allowing for greater voice for developing nations in the formation of international tax policies.

Lacking the signals provided by prices, profit, and loss, agents within bureaucracies must rely on other types of information to achieve their stated goals, including cost-benefit analysis which attempts to estimate the costs and benefits of a given regulation or program. In chapter 9, "Knowledge and the Efficacy of Energy Efficiency Programs," Arthur Wardle explores how randomized control trials (RCTs) might be used to evaluate the performance of energy efficiency programs on reducing the impact of climate change. Depending on their effectiveness in providing accurate information, incorporating RCTs into agencies' program evaluations would allow agencies to identify wasteful programs before revenues are allocated.

In chapter 10, "Majority Opinions and the Entrepreneurial Pursuit of Judicial Power," Christian McGuire considers how entrepreneurial activity occurs in the American federal judiciary. Using a case study approach, McGuire examines the Supreme Court's decision to replace seriatim opinions with majority opinions to illustrate the manner in which judges act as public-sector entrepreneurs. The Court's decision to abandon seriatim opinions in favor of majority opinions illustrates how judges act to expand their influence, even through licit means.

Finally in chapter 11, "Urban Deindustrialization and Its Discontents: A Commentary on the Social Policy Education of President Barack Obama," Michael Lachanski takes an intellectual history approach to show how the Austrian critique of central planning influenced the intellectual formation of Barack Obama as a student at Harvard Law School. Elite institutions and networks act as vectors for ideas and knowledge, shaping culture and ultimate public policies. In this case exposure to the Austrian school may have affected Obama's conception of urban policy bringing his views closer to the then-emerging neoliberal consensus on the failures of central planning, and inadequacy of an industrial planning approach as a response to the Post War economic decline of many urban centers.

Our hope is that this collection of interdisciplinary research will offer insight into the connection between knowledge, entrepreneurship, and public policy. While the authors offer novel insight into their specific topics of study, their scholarship also provides an entry point for further research on these, and related, topics.

REFERENCES

Aligica, Paul Dragos. 2018. *Public Entrepreneurship, Citizenship, and Self-Governance*. New York: Cambridge University Press.

Aligica, Paul Dragos, Peter J. Boettke, and Vlad Tarko. 2019. *Public Governance and the Classical Liberal Perspective: Political Economy Foundations*. New York: Oxford University Press.

Boettke, Peter J. 2014. "Entrepreneurship, and the Entrepreneurial Market Process: Israel M. Kirzner and the Two Levels of Analysis in Spontaneous Order Studies." *Review of Austrian Economics* 27 (3): 233–247.

———. 2018. "Economics and Public Administration." *Southern Economic Journal* 84 (4): 938–959.

Boettke, Peter J., and Christopher J. Coyne. 2003. "Entrepreneurship and Development: Cause or Consequence?" *Advances in Austrian Economics* 6: 67–88.

———. 2009. "Context Matters: Institutions and Entrepreneurship." *Foundations and Trends in Entrepreneurship* 5 (3): 135–209.

Boettke, Peter J., and Virgil Henry Storr. 2002. "Post-Classical Political Economy: Polity, Society, and Economy in Weber, Mises and Hayek." *The American Journal of Economics and Sociology* 61 (1): 161–191.

Cole, David H., and Michael D. McGinnis (Eds.). 2014. *Elinor Ostrom and the Bloomington School of Political Economy, Volume 1, Polycentricity in Public Administration and Political Science*. Lanham, MD: Lexington Books.

Hayek, Friedrich A. 1948. *Individualism and Economic Order*. Chicago, IL: University of Chicago Press.

Kirzner, Israel M. 1973. *Competition and Entrepreneurship*. Chicago, IL: University of Chicago Press.

———. 1979. *Perception, Opportunity, and Profit*. Chicago, IL: University of Chicago Press.

———. 1992. *The Meaning of Market Process*. New York: Routledge.

Mises, Ludwig von. 1944. *Bureaucracy*. New Haven, CT: Yale University Press.

———. 1949. *Human Action: A Treatise on Economics*. New Haven, CT: Yale University Press.

North, Douglass C. 1990. *Institutions, Institutional Change and Economic Performance*. New York: Cambridge University Press.

———. 2005. *Understanding the Process of Economic Change*. Princeton, NJ: Princeton University Press.

Ridley, Matt. 2020. *The Rational Optimist: How Prosperity Evolves*. New York: Harper Collins.

Tarko, Vlad. 2016. *Elinor Ostrom: An Intellectual Biography*. New York: Roman and Littlefield.

Tullock, Gordon. 1965. *The Politics of Bureaucracy*. Washington, DC: Public Affairs Press.

Wagner, Richard E. 2016. *Politics as a Peculiar Business: Insight from a Theory of Entangled Political Economy*. Northampton, MA: Edward Elgar Publishing.

Section I

HOW PUBLIC POLICY SHAPES ENTREPRENEURSHIP IN THE PRIVATE SECTOR

Chapter 1

Framing Our Thinking about Entrepreneurship and Public Policy

Abigail R. Hall

Thank you for letting me present these ideas to you today.[1] It allowed me to do a lot of thinking about my work and how it relates to the topics of entrepreneurship and public policy. It also helped me rediscover threads in schools of thought I know well but may have forgotten or otherwise neglected.

I want to begin by starting to talk about what I was like before I was an economist. I grew up in Kentucky and started working from a young age. While I was an undergraduate student, I had a very, what you might call, a "Kentucky job." What does that mean? No, I wasn't a farrier shoeing horses. I didn't work making Louisville Slugger baseball bats. I worked for a tobacconist—primarily selling cigars, cigarettes, and other tobacco products. I have to say that I learned more about entrepreneurship in practice from this job, and learned more about entrepreneurship and its relationship to public policy through working in this particular job, than I ever learned from any paper or any book. In thinking back over the four years I worked for this tobacconist, I learned a lot of different things.

The first thing I learned about was entrepreneurship and risk. The owner of the shop was someone who worked for a competitor in the same industry. He decided to strike out on his own. He saw the profit potential, he took the risk, and he opened his own business. I watched the profit motive incentivize his behavior. The choices he made after that initial opening, from adding inventory, to changing business hours, were all influenced by the signals he received from his customers.

The second thing I saw in this job was the price mechanism in action. It's one thing to learn about prices. It's one thing when you talk to your students about how it is that prices work. It's another thing to watch those prices function in action and to think about it retrospectively. A couple of examples illustrate what I'm talking about. I watched as consumers effectively pushed up the price of certain items. There was one specific type of cigar made by a company called Arturo Fuente—the *Hemingway Short Story*. They're a relatively small cigar and take about 45 minutes to smoke. They were (and still are) immensely popular and cost about $5–$6 apiece. As soon as we would get them in the shop, they would be gone. We couldn't keep them on the shelf. What eventually started happening was people would call my boss, and they would say "Hey, Jason, do you have any *Short Stories*?" and of course, the answer would be "No, you know we don't have any of those." The person on the other end of the phone would say something like this: "If you hold them for me, I'll pay an extra $20 on the box [of cigars]." I would come in for my shift and my boss would say, "[this person] is coming in to pick these up. This is how much to ring up on the register. If somebody else asks if we have them the answer is, 'no.'" So that's how it went. Enough people started making him that offer, to pay over the listed price for the cigars, he eventually saw it made sense to push up the price of those particular cigars. Sure enough, people made the same offer after the price increase. I'd come in for my shift and receive the same instructions as before. Once again, he'd raise the price.

On the flip side of that, I also saw how this dynamic worked in reverse: dropping prices to move inventory. For a while, we sold hookah tobacco. In case you're unfamiliar, a hookah is a type of water pipe. Perhaps shockingly, not a lot of people want watermelon-flavored tobacco! So, it just *sat there.* Sitting inventory doesn't make any money. What's worse is that it takes up space from something that could make money. So, what do you do? You try to get that inventory out the door. You drop the price until it eventually clears (or maybe you give it away to some eighteen-year-olds, I'm not ultimately sure).

During my time in this job, I was *acutely* aware of regulations. Specifically, the regulations that made my boss's life particularly difficult. I also saw how entrepreneurs worked to get around the regulations. As you might imagine, working in a cigar shop, people would often come in, they would look over their shoulder, they would lean very close to me, and they would say the following phrase: "Do you have any Cubans?" referring to Cuban cigars. It was always like they were asking for something particularly nefarious. The answer to that question was often, perhaps surprisingly, "yes." One of the things that I learned from that job was that it was *legal* to sell Cuban cigars as long as they were imported *before* the embargo. Now, that meant that you were smoking very, very, old tobacco considering that this embargo was put in place in February of 1962. Now, assuming that everything is kept properly, tobacco mellows as it ages and so some of these old cigars are quite good, even if relatively expensive. But as you might imagine, it's kind of hard to keep the product fresh for that long, so smoke at your own risk. I won't tell you whether, or not, we had anything that was imported after the embargo.

My employer and our competitors responded to other regulations as well. For example, our customers liked the pairing of bourbon and cigars. But to sell bourbon, however, we had to have a liquor license. There were too many businesses that had liquor licenses in our area, and we were located too close to an elementary school, so my boss was prohibited from getting one. How did we potentially get around this? We couldn't sell it, but we could offer bourbon tastings for free. So we did.

Other things we had to consider were regulations on *where* people were allowed to smoke. In 2008 the city of Louisville implemented a blanket ban on indoor smoking. Taking effect in 2022, now retailers who sell any kind of cigarette whether it is traditional tobacco, or an e-cigarette must have a local license to operate within the county. My boss still has his shop and has been open for about fifteen years now. So, he's navigated these transitions in his own way. While he still can't allow people to smoke inside his shop, there was nothing prohibiting him from creating a nice porch outside where people could smoke when the weather was nice or when folks wanted to brave the elements.

Others have navigated these regulations as well. New and existing entrepreneurs are adapting to these regulations in other ways. Again, consider the smoking ban. I recently came across a news story about a new business in Louisville called Smokeasy. So remember we have an indoor smoking ban? It bans smoking in buildings, but it *doesn't* ban smoking in vehicles. Smokeasy is described as an 8 ½' by 24' bar on wheels (Jones 2022). With customized humidors, a full bar, hardwood floors, leather seats, and four large TVs, it can be rented out for things like events, weddings, birthdays, or Tuesday afternoons, whatever the occasion may be. These entrepreneurs have figured out a way to bring this product to their customers despite the regulations.

I left that job after four years to come to George Mason for graduate school and largely put the lessons I learned at the shop out of my mind. I will have to admit that for a while if you had asked me what the connection was between my research and the ideas of entrepreneurship, my answers probably would have come up a little flat. To be honest, I didn't necessarily see the connection. Now that connection is remarkably clear. Entrepreneurship in my contemporary research looks a little bit different than the entrepreneurship I experience as an undergraduate student, but the core is the same.

There are many examples I could point to, but I'll mention just a few. Take unmanned aerial vehicles (UAVs), or what are colloquially known as drones, for instance. These pieces of technology have a very long history but came to prominence within the context of the War on Terror. Would it surprise you to learn that right around the same time that these UAVs were being deployed in places like Afghanistan and Iraq, they were also being deployed along the U.S.'s southern border primarily by Customs and Border Patrol? I would submit to you that this action is just as entrepreneurial as my boss's actions. It's entrepreneurship in a different context. Another example would be the implementation, or the integration, of tactics used by Elite Force Reconnaissance units in Vietnam, in Los Angeles. Seeing an opportunity to improve the efficiency of the Los Angeles Police Department, a man by the name of John Nelson suggested modeling a unit in the LAPD after these military forces. His idea formed the basis for the first SWAT team, and idea which proliferated across police departments throughout the country.

The commonality between all these examples I've just mentioned is that they represent entrepreneurship in response to public policy. My boss at his cigar shop and Smokeasy, both of those are examples of entrepreneurial adaptation in response to public policy. In the same way, the integration of UAVs, the importation of military tactics into police departments, are also entrepreneurship in response to public policy, even though the arrow linking policy and these actions might not be as clear. What I propose is that when we're thinking about the relationship between entrepreneurship and public policy, we consider two primary veins of inquiry. Before we discuss these veins, however, we must first understand several core ideas, all of which are intimately connected to the methodology associated with the Austrian School of Economics.

So, what are these ideas, or what are these core concepts that we need? There are three. First, we need to know about the science of human action. Second, we must develop an appreciation of the nature of knowledge and its dissemination. Third, and finally, we must have some conceptualization of entrepreneurship. I'll turn to each of these pieces individually before returning to my two proposed areas of inquiry.

FRAMING OUR THINKING

Praxeology

We want to start off thinking about praxeology. Praxeology is, simply put, the science of human action. It was pioneered by and most closely associated with Ludwig von Mises, one of, if not the most, well-known Austrian economist. Mises (1949) talks about praxeology in multiple places, but the first 100 pages of *Human Action* are where the magic is happening. In thinking about and discussing why it is that people act, we first need to talk about five different prerequisites for action. It's these prerequisites that for Mises, and for us, allow us to conceptualize how humans behave.

The first prerequisite for human action is that there is some kind of felt uneasiness in our current state and there is a desire for improvement. We say to ourselves, "I don't like where I am, and I would like to be someplace better." The second is some conceptualization of an alternative state of affairs. So again, we feel this uneasiness and we would like to be someplace else. Note this might not be a physical place, but rather, we can imagine some alternative state where we are better off. Third, we have some kind of expectation about the means. "Means" in this case is simply a synonym for the word action. Note here that the actions in question can vary considerably. When I explain this idea to my undergraduate students, I point out that "means" can be very simple actions. Alternatively, when we discuss means we might also talk about grand policies. Fourth, we have some conceptualization of time, of past, present, and the future. Fifth and finally, we have ideas regarding causality. Feeling some uneasiness, conceiving of some alternative, I undertake some action now that I believe will, at some point in the future, cause me to arrive at some alternative, preferred state.

We can use this framework, this idea of means being taken to achieve particular ends in quite literally an infinite number of scenarios from things that are incredibly mundane, to things that undeniably alter the course of human history. Allow me to give you two brief examples, to illustrate this point, highlighting those five prerequisites I mentioned a moment ago. We'll start with something easy. Let's say I feel my stomach rumbling—I am uncomfortable—it's a *felt uneasiness*—that's prerequisite one. I can conceptualize some alternative state where I am no longer hungry—prerequisite two. I have some expectation about means. There are means available to me, that will allow me to no longer be hungry—prerequisite three. I have some concept of time: I know I'm hungry right now, I wasn't hungry earlier, and I hope to not be hungry later—prerequisite four. Then lastly, prerequisite five, causality: some action will allow me to achieve my goal. So, what do I do? I eat a sandwich. Yes, I know this seems to be a very deliberate and calculated way to discuss something very simple. Perhaps a more complex example will help further illustrate the power of this framework.

For this next example, I'll utilize a character figuring into some of my contemporary research, Simón Bolívar, frequently known as "The Liberator" of South America. For perspective, Bolívar was a contemporary of President Andrew Jackson. Anyway, Bolívar looks at his home country of Venezuela and feels uneasy. He sees hundreds of years of Spanish colonial rule and is distressed about the continued subjugation of South America. He can conceptualize an alternative state: something where South America looks kind of like the United States, an interstate federation in which South America is united. He has expectations about means—he believes actions exist that can move him and his countrymen from this less preferred state to a more preferred state. Bolívar understands time—past, present, and future—he comprehends past and contemporary subjugation and a future in which individuals may be free. He believes that means causal—that some action can achieve the desired outcome. So, what does he do? He raises an army and systematically conquers six different countries one of which is now named after him. You know it as Bolivia.

Epistemology

Understanding praxeology is necessary, but insufficient for our purposes. We must also discuss epistemology, or knowledge. Here we draw upon the work of F. A. Hayek. Building off the work of Mises, Hayek asked fundamental questions regarding knowledge: When individuals act, what is it that they know? How do they take the information that they know and transfer it to other people? How, for instance, to I transfer my knowledge to you? How do you transfer your knowledge to me? How does the knowledge from multitudes of people come together to bring about the coordination we observe in the market? This is a remarkably difficult question. You might think, "well, we talk about things." And while we may share some information through discussions of differing varieties, we certainly don't talk about everything, and yet, we are still able to convey information. So how is it that we do that?

Importantly, for Hayek ([1937] 2014, [1945] 2014), knowledge is *decentralized.* We are all repositories of knowledge. We have our knowledge of time and place. For Hayek, knowledge is often what's referred to as *tacit* or inarticulate. Now, given the fact that, for Hayek, knowledge is often inarticulate, you will forgive me if this concept is a bit tricky to explain. But I'm going to do my best.

If you have ever taught a class before, or if at any point you ever run a meeting, you will, at some point, have this realization that the group you are speaking to is *just done.* You'll look at them and know, *just know* that their brains are completely saturated. They can't take in any more information. Every teacher I've ever met knows this feeling very well, but if you were to ask them, or me, to write down what it is that I see or feel in my classroom, I would have a really difficult time telling you.

Here's a second example. Thinking back to when I worked at the cigar shop, there were times we'd get in some new product, and I'd think about one of my regular customers. The next time they'd walk into the shop I'd say something like, "I'm glad to see you. We got something new in and *I know* you'll like it." How did I know they'd like it? If you had asked me to write down how I knew, I would have certainly failed. But I *knew.*

Since knowledge is dispersed and tacit, this implies for Hayek that planning should be decentralized. This makes sense when we think about the broader context in which Mises and Hayek were having these discussions within the broader social calculation debate within the 1930s, 1940s, and beyond. Decentralized planning, or bottom-up planning we might say, allows us to take advantage of dispersed knowledge. It's important here to throw in one particular caveat—decentralization of knowledge is *necessary* for us to transfer knowledge, but it's not *sufficient* for us to transfer knowledge. Put in a slightly different way, decentralized planning doesn't guarantee that knowledge is going to be transferred.

How can we know if a resource is being used in a way that best satisfies or best achieves those goals that we have set out for ourselves? Again, whether those goals can be small, large, mundane, profound, or anything in between. For that, we need to bring in our third main puzzle piece.

Entrepreneurship

We need a clear conceptualization of entrepreneurship. I'm going to spend most of my time here, focusing on one particular economist—Israel Kirzner—who has dedicated his career to the study of entrepreneurship. Kirzner is very well respected within the Austrian school and beyond. He has worked carefully to tie together some of these threads, particularly those laid down by Mises and Hayek. I've heard it said, but I can't remember exactly where, that Kirzner provides a "Misesian answer to a Hayekian question." Hayek argued that markets allow people to better coordinate with one another. Markets are a social learning process.

Now, the question is this: How does this process take place? What causes knowledge to spread within markets and allows this learning to take place? It's relevant here to pause for a second and talk a little bit more about what Kirzner is doing with his overarching project. Kirzner is a student of Ludwig von Mises. His most well-known book is probably *Competition and Entrepreneurship*, which was published in 1973. In this book and elsewhere, he proposes a theory of entrepreneurship that is based on the Austrian tradition, and he's showing within his work how the Austrian tradition and its methodology is both similar and dissimilar from other frameworks when discussing entrepreneurship.

We're going to contrast what it is that Kirzner says with the standard neoclassical model. It is important to note that Kirzner does retain the idea of equilibrium. Those of you who have had an economic principles course will know this idea well. You can conceptualize some downward-sloping demand curve, some upward-sloping supply curve, and at the intersection of those two lines we find there is some price point that exactly coordinates the two sides of the market. At some price, "X," consumers are willing and able to buy the exact amount that suppliers are willing and able to produce. The important thing for Kirzner is the idea of *coordinating* buyers and sellers, how individuals change and adapt their behavior to better achieve their goals.

This is different from the neoclassical conceptualization. In the neoclassical model all things are static. The work is done. If we're in equilibrium, we have no incentive to move or change. Now we talk about people like Joseph Schumpeter (1942) who think about entrepreneurship as this *disequilibrating* event where, through some, often technological shock, we are broken out of one equilibrium and moved to another. We move from one static point to another static point. But the focus for Kirzner is again not on that static equilibrium point, but the *dynamic process* by which people are coordinating their plans.

Hayek in his writing makes it clear that the price system is the mechanism through which knowledge is conveyed, but in Hayek's work, he doesn't discuss who or what is the agent of change. Kirzner attempts to answer this question. He does this in a very interesting way, by bringing Misesian arguments into Hayek. Kirzner takes Mises's discussion in *Human Action* about entrepreneurship and applies it to discussions in Hayek about knowledge in markets. For Kirzner, entrepreneurship is *alertness* to opportunities that, in his words, allow us to "grasp pure profit" and for knowledge to spread (2002, 19). So, through this entrepreneurial alertness, the entrepreneur sees some new way of doing things that has previously been overlooked or otherwise ignored. This is entrepreneurship in the Kirznerian sense. It is this entrepreneurship that allows knowledge to spread and be transmitted.

An example may be helpful. Consider the case of Samuel Zemurray, otherwise known as Sam the Banana Man—someone who is an incredibly important figure in not only United States, but Latin American history.[2] You may have never heard of him, but chances are if you lived in the early 1900s you would know this name. It would be like if today I talked about Jeff Bezos of Amazon. Samuel Zemurray was an immigrant to the United States and was remarkably poor. In the summer of 1893, he encountered bananas. Now for us, bananas are not particularly exciting, you may have had one at breakfast this morning. At breakfast, my toddler will often ask for one, and there's a good chance she'll eat none of it—but I don't lose any sleep over it. But in Sam's time, bananas were new to the United States and were an exotic delicacy.

Zemurray, keen on entering this trade in this new exotic fruit, goes to Mobile, Alabama, and spends an incredible amount of time just watching the banana traders, watching bananas come off the boats, and watching them getting loaded into train cars. But, before they were loaded, he watched how the bananas were sorted. Remember we're talking late 1800s—there was no refrigeration, and things weren't moving by plane or by a semitruck on a highway system. They were being moved by train. So, this separation is critically important.

If you've ever bought bananas, which ones you select will depend on when you want to eat them. If you want bananas for later in the week, you buy bananas that are still green. If you want to eat one today, you get something that maybe has a few brown spots. But within this context in the late 1880s, absent refrigeration, and potentially being on a train for several days, what did the selection process look like for banana traders? The green bananas are the ones that are going to survive transport the longest; those are the good bananas, so they get put on the train. There's another category of bananas that were referred to as "turnings": those were the bananas that were still good, they had a few days left, but they needed to be moved quickly because within a few days they were going to go bad. Then there was a third category—what were called "ripes." So ripes were those bananas that, as the name might indicate, were already ripe, or about be ripe.

To the banana producers at the time, ripes were worthless, because they wouldn't make it to market in time. And so, they threw them away. Here is where we see a prime example of Kirznerian entrepreneurship. Samuel Zemurray, as a young man, watched them load these bananas onto trains and throw away these large quantities of bananas that were seen as worthless. So, he went to the bananas trader and said, "I'd like to buy those ripes." He bought them for a very cheap price. He put them on a train car, and the short version of the story is that he managed to get telegraphs sent to the train stations ahead and people were made aware that he's going to have these tropical delicacies for sale at very cheap prices. Starting with only $150, keeping in mind again this is 1893, by the time Samuel Zemurray was twenty-one, he earned and saved $100,000—an incredible amount at the time. His success earned him the nickname "Sam the Banana Man." Sam would later turn around and through a complex story, wind up being the head of United Fruit. He and his company would play substantial roles in civil wars and other conflicts throughout Central America. You have likely bought bananas from United Fruit's offspring—Chiquita Banana.

There are four important things to note about Kirznerian entrepreneurship. First, for Kirzner, entrepreneurship is not some maximization problem. It's not something where you have cost curves and revenue curves that are just given to you. When we teach these ideas to our students, we assume a great deal. We assume that cost curves are known and given. Revenue curves are given. It's assumed, explicitly, that firms already know what it is that they are going to produce! This is the neoclassical idea. In this sense, firms are acting passively. There's no room for entrepreneurship. This is even indicative in the terminology that we use to refer to them, we refer to them in many contexts as price searchers. They—meaning individuals in these firms with their known cost and revenue curves—are searching for some mythical price that will maximize profit. There's no choice involved. There's no real action.

Second, entrepreneurship from Kirzner's perspective is about seeing new ways of doing things. It's about finding new means-ends relationships. Third, for Kirzner, entrepreneurship is about *discovery*. It's about finding something new, something that you didn't know before. This is distinctive from the idea of *search*. An example might be helpful, let's say I'm looking up a reference for a journal article. I'm actively looking for that. That is an example of a search. But let's say within the context of that searching I find out that there is an article related to something I research, a new person or a new paper I didn't know about. That is discovery. I wasn't looking for it, I didn't know that it was out there, it came as a surprise. Fourth and finally, if we utilize Kirzner's conceptualization of entrepreneurship, then entrepreneurship alone cannot explain the wealth of nations. Why? Because entrepreneurship in the sense that Kirzner is talking about it, is everywhere (Boettke and Coyne 2003). Entrepreneurship is not some characteristic that is possessed by only a few people. Instead, entrepreneurship is an ever-present condition of mankind.

OUR VEINS OF INQUIRY

Now that we have these ideas firmly in the front of our mind, discussions related to epistemology or knowledge, praxeology or the study of the science of human action, and our conceptualization of entrepreneurship, I'd like to return to my proposed two main veins of inquiry when talking about entrepreneurship and public policy and the intersection between the two.

The first vein of inquiry relates to entrepreneurship in response to public policy. Consider again one of my earlier examples. How did Smokeasy—our 8 ½' x 24' bar and cigar lounge on wheels—come to be? As a result of regulation! They viewed the regulatory landscape, saw that regulation (namely, the indoor smoking ban) was preventing mutual gains from trade. They were alert to a new opportunity and they took it.

There are plenty of other examples we could think of as well. Consider, for instance, the start of the COVID-19 pandemic, think March–April of 2020. This was the time that many state governments were shutting down large segments of the economy, particularly bars and restaurants. My family and I in Tampa, Florida, started seeing something interesting happening as a result. Prior to the start of the pandemic, many restaurants in the city were in-person only. When government decreed they could no longer serve their customers indoors, they became alert to new and innovative ways to reach their customer base. For instance, our favorite pizza place started making kits where people could make pizza at home. Not only could you enjoy their product, but it would often give you something to do when you couldn't go out and were tired of watching television. Other restaurants in the area started allowing people to sign up for virtual cooking classes. Again, these individuals were entrepreneurially alert—responding to this public policy of shutting down restaurants. There are lots of other potential examples that we could talk about within the context of the pandemic—contactless delivery for all kinds of goods, people innovating new ways to connect remotely, more reliably, more securely. It's entrepreneurship in response to public policy.

Policy is important because it alters the landscape in which people find themselves. Policy alters markets, and it changes the profitability of some ventures. Some previously profitable ventures may become unprofitable. This is wasteful in an economic sense because, otherwise, these trades would have taken place. Alternatively, public policy makes exchanges that would have otherwise been profitable, unprofitable. So, they no longer take place (Kirzner 1985). An example may be illustrative. Again, I'll return to my time in the cigar shop. We would frequently have customers who would come in, typically after returning from a trip to Europe, and they would ask for a couple of specific brands of cigarettes—usually French ones. We weren't allowed to sell them. If we attempted to jump through the myriad of regulatory hoops to be able to sell them, we would have inevitably had to pass those costs onto our customers. The result would have been prices so high that no one would have bought them. Regulation made what would have been profitable, unprofitable. Similarly, with bans on things like flavored cigarettes, people who were interested in those could no longer purchase them.

In response to regulation, we also see the emergence of things like illicit or "black markets." Think again about things like cigars and cigarettes. If you've ever attempted to buy a pack of cigarettes in a place in New York City, you know that they are very expensive. Why are they so expensive? They are heavily regulated and heavily taxed. You may or may not know that there is a robust underground economy in New York working to provide cheaper cigarettes by avoiding the regulation. In particular, smugglers work to bring in cheaper goods from neighboring states and take care to put fake seals on the packing so it looks like the bootlegged items have been subjected to the levied taxes. You also see examples of entrepreneurial activity in regulated markets that isn't expressly illegal. Take, for example, Uber, Lyft, and Airbnb. These companies were remarkably innovative, but also patently disruptive of the environment created by the regulatory landscape. Uber and Lyft disrupted the market which had for decades been dominated by taxicabs and medallions. Airbnb disrupted the market for lodging, becoming the largest purveyor of places to stay—but they own no hotels. Each of these are examples of entrepreneurship where someone recognized a new means-ends combination, a new way of doing things that was previously unseen.

My proposed second vein of inquiry is different. Not only can we examine how entrepreneurs respond to public policy, but we can also analyze policies intended to generate entrepreneurship. We don't have to look very far to find examples of these policies. Entrepreneurship is recognized as a critical component of economic development. Scholars have asked and analyzed the question of whether entrepreneurship is the cause or consequence of economic development. Regardless of where you come down on that question, we can agree that entrepreneurship is seen in one way or another as a critical component of this economic development puzzle (Boettke and Coyne 2003). As a result, governments will often attempt to facilitate or otherwise kickstart entrepreneurship. We see this in many different capacities. Local and state initiatives try to induce entrepreneurship—think about your downtown revitalization programs in large cities or small towns. Think about state funding programs for generating entrepreneurship in specific areas. There are national initiatives, and even international programs to generate new ideas, new businesses, etc. Think of the sheer number of programs implemented by agencies like the International Monetary Fund or the World Bank. These initiatives are everywhere.

How can we think about these attempts to spark entrepreneurship in light of what we know from the likes of Mises, Hayek, and Kirzner? The first thing we know is that policymakers cannot solve the problems of knowledge discussed by Mises and Hayek. Think again about the nature of knowledge. It is tacit and dispersed. How is this knowledge learned and transmitted? Through the entrepreneur within the context of the market process. There's not an equivalent mechanism available to planners. The mechanisms of the market are distorted or absent whenever we encounter centralized planning, whether it be comprehensive orwithin "microcosms of planning," where government planners attempt to top-down arrange some segment of the economy. This idea is discussed in greater detail by the late Don Lavoie (1985), who talks about this idea of non-comprehensive economic planning. Using a similar line of reasoning to Mises and Hayek, he illustrates why this sort of piecemeal planning will be ineffective.

We should also think about Kirzner (1985) within this second vein of inquiry. In particular, we should bring to bear those ideas I referenced a moment ago—stifled discovery and superfluous discovery. With these various initiatives to spark entrepreneurship, we see government, intentionally or unintentionally, changing the relative profitability of certain activities. Some things that would have been learned are left unknown and unutilized because it's no longer profitable for them to seek out those opportunities. On the other hand, we have superfluous discovery as a result of these policies—people are now looking in areas that they would not otherwise have been.

The Appalachian Regional Commission gives us a great example of this dynamic. The Appalachian Regional Commission, or ARC, is the second oldest regional development organization in the United States. The Appalachian region of the United States is a particularly interesting area of study within the context of economic development. In his book *The Elusive Quest for Growth*, economist William Easterly talks about five ethnogeographic poverty clusters in the United States, ethnically similar, geographically concentrated areas of poverty. Most of these groups are unsurprising. He talks about (1) southern Blacks, (2) inner-city Blacks, (3) Hispanics in the southwestern United States, and (4) Native Americans primarily in the northern plains states. But there is a fifth group—and this group is the worst off economically out of the five. This group is predominantly white and located in the central region of Appalachia—eastern Kentucky, southern West Virginia, and parts of northeastern Tennessee.

This is an interesting development puzzle because we lack explanatory mechanisms we could employ in discussing the other groups. We can't point to racial bias or other systemic discrimination. We also lack other explanations for their poverty like we'd see in international contexts. The Appalachian region has a stable rule of law, for example. And yet, this region is remarkably poor. Recognizing the economic status of the area, President Kennedy commissioned a report in 1964 to evaluate the region. President Johnson continued on this endeavor and created ARC with the explicit goal of developing the region. So, from 1964 to today, ARC has undertaken numerous initiatives to develop the region, including programs to try and spark entrepreneurship. ARC has received and allocated millions of dollars to hundreds of different projects over this time. And what does the region have to show in terms of economic progress? Nothing. Gains that are accrued, get wiped out almost instantaneously from one year to the next. This region gets hit harder by recessions and takes longer to recover.

So why hasn't ARC been able to spawn consistent, sustained development? Why haven't they been able to generate entrepreneurship? It's because they lack the knowledge to be able to do so! They're not able to consistently pick winners in this region. They have no market mechanism to refer to in their efforts. They are unable to solve the knowledge problem.

There are other issues as well. For instance, there are a variety of incentive problems. One of the particularly problematic things about ARC is that they're not allowed to give any kind of funding to a for-profit entity. So, if you have someone in McCreary County, Kentucky, who says, "You know what my county needs? A taco truck," he can't go out and get that loan from the Appalachian Regional Commission because he's a for-profit entity. So, what do you wind up with? You wind up with government-bureau-to-government-bureau transfers. The dollars intended for entrepreneurial ventures wind up getting funneled into things like sewage systems and roads, but not to entrepreneurs, to people who might have the tacit and dispersed knowledge necessary to engage in activities that would actually generate sustained economic development.

EXTRA-MARKET ENTREPRENEURSHIP

I want also to address the concept of entrepreneurship outside of the market context. I mentioned how regulation can push entrepreneurial behavior into black or illicit markets. Certainly, we can think about those individuals as being entrepreneurial, even if we may potentially find the markets in which they are operating to be repugnant. I would draw us back again to Kirzner, and particularly Kirzner's ideas regarding entrepreneurship and institutions. Outside of the market context, do we see entrepreneurship? The answer for Kirzner is "Of course!" Entrepreneurship again is not the sole possession of some individuals, but instead a quality or something that we all possess. We all have entrepreneurial moments. But for Kirzner, institutions are incredibly important. When Kirzner discusses markets, he says they do an exceptional job of funneling or channeling individuals' behavior toward efficient outcomes. Outside of the market context, Kirzner cautions us against thinking that individuals will be driven toward an efficient outcome, or that they will be driven there in any way that is necessarily fast. So outside of markets, we can't guarantee or have no reason to believe that order will emerge quickly, or that it will result in good outcomes.

So, the institutional structures in which people are engaging are profoundly important. Because the institutions, or what you might also have referred to as the "rules of the game," (North 1990) are what direct people's behavior. Institutions determine the relative costs and benefits of particular courses of action. A couple of examples here are relevant. Take, for example, the implementation of "clean torture" techniques in U.S. prisons. This integration was sparked by public policy—particularly international policy and war. If you go back to the 1960s–1970s, into the Vietnam era, you see this transition from militaries, particularly advanced militaries, from using traditional torture to techniques referred to as "clean" ones. So, what does a clean torture entail? If done correctly—from the perspective of the torturer—these techniques do not leave physical marks on the victims. This is potentially helpful to somebody who wants to use torture but must conceal it due to international law or other restrictions. As my coauthor and I discuss (Coyne and Hall 2018), individuals involved in developing and honing these techniques abroad eventually brought these tools back home. Why? They were behaving entrepreneurially. They recognized the opportunity for new means-ends connections, a "better" way of doing things. This example is related to Chicago and a man by the name of John Burge, who, while working for the Chicago Police Department, implemented various clean torture techniques in an attempt to extract confessions, primarily from black men, over approximately twenty years. To give an indicator of where it is exactly that this technique came from, or what sparked this entrepreneurial idea, it was said in a court deposition, that one of the torture techniques that they used—electrocution using a modified field telephone—was referred to as "the Vietnam special" (see Coyne and Hall 2018, 163–166).

The second example that I would offer to you to illustrate entrepreneurship in contexts outside of markets is again related to the idea of international policy regarding war. Within the context of the larger War on Terror, you see two things. First, you see an increase in the number of military deployments. Second, you see that the number of enlisted military personnel remains relatively flat. This presents a real issue where military officials are concerned about making sure they can fill their ranks. So, what do they do? They relax their recruitment standards, particularly along the lines of things like tattooing. So, someone who may have held an ideology that would be considered objectionable at a best-case scenario, or extremist and other cases, or someone who walked in with a swastika tattoo may nevertheless have been allowed to enlist in the military if they said something like well, "I just like the way it looked." As a result, what happened? Extremist individuals enlisted, acquired training, and were entrepreneurial upon their return. They are alert to new opportunities, alert to the ability to use these tools and tactics to gain status within their organizations, to make their organizations more effective. And so, you see things like extremist groups forming around military hierarchical structures or importing military tools and tactics into their organizational structures to either enhance efficiency or for personal gain within that organization (Hall et al. 2021). We would classify these actions as being entrepreneurial, just as we would qualify, or we would think about Samuel Zemurray acting as an entrepreneur. We would think about my boss's cigar shop as acting entrepreneurially, but the institutional structures in which they are operating are profoundly different.

CONCLUDING THOUGHTS

When we think about entrepreneurship, our view is often quite limited. If you ask a man on the street to define entrepreneurship, he's probably going to talk about opening a business, which is certainly entrepreneurial. But entrepreneurship is so much more than the act of opening a new brick-and-mortar business. It's something that we are all capable of doing, and we all do throughout our lives. When it comes to thinking about government and entrepreneurship, and government activities as they relate to policy can and does impact individuals. Public policy sets up incentives such that people will change their behavior. They pursue some activities instead of other activities in response to these policy changes. When we go out to analyze entrepreneurship, and that intersection of entrepreneurship and public policy, it's important for us to not only to think about these institutional constraints but also to keep in mind what it is that we've been taught by the likes of Mises, Hayek, and Kirzner—things like praxeology, things like the epistemological constraints faced by policymakers, how it is that people convey that tacit and dispersed knowledge, and thinking about the institutional structures in which these types of activity should be placed.

NOTES

1. This chapter is a transcript from a lecture given on February 18, 2022, to the participants of the Frédéric Bastiat Fellowship Research Sequence.
2. For a comprehensive biography of Zemurray, see Cohen 2012.

REFERENCES

Cohen, Rich. 2012. *The Fish that Ate the Whale: The Life and Times of America's Banana King*. New York: Picador.

Coyne, Christopher J., and Abigail R. Hall. 2018. *Tyranny Comes Home: The Domestic Fate of U.S. Militarism*. Stanford, CA: Stanford University Press.

Boettke, Peter J., and Christopher J. Coyne. 2003. "Entrepreneurship and Development: Cause or Consequence?" In *Advances in Austrian Economics, Volume 6: Austrian Economics and Entrepreneurial Studies,* edited by Roger Koppl, 67–87. New York: Elsevier Science, JAI.

Easterly, William. 2002. *The Elusive Quest for Growth: Economists' Adventures and Misadventures in the Tropics*. Cambridge, MA: MIT Press.

Hayek, Friedrich. A. 2014. "Economics and Knowledge (1937)." In *The Collected Works of F. A. Hayek, Volume 15: The Market and Other* Orders, edited by Bruce Caldwell, 57–77. Chicago, IL: University of Chicago Press.

———. 2014. "The Use of Knowledge in Society (1945)." In *The Collected Works of F. A. Hayek, Volume 15: The Market and Other* Orders, edited by Bruce Caldwell, 93–104. Chicago, IL: University of Chicago Press.

Hall, Abigail R., Jerod T. Hassell, and Chivon H. Fitch. 2021. "Militarized Extremism: The Radical Right and the War on Terror." *The Independent Review* 26 (2): 225–242.

Jones, Michael L. 2022. "New Louisville Mobile Cigar Lounge Is a Throwback to the Days of Speakeasies." *Louisville Business First*, January 16. Online: https://www

.wlky.com/article/new-louisville-mobile-cigar-lounge-is-a-throwback-to-the-days-of-speakeasies/38785727.

Kirzner, Israel M. [1973] 2013. *Competition and Entrepreneurship*. Indianapolis, IN: Liberty Fund.

———. 1985. *Discovery and the Capitalist Process*. Chicago, IL: University of Chicago Press.

———. [1992] 2002. *The Meaning of the Market Process*. New York: Routledge.

Lavoie, Don. [1985] 2016. *National Economic Planning: What Is Left?* Mercatus Center Edition. Arlington, VA: Mercatus Center, George Mason University.

Mises, Ludwig von. [1949] 2007. *Human Action: A Treatise on Economics*. Indianapolis, IN: Liberty Fund.

North, Douglass C. 1990. *Institutions, Institutional Change, and Economic Performance*. Cambridge: Cambridge University Press.

Schumpeter, Joseph. *Capitalism, Socialism, and Democracy*. New York: Harper & Bros, 1942.

Chapter 2

Moral Entrepreneurship

Integrating Equity within Antimicrobial Resistance Innovation

Ximena Benavides

The discovery of antibiotics nearly a hundred years ago led to the elimination of many serious and fatal infections worldwide. Over time, however, bacteria can adapt to environmental conditions and develop resistance to antibiotic treatments, diminishing their ability to treat infections. The rise of antimicrobial resistance (AMR) and, in particular, resistance of bacteria to known antibiotics, poses an urgent threat to global health systems. Untreated, AMR infections lead to longer hospitalizations, higher medical costs, and increased mortality, issues which disproportionately affect populations in the Majority World, commonly referred to as the global South.[1] Each year, 700,000 people die globally from antibiotic-resistant infections (RAR 2016). In the United States alone, the Centers for Disease Control and Prevention (CDC) estimates that close to three million people develop antibiotic resistance each year (CDC 2019), and someone dies of a difficult-to-treat infection every fifteen minutes (Moss 2021). According to global health organizations, untreatable bacterial infections could become the existential global public health crisis of the century and account for the deaths of as many as ten million people annually by 2050 (World Bank 2017).

The research and development (R&D)[2] pipeline for new antibiotics falters in the face of this hallmark healthcare threat (So 2011, 89). Despite widespread recognition that developing new antibiotics is a primary global public health priority, market interest in producing new antibiotics remains low in the private sector; the last time a new class of antibiotics was developed was in 1987 (Moss 2021; Deak et al. 2016). Disengagement from antibiotic-focused biotech ventures is justified with a host of market failures (Renwick et al. 2016) beginning with high financial risks and the steep costs of developing new antibiotics (Ledley et al. 2020).[3] To begin, antibiotics are administered acutely in contrast to chronically, which makes these drugs a less economically wise investment and drives large pharmaceutical companies toward more lucrative drugs (Ventola 2015). Developing an antimicrobial can require more than a billion dollars and take longer than a decade to move from discovery to market (Patel 2023). Around 80 percent of antimicrobials in clinical development are in the hands of small and mid-size biotech companies with limited resources (Thomas and Wessel 2022, 14). Biopharmaceutical firms refer that the costs of late-stage R&D of novel antibiotics are too high to be recouped later in sales and fear the limited market potential of new antibiotics could lead to bankruptcy.[4] Thus, the lack of commercial sustainability of antimicrobial treatments increases the risk for a valley of death between invention and timely access to life-saving medicines. On the other hand, governments usually do not engage in biopharmaceutical manufacturing themselves. Nonetheless, governments regularly play the role of funders of basic research of scientific foundation and drug discovery (Moses et al. 2015).[5] Studies examining the most impactful or transformative drugs since 1965 have observed that half to two-thirds of them were associated with public contributions, especially for basic science (Cockburn and Henderson 2001; Chakravarthy et al. 2016; Zycher et al. 2010). Public contributions have also increased over the years. All drugs approved by the U.S. Food and Drug Administration (FDA) from 2010 to 2016 were based on publicly funded research (Cleary et al. 2018). In the development of mRNA COVID-19 vaccines, public investment was extraordinary compared to other publicly funded health technologies (Benavides 2023). Pre-pandemic, the National Institutes of Health invested in mRNA vaccine technology and the Biomedical Advanced Research and Development Authority (BARDA) and the Department of Defense invested in vaccine development (Lalani et al. 2023), totaling $31.9 billion in U.S. government investment to develop, produce, and purchase mRNA COVID-19 vaccines.

In recent years, AMR initiatives in the United States and globally are emerging under seemingly new collaborations that promise forward-thinking policy action of public and private actors to develop alternative treatments and new antibiotics. The Combating Antibiotic-Resistant Bacteria Biopharmaceutical Accelerator (CARB-X)[6] and the Global Antibiotic Research and Development Partnership (GARDP)[7] promise AMR research and development of new therapeutics, vaccines, and diagnostics—the "5 by 25" Initiative, for example, commits to deliver five new treatments by 2025. The AMR Action Fund, established in 2020, works as a public-private investment fund that provides temporary funding to support companies developing new antimicrobial therapeutics.[8] Founded in 2016, the AMR Industry Alliance serves as an industry-led organization that promises to advance partnerships across the public and private sectors and a common framework for accountable antibiotic manufacturing.[9] In parallel, some government-led efforts, predominantly in Europe, have been focusing on addressing short-term market challenges by offering the industry a different set of pull incentives (Patel 2023).[10]

While many of these initiatives could attract private investment into the AMR field and stimulate the invention of AMR products, I argue they still replicate traditional collaborative models and governance strategies that have proven unsuccessful in addressing public health crises in the past.[11] By predominantly focusing on creating meaningful incentives for innovation in AMR to flourish, these initiatives may come up short in terms of addressing the underlining market failures favored by patent and IP laws that prevent equitable access to biopharmaceutical products. The COVID-19 pandemic made plain the need to rethink the public and private governance structures for biopharmaceutical innovation. Business as usual is insufficient (Torreele 2020). The inequitable global distribution of COVID-19 vaccines resulted from low production and delayed distribution of safe and effective vaccines. The scarcity and access problems fundamentally were symptoms of policy choices with political and moral dimensions. Biopharmaceutical innovation is highly dependent on the production capacity and business motivations of a few biopharmaceutical firms, mostly based in the United States, raised up in a strong patent culture (Benavides 2023; Santos Rutschman 2021, 177) that allows them to consolidate their market power. As it is, the patent culture feeding the biopharmaceutical market is failing to produce AMR drugs and will fail to provide equitable access to them. Today's challenges to speeding up novel antibiotics' R&D and production do not exclusively represent scientific and financial barriers, but structural ones stemming from, what I refer to be, a *power silo problem.* Market and political power are concentrated in the hands of a few actors via regulatory capture, informational capitalism, and licit lobbying for protections and special treatment. The pharmaceutical industry is viewed as one of the most politically powerful industries today in the United States (Florko and Facher 2019), with one of the greatest market powers of informational capitalism (Kapczynski 2020; Kapczynski 2022) and the largest lobbying in the country (Wouters 2020).

The AMR public health crisis could be regarded as a policy forward-thinking moment where, with realistic expectations of antimicrobial inventions, governance initiatives develop new value-based investment incentives that do not rely on the patent culture as the financial model and pay real attention to equitable access strategies. Pressing concerns include how R&D is financed, why manufacturing capacity is so consolidated, why R&D efforts and benefits are not equitably distributed, and whether the current biopharmaceutical production model is serving to address public health interests.

Ultimately, how can the invention of therapeutic interventions excel while improving, rather than sacrificing, equitable access to lifesaving products? In this chapter, I argue it is urgent to integrate equity into the structure, funding, and governance of firms and collaborative initiatives when designing antimicrobial innovation business models. By equity, this chapter calls for securing equitable access to effective antibiotics as a central objective of research and production, ensuring access without excess to prevent antibiotics misuse. By focusing on a few of the emerging AMR initiatives, this chapter critically examines their power dynamics and suggests equity-based governance strategies to mediate the tension between production and accessibility of novel AMR treatments.

This chapter is structured as follows. The second section explores Hayek's liberal thinking of entrepreneurship inefficiency and social justice. According to Hayek, the pursuit of social justice required social control and central planning that would inevitably undermine the rule of law and sacrifice liberal democracy. However, a contemporary perspective suggests that social justice is attainable in market-led environments through a balanced distribution of political roles of powerful stakeholders, for example, preventing vertical forms of power over the political process that confers the industry with regulatory capture that helps entrench the status quo of drug manufacturing control. The third section examines the *power silo problem* in biopharmaceutical R&D. Drawing from the inequitable production and distribution of mRNA COVID-19 vaccines, this section provides a critical account of the risks and actual harms that market and political power concentrations create over public health, fueled by a patent culture. Finally, by looking closely at the organizational and financial challenges of emerging AMR initiatives, the fourth section offers possible ways to treat the power silo problem with equity-based private governance strategies.

ENTREPRENEURSHIP, EQUITY, AND HAYEK'S SOCIAL JUSTICE

A central normative claim of this chapter is that of holding *equity* as a central, shared stakeholders' objective of AMR entrepreneurship. Although understood as a value of social justice, the attainment of equitable access to effective medicine has been rather marginal to the efficiency of markets. The evolution of human rights during neoliberalism evidenced the moral and political dimension of markets rather than one that is strictly economic (Whyte 2019). As the human rights movement and neoliberalism flourished together, many aspects of human life were economized (Moyn 2015). In the economic rationale of neoliberalism, values of equality and justice were subordinated to efficiency, and human rights violations were considered market mistakes rather than policy choices "that served clear political and economic ends" (Klein 2007, 147). Political problems were allegedly solved through the market (Brown 2006, 692; Brown 2015), without critical judgement about the motivations of those actors who exercised political power to create the market rules (Grewal and Purdy 2014). The concern of the growing scholarship on social justice has been economic systems not addressing but expanding the social problems that imbalanced economic power and political capital create (Duff et al. 2013; Reisch 2002; Jackson 2005; Bankston 2010).

Friedrich A. Hayek was critical of the application of social justice to market theory. In his major statement of political philosophy of markets, Hayek described the pursuit of social justice—defined as economic injustices addressed through redistribution remedies—as an effort that necessarily involves the use of tools of social control (Hayek 1976). Hayek distinguished two possible scenarios for the quest for social justice: one where governments treat "all citizens according to the same rules" and another where governments "place the different citizens in equal (or less unequal) material positions" (Hayek 1976, 82). To Hayek, the second scenario, governments treating citizens differently to compensate for those disadvantages and differences they could not directly solve, would ultimately undermine the rule of law and liberal democracy (Boettke 2019, 222). Hayek feared the promotion of social justice might introduce justified manipulations that corrupt the process of redistribution of power and wealth and worsen inequality. He observed that in the name of social justice many calls for reform have led to "special interests seeking privileges from government" as part of strategies to consolidate their current market positions (Haeffele and Storr 2019, 146). Redistribution is "irreconcilable with the rule of law, and with that freedom under the law which the rule of law intended to secure. The rules of distributive justice cannot be rules for the conduct toward equals, but must be rules for the conduct of superiors toward their subordinates" (Hayek 1976, 86). As such, Hayek envisioned an unavoidable tradeoff between social justice and liberty, where liberty was sacrificed.

Hayek's critical view of social justice is grounded on two major assumptions. First, Hayek's thinking envisions *well-functioning markets*. Hayek believed that injustice lies not in the institution of markets but in the individuals acting within them. According to Hayek's view, only if players of the market play unmorally, the outcome of the game could be called just or unjust (Hayek 1976, 72). As such, to Hayek unfairness is an individual problem, which can be remedied "only when you can pinpoint who precisely is acting unjustly" (Haeffele and Storr 2019, 148). Injustices are unlikely to be systematic, and, hence, solutions should be a matter of individual justice, not of social justice. However, the outcome of the game might be unjust even when none of the participants break the rules and the referees impartially enforce them (Haeffele and Storr 2019, 149). A grounding assumption of Hayek is that the market order is a "constellation of games" rather than one single game that everyone must but might not be able to play (Haeffele and Storr 2019, 151). In reality, though, there is only one set of rules governing the market order. If there are individuals who are unlikely to ever win the economic game, for whatever reason, then the market might be an unjust environment and produce unjust outcomes (Haeffele and Storr 2019, 150). Furthermore, markets are rife with political capitalism. Political interventions by individuals in the construction and operation of the market rules create rigid and hierarchical economic systems, where referees of the economic system may act in ways that are biased or discriminatory (Holcombe 2018), producing an unfair environment that disfavors mutual cooperation and give a few at the top opportunities to write the rules that shape the game in their favor and win at the expense of the rest of society (Wagner 2016; Stiglitz 2012, 39–40, 59). The critique is not about conceiving an economic order where players will lose (that still can be a fair game), but instead uncritically accepting that the distribution of rewards is not skewed and rejecting the fact that rules, as creatures of biased referees, can allow advantageous positions to some and not others in the market (Haeffele and Storr 2019, 152).

A second main assumption of Hayek's thinking is a clear *dichotomy of state and market*, where only states, through a centrally directed economy, can take action toward social justice. In this view, social justice comes at the cost of the liberty represented in market settings (Hayek 2014, 219). But as Elinor Ostrom reminds us, such a dichotomy is partial and narrow (Ostrom 1990). In reality, multiple and complementary levels of governance coexist, with a plurality of interdependent decision-makers managing a given resource (Ostrom 2010). Despite the decades-long efforts of public health advocates, avoidable health disparities persist (Harris and Pamukcu 2020, 766–67; Benfer et al. 2020). Contemporary health justice scholars attribute this persistence to the unconfronted policies, practices, and culture that hold down one social group while benefiting another and transform disparities into structural inequities (Harris and Pamukcu 2020, 770). The health of individuals and populations rely on broader social and economic environments (e.g., living in a more equal society) as well as the commercial conditions shaping them, including the regulatory systems, the articulation of social and economic power, and the neoliberal and capitalist ideologies themselves (de Lacy-Vawdon et al. 2022; Buse 2017; Millar 2013).[12] And as power differentials grow and superstructural dynamics are replicated even systemically and organically across healthcare systems, health disparities endure and expand (Pistor 2021; Williams 2019). As such, health inequities are embedded in complex systems with many unclear interdependencies (Wegner 2009, 871).

They are rooted in concurrent social, economic, and political power differentials at the interpersonal to global level (Benfer et al. 2015, 52). As "wicked problems,"[13] health inequities require solutions that transcend the borders of traditional policy domains and involve a variety of actors across scales (Termeer et al. 2019, 167–68).

Hayek's view that social justice requires coercion, at the risk of undermining a free society, has been criticized on multiple fronts. To some scholars, Hayek relies on a too optimistic assessment of markets while some of his policy concessions, like supporting a minimum income wage, weaken his own claim of central planning—and the knowledge and incentive problem prevalent to it (Hayek 1976, 99; Coyne 2013)—as well as the redistribution of wealth (Feser 1997; Johnston 1997; Lukes 1997; Tebble 2009). Contemporary liberal accounts also recognize some inconsistencies in Hayek's approach (Haeffele and Storr 2019, 147). Their emphasis is on the unjust referees of the game, who may favor the powerful—and themselves—with the rules of the socioeconomic game, preventing "the chances that the least advantaged will rise to the top" (Haeffele and Storr 2019, 147). They examine ways to pursue social justice and economic opportunity other than through central planning and social control. These renovated perspectives rethink resource management not only *efficiently* but *equitably*. Stephanie Haeffele and Virgil Storr encourage policymakers to think critically about the rules of the market; whether they are inclusive, adaptable, and fairly enforced (Haeffele and Storr 2019). These scholars assert that a liberal order has to be actively maintained by learning about the ways in which political roles and social practices can potentially generate social injustices. The modern notion of social justice is about power balancing; it is about the fair distribution of wealth and essentially of power. Haefelle and Storr's narrative recognizes a power problem in addition to the knowledge problem that, according to Hayek, would prevent social justice through government intervention. Their account also suggests social justice might have been seen as secondary to economic growth by liberal thinkers.

The law-and-political-economy (LPE) project makes a similar end-claim with respect to the efficiency of markets, yet from a different angle. The LPE project urges scholars to unearth the political foundations of neoliberal laws and the ways in which power speaks through law (Britton-Purdy et al. 2020; McCluskey et al. 2017; Pasquale et al. 2019; Harris and Varellas 2020). Essentially, LPE scholarship questions the prominence given to furthering the *efficiency* of markets, emphasizing that markets are not neutral nor the economy is separate from politics. The project argues that political order affects the democratization of markets as much as the democratization of politics. As creatures of law and policy choices, markets represent political order and representative democracy at a moment in history. Ultimately, the

LPE project contests the idea of a free, spontaneously competitive market order and claims that, therefore, neoliberal efficiency offers no means to analyze "contemporary concentrations of wealth and power, except insofar as they interfere with overall efficiency" (Britton-Purdy et al., 2020: 1790).

Whether it is market or political power, or any other new, dynamic form of power (Kapczynski 2022), the modern notion of social justice and the LPE analysis of markets commonly recognize that any reform to foster economic opportunity and agency equitably needs to grapple with all sources of power and the dynamics present in the current economic order that reinforce one another.

THE POWER SILO PROBLEM

Once the novel COVID-19 mRNA vaccines were developed, produced, and approved for emergency use, questions of when and who gets vaccinated were predominantly informed by market accessibility and affordability (Blanco et al. 2022). As a result, underserved populations in the Majority World were queued up last. Two problems were notorious in the inequitable production and allocation of the mRNA COVID-19 vaccines during the pandemic: *scarcity* of safe, effective, and quality vaccines and lack of timely *access* to all populations in need. Both production and allocation problems rely on supply-driven regulations and market-driven mechanisms that largely remain at odds with public health needs. Prior to and during the pandemic, the control exerted by large, multinational pharmaceutical companies over when, which and how many products to manufacture, for what populations, and at what price, has made biopharmaceutical innovation highly dependent on the production capacity and commercial motivations of a few biopharmaceutical firms (Maxmen 2022). On the other hand, the wealthiest countries of the minority world, where these firms are commercially active, have contributed, whether actively or passively, to ossifying harmful power concentrations. The most notorious examples during the COVID-19 pandemic were governments failing to waive TRIPs or exercise compulsory licenses and, generally, validating the highest lobbying expenditures coming from the drug industry (Furlong et al. 2022; Benavides 2023). As a result, in practice, biopharmaceutical production is controlled by a handful of powerful pharmaceutical firms and at the same time hoarded by wealthy nations who compromise supply with pre-marketization agreements and sovereign power exercise.

Patent Culture

Power concentrations in drug manufacturing are favored by a *patent culture* primarily shaped by intellectual property (IP) laws and related policies. In law-and-economics terms, IP rewards inventors with guaranteed temporary market exclusivity to incentivize investment of time and financial resources in R&D of hard to make, new and innovative products that are useful to society (Posner 2002).[14] No one else can manufacture or sell the patented product without the permission of the patent holder until, for example, the twenty-year temporary exclusivity term expires.[15] At this point, the rights to the invention are transferred to the public and the invention becomes part of the public domain. Some scholars have noted that IP rules do not always work as law-and-economics theory suggests (Levin et al. 1987)[16]; others have asserted that patents sacrifice social utility and efficiency (Rahmatian 2013; Kapczynski 2017).[17] A medical product can be supported by a web of patents, which can extend exclusivity for decades.[18] Reaching an optimal balance between exclusive rights valuable enough to be a spur to invention, but not so extensive in scope or duration as to prevent public access in the future is one of the main challenges of the patent model. As it is, the patent model provides drug makers with "perfectly rational reasons to restrict supply" by prioritizing drugs for those who can afford them and "keeping the know-how secret to control the market for [drugs] in the long run" (Kapczynski 2021; Wirtz et al. 2017). Disease prevention and vaccines are often sidelined over high-incidence chronic or life-long medical treatments as the latter represent better prospects for sales (Thissen 2014). Studies published over the last two decades show how drug makers' *commercial bias* affects drug design and clinical testing (UCL Institute for Innovation and Public Purpose 2018, 17). Recent studies on conflicts of interest in biomedical research show that infectious diseases were marginal in research agendas between 1999 and 2018 (Testoni et al. 2021).[19] More recently, the Access to Medicine Foundation 2022 report reveals that only a fourth of the companies covered by the report engage in bolstering R&D pipelines for most emerging infectious diseases other than COVID-19, including AMR (AMF 2022). The high demand for therapeutical treatments for diseases to which the Western market is prone, and hence with higher payment value, make them more attractive to develop and manufacture. Governments attempt to address the risk of underproduction of new pharmaceutical products through a combination of tools (prizes, patents, and R&D grants); yet, concerns remain that "too few resources are devoted to [. . .] vaccines or therapies aimed at infectious diseases" and that underproduction increases the risk of global health disparities (Fisher III 2016, 256–60).

With rare exceptions, the set of entitlements that patents and other IP laws create has grown steadily and dramatically since the eighteenth century (Fisher III 1999). By the end of the twentieth century, the number of patents expanded as a result of the Trade-Related Intellectual Property Rights (TRIPS) Agreement, the main legal international IP framework implemented by essentially all countries,[20] that mandates patents in all fields of technology—including medicine—with visible impacts on access to drugs.[21] The 2001 Doha Declaration introduced "TRIPS flexibilities,"[22] which marked a change in thinking about patents and medicine by suggesting the reformulation of IP protection as a social policy tool rather than a mechanism to protect makers' commercial interests ('t Hoen 2016).[23] With the Doha Declaration, certain initiatives emerged to counterbalance the expansion of monopolies and improve access to patented medicine, but most of those initiatives are voluntary and rely on political and corporate will ('t Hoen 2009). TRIPS flexibilities still do not eliminate the heavy dependence of the pharmaceutical system on patents as the main mechanism for financing innovation. Moreover, drug makers have used flexibilities to extend their exclusive rights beyond the statutory twenty-year term (Kapczynski 2008),[24] which has led to the formation of power silos and abusive market exclusivity positions. Even when economists of classical liberal thought refuse to compare patent exclusive rights to monopolies (Meiners and Staaf 1990; Kitch 1990), a set of non-IP rules and policies jointly shape the patent culture and favor the concentration of market and political power in a handful of large biopharmaceutical firms (Kapczynski 2022).[25] Unlimited lobbying, tax benefits and exemptions, corporate flexibilities, unconditional R&D public funding, among other regulations, have established a *too friendly* business model that prioritizes profits over populations' health needs (Benavides 2023). mRNA COVID-19 makers justified their supply control power on the basis of innovation nationalism (Kumar 2019, 208–09; Santos Rutschman 2021, 183).[26] Although the IP model applicable to biopharmaceutical innovation already offers generous commercial incentives to bear the exorbitant AMR-related costs, it has not successfully stimulated AMR development enough. Instead, biopharmaceutical companies interested in investing in AMR-based products demand more commercial incentives (AMRIA 2020, 7, 13 and 46).

Ultimately, the patent culture is driving a disconnected set of goals among firms, regulators, funders, and other biopharmaceutical actors, yet all are suppressing a public health need-based discourse. The proliferation of examples where science development is guided almost exclusively by profit maximization rather than the public value science can offer, excluding one another, is troubling. The uneven global distribution of lifesaving vaccines during the COVID-19 pandemic and the unaffordability of treatments for diseases considered top U.S. mortality causes, like cancer or diabetes, are only a few examples that illustrate the stark inequities in medicines access, and their global impact, under patent culture.

Addressing the Power Silo Problem

A deep-rooted understanding of drug manufacturing regulation as a consumer protection issue has favored a dominant "product-focused" approach to biopharmaceutical innovation (Carpenter 2010; Kapczynski 2018). The U.S. medical products regulatory agency—the FDA—has historically played the role of protecting users from harmful medicines by focusing on the safety and efficacy of therapeutics. Likewise, a market-driven U.S. pharmaceutical industry immersed in the dangerous patent culture described earlier, has encouraged maximization of returns and efficiency over all other motivations. Biopharmaceutical innovation priorities are often determined by the demand of those who can afford and have market access to a novel medical product instead of the social value of science. This supply-driven perspective shaping medical manufacturing casts equitable access to medicines to the periphery. Certainly, it is an efficient outcome if even one percent of the global population have access to the most essential, life-saving drugs. However, when knowledge to manufacture safe and effective new medical interventions is hidden rather than shared to expand widely production, access to the benefits of science becomes a privilege, at the risk of displacing the social value of science.

The scarcity and access problems that explained the inequitable production and allocation of COVID-19 vaccines are ultimately symptoms of policy choices with a moral dimension. Our innovation ecosystems are suitable for efficient results but disregards the moral value of the markets. The moral dimension of markets is not distant from Adam Smith's concern of the moral costs associated with life in market societies, even when he celebrated markets (Smith [1776] 1981). Smith claimed that "markets are the reason that countries are wealthy and are also potentially corrupting" (Storr and Choi 2019, 181). Contemporary market scholars similarly assert "[m]arkets cannot thrive if entrepreneurs are comfortable with circumventing the rules of the game or are principally engaged in political entrepreneurship (i.e., rent seeking)" (Storr and Choi 2019, 182). Although for Storr and Choi moral people are necessary yet not sufficient for markets to drive, they recognize the virtue of temperance, which encourages market actors to tame their vested impulses, and justice, which cheers actors "to pay willingly for good work, to honor labor, to break down privilege" (McCloskey 2006, 508).

Holding the position of market actor and referee simultaneously represents a grand moral problem that corrupts markets. To modern economist Randall G. Holcombe, who develops the idea of political capitalism, when the same actors hold both economic and political power—like drug makers, who in practice control drug production and price as patent holders and lobby to maintain the status quo—the result is stagnation, in contrast to progress through cooperation when economic and political power are separate (Holcombe 2020).

High levels of inequality present in the market systems suggest markets are not perfect incubators of cooperation (Storr and Choi 2019). Civilizations cannot endure on transactional exchange alone. Markets require ethical preconditions (Collins 2020). Equity cannot be an either-or concern to markets. Power balancing in the biopharmaceutical innovation realm is justified in everyone's right to benefit from science.

THE CHALLENGES OF NEW AMR INITIATIVES

Hayek's understanding of social justice as an avoidable trade-off between the values of liberty and equality may make it difficult to understand exactly what equity might look like in practice. Is it possible to constrain vested interests and profits and still make progress? How can privately led initiatives, such as the AMR Action Fund, integrate equity into their traditional governing structure and ways of operating? What can initiatives to move the industry forward, such as the AMR Industry Alliance, do differently to address the organizational and financial barriers to secure *efficient and equitable* drug innovation? Social science scholars in the business organizational realm, who advocate for power balancing to mitigate distrust in capitalism to solve social problems, propose consistent and concerted efforts to balance the interests of multiple actors (Holmes Jr. et al. 2022, 986). How can power-balancing efforts be successfully propelled when a strong patent culture consolidates power silos and its abuses constitute barriers to global equitable access to healthcare?

This section explores the balancing of power strategies to address the power silo problem in AMR medical innovation by examining the ways in which AMR businesses and initiatives are structured, developed, and overseen. To that end, this section outlines specific organizational and financial challenges at the intersection of corporate motivations and public health interests, and it suggests integrating equitable access as a core principle into private governance to restore power balancing and prevent power-abusive dynamics.

Organizational Challenges

In this section, I cover two main organizational challenges that might essentially frustrate the promise to develop innovative AMR solutions for the benefit of all. On the one hand, those actors running and making the key decisions for AMR initiatives fuel a trust gap. The 2022 Gallup report on confidence in U.S. institutions shows that the pharmaceutical business sector has a major-level negative rating—its lowest in at least three decades of measurement—coinciding with the low confidence in major nation's institutions, including the medical system (Jones 2022; Brenan 2022). On the other hand, collaborations with less established actors from the Majority World may become an empty promise unless initiatives are organized within the larger target of promoting economic agency of all actors.

Trust Gap in Powerful Actors

Even before the pandemic, the U.S. pharmaceutical industry was "the most poorly regarded industry," and it ranked below the federal government, showing the lowest negative ratings since Gallup first started polling industries in 2001 (McCarthy 2019). A 2018 RepTrak's reputational rank of pharmaceutical companies in the United States shows that Pfizer has the lowest reputational score (Hu 2018), and after the industry developed a COVID-19 vaccine, the pharmaceutical industry rated even lower, showing only a 31 percent positive rate. Such low ratings then and now are fundamentally explained by the fact that the United States has the highest pricing and cost of drugs in the world.[27] The general public condemns the industry for not committing to limit drug price increases and disclose drug costs. Drug pricing has represented a significant increase in lobbying spending and in the number of companies lobbying in the last decade, reaching record-breaking numbers with the pandemic (McFadden 2021; Suter 2021). The U.S. pharmaceutical industry is by far the largest lobby in the country showing its largest campaign contributions near in time to legislative events where drug pricing was a key concern (Wouters 2020).

While high drug prices segment access to health, they also put at risk manufacturers' reputations, social licenses to operate, and ethical corporate values (Singer 2022). It is critical for AMR initiatives to recognize these high levels of distrust when designing their organizational structure along with implementing trust-building strategies. Equity must be baked into biopharma's organizations' DNA, not just into the access to the final product. Considering who are in charge of the decision-making process and shape the day-to-day functions of AMR innovative initiatives is an important equity-building factor. By adopting a new organizational vantage point, biopharma actors will be better able to make business decisions that leverage science-based, high-tech innovation while securing equitable access to new science.

In recent years, collaborative initiatives in the United States and globally have surged, promising to overcome the AMR problem. The AMR Action Fund, launched in July of 2020 with the goal to discover and produce two to four new antibiotics by 2030, groups more than twenty leading pharmaceutical companies from the United States, Europe, and Japan, including large pharmaceutical companies highly criticized for directing the inequitable distribution of mRNA COVID-19 vaccines based primarily on wealth (Furlong et al. 2022; Maxmen 2022). The collective venture receives public funding and is developed in collaboration with the World Health Organization (WHO), the European Investment Bank, and the Wellcome Trust. The fund aims to provide a "temporary bridge" to AMR innovation by funding biopharmaceutical companies with the expectation that regulators, in the meantime, will address "the larger economic issues" hampering antibiotic market development (Dall 2022). The AMR Industry Alliance, in turn, is an industry-led collaborative initiative founded in response to the 2016 UN AMR call for action and includes over a hundred biopharmaceutical companies. The Alliance 2020 second biennial progress report included large biopharmaceutical companies who played a dominant role in the inequitable development and distribution of COVID-19 vaccine (AMRIA 2020, 7, 13 and 46; Blanco et al. 2022).

As indicated, the declining trust in these large drug firms spans prior to the pandemic, and the biopharmaceutical industry is not an exception. An interesting analysis to the content of news stories about the pharmaceutical industry in 2017 shows that the biggest conversation around big pharma were centered around a profits-over-patients discourse, where pharmaceutical companies "ignore the needs of those who rely on their drugs" (Cate 2017). The second major conversation topic covered how the industry provided "needed support and funding to treat the world's worst diseases" (Cate 2017). While there is a positive perception of the role that the biopharmaceutical industry plays in medical innovation, a negative perception on their inequitable business outcomes is predominantly larger.

Powerful actors have a vested interest in preserving the status quo (Nik-Khah 2014). Of course, innovation both run by the industry or led by government present their own set of conflicts of interest. Governments represent the risk of exercising nationalism and hoarding medicine production, in addition to potential conflicting interests stemming from their dual role as referees and manufacturers. In turn, the industry represents the risk of maximizing profiteering over meeting populations' health needs. Nonetheless, even if opportunities to mitigate the risks of conflicts of interest stemming from the industry were greater than to those available if R&D were carried out by the government, political capitalism in the pharmaceutical sector is hard to overcome and requires strong willingness of policymakers.

Collaboration versus Capacity Building

The goal of biomedical innovation is to accelerate the production of new life saving interventions. This is quite impossible, however, if innovation remains clustered in informational ecosystems geographically controlled by a few market actors. Every region of the world must be able to produce its own novel medical products (Maxmen 2022). Otherwise, the Majority World will forever be sentenced to heavily rely on importing medicines from wealthy producers, contingent to the promise of not hoarding supply or selling it to more profitable buyers. To date, scaling up the production of medical products to meet global demand is impossible because the details of the manufacturing process remain secret despite the technological capacity in the Majority World.

Collaborations that are presented as opportunities predominantly to share insights with the best innovators, who share common goals and are part of the same cluster, represent a risk in practice: preserving collaboration only among a close group of actors. Outside of the elite cluster, collaboration tends to be offered in the form of donations. The production of COVID-19 vaccines evidenced that the strictly voluntary approach to technology transfer was not enough to deliver. Neither the environment that fostered collaborations among private biopharmaceutical innovators was healthy (Herder et al., 2022).[28] The outcome, an inequitable distribution of treatments, is not new. A story of health disparities repeats cyclically across public health crisis: the poorest and those hardest hit by diseases do not have access to health innovation or innovation reaches them too late. Five decades ago, Julian T. Hart developed the inverse equity theory that explains how "the availability of good medical care tends to vary inversely with the need for it in the population served" (Hart 1971, 405), a theory ignored in practice despite well expanded (Marmot 2018; Cookson 2021) and the ample evidence of health disparities in access to medicine.

The AMR Action Fund was established in 2020 as an international public-private partnership between the International Federation of Pharmaceutical Manufacturers and Associations, the World Health Organization (WHO), the European Investment Bank, and the Wellcome Trust, aimed to fund through equity investments clinical-stage small and mid-size biotechnological companies in the development of new antimicrobial therapeutics. The Fund goal is to serve as a "temporary bridge" toward AMR innovation in response to "the larger economic issues" hampering antibiotic market development (Dall 2022). The AMR Action Fund presents itself as a collaborative initiative between the largest and the emergent pharmaceutical companies of the world, offering the emergent access to deep expertise and resources that would strengthen them and accelerate the production of novel anti-microbial medicines.[29] In April 2022, the Fund announced U.S. biopharmaceutical companies Adaptive Phage Therapeutics and Venatorx Pharmaceuticals to be the first recipients of funding to primarily support AMR-related clinical trials. Collaborations are intended to occur fundamentally among members of the industry, from big pharmaceuticals to clinical-stage companies. Making the group of entrepreneurs larger in number, including young actors from the industry and the minority world, does not guarantee alone higher collaboration. Structured as such, collaborations cannot promise *expanding capacity* for medical innovation outside of clusters. Similarly, the AMR Industry Alliance promotes collaborations among experienced and young biopharmaceutical companies. Inclusion of biopharmaceutical entrepreneurs of the Majority World is, again, mostly inexistent.[30]

Promoting and achieving equity through collaborations remains a challenge despite the many empirical studies documenting inequity and providing critical insights on what is required to advance equity across global actors (Faure et al 2021). When promoting public value through innovation, it is essential to foster collaborations that build capacity and share knowledge including actors of the global South and LMICs, and even promoting South-to-South collaborations. Too frequently cooperation with actors of the global South is limited or practically inexistent, which seems falsely justified on the fact that biopharmaceutical innovation is predominantly government-led in the South—yet, biopharma innovation in the developed world is primarily economically supported with public funds. Looking at the conditions that conciliate scientific research and the rights and welfare of individuals, Alex London encourages to encompass a wider array of actors who co-labor in the social undertaking of biomedical knowledge production, reflecting critically on the roles and contributions of pharma firms, philanthropic organizations, and other stakeholders and affected communities (London 2021). Intentional synergies and partnerships with less wealthy actors, that focus on capacity building rather than risk management (Crane 2020), can promise broader innovation production. When building capacity, all healthcare-related actors must be treated as partners. That is, fostering fair partnerships by which power-diverse actors become competent to manufacture and respond effectively and faster to the medical needs of their populations (de Vries et al. 2015).

Financial Challenges

In this section, I cover equity-based strategies for funding innovation mindful of the object to fund and the purpose of funding. As research funding primarily originates from the global North, either governments or private actors, which translates into influencing power of elite actors, funding becomes a central determinant of equity (Faure 2021). Dependency on elite funders affects the scope of the innovation research (e.g., whether it addresses specific health needs) and limits access to innovation of less privileged populations.

Sustainable Financing

There is wide acknowledgement that the overall level of investment in AMR R&D is insufficient to deliver the novel treatments needed. Studies on the antibacterial R&D pipeline indicate that the success of "crossing the valley of death" during the screening for antibacterial drug candidates relies on "the size of the medicinal chemistry effort that can be mounted, and (. . .) the available financial resources, as well as the opportunity costs, of undertaking this" (So 2011, 89). The AMR Industry Alliance 2018 progress report showed exits of large research-based biopharmaceutical companies (e.g., Novartis, Sanofi, and AstraZeneca) and biotechnology companies (e.g., Achaogen's bankruptcy) in AMR-related investments (AMRIA 2018). There is no single source reporting on total AMR R&D funding across public and private sectors and, still, it is unsafe to say that the innovation required to address AMR public health needs can be sustained by private or public financing alone. The AMR Industry Alliance and the Global AMR R&D hub reported between $1.6 billion and $1.8 billion investment in AMR product development in 2018 from private-non-profit, government, public-private partnerships, and other public sources (AMRIA 2020, 13).

AMR research needs *more* funding, but, fundamentally, *equity-principled* funding. That is, aligning commercial interests and public health needs in a way that ensures the investment needed for AMR research and equitable access to novel treatments. An equity-principled funding model would urge AMR business models to delink antimicrobial making exclusively from profits but to public value (CIDRAP 2022). The idea of public value relates to the broader concept of a mission-oriented healthcare model that values medicine as *public goods*, understood based on the benefits that consumption infuses into the community (Kutz, unpublished). Different incentives have been used to promote AMR research investment. Antibiotics as a class already enjoy among the fastest clinical approval times and highest approval rates of the U.S. FDA across therapeutic categories (AMRIA 2020, 13); however, the few tight margins on clinical trials lead firms to perceive the approval process as unpredictably costly. Yet, accelerating approvals may lead to increase false-positive results and compromise safety, leading to a post-marketing, subsequent withdrawal from the U.S. market (Food and Drug Administration 2010; Outterson 2010). Some pull incentives have been in place in addressing short-term market challenges, especially in Europe, introducing reimbursement schemes or reducing reliance on sales (Patel 2023). Earlier to the AMR Action Fund, the United Kingdom launched a five-year national plan to contain and control the AMR crisis by 2040 (UK Department of Health and Social Care 2019a; 2019b). The UK announced to be the first country in the world to have a scheme that pays companies for antimicrobials by assessing their health technology value to the UK-National Health System (NHS), as opposed to the antimicrobials volume usage. The plan offers a subscription-style payment model for antibiotics to guarantee upfront income to pharmaceutical companies participating in new antibiotic development (UK DCSC 2020). An upfront or pre-commitment payment strategy per se is not a novel proposition, but setting revenues based on contributions to health outcomes. These policy strategies are still considered not enough to "address the long-term realities of AMR" with bacteria continually evolving and treatments becoming ineffective (Patel 2023).

This chapter has a further claim to AMR innovation funding. Sustainable AMR funding is not only securing invention ecosystems in the long run but the accessibility of knowledge, technology, and the novel treatments to all people (Graham 2023). The production and distribution of COVID-19 vaccines is an illustrative example of funding misaligned from equitable access. Vaccine producers like Pfizer did not deny that profits exclusively govern their vaccine allocation plans.[31] Supply allocations were exclusively based on volume and buyers' capacity to pay vaccine prices instead of, for example, a country's incidence of COVID-19 (e.g., prioritizing vaccination in countries with the highest death tolls or where deadly variants originated). Pfizer's profit-seeking strategy might be justified in aligning marketing decisions to the interests of manufacturers' shareholders instead of all stakeholders' needs. These expectations are lineal to the corporate anatomy of large pharmaceutical firms. Pfizer's largest shareholder is an investment management firm and more than half of the company's disseminated stock is held by institutional investors, which feeds the prioritization of profit maximization in the short run.[32] With a fragmented clinical trial network that has been the target of private equity firms in the last years (Pradhan 2022), it is not surprising a board's push to align companies' decisions with the interests of the shareholders with the largest ownership position either. The 'more-like-a-fund-than-a-medical-research-company' mindset is consistent with the broader pharmaceutical industry's practices. A U.S. Government Accountability Office report (GAO 2017) revealed that the pharmaceutical industry is increasingly inclined to buy smaller firms to *acquire knowledge* about drugs already invented and maximize returns by increasing medicine prices over the patent lifetime.[33] The moral political economy of this form of informational capitalism is the public funding component. Research funding from the public sector is untied to any strings that secure equitable access to treatments. The transition from free-access to COVID-19 mRNA vaccines to their commercialization in the United States is expected to increase vaccine prices, which reveals a moral problem considering mRNA R&D was publicly funded.

Exceptionally and recently, a number of institutional investors urged the boards of several large drug firms to establish concrete metrics for linking executive compensation with policies that widen access to medicines to low- and middle-income countries (Silverman 2022). The grounding principle of medical innovation decision-making leans toward lining up R&D and manufacturing decisions not only to the interests of manufacturers' shareholders but to other multiple constituencies' interests. Failing to determine criteria to public-value goals can prevent decision-makers from optimally setting innovations, their prices, and opportunity costs, which means missing the greatest social value of innovation.

Access Strategies

Allocating financial resources in initiatives for the development of AMR-based products requires designing important reward incentives strategies, for example, before and after products approval. One way to set equity-based goals can be at the time the government or investors provide funding to the R&D initiative, in addition to rewarding makers over time after drug approval. For example, funding provided by the government may be conditioned to submitting and enforcing access plans (e.g., plans to determine levels of investment in addressing public health needs, local to global allocation plans to be executed once products are approved, plans of the drug cost and price determination). Incentives in the form of prizes or rewards can be set up for achieving a specific goal prior to the products' approval, under a set of conditions and principles (e.g., facing scarcity of supplies or an increased disease impact over certain populations), which may be revised or updated during the product allocation.

One of the founding promises of the AMR Industry Alliance is driving and measuring the industry progress to curb AMR. To that end, allies are encouraged to advance proactive partnerships across the public and private sectors and enable coordination across subsectors. The alliance has developed a common framework for responsible antibiotic manufacturing that encourages members of the industry to put in practice several equity-based business strategies: registering medicines with regulators in other countries; conducting clinical trials in more countries to favor wide marketing of medicines; committing to making more donations and waiving patents; applying equitable pricing plans; engaging in technology transfers; and agreeing to voluntary licensing. Most of these strategies, if not all, have been discussed in the literature in different ways and extents and specially urged amidst the pandemic, yet they have been barely implemented as its voluntary nature makes them toothless. By 2020, just 44 percent of all alliance manufacturing member-owned sites reported meeting the framework requirements to meet those strategies (AMRIA 2020, 6). The AMR Industry Alliance 2020 report also showed that, still, 84 percent of companies who were in late-stage R&D or had at least one AMR-relevant commercial product and platform in clinical development declared having access strategies in place (AMRIA 2020, 6). A year after, the AMR Industry Alliance 2021 report showed that 85 percent of members involved in AMR-products manufacturing were assessing their sites to the coalition manufacturing framework (AMRIA 2022).

The AMRIA reports, which are based on independent research yet financed by members' contributions, suggest that the industry involved in AMR-related investments are expressing interest in implementing private equity-based governance strategies. Still, lessons from federal funding support in developing key technology used in mRNA COVID-19 vaccines point toward the need for greater federal oversight and further regulatory push incentives for private action, especially before marketing approval of drugs of uncertain value (Herder 2019). Integrating equity in medical innovation business models is particularly critical when R&D efforts are publicly funded—and when despite public funding drug makers get additional benefits from tax income exemptions (NCHS 2021), among other many benefits stemming from a patent culture driving biopharmaceutical ecosystems. While patents may encourage needed invention and innovation during public health and life-threatening circumstances, they do not necessarily encourage innovation *expansion*. Patents, and the patent culture around them, can stand in the way of quick and wide global access to antimicrobials. Thus, access plans and equity-based strategies integrated into AMR business plans may need higher government intervention than relying on firms' expressions of interest. Notwithstanding, a claim for greater government intervention, without addressing the political capitalism of the pharmaceutical industry, does not necessarily tackle the declining trust and growing concerns in large pharmaceutical firms to incorporate health equity demands to their business plans.

CONCLUSION

More investment in antimicrobial innovation—and biopharmaceutical products in general—is needed. Equally, or more important, is to remember that the goal of drug innovation reaches beyond maximization of financial returns. Efficiency and equity should, on equal footing, play a role as drivers of biopharmaceutical innovation. To that end, identifying the power silo problem embedded in the way in which ventures for biopharmaceutical innovation are structured, funded, governed, and oversight is critical. Balancing of power in the form of intentional partnerships, building-capacity strategies across private and public sectors and between actors of the Majority World, purposeful financing to satisfy public health needs, and equity-based access plans are promising governance strategies to address the power silo problem and rebalance power dynamics of the U.S. patent culture.

NOTES

1. The author acknowledges and recognizes that binary classifications such as "global South/global North," "developed/developing," this chapter uses at times, follow a prevailing global health discourse rooted in racism and colonialism that perpetuates hierarchies among countries and regions of the world. On global South and global

North world classifications, see Themrise Khan et al., "How We Classify Countries and People—and Why It Matters," *BMJ Global Health* 7, no. 6 (2022), http://dx.doi.org/10.1136/bmjgh-2022-009704; Anne Garland Mahler, *Global South*, ed. Eugene O'Brien (New York: Oxford University Press, 2017), 9. The essay uses the term 'Majority World,' coined by Bangladeshi photographer, writer, and social activist, Shahidul Alam, named a Time magazine Person of the Year in 2018. See Shahidul Alam, "Majority World: Challenging the West's Rhetoric of Democracy," 34(1) *Amerasia Journal*, 88–98 (2008).

2. R&D is the initial stage in the process of innovation and invention of medicine and medical treatments that leads to the development and production of drugs.

3. Compares research and development expenses of pharmaceutical companies and S&P 500 companies. The difference in median profits was close to 4 percent, where pharmaceutical companies were not more profitable.

4. Statement from Thomas Cueni, Director of the International Federation of Pharmaceutical Manufacturers & Associations (IFPMA) at the AMR Action Fund launch event in Tokyo on July 10, 2020. Available at https://www.ifpma.org/resource-centre/video-message-from-thomas-cueni-at-amr-action-fund-launch-event-in-tokyo-on-10-july-2020/ (last accessed, December 27, 2022). Examples of biotech bankruptcy for antibiotics include Achaogen and DeInove.

5. Basic research funded by governments is performed principally by academic institutions or government laboratories, which findings are then transformed to the private sector for development.

6. See https://carb-x.org. Carb-x is global non-profit partnership accelerating antibacterial products to address drug-resistant bacteria funded by a global consortium of governments and foundations (including the governments of the United States, United Kingdom, and Germany, Wellcome Trust and the Bill & Melinda Gates Foundation), headquartered in Boston University.

7. See https://gardp.org. GARDP brings together private, public, and non-profit partners for the development of treatments for drug-resistant infections. It is governed by a Board of representatives of donor countries, including the United States, Norway, Switzerland, Germany, Japan, South Africa and One Health Trust; with observers from the WHO and DNDi.

8. See https://www.amractionfund.com. The fund works with the International Federation of Pharmaceutical Manufacturers and Associations, the WHO, the European Investment Bank, and the Wellcome Trust.

9. See https://www.amrindustryalliance.org. The AMR Industry Alliance is a large private sector coalition, including over a hundred biotech, diagnostics, generics and research-based pharmaceutical companies and associations that work on AMR R&D, manufacturing and access.

10. Sweden offers revenues with a reduced reliance on sales; Germany and France offer reimbursement schemes; and the United Kingdon has tried out incentive schemes based on innovation, access, and valuation.

11. For example, Ebola, communicable diseases like Zika and SARS, HIV, and most recently, COVID-19.

12. Buse et al. assert commercial determinants of health can influence health outcomes to the extent diet disorders and alcohol and tobacco abuse, for instance, are considered profit or corporate-driven diseases.

13. In social science literature, wicked problems are hard to fully predict, prevent, and deal with because of their complex nature. On health inequities as wicked problems, see generally Claes Andersson & Petter Törnberg, "Wickedness and the Anatomy of Complexity," 95 *Futures* 118 (2018); Brian W. Head, "Problem Definition and the Policy Process: Wicked Problems," *Oxford Research Encyclopedia of Politics* (2017).

14. Other substantive theories that support IP include (1) the personality theory, focusing on the personality of creators and (2) the Lockean labor theory, focusing on the fruits of the creator. Two sets of economic incentives—promoting worthwhile investments in research versus widespread diffusion of the benefits of innovation—ought to reach balance with a temporary *monopoly* for twenty years over the invention and its later diffusion in competitive terms.

15. 35 U.S.C. § 154.

16. Levin et al. suggest that imperfect appropriability may lead to under-investment in new technology and less economic growth.

17. Rahmatian argues that particularly in patents "the relevant [efficiency] test is not supposed to be whether the invention is worth a monopoly (the classical patent 'reward'' idea), but whether the invention is information whose significance should be further investigated." Kapczynski claims IP law in the form of patents neglects the values of equity and justice that should underpin efficient allocation of live-or-die innovation.

18. For example, drug Humira benefits from 132 patents, which protect it from competition until 2037 although the FDA approved it in 2002. See Knox & Curfman, 2022.

19. The study also shows that health and biomedical sciences research agenda prioritizes research on pharmacological intervention over research on socio-environmental factors influencing disease onset or progression.

20. TRIPS: Agreement on Trade-Related Aspects of Intellectual Property Rights, Apr. 15, 1994, Marrakesh Agreement Establishing the World Trade Organization, Annex 1C, 1869 U.N.T.S. 299, 33 I.L.M. 1197 (1994).

21. The TRIPS Agreement's implications for health care were first visible during the HIV-AIDS crisis. The high cost of medicine drew attention to the relationship between patents and high drug prices. See 't Hoen 2009.

22. Declaration on TRIPS and Public Health in Doha, Qatar, DOHA WTO MINISTERIAL 2001: TRIPS, WT/MIN(01)/DEC/2, November 20, 2001.

23. Ibid.

24. Kapczynski refers that the fact that patents have been made increasingly hard to license and too easy to renew has translated into a system that is prone to gaming by pharmaceutical companies by, for instance, tweaking patented drugs with trivial changes to look like new ones to fit the IP rights checklist. See also Lindsey, 2021., referring that the U.S. patent system is off-balance. The number of exclusive monopolies has skyrocketed over the past few decades without a commensurate acceleration of competitive environments that advance innovation or productivity, discouraging public access of the invention.

25. Kapczynski claims attempts to reform the pharmaceutical industry must grapple with four sources of power, which tend to reinforce one another: power property, vertical power over politics, ideational power, and material power.

26. Santos Rutschman refers that a patent-intensive culture has favored COVID-19 vaccine nationalism in the form of preproduction commitments during the vaccine R&D stage.

27. The 2022 Gallup report refers to the massive lobbying to politicians, patent protection laws, and the origin of the opioid crisis linked to the pharmaceutical industry as other likely reasons.

28. Herder et al., draws upon the example of the lipid nanoparticle delivery technology, developed in and around the University of British Columbia and incorporated into the Pfizer/BioNTech COVID-19 vaccine and the litigations and rivalries among researchers and makers.

29. Statement by president and CEO of PhRMA at the AMR Action Fund global launch in Washington D.C., on July 9, 2020.

30. According to information on the AMR Industry Alliance website as of November 11, 2022.

31. For example, in November 2021, Pfizer's chief executive officer said the company decides "vaccine allocation in relation with how many doses [Pfizer] had and who wants to get them . . . mainly with high income." See Stephanie Baker & Vernon Silver, "Pfizer Fights to Control Secret of $36 Billion COVID Vaccine Recipe," *Bloomberg* (Nov. 14, 2021), https://www.bloomberg.com/graphics/2021-pfizer-secret-to-whats-in-the-COVID-vaccine/?sref=qneqM2kv?srnd=premium-europe.

32. With no dominant shareholder, the top twenty-five shareholders collectively control less than half the shares. General public investing in Pfizer represents a considerable aggregated ownership, yet it is not strong enough to change company's policies. See "How Many Pfizer Inc. Shares Do Institutions Own?" *Nasdaq* (September 3, 2021) https://www.nasdaq.com/articles/how-many-pfizer-inc.-nyse:pfe-shares-do-institutions-own-2021-09-03

33. The world's most lucrative drug before the COVID-19 vaccine, Humira, is a treatment for autoimmune diseases owned by AbbVie after a buyout. See U.S. Congress, 2021. U.S. House of Representatives, Comm. on Oversight & Reform, Drug Pricing Investigation: Industry Spending on Buybacks, Dividends, and Executive Compensation (2021).

REFERENCES

Adler, Paul S. 2019. *The 99 Percent Economy: How Democratic Socialism Can Overcome the Crises of Capitalism.* New York: Oxford University Press.

Access to Medicine Foundation (AMF). 2022. *Access to Medicine Index 2022.* Amsterdam, Netherlands: Access to Medicine Foundation. https://accesstomedicinefoundation.org/medialibrary/2022-access-to-medicine-index-1668514482.pdf.

AMR Industry Alliance (AMRIA). 2018. *Tracking Progress to Address AMR.* Geneva: The AMR Industry Alliance. https://www.amrindustryalliance.org/wp-content/uploads/2018/01/AMR_Industry_Alliance_Progress_Report_January2018.pdf.

———. 2020. *2020 Progress Report*. Geneva: The AMR Industry Alliance. https://www.amrindustryalliance.org/wp-content/uploads/2020/01/AMR-2020-Progress-Report.pdf.

———. 2022. *AMR Industry Alliance Progress Report: 2021 Member Survey*. Geneva: The AMR Industry Alliance. https://www.amrindustryalliance.org/progress-report/.

Bankston, Carl L., III. 2010. "Social Justice: Cultural Origins of a Perspective and a Theory." *The Independent Review* 15 (2): 165–178.

Benavides, Ximena. 2023. "Inequitable by Design: The Patent Culture, Law and Politics Behind COVID-19 Vaccine Global Access." *University of Michigan Journal of Law Reform* 56 (2): 4551541.

Benfer, Emily A. 2015. "Health Justice: A Framework (and Call to Action) for the Elimination of Health Inequity and Social Injustice." *American University Law Review* 65 (2): 275–351.

Benfer, Emily A., Seema Mohapatra, Lindsay F. Wiley, and Ruqaiijah Yearby. 2020. "Health Justice Strategies to Combat the Pandemic: Eliminating Discrimination, Poverty, and Health Disparities During and After COVID-19." *Yale Journal of Health Policy, Law, and Ethics* 19 (3): 122–171.

Benfer, Emily A., James Bhandary-Alexander, Yael Cannon, Medha Makhlouf, and Tomar Pierson-Brown. 2021. "Setting the Health Justice Agenda: Addressing Health Inequity & Injustice in the Post-Pandemic Clinic." *Clinical Law Review* 28: 45–84.

Blanco, Erin, Ashleigh Furlong, and Lennart Pfahler. 2022. "How Bill Gates and His Partners Took Over the Global COVID Pandemic Response." *Politico*, September 14. https://www.politico.com/news/2022/09/14/global-COVID-pandemic-response-bill-gates-partners-00053969.

Boettke, Peter J. 2019. *F. A. Hayek: Economics, Political Economy and Social Philosophy*. London: Palgrave Macmillan.

Braveman, Paula. 2014. "What Are Health Disparities and Health Equity? We Need to Be Clear." *Public Health Reports* 129 (2): 5–8.

Brenan, Megan. 2022. "U.S. Business Sectors Raying Worst Since 2008." *Gallup News*, September 9. https://news.gallup.com/poll/400835/business-sector-average-rating-worst-2008.aspx.

Britton-Purdy, Jedediah, David Singh Grewal, Amy Kapczynski, and K. Sabeel Rahman. 2020. "Building a Law-and-Political-Economy Framework: Beyond the Twentieth-Century Synthesis." *The Yale Law Journal* 129 (6): 1784–1835.

Brown, Wendy. 2006. "American Nightmare: Neoliberalism, Neoconservatism, and De-Democratization." *Political Theory* 34 (6): 690–714.

———. 2015. *Undoing the Demos: Neoliberalism's Stealth Revolution*. Cambridge, MA: The MIT Press.

Buse, Kent, Sonja Tanaka, and Sarah Hawkes. 2017. "Healthy People and Healthy Profits? Elaborating a Conceptual Framework for Governing the Commercial Determinants of Non-communicable Diseases and Identifying Options for Reducing Risk Exposure." *Global Health* 13 (34): 1–12.

Carpenter, Daniel. 2010. *Reputation and Power. Organizational Image and Pharmaceutical Regulation at the FDA*. Princeton, NJ: Princeton University Press.

Cate, Reinhard. 2017. "What Beliefs Drive Negative Coverage of 'Big Pharma.'" *Protagonist* (Blog), August 1. https://www.protagonist.io/what-beliefs-drive-negative-coverage-of-big-pharma/.

Centers for Disease Control and Prevention (CDC). 2019. *Antibiotic Resistance Threats in the United States, 2019*. Atlanta, GA: U.S. Department of Health and Human Services, CDC.

Chakravarthy, Ranjana, Kristina Cotter, Joseph DiMasi, Christopher-Paul Milne, and Nils Wendel. 2016. "Public- and Private-Sector Contributions to the Research and Development of the Most Transformational Drugs in the Past 25 Years: From Theory to Therapy." *Drug Information Journal* 50 (6): 759–768.

Cleary, Ekaterina G., Jennifer M. Beierlein, Navleen Surjit Khanuja, and Fred D. Ledley. 2018. "Contribution of NIH Funding to New Drug Approvals 2010–2016." *PNAS* 115 (10): 2329–2334.

Cockburn, Iain, and Rebecca M. Henderson. 2001. "Publicly Funded Science and the Productivity of the Pharmaceutical Industry." *Innovation Policy and the Economy* 1: 1–34.

Collins, Gregory M. 2020. *Commerce and Manners in Edmund Burke's Political Economy*. Cambridge: Cambridge University Press.

Cookson, Richard, Tim Doran, Miqdad Asaria, Indrani Gupta, and Fiorella Parra. 2021. "The Inverse Care Law Re-Examined: A Global Perspective." *The Lancet* 397 (10276): 828–838.

Coyne, Christopher J. 2013. *Doing Bad by Doing Good: Why Humanitarian Action Fails*. Stanford, CA: Stanford University Press.

Crane, Johanna T. 2020. "Dreaming Partnership, Enabling Inequality: Administrative Infrastructure in Global Health Science." *Africa* 90 (1): 188–208.

Dall, Chris. 2022. "AMR Action Fund Announces Its First Investments." *CIDRAP News*, April 4. https://www.cidrap.umn.edu/amr-action-fund-announces-its-first-investments.

de Lacy-Vawdon, Cassandra, Brian Vanderberg, and Charles H. Livingstone. 2022. "Recognising the Elephant in the Room: The Commercial Determinants of Health." *BMJ Global Health* 7: 2–4.

de Vries, Jantina, Paulina Tindana, Katherine Littler, Michèle Ramsay, Charles Rotimi, Akin Abayomi, Nicola Mulder, and Bongani M Mayosi. 2015. The H3Africa Policy Framework: Negotiating Fairness in Genomics." *Trends in Genetics* 31 (3): 117–119.

Deak, Dalia, Kevin Outterson K, John H. Powers, and Aaron S. Kesselheim. 2016. "Progress in the Fight Against Multidrug-Resistant Bacteria? A Review of U.S. Food and Drug Administration-Approved Antibiotics, 2010–2015." *Annals of Internal Medicine* 165 (5): 363–372.

Department of Care and Social Care. 2020. "World-First Scheme Underway to Tackle AMR and Protect UK Patients." *UK Government News*, June 17. https://www.gov.uk/government/news/world-first-scheme-underway-to-tackle-amr-and-protect-uk-patients.

Duff, Wendy M., Andrew Flinn, Karen E. Suurtamm, and David A. Wallace. 2013. "Social Justice Impact of Archives: A preliminary Investigation." *Archival Science* 13 (4): 317–348.

Faure, Marlyn, Nchangwi S. Munung, Ntobeko A.B. Ntusi, Bridget Pratt, and Jantina de Vries. 2021. "Considering Equity in Global Health Collaborations: A Qualitative Study on Experiences of Equity." *PLOS One* 16 (10): e0258286.

Feser, Edward. 1997. "Hayek on Social Justice: Reply to Lukes and Johnston." *Critical Review* 11 (4): 581–606.

Fisher III, William W. 2006. "The Growth of Intellectual Property: A History of the Ownership of Ideas in the United States." In *Intellectual Property Rights: Critical Concepts in Law*, edited by David Vaver, 265–291. New York: Routledge.

———. 2016. "Regulating Innovation. A Response to Ian Ayres and Amy Kapczynski, Innovation Sticks: The Limited Case for Penalizing Failures to Innovate." *The University of Chicago Law Review Dialogue* 82, (1): 251–267.

Florko, Nicholas, and Lev Facher. 2019. "How Pharma, Under Attack from All Sides, Keeps Winning in Washington." *Stat News*, July 16. https://www.statnews.com/2019/07/16/pharma-still-winning/.

Food and Drug Administration (FDA). 2010. "FDA Drug Safety Communication: Increased risk of Death with Tygacil (tigecycline) Compared to other Antibiotics Used to Treat Similar Infections." *U.S. Food and Drug Administration*, September 1. http://www.fda.gov/Drugs/DrugSafety/ucm224370.htm.

Furlong, Ashleigh, Sarah Anne Aarup, and Samuel Horti, 2022. "Who Killed the COVID Vaccine Waiver? The Inside Story of Lobbying, Threats and the Desire to Protect Industry Gutted a Proposal That Was Meant to Make Vaccines Widely Available in Poorer Countries." *Politico*, November 10. https://www.politico.eu/article/COVID-vaccine-poor-countries-waiver-killed/.

Government Accountability Office (GAO). 2017. *Drug Industry: Profits, Research and Development Spending, and Merger and Acquisition Deals*. Washington, DC: GAO. https://www.gao.gov/assets/gao-18-40.pdf.

Graham, David. 2023. "AMR in the Environment." Interview by Dr. Alex Lathbridge. *Brought to you by chemistry*, Royal Society of Chemistry, February 15. Audio, 50:59. https://open.spotify.com/episode/6SG4xZlXzIqzJ1OrIpnywL?si=JG4H9d0FSUKhFQlc7x_xug.

Grewal, David, and Jedediah Purdy. 2014. "Introduction: Law and Neoliberalism." *Law & Contemporary Problems* 77 (4): 1–23.

Haeffele, Stephanie, and Virgil Storr. 2019. "Is Social Justice a Mirage?" *The Independent Review* 24 (1): 145–154.

Harris, Angela, and Aysha Pamukcu. 2020. "The Civil Rights of Health: A New Approach to Challenging Structural Inequality." *UCLA Law Review* 67 (4): 758–832.

Harris, Angela, and James J. Varellas. 2020. "Introduction: Law and Political Economy in Times of Accelerating Crises." *Journal of Law and Political Economy* 1 (1): 1–27.

Hart, Julian Tudor. 1971. "The Inverse Care Law." *The Lancet* 297: 405–412.

Hayek, Friedrich A. 1976. *Law, Legislation and Liberty, Vol 2. The Mirage of Social Justice*. London: Routledge & Kegan Paul.

———. 2014. *The Collected Works of F.A. Hayek Vol. XV: The Market and Other Orders*. Edited by Bruce Caldwell. Chicago, IL: University of Chicago Press.
Herder, Matthew. 2019. "Pharmaceutical Drugs of Uncertain Value, Lifecycle Regulation at the S Food and Drug Administration, and Institutional Incumbency." *The Milbank Quarterly* 97 (3): 820–857.
Herder, Matthew, E. Richard Gold, and Srinivas Murthy. 2022. "University Technology Transfer Has Failed to Improve Access to Global Health Products During the COVID-19 Pandemic." *Healthcare Policy* 17 (4): 15–25.
Holcombe, Randall G. 2020. *Coordination, Cooperation, and Control: The Evolution of Economic and Political Power*. Springer International Publishing.
———. 2018. *Political Capitalism: How Economic and Political Power Is Made and Maintained.* Cambridge: Cambridge University Press.
Holmes Jr., R. Michael, David A. Waldman, Donald S. Siegel, and Justin A. Pepe. 2022. "Declining Trust in Capitalism: Managerial, Research, and Public Policy Implications." *Academy of Management Perspectives* 36 (4): 984–1006.
Hu, Charlotte. 2018. "These Are the Most—and Least—Reputable Drug Companies in the U.S." *Business Insider*, June 19. https://www.businessinsider.com/pharmaceutical-company-reputation-rankings-2018-6.
Jackson, Ben. 2005. "The Conceptual History of Social Justice." *Political Studies Review* 3 (3): 356–373.
Johnston, David. 1997. "Hayek's Attack on Social Justice." *Critical Review* 11 (1): 81–100.
Jones, Jeffrey M. 2022. "Confidence in U.S. Institutions Down; Average at New Low." *Gallup News*, July 5. https://news.gallup.com/poll/394283/confidence-institutions-down-average-new-low.aspx.
Kapczynski, Amy. 2008. "The Access to Knowledge Mobilization and the New Politics of Intellectual Property." *The Yale Law Journal* 117 (5): 804–885.
———. 2018. "Dangerous Times: The FDA's Role in Information Production, Past and Future." *Minnesota Law Review* 102: 2357–2382.
———. 2021. "How to Vaccinate the World, Part 1." *The Law and Political Economy Project*, April 30. https://lpeproject.org/blog/how-to-vaccinate-the-world-part-1/.
———. 2020 "The Law of Informational Capitalism." *The Yale Law Journal* 129 (5): 1460–1515.
———. 2022. "The Political Economy of Market Power in Pharmaceuticals." *Journal of Health Politics, Policy and Law* 48 (2): 215–239.
———. 2017. "Why 'Intellectual Property' Law?" The Law and Political Economy Project, November 6. https://lpeproject.org/blog/why-intellectual-property-law/.
Kitch, Edmund W. 1990. "Property Rights in Inventions, Writings, and Marks." *Harvard Journal of Law and Public Policy* 13 (1): 119–124.
Klein, Naomi. 2007. *The Shock Doctrine: The Rise of Disaster Capitalism.* New York: Picador.
Knox, Ryan, and Gregory Curfman. 2022. "The Humira Patent Thicket, the Noerr-Pennington Doctrine, and Antitrust's Patent Problem." *Nat Biotechnology* 40 (12): 1761–1763.
Kumar, Sapna. 2019. "Innovation Nationalism." *Connecticut Review* 51 (2): 205–246.

Kutz, Christopher. Unpublished. *The Improvisational Public*. https://www.law.nyu.edu/sites/default/files/NYU%20paper%20-%20Improvisational%20Public%2010-16%20KUTZ.pdf.

Lalani, Hussain S., Sarosh Nagar, Ameet Sarpatwari, Rachel E. Barenie, Jerry Avorn, Benajmin N. Rome, and Aaron S. Kesselheim. 2023. "US Public Investment in Development of mRNA COVID-19 Vaccines: Retrospective Cohort Study." *The BMJ* 380: e073747.

Ledley, Fred, Sarah Shonka McCoy, Gregory Vaughan, and Ekaterina Galkina Cleary. 2020. "Profitability of Large Pharmaceutical Companies Compared with Other Large Public Companies." *The Journal of the American Medical Association* 323 (9): 834–843.

Levin, Richard C., Alvin K. Klevoric, Richard R. Nelson, and Sidney G. Winter. 1987. "Appropriating the Returns from Industrial Research and Development." *Brookings Papers on Economic Activity* 18 (3): 783–832.

Lindsey, Brink. 2021. "Why Patents and Pandemics Don't Mix." *Brookings*, June 3. https://www.brookings.edu/blog/up-front/2021/06/03/why-intellectual-property-and-pandemics-dont-mix/.

London, Alex John. 2021. *For the Common Good: Philosophical Foundations of Research Ethics*. London: Oxford University Press.

Lukes, Steven. 1997. "Social Justice: The Hayekian Challenge." *Critical Review* 11 (1): 65–80.

Marmot, Michael. 2018 "An Inverse Care Law for Our Time." *The BMJ* 362: p.k3216.

Maxmen, A. 2022. "The Radical Plan for Vaccine Equity." *Nature*, July 13. https://www.nature.com/immersive/d41586-022-01898-3/index.html.

McCarthy, Justin. 2019. "Big Pharma Sinks to the Bottom of U.S. Industry Rankings." *Gallup News*, September 3. https://news.gallup.com/poll/266060/big-pharma-sinks-bottom-industry-rankings.aspx.

McCloskey, Deirdre. 2006. *The Bourgeois Virtues: Ethics for an Age of Commerce*. Chicago, IL: University of Chicago Press.

———. 2016. *Bourgeois Equality: How Ideas, Not Capital or Institutions, Enriched the World*. Chicago, IL: University of Chicago Press.

McCluskey, Martha T., Frank Pasquale, and Jennifer Taub. 2017. "Law and Economics: Contemporary Approaches." *Yale Law and Policy Review* 35 (1): 297–308.

McFadden, Alyce. 2021. "Pharma Loses Vaccine IP Battle Despite Record Q1 Lobbying." *Open Secrets*, May 4. https://www.opensecrets.org/news/2021/05/big-pharma-shatters-q1-lobby/.

Meiners, Roger E., and Robert J. Staaf. 1990. "Patents, Copyrights, and Trademarks: Property or Monopoly?" *Harvard Journal of Law & Public Policy* 13 (3): 911–925.

Millar, John S. 2013. "The Corporate Determinants of Health: How Big Business Affects Our Health, and the Need for Government Action!" *Canadian Journal of Public Health* 104 (4): 327–329.

Moses III, Hamilton, David H. M. Matheson, Sarah Cairns-Smith, Benjamin P. George, Chase Palisch, and E. Ray Dorsey. 2015. "The Anatomy of Medical Research: US and International Comparisons." *JAMA* 313 (2): 174–189.

Moss, Molly. 2021 "Antimicrobial Resistance: Warnings of the Next Pandemic." *United Nations Foundation*, May 10. https://unfoundation.org/blog/post/antimicrobial-resistance-warnings-of-the-next-pandemic/.

Moyn, Samuel. 2014. "A Powerless Companion: Human Rights in the Age of Neoliberalism." *Law and Contemporary Problems* 77 (4): 147–169.

National Center for Health Statistics. 2021. *Health, United States, 2019*. Hyattsville, MD: U.S. Department of Health and Human Services.

Nik-Khah, Edward. 2014. "Neoliberal Pharmaceutical Science and the Chicago School of Economics." *Social Studies of Science* 44 (4): 489–517.

Ostrom, Elinor. 1990. *Governing the Commons: The Evolution of Institutions for Collective Action*. Cambridge: Cambridge University Press.

———. 2010. "Beyond Markets and States: Polycentric Governance of Complex Economic Systems." *The American Economic Review* 100 (3): 641–672.

Outterson, Kevin, Rosa Rodriguez-Monguio, Enrique Seoane-Vazquez, and John H Powers. 2010. "Analysis of Systemic Antibiotics Approved in the U.S. Between 1980 and 2009." Conference paper at 138st APHA Annual Meeting and Exposition 2010, Denver CO, November 8–10.

Pasquale, Frank, Lenore Palladino, Martha T. McCluskey, John D. Haskell, Jedidiah Kroncke, Jamee K. Moudud, Raúl Carrillo, Rohan Grey, James J. Varellas III, Reza Dibadj, and Sandeep Vaheesan. 2019. "Eleven Things They Don't Tell You About Law and Economics: An Informal Introduction to Law and Political Economy." *Minnesota Journal of Law & Inequality* 37 (1): 97–147.

Patel, Deepali. 2023. "Why Pull Incentives Are Key to Catalysing Private Investment into Antibiotics." *The EFPIA View*, March 21. https://efpia.eu/news-events/the-efpia-view/blog-articles/why-pull-incentives-are-key-to-catalysing-private-investment-into-antibiotics/.

Pistor, Katharina. 2021. "Joe Biden's Pro-Market Agenda." *Project Syndicate*, July 20. https://www.project-syndicate.org/commentary/biden-promoting-competition-in-the-american-economy-by-katharina-pistor-2021-07.

Posner, Richard A. 2002. "The Law & Economics of Intellectual Property." *Daedalus* 131 (2): 5–12.

Pradhan, Rachana. 2022. "The Business of Clinical Trials Is Booming. Private Equity Has Taken Notice." *Kaiser Health News*, December 2. https://kffhealthnews.org/news/article/business-clinical-trials-private-equity/.

Rahmatian, Andreas. 2013. "International Intellectual Property Scholars Series: A Fundamental Critique of the Law-and-Economics Analysis of Intellectual Property Rights." *Marquette Intellectual Property Law Review* 17 (2): 191–229.

Reish, Michael. 2002. "Defining Social Justice in a Socially Unjust World." *Families in Society* 83 (4): 343–354.

Renwick, Matthew J., David M. Brogan, and Elias Mossialos. 2016. "A Systematic Review and Critical Assessment of Incentive Strategies for Discovery and Development of Novel Antibiotics." *The Journal of Antibiotics* 69 (2): 73–88.

Review on Antimicrobial Resistance (RAR). 2016. *Tackling Drug-Resistant Infections Globally: Final Report and Recommendations*. London: Government of the United Kingdom.

Santos Rutschman, Ana. 2021. "The COVID-19 Vaccine Race: Intellectual Property, Collaboration(s), Nationalism and Misinformation." *Washington University Journal of Law and Policy* 64: 167–201.

Silverman, Ed. 2022. "Dozens of Institutional Investors Urge Drugmakers to Link Executive Compensation to Access to Medicines." *STAT News*, October 20. https://www.statnews.com/pharmalot/2022/10/20/compensation-health-inequity-COVID19-merck-pfizer-jnj-lilly-moderna-biogen-novartis-abbvie-gilead-astrazeneca/.

Singer, Peter. 2022. "Investors Must Tackle Vaccine Inequity." *Jackson Hole Economic*, January 24. https://jheconomics.com/investors-must-tackle-vaccine-inequity/.

Smith, Adam. [1776] 1981. *An Inquiry into the Nature and Causes of the Wealth of Nations*. Indianapolis, IN: Liberty Fund.

So, Anthony D., Neha Gupta, Samir Kumar Brahmachari, Ian Chopra, Bernard H. Munos, Carl F. Nathan, Kevin Outterson, Jean Pierre Pacaud, David J. Payne, Rossana Peeling, Melvin Spigelman, and Johan Weigelt. 2011. "Towards New Business Models for R&D for Novel Antibiotics." *Drug Resistance Updates: Reviews and Commentaries in Antimicrobial and Anticancer Chemotherapy* 14 (2): 88–94.

Stiglitz, Joseph E. 2012. *The Price of Inequality: How Today's Divided Society Endangers Our Future*. New York: W.W. Norton and Company.

Storr, Virgil Henry, and Ginny Seung Choi. 2019. *Do Markets Corrupt Our Morals?* New York: Palgrave Macmillan.

Suter, Tara. 2021. "Lobbying Efforts by Companies Making COVID-19 Rapid Tests and Vaccine Fluctuate." *Open Secrets*, November 8. https://www.opensecrets.org/news/2021/11/lobbying-efforts-by-companies-making-COVID-19-rapid-tests-and-vaccines/.

't Hoen, Ellen F.M. 2016. *Private Patents and Public Health Changing Intellectual Property Rules for Access to Medicines*. Amsterdam, Netherlands: Health Action International.

———. 2019. *The Global Politics of Pharmaceutical Monopoly Power: Drug Patents, Access, Innovation and the Application of the WTO Doha Declaration on TRIPS and Public Health*. Diemen, Netherlands: AMB Publishers.

Tebble, Adam. 2009. "Hayek and Social Justice: A Critique." *Critical Review of International Social and Political Philosophy* 12 (4): 581–604.

Termeer, Catrien J.A.M., Art Dewulf, and Robbert Biesbroeket. 2019. "A Critical Assessment of the Wicked Problem Concept: Relevance and Usefulness for Policy Science and Practice." *Policy and Society* 38 (2): 167–179.

Testoni, Federico E., Mercedes Garcia Carrillo, Marc-André Gagnon, Cecilia Rikap, and Matias Blaustein. 2021. "Whose Shoulder Is Health Research Standing On? Determining Key Actors and Contents of the Prevailing Biomedical Research Agenda." *PLOS One* 16 (4): e0249661.

Thissen, Elvira. 2014. "Focus on Pharma: Creating a Market for Disease Prevention." *GreenBiz*, December. https://www.greenbiz.com/article/focus-pharma-creating-market-disease-prevention.

Thomas, David, and Chad Wessel. 2022. *The State of Innovation in Antibacterial Therapeutics*. Washington, DC: Biotechnology Innovation Organization. https://

www.bio.org/sites/default/files/2022-02/The-State-of-Innovation-in-Antibacterial-Therapeutics.pdf.

Torreele, Els. 2020. "Business-as-Usual Will Not Deliver the COVID-19 Vaccines We Need." *Society for International Development* 63 (2): 191–199.

UCL Institute for Innovation and Public Purpose. 2018. *The People's Prescription: Re-imagining Health Innovation to Deliver Public Value*. London: IIPP, Global Justice Now, Just Treatment, STOPAIDS. https://www.ucl.ac.uk/bartlett/public-purpose/wp2018-10.

UK Department of Health and Social Care. 2019a. *Tackling Antimicrobial Resistance 2019–2024. The UK's Five-Year National Action Plan*. January 24. https://www.gov.uk/government/publications/uk-5-year-action-plan-for-antimicrobial-resistance-2019-to-2024.

———. 2019b. *Contained and Controlled. The UK's 20-Year Vision for Antimicrobial Resistance*, January 24. https://www.gov.uk/government/publications/uk-20-year-vision-for-antimicrobial-resistance.

U.S. House of Representatives, Committee on Oversight and Reform. 2021. *Drug Pricing Investigation Industry Spending on Buybacks, Dividends, and Executive Compensation*. Washington, DC: Committee on Oversight and Reform, U.S. House of Representatives.

Ventola, C. Lee. 2015. "The Antibiotic Resistance Crisis." *P&T* 40 (4): 277–283.

Wagner, Richard E. 2016. *Politics as a Peculiar Business: Insights from a Theory of Entangled Political Economy*. Cheltenham: Edward Elgar Publishing.

Wegner, Judith Welch. 2009. "Reframing Legal Education's Wicked Problems." *Rutgers Law Review* 61 (4): 867–1008.

Williams, David R., Jourdyn A. Lawrence, Brigette A. Davis, and Cecilia Vu. 219. "Understanding How Discrimination Can Affect Health." *Health Services Research* 5 (2): 1374–1388.

Wirtz, Veronika, Hans V. Hogerzeil, Andrew L. Gray, Maryam Bigdeli, Cornelis P. de Joncheere, Margaret A. Ewen, Martha Gyansa-Lutterodt, Sun Jing, Vera L. Luiza, Regina M. Mbindyo, Helene Möller, Corrina Moucheraud, Bernard Pécoul, Lembit Rägo, Arash Rashidian, Dennis Ross-Degnan, Peter N. Stephens, Yot Teerawattananon, Ellen F.M. 't Hoen, Anita K. Wagner, Prashant Yadav, and Michael R. Reich. 2017. "Essential Medicines for Universal Health Coverage." *The Lancet* 389: 403–476.

Whyte, Jessica. 2019. *The Morals of the Market: Human Rights and the Rise of Neoliberalism*. London: Verso.

World Bank. 2017. *Drug-Resistant Infections: A Threat to Our Economic Future*. Washington, DC: International Bank for Reconstruction and Development/The World Bank. https://documents.worldbank.org/en/publication/documents-reports/documentdetail/323311493396993758/final-report.

Wouters, Olivier J. 2020. "Lobbying Expenditures and Campaign Contributions by the Pharmaceutical and Health Product Industry in the United States 1999–2018." *JAMA Internal Medicine* 180 (5): 688–697.

Zycher, Benjamin, Joseph A DiMasi, and Christopher-Paul Milne. 2010. "Private Sector Contributions to Pharmaceutical Science: Thirty-Five Summary Case Histories." *American Journal of Therapeutics* 17 (1): 101–120.

Chapter 3

Successful Evasive Entrepreneurship

Nature or Circumstance? Three Case Studies in the Area of Health and Safety Regulation

Alexander Köhler

The digital age is driven by ambitious and confident entrepreneurs—young companies that influence, mold, and facilitate human relationships and interactions. From instant messaging or online dating, to the way we engage with our environment, to innovative mapping services or app-based taxi hailing, the businesses and the entrepreneurs behind them are often iconic, and occasionally infamous, for their relentless drive to innovate and expand. The mechanisms these companies and their leaders employ to carve out, maintain, and increase their market share in digital and physical markets have gained increasing public and regulatory attention.

Today, the most commonly referenced scenario in evasive entrepreneurship is the use of tools by tech-sector startups, ranging from unorthodox interpretations of existing regulation to rule-bending, and ultimately, to deliberate rule-breaking, aimed at achieving growth in heavily regulated and formerly analogue markets. Such behavior may not necessarily be ill-motivated, but it does stem from the perception that deficient legal frameworks are often made for, and therefore privileging existing (pre-digital), businesses and their products and services, while simultaneously disadvantaging new and emerging players who offer novel, often digitally driven, evolutions of the incumbent industry leader's product. *Evasive Entrepreneurship*, made popular as a term by economists such as Magnus Henrekson (2007), Coyne and Leeson (2004), Peter Boettke (2014), Adam Thierer (2020), Tino Sanandaji (2011) and many others, is defined as "entrepreneurial practices aimed at circumventing existing institutional frameworks" (Ufere and Gaskin 2021, 1), and has become common practice for today's heavy weights of the digital economy. Eccentric strategies to increase market share are, however, neither a new phenomenon, nor are they limited to tech companies. Social entrepreneurs and businessmen and -women of other manufacturing industries have made use of evasive tactics in the past, and continue to do so, differing greatly in both the nature of the entrepreneurial activity and the historical and socioeconomic context of the market in which it is tried.

Ride-hailing app Uber is one of the most prominent examples of successful evasive entrepreneurship, having shifted employment laws and taxi regulation in many countries to allow for its business to thrive. E-scooter businesses, on the other hand, such as Lime, Voi, or Tier, similar to Uber in that they are built on the idea of offering convenient and app-based individual mobility solutions, have, after widely successful market entries, faced strong regulatory backlash, especially in Western Europe. E-scooter providers exploiting regulatory gaps are now facing forced shutdowns in major cities like Paris, and while Uber, Bolt and Lyft are continuously growing, the question remains as to why some of these evasive entrepreneurs succeed and others fail. This chapter assesses one possible answer to this question; how the interplay between the type of evasive entrepreneurial undertaking—whether it is for-profit or altruistic, digital or analogue—and broader socioeconomic circumstances may affect its chances of prevailing and success.

The COVID-19 pandemic put a spotlight on health and safety regulation worldwide, especially concerning its ability to equally adapt to an everchanging pandemic environment as well as the increasingly dynamic developments of social, technological, and economic trends and necessities. I have chosen to place case studies of evasive entrepreneurship revolving around health and safety regulation at the center of my analysis because they provide timely entrepreneurial examples and simultaneously allow for a cross-sectoral analysis with their wide range of application. The chapter is not an exhaustive study of evasive entrepreneurship but a qualitative review of evasive business practices that touch upon the nexus of health and safety regulation and their respective socioeconomic circumstances.

Evasive entrepreneurship is far from a recent phenomenon. The eighteenth-century political economist Adam Smith already listed the entrepreneur's capability to overcome obstacles in form of human-made laws as a necessity to achieve economic progress, besides other traditional liberal ideals of freedom and security (Smith [1776] 1977, 540). Evasive entrepreneurs may serve a crucial role in a functioning constitutional state as they provide incentives for legislators to adapt laws. They can ensure the "health" of economies by driving innovation and economic evolution. Elert and Henrekson (2014) detail the evasive entrepreneur's particular purpose in a growing economic system, rearranging the top-down conception of entrepreneurship as being conditional on institutional regulation, toward a reciprocal and living relationship between private and public actors. Works such as Thierer's "Evasive Entrepreneurs" (2020) and Henreksons and Sanandaji's

"Institutional Entrepreneurship" (2012) have aimed to shed a light on how institutions under pressure by entrepreneurs interact with them, especially as the entrepreneur has reemerged as an important economic player of the twenty-first century.

Literature on evasive entrepreneurs and ideal business conditions highlights a conflict between what is commonly understood as circumstances that are conducive to innovation and the practice that many evasive entrepreneurs follow. As Boettke (2014) notes, one of the main factors that creates an environment friendly toward innovation and entrepreneurship is the rule of law—that is a clear and enforceable legal framework which renders risk analyses (at least the regulatory part) more tangible and, together with the protection of intellectual property, allows businesses to thrive free from intellectual theft and arbitrary legal obstacles.

At the same time, however, many of the innovative disruptors of the past two decades succeeded not because of legal frameworks, but *in spite* of them. Uber may be the most prominent example, with a business model that was at least partially outside of what was widely considered the legal boundaries of formal employment and taxi businesses. The company was so successful that, with public support, regulators had to follow suit and adapt to the ride-sharing giant's needs (Thierer 2020). One may presume that both Thierer and notorious Uber cofounder Travis Kalanick would agree with Boettke on the importance of the rule of law, a fact that points toward a complicated intersection of stable regulatory environments and what is understood to be successful evasive entrepreneurship. Undoubtedly, some laws must be more bendable than others, while some remain comparatively static. This difference, the likelihood of rules shifting under pressure, depends on regulatory stickiness, that is, how quickly rules can be changed or adapted. Whether a law is based on a single yes-or-no decision and is therefore static, or built on a "series of multiple partial sequential decisions informed by monitoring and review" (Bennear and Wiener 2019, 1), and therefore adaptive, influences its stickiness. The rich history of evasive entrepreneurship and its academic study highlights the fact that as a concept, it precedes the modern, fast-growing tech business.

The rest of the chapter proceeds as follows. After defining entrepreneurship, as well as regulatory stickiness and adaptability as integral concepts to the study of evasive entrepreneurship, the chapter develops a broad theoretical framework of factors that influence the success of evasive entrepreneurial activity, based on which it then compares three case studies. The case studies include the French digital healthcare platform Doctolib, a case of social evasive entrepreneurship based on Greek solidarity clinics, and lastly the unsuccessful food business "Chowdy" which blurs the lines between conventional business and a gig-economy startup. Doctolib, Greek solidarity clinics, and food start-up Chowdy represent innovative entrepreneurial undertakings in diverse settings that have made use of evasive strategies, and their study helps us to develop an analysis of the stickiness of health and safety regulation and why evasive activities are more successful in some cases than in others.

The case selection set forth in this chapter therefore distinctly transcends the realm of technology start-ups, a sector which has gained notoriety for evasive entrepreneurial tactics and tends to overshadow the many less controversial but nevertheless influential cases of non-tech evasive entrepreneurs. Approaching the topic through a qualitative review of case studies allows for a detailed exploration of the mechanisms that contribute to the success of an evasive entrepreneurial undertaking, capturing intricacies that a quantitative analysis might overlook, allowing me to explore a complex phenomenon that cannot be easily measured.

ENTREPRENEURS AND ENTREPRENEURSHIP

Definitions of entrepreneurship as an economic concept differ; for the purpose of this chapter, it is understood as the founding and establishing of a new enterprise (Low & MacMillan 1998). The level at which entrepreneurial activities have been analyzed ranges from microeconomic considerations of the success and viability of the business model (Barreto 2013) to macroeconomic approaches which aim to determine an entrepreneur's value for economic progress in a given economic system (Quadrini 2009), to Schumpeterian innovation-centered approaches (Schumpeter 1934). Hanoteau and Vial (2020) argue that whether business practices are conforming or evasive must be the starting point of any analysis of entrepreneurship. The definition of evasive varies—Hanoteau and Vial specifically address corruption to evade applicable regulation, others simply refer to the disregard of existing laws and rules. They argue that evasion is only the second-best option chosen in the face of regulatory adversity, while generally, the favored response of entrepreneurs to regulation is conforming. Bribery and corruption as "hard" evasive techniques are commonly seen as both morally wrong and prosecutable; evasive entrepreneurs, however, especially in the tech sector, tend to resolve to more intricate, "soft" forms of rule-bending. This analysis understands evasive entrepreneurship as behavior that utilizes loopholes in existing regulation, taking advantage of legal grey zones or simply defying laws by introducing innovative products and services which current legal frameworks are not equipped to grasp.

In theory, successful evasive entrepreneurship may render the institution that is being evaded obsolete, highlighting its irrelevance regarding contemporary businesses, or increasing the pressure for political and regulatory reform (Henrekson and Sanandaji 2011). This may be especially relevant in notoriously slow regulatory environments, such as the European Union. The inter-institutional dialogue between the European Parliament and the Commission takes almost two years on average to pass new regulation because they must take into account the sensitivities of each member state. The nearly forty-year-long process of implementing the "Societas Europaea (SE)," the standard of a public company registered according to the EU's corporate law, was infamous. In the fast-paced and potentially disruptive entrepreneurial field of technology and information services and products, two years may very likely be longer than the lifespan of a new tech-startup. Audio-based social platform Clubhouse, for example, heavily criticized for its use of private data and hate speech policy, has been nearly forgotten since its launch and hype in 2020, well before new privacy and market regulation could be implemented.

Contemporary debates around evasive entrepreneurship in academia, in popular literature and in the media largely focus on gig-economy "icons." These are not the only examples, however. One may think of how the first carmakers resisted and defied societal and regulatory pressure against their "devilish" machines (Kline and Pinch 1996), or the many community-based social entrepreneurs who continue their work despite legal troubles and social stigma (Elahi and Malik 2021).

Either way, evasive entrepreneurs are polarizing—hated by those who consider it paramount to respect the state's regulatory might, admired by technophiles that value innovation and idolize entrepreneurial archetypes as those who lead the way toward a fully integrated digital society. Current scholarship appears similarly binary in its assessment of said entrepreneurs and their businesses, focusing mostly on successful examples, for example, ride-hailing giant Uber, or foreshadowing the end of a state-led and rule-based economy as the GAFAs (Google, Apple, Facebook, Amazon) and other gig economy players become too big to fail, and too powerful to be regulated. Beyond critique or praise for evasive entrepreneurs, it remains necessary to shed light on the phenomenon and its different forms in their juridical-cultural context.

STICKINESS AND ADAPTABILITY

Regulation and the rule of law are generally accepted as part of the social contract in democratic nations, facilitating fair competition while protecting private and public interests. A considerable number of clauses and paragraphs, however, sit idle in the bookshelves of regulators and lawyers, unused, outdated or otherwise irrelevant to the lives of citizens and entrepreneurs.

Many are simply obsolete, such as §27 of the German road traffic act, which forbids marching on bridges, a remnant of World War II where soldiers would accidentally collapse small bridges as they crossed marching in step (§27 (6) StVO). Others are overlooked, like the prohibition to apply stamps with the Queen's portrait upside-down in the United Kingdom (e.g., see the UK's Treason Felony Act of 1848). Examples are plenty, and new additions are not unlikely. The state of California introduces roughly one thousand new pieces of legislation each year, and Switzerland reaches a record-worthy 5,500 newly passed laws per annum. Many are not thought out; they are too niche to have a tangible effect, or simply lagging behind the speed of social evolution and technological revolution in citizen's lives and the new services and devices that penetrate homes, workplaces, and the public realm.

Not all regulation therefore has an evident purpose, a reality that provides a potent tool to attack the presumed "regulation mania" of legislators. Instead of proving the needlessness of rules, however, obsolete laws can rather serve as a reminder that legislation needs to evolve and adapt, as it may otherwise turn into merely an obscure anecdote. It equally shows that legislators are not quick to update existing regulation or evaluate its necessity beforehand, providing evidence that the rationale of evasive entrepreneurs may be without alternative in certain cases.

Sticky regulations are those which are hard to change—the stickiness of a law, a technical standard or a policy determines how dynamic and flexible it is. Stickiness may appear negative at first, government and legislative bodies are frequently criticized for their inability to adapt to new realities, changing markets and societal progress. Aaron Nielson (2018) challenges this view as he highlights that one of the most important factors in creating an environment conducive to investment and growth is regulatory stability and the rule of law. As business decisions are often made with regards to long-term effects and potentials for future revenue streams, the relative stability and predictability of regulatory frameworks become determining factors. A billion-dollar investment into a nuclear powerplant is only a sound business decision if it is to be expected that nuclear energy is not going to be outlawed before the plant recuperates its cost.

Beyond a safe and predictable investment climate, sticky regulations may also simply be born out of extensive testing periods—one may be reminded of regulations regarding fire safety, which are relatively stable because standards have proven to be practical and efficient in saving lives. Similarly, laws may be sticky because they achieve some form of socially desirable outcome. Labor laws are an example of such a rationale behind inflexible regulation, safeguarding the income and livelihoods of employees at the extent of a firm's ability to adapt to a changing market environment, or from implementing its business model in the first place if its structure does not reflect common, legally established forms of employment. Nielson (2018) refers to the process of manifesting and maintaining regulations against a changing environment as ossification, a borrowed medical term that typically describes the natural process of bone formation.

Boettke, Coyne, and Leeson (2008, 332) discuss institutional path dependence and the "lock-in" effect stickiness results in. Traditionally, the lock-in effect describes costly obstacles which market actors implement to disincentivize customers from switching to other products or services, either through high fees or other barriers such as the prohibition to carry over data. The outcomes are economically suboptimal—customers are barred from using the best available service, while providers are disincentivized to innovate and improve their products and services. Similarly, "locked-in institutional arrangements" (Boettke, Coyne, and Leeson 2008, 332) may result in stickiness of regulation that is inadequate for current economic developments and market-customer needs. Lock-in effects in products and services are usually resolved through regulatory initiative, for example, the prevention of mergers and acquisitions or forced break-up of tech giants by competition authorities. Smaller market interventions, such as the recently adopted Digital Markets Act of the European Commission, already aim to lessen market power and lock-in effects of big tech players by implementing rules on level-playing fields and access of outsiders to online marketplaces (European Commission 2022). Evasive entrepreneurship puts this logic on its head, using business tactics to create an "exogenous 'shock' necessary to break society out of the suboptimal scenario" (Boettke, Coyne, and Leeson 2008, 332), meaning that the lock-in effect of inflexible, path-dependent regulation is challenged and, if successful, alleviated by evasive entrepreneurial action.

Change, progress, and innovation require flexible lawmakers and adaptable laws. Many of today's most valuable and innovative firms have business models which are based on the disruption of traditional and sometimes century-old products, services, and their distribution. Therefore, the more static a regulation, the less it may allow for viable innovation and progressive, disruptive business models. This further illustrates the complex relationship between the stickiness and adaptability of laws and the ability of an economy to innovate and develop. It requires a trade-off, where occasionally given rules and regulatory stability bend for evasive entrepreneurial endeavors, while at other times, the legislative status-quo prevails over the interests of innovators, and regulations are maintained at the expense of possible economic growth.

As a regulatory sector, health and safety laws and their (non-)adaptability have received increased attention in recent years. While the COVID-19 pandemic struck the world, regulation concerning health and safety swiftly became the center of discussion in private and public discourse. Questions of where and when to wear masks, vaccination mandates, how to protect vulnerable groups or how to keep schools open, affected virtually every person – all these issues were contingent on regulatory decisions.

The health sector is possibly one of the most regulated business areas; certificates and licenses are critical in that they ensure the wellbeing, and survival, of both patients and practitioners. The regulatory reach of health and safety legislation spans much wider than just medical care, emergency services, and hospitals; it includes pollution caps for inner cities, workplace health and safety standards or the regulation of restaurants and food producers. An array of regulations is established to ensure and enforce citizens' safety throughout all spheres of life—aforementioned laws regulating fire safety, those dealing with road safety and standards for cars, food safety, the safety of pharmaceutical products, and so forth. The stickiness of a law may increase the more it is perceived to ensure safety—path dependency has proven particularly strong in health policy and regulation (Bali, He, and Ramesh 2022). The more a legislative change is seen to infringe on citizens' safety the less adaptable a law may be. This is especially relevant regarding technological innovation—remembering both the first trains and the introduction of cars, it was safety concerns (together with people's conviction that these new forms of transport were the devil) that proved the hardest to overcome. Health innovators may especially struggle with this, as relevant regulations tend to be exceptionally strict.

Health and safety regulation is unique also because its necessity is almost universally accepted. "Most observers acknowledge that some form of oversight is needed when factors as essential as life and health are involved. Even those who are especially suspicious of heavy-handed government bureaucracy see a public interest in some form of external supervision of this field," Robert Field (2010, 607) writes.

THEORETICAL CONSIDERATIONS

While many factors may contribute to stickiness or adaptability of laws, I contend that five are of particular interest and offer a more robust base to understand and compare different cases of evasive entrepreneurship and their outcomes. The first of these variables is time. Time contributes to norm stickiness; the longer a law or regulation has been in force, the more entrenched it may become in a given legal framework, as well as in the minds of legislators and constituents (Bernstein 2006). This is often the case with laws that have been in place for a long time and have deep-seated support from particular interest groups and other stakeholders. Laws that have been in place for a long time may also be seen as more legitimate, and therefore stickier, because they have been tested and proven to be effective over time. Time can also influence the stickiness of legislation through the political and administrative process. Laws that pass through the legislative process quickly, without sufficient debate or consideration, are likely to be less sticky than those that are the result of a more deliberate and thoughtful process. Equally, however, long-standing laws may become outdated or irrelevant due to changes in technology, the economy, social, or moral values. This can lead to a lack of enforcement or compliance, making the laws less sticky.

The second variable to consider is political context. The political context and a society's perception of a particular piece of legislation can also play a role in how sticky said legislation is. If a law is highly controversial or unpopular, it may be more likely to be repealed or changed over time, while a law that is widely accepted and supported is more likely to remain in place. One example may be the German Autobahn and the lack of a speed limit—it exemplifies a regulation which over time has become intertwined with a culturally distinct understanding of freedom, to the point that attempts to introduce a speed limit have failed time and again, even though to outsiders it may seem as a backward and dangerous lawlessness. Similarly, the constitutional protection of gun ownership in the United States is at least partly explained by the Second Amendment's over 200 year-long history.

Time is closely linked to a third critical variable—custom and culture. The Autobahn is again illustrative. Traditions and customs are certain behaviors, practices, and beliefs that are said to occur among a previously defined group and are passed on through generations (Merriam-Webster Dictionary 2023). Group membership may be contingent on nationality, ethnicity, or religion and is highly dynamic (Namenwirth and Weber 1987). It may also rest "simply on the claim that certain cultural elements are rooted in the past" (Lewis and Hammer 2007, 3). Certain laws and regulations can grow to represent the identity of a country and its citizens, or at least a part thereof. Customs and traditions can shape the values and beliefs of a society, which in turn can influence the laws that are passed (Kitching, Mashruwala, and Pevzner 2016). Tradition can also be used as a justification for certain laws to be introduced, or as a basis for legal precedents—in turn, it may also be a source of resistance to change, which can make it difficult to pass new laws or reform existing ones. This may include cultural or religious particularities—examples of the latter are regulations regarding abortion rights or same-sex marriage. Theological or cultural rationales behind legal texts therefore contribute to their stickiness.

The fourth variable to consider is a country's economic system and political philosophy. Legal frameworks may originate in different economic and political ideologies: nations subscribe to capitalism or socialism, some economies are based on a social market system, and many others might have some combination of these concepts—different political and economic ideologies around the world may show regulatory ossification in different areas. Political ideology and systemic realities then equally determine how strong the effect of the nature of entrepreneurial undertaking on its success is—most obviously it is harder to imagine a tech-startup in a communist country while a social entrepreneur may struggle in an authoritarian state. One may also assume that a nation based on a capitalist economic and political system will show increased stickiness regarding laws that protect intellectual property and protection of property in general, as well as freedoms that pertain to conducting business. Labor laws, on the one hand, may be more adaptable in such a system, equally as universal health care for example, as they are in conflict with the individualistic and non-paternalistic philosophies of such a state. A socialist country, on the other hand, may show regulatory stickiness in areas of employment and state benefits, while property rights may be more adaptable (Jingyao and Lai 2018).

Fifth and finally, stickiness may also change due to shocks to an economic system. Such exogenous shocks, defined by the International Monetary Fund (IMF) as "sudden event[s] beyond the control of the authorities that [have] a significant negative impact on the economy" (Geithner 2003, 4), require authorities and governments to rethink and restructure policy tools, policy implementation, and evaluation (Röglinger et al. 2020). Sudden events such as natural disasters or economic downturns may create new risks and uncertainties, prompting regulators to create new rules to address them or to amend existing ones. In extreme situations, regulators may suspend some regulations to allow for a more rapid response to the shock; in other cases, the shock may cause regulators to reevaluate the relative importance of various regulations and adjust their enforcement priorities accordingly. Exogenous shocks may also influence regulatory bodies by changing public opinion, affecting the political will to enforce existing regulations or create new ones. Exogenous shocks are the topic of thorough academic enquiry, and as Boettke, Coyne, and Leeson (2008) write, evasive entrepreneurship can be understood as an exogenous shock in and of itself. "Traditional" exogenous economic shocks can push regulators to allow for quick change, and therefore support evasive entrepreneurs in their mission to create a legislative environment conducive to their business (Bonciani and Van Roy 2016). As catastrophes, pandemics or recessions change the foundation and basic assumptions on which regulation was formulated, and existing legislation is perceptibly ill-suited to maintain the health and safety of citizens; the immediate pressure of the crisis adds to that exercised by the entrepreneur, and consequently probabilities of change increase.

The above is, by far, not an exhaustive list of factors that may influence the adaptability or stickiness of regulations. It aims to provide an overview of the different dimensions that altogether may give an indication of a nation's or regulatory sector's affinity to adapt regulations to the needs of innovative entrepreneurs. A *disruptive* entrepreneur's success depends on their ability to decrease regulatory stickiness in their field as previous laws hinder their business model. It therefore complements or precedes the idea of evasive entrepreneurship—both concepts are however inherently interrelated. Evasiveness is only required if a legal framework proves to be too sticky to change by "traditional" means, and it is only successful if the respective regulation is not sticky enough to prevail.

CASE STUDIES

Evasive entrepreneurship is not limited to a certain sector, region, or a specific business model. Equally, the rules and regulations that are being evaded or undermined are not confined to one area of law—a tech start-up may be at odds with existing labor laws, while an industrial company is eluding environmental regulations, or vice versa. As a set of tools to further economic interests of entrepreneurs and firms, evasive entrepreneurial techniques may be deployed in different ways, at any time and by any actors. To allow for a fruitful comparison between different instances of evasive entrepreneurship I utilize cases which are exclusively related to health and safety regulation, precisely because such regulation typically finds cross-sectoral application and therefore allows for a broader analysis. All case studies occurred within the past decade, differed in their success and were not in competition with each other to control for regular market mechanisms. I have set out to compare (A) Doctolib, a case of a modern, successful, technology-driven disruptive entrepreneurial activity that evades existing standards and reflects what is publicly and most prominently understood as evasive entrepreneurship, (B) Chowdy, a case of a recent, technology-driven and convenience-based start-up that yielded commercial success yet failed to materialize institutional change and hence collapsed, and (C) Greek Alternative Health System, a case of social evasive entrepreneurship, which exemplifies a form of rule bending and breaking, is not primarily governed by economic objectives and distinctly tolerated by regulators.

Case Study A: Doctolib

Doctolib is a French start-up which provides an online platform that allows patients to book appointments at participating general practitioners and specialists, using an appointment management software for practitioners as well as a software for virtual medical consultation. Services are mainly offered in medium and large German and French cities. Both countries offer universal healthcare to citizens, and both systems are notoriously analog—digital technology to improve administration, data availability and provision of services lags far behind the technologically possible, mainly due to strict data protection laws. The European Union mainstreamed the ways in which personal data of European citizens may be shared and monetized under the General Data Protection Regulation (GDPR) of 2018, with especially stringent rules in high-risk sectors that include sensitive personal information, such as healthcare.

As detailed previously, historical and cultural context may permeate entrepreneurial activity in a given country or region (McGrath, MacMillan, Yang, and Tsai 1992). Germany's cultural heritage and historical context have made people wary of giving access to personal data for governments and businesses, German citizens tend to share less data that allows for personal identification compared to citizens of other industrialized countries (Wadle et al. 2019). The experiences of the secret police of the Nazi regime included spying on and categorizing people according to their physical and mental health, a system of denunciation, and an omniscient state apparatus in the German Democratic Republic, as well as state surveillance and state control, which all remain present in the collective memory of the German population and have had lasting effects on wellbeing and the willingness to grant access to personal data (Neuendorf 2017). Not surprisingly, German law requires the use of certified software as opposed to the regular video-chat platforms customers might be accustomed to, both for handling patient data as well as facilitating virtual medical consultation.

Pre-pandemic, the uptake of said services was limited as both patients and practitioners were hesitant to share or request personal data on unknown platforms, while authorities remained unsupportive of innovative healthcare delivery methods due to a perceived lack of necessity. The COVID-19 pandemic however kickstarted an exponential increase in online consultations, which skyrocketed from a few thousand in 2019 to 2.7 million in 2020 (McKinsey 2021). Concerns about safety from a highly contagious, and at that time unknown, disease needed to be balanced against data privacy concerns—the former became a defining factor of the stickiness of health and health consultation regulation. Both patients and doctors were conscious to minimize situations of possible exposure to the novel virus, which lowered barriers and helped in de-mystifying the concept of a virtual medical consultation.

Pre-digital solutions prevailed in all sectors; in 2020, only 30 percent of transactions in Germany were made electronically or by credit and debit card (Deutsche Bundesbank 2021), compared to around 80 percent in the United States (McKinsey 2021). Despite this, in the face of the pandemic as an exogenous shock to the German public health system, former German minister of health Jens Spahn introduced draft legislation to allow for digital prescriptions under the Digital Care and Nursing Modernization Act (DVPMG) in 2020, which would allow for entire medical transactions, from booking an appointment to the actual consultation and the prescription of medication, to be handled digitally via a platform such as Doctolib, a significant success for the entrepreneurial endeavor.

The case of Doctolib and health regulation shows that the stickiness of regulation may be turned upside down in the event of an unpredictable crisis or an exogenous shock—formerly extremely rigid regulation may be adapted if it is perceived to serve common safety and public health. Dynamics may shift entirely; as vaccines became widely available in the European Union and needed to be distributed quickly, France and several German states, including Berlin, used Doctolib as a platform for citizens to book vaccination appointments, both at general practitioners and at official vaccination sites. Official endorsement of Doctolib's service allowed the company to access an enormous new customer base and functioned as free marketing and a certificate of trust, while at the same time aiding authorities in executing an unprecedented vaccination drive.

Simultaneously, however, Doctolib faced criticism for mishandling of patient data, such as storing it on Amazon servers in the United States, presumably violating rulings about data transfers outside of the European Union and the so-called privacy shield (CJEU 2020). French courts dismissed this criticism and saw the service in compliance with data protection law (Legifrance 2021). The evidence suggests that the necessities of the COVID-19 pandemic took precedence over previous public and private reservations concerning data protection and the privacy of citizens.

In pre-pandemic years, digital novelties in the German health care sector appeared to be a distant reality. The political and communicative efforts of Doctolib to aid digital transformation were limited in success, and its collection of user data and subsequent monetization put the company in hot legal water. Through the exogenous shock of COVID-19 on authorities, doctors, and patients however, Doctolib was in a position of offering a platform as a "quick-fix," legal uncertainties became secondary and were later resolved through new legislation.

Case Study B: Chowdy

In 2014, a group of Canadian young professionals, who had become increasingly dissatisfied with the prices of food in Toronto, had the idea to hire a chef. What started as a cost-saving measure for a group of twenty people quickly ballooned into a meal pick-up and delivery service that generated over $100,000 a month. Instead of having a fixed space with overhead costs such as staff and furniture, Chowdy grew to employing chefs by the hour, renting a commercial kitchen by the hour, and allowing for customers to pick-up their lunches from several hubs dispersed throughout the city. These third-party hubs would store pre-made meals for between 8 to 36 hours, ready-made for price-savvy customers who do not cook. This model, which kept costs low while providing flexibility and convenience to clients who could pick up their order anytime instead of having to wait for it to be delivered, landed the company in regulatory trouble with the health department of the city of Toronto.

The storing of food in spaces that were not under the direct oversight of the company was deemed too risky and potentially unhygienic by the department. Food premise operators in the Province of Ontario are obliged to follow the Ontario Food Premises Regulation (Ontario Regulation 1990), which details the duties of a premise operator, such as protection of the food from contamination and adulteration (§26 (1)) or that its temperature may be kept either below or at 4°C or above or at 60°C. What it does not detail is how these obligations are to be met when vendor and storage facility are independently operated as separate entities. The legal code of Ontario simply does not cover Chowdy's business model, and although not distinctly illegal, its business operated in a regulatory grey area, and combined with the specificities of the food industry and its individual health and hygiene requirements, health authorities were prompted to use their ability to interpret codes at their discretion and to the disadvantage of the young and successful start-up.

Despite lengthy discussions between the company and the authorities, which Chowdy's founder Steven Long (2018) detailed in a blogpost on the industry news page Failory, a compromise, which would have allowed for the survival of the company, did not materialize. The startup subsequently shut down in 2016, two-and-a-half years after its inception. Chowdy fulfilled many of the common characteristics of a successful gig-economy startup, creating a digitally enabled service that is low in fixed costs and provides added convenience at a competitive price for customers. It did so in a legal gray zone, hoping regulators would adapt applicable legislation that includes its business model—as they had in previous cases, for example, regarding Uber. Highly entrenched health and safety regulation which had grown over time, however, made regulators and institutions resistant to adapt in a way which would allow Chowdy to survive economically.

The authorities had specifically allowed for the continuation of the company's delivery service, which had been distributing the ready-made meals directly from its rented kitchens to customers in suburban areas where the model of third-party hubs for self-pick up was not viable. Yet the delivery business was only an add-on to the start-up's core product and created virtually no profit – not least because the competition in the food delivery industry is fierce and backed by large, capital-heavy players such as Uber's in-house delivery service UberEats.

Case Study C: Greek Alternative Health System

The entrepreneur is commonly imagined as a "go-getter," someone who starts a new business, taking on financial risk with the intent of creating revenue—someone who wants to "make money." This somewhat narrow definition fails to capture an increasingly prevalent form of entrepreneurship that may follow traditional parameters of entrepreneurship, such as opportunity, drive, price, and cost consciousness, but focuses on creating or maintaining a public good or service instead of revenue generation and profit maximization. The social entrepreneur is one who engages in an entrepreneurial activity that seeks to work innovatively, pragmatically, and in the long term to solve social problems or, more generally, to bring about significant, positive change in a society, towards so-called meta-economic overarching goals.

Much like the narrowly defined entrepreneur, the social entrepreneur may find him- or herself obstructed by laws that render the entrepreneurial activity illegal or outside of existing regulatory frameworks. Unsurprisingly, these obstructions are more prevalent in health- and safety-related cases of social entrepreneurship. Often, community gardens or co-op stores come into mind as one thinks of social entrepreneurs, yet in reality, business-minded individuals with altruistic motifs operate in many sectors, especially in those where the absence of state interest and involvement is harming communities.

One example of evasive social entrepreneurship in the health sector is that of the Greek Alternative Health System, topic of widespread media coverage in the aftermath of the financial crisis of the late 2000s (Gordeljevic 2015; Alderman 2012). Under the Greek Alternative Health System volunteers, medical practitioners, and pharmacists created so-called "underground" clinics which served a growing number of previously publicly insured patients, who found themselves unable to pay dramatically higher out-of-pocket sums as austerity measures cut especially deep into the country's public health budget.

As discussed, the health sector is one of the most heavily regulated, and those performing pro-bono consultations and giving out free medicine subsequently found themselves in legal difficulties. For example, the Solidarity Clinic of Arta in the West of Greece's mainland was publicly accused by the local medical association of providing illegal and unlicensed medical care to patients (Solidarity4all 2015). In 2015, around ninety-two active solidarity clinics existed in Greece, out of which a majority listed legal status as a main problem of their undertakings (Evlampidou and Kogevinas 2019). As social entrepreneurs, the providers of Greece's alternative solidarity-based public health system were offering an innovative service that bridged a gap in an underperforming market. At times, one third of Greeks had no access to public health services (Evlampidou and Kogevinas 2019). Nevertheless, traditional state-licensed healthcare providers decried the unfair competition they saw themselves up against and highlighted the illegality of individual doctors and pharmacists practicing in make-shift clinics without conventional contracts or licenses.

It is hard to imagine an industrialized country with a centralized public health system that allows for unlicensed clinics to operate freely. Yet many of Greece's underground solidarity clinics were operating out of official buildings or state-owned facilities, such as MCCH (Metropolitan Community Center Helliniko) in Athens which was housed in a part of the old airport and supported by the Helliniko municipality, without an official lease on the premises nor any contracts with utility suppliers (Cottica 2015; Keep Talking Greece 2018). The municipality simply continued to pay water and telephone bills as the solidarity clinic was providing services it was no longer able to provide itself.

What made it possible for the solidarity entrepreneurs, decidedly operating outside of the realm of what is permitted under health regulation, if not against it, to do so successfully and under the eyes of authorities? It is the socioeconomic context and the exogenous shock of the crisis in financial markets that started in 2007 and worsened over time, of which Greece became a prominent victim. This shock put pressure on the public health sector and on authorities, which explains them turning a blind eye on what solidarity clinics do and how they are run. Consequently, the pressure on regulatory systems generated by the evasive entrepreneur in this case is a downstream effect of an initial shock to the system—that of the financial crisis and following austerity measures.

Discussion

Comparing all three case studies, one notices great variations in the nature of the demonstrated evasiveness as well as the specific social and economic circumstances. While Doctolib and Chowdy are both classic business endeavors, solidarity clinics in Greece operated on a non-profit basis. The clinics and Doctolib, however, both directly deal with the provision of health care services, while Chowdy's relevance for health and safety regulation stems from food hygiene. The comparison shows that rigid health regulation is likely to prevail, despite the economic benefits of lower cost and customer happiness. Exponential growth and a popular business idea do not suffice as exogenous shocks to make rules and regulators bend, especially since Chowdy did not provide any health or safety benefit for customers, besides offering an alternative to fast food.

Many aspects of a social evasive entrepreneur overlap with those of a traditional evasive entrepreneur. A major difference between the case of Greek solidarity clinics and Doctolib or Chowdy, however, is that the survival of the latter two depended on their ability to change regulation in the long or short run, while the former case of social evasive entrepreneurship never had the stated goal of adapting legislation, but to be allowed to carry out what was widely seen as essential services, without government interference.

Herein lies the conceptual difference between both forms of evasive entrepreneurship: one engages with institutions to adapt current laws to their economic benefit, sometimes more or less aggressively, while the other may hope to be tolerated by lawmakers, but ideally wants for official institutions to claim or reclaim the gap which the social entrepreneur occupies out of perceived necessity. This difference becomes starkly obvious on the two examples given, Doctolib has no interest in a state-owned app for doctors' appointments being introduced as a response to its evasive business tactics, while those who work in and for solidarity clinics in Greece are desperately waiting for public institutions to reinstate health insurance policies and ramp up funding for existing infrastructure and personnel.

For Doctolib it was the advent of COVID-19 and the radical shift in the perception of what is possible and what is necessary in the online realm that allowed for its business model to fully take off and be incorporated into the legal canon of its European markets. For Greek solidarity clinics, the only reason they exist is the exogenous shock of austerity measures, and the reason Greek authorities allowed them to operate, despite a complete lack of official organization, licensing, and contractual agreements.

For Chowdy, a comparable secondary shock was absent—authorities had no reason to bend in a market already saturated with delivery options, a cheaper pick-up solution was of little interest to policy makers. A promising socioeconomic context did not appear to work in its favor. At the same time, it is perfectly imaginable that a similar business idea in 2020, the first year of the COVID-19 pandemic, may have been met by much more flexible authorities that use their leeway to the benefit of entrepreneurial activity. Many restaurants affected by lockdowns adopted the offering of pick-up options for customers to survive, envisaging a company facilitating such, much like others facilitate delivery, does not appear far-fetched. Such speculation, however, is not the purpose of this chapter.

Other dimensions that contribute to stickiness appear to pale against the backdrop of exogenous shocks and socioeconomic circumstance when concerning health and safety regulation. Customary and historical truths prove flexible if dramatic occurrences require immediate action, state philosophy and legal frameworks lose their definitive character if found unequipped to deal with immense social and macroeconomic pressure. Equally, powerful incumbent stakeholders, such as Greek private practitioners, find themselves sidelined if they are perceived as unable to provide remedies against urgent exogenous shocks. The absence of such a shock in Chowdy's case shows how the previously defined dimensions of regulatory stickiness regarding health and safety prevail, even if a business model has proven its economic viability.

CONCLUSION

Many factors may contribute to the success of an evasive entrepreneur's undertakings, some of which are hard to measure and even harder to generalize. Personal drive, the political and economic situation of a given jurisdiction, or the viability of a business model may all play a role in determining whether the evasion of regulation is fruitful or doomed. As set forth, health industries are some of the most heavily regulated business areas around the globe, and understandably so, as they may potentially affect the life and death of a consumer. Evasive entrepreneurial activity, which touches on the health and safety of consumers, appears to face distinct challenges when it comes to the stickiness of regulation, becoming a determining factor of the evasive entrepreneur's economic fate.

The conducted investigation, however, proved this assumption is anything but forthright. As Boettke et al. (2008) describe how evasive entrepreneurs provide the exogenous shock needed for gridlocked regulatory environments to adapt and evolve, the case studies put forth provide evidence that evasive entrepreneurship, even in notoriously sticky regulatory areas which concern health and safety, may be able to unravel its potential and not be suffocated by regulatory tenacity if preceded by an exogenous economic and societal shock. The nature of the entrepreneurial undertaking, that is whether it is providing a public service, purely a tech-startup or simply innovating an existing business model, appears to be less instrumental for its success compared to the socioeconomic realities facing the evasive entrepreneur. A further, empirical analysis of comparable cases is warranted to confirm these observations.

REFERENCES

Alderman, Liz. 2012. "Amid Cutbacks, Greek Doctors Offer Message to Poor: You Are Not Alone." *The New York Times*, October 25. https://www.nytimes.com/2012/10/25/world/europe/greek-unemployed-cut-off-from-medical-treatment.html.

Bali, Azad Singh, Alex Jingwei He, and M. Ramesh. 2022. "Health Policy and COVID-19: Path Dependency and Trajectory." *Policy and Society* 41 (1): 83–95.

Barreto, H. 1989. *The Entrepreneur in Microeconomic Theory: Disappearance and Explanation*. London: Routledge.

Bennear, Lori S., and Jonathan B. Wiener. 2019. "Adaptive Regulation: Instrument Choice for Policy Learning over Time." Working Paper, Harvard University.

Bernstein, Gaia. 2006. "When New Technologies are Still New: Windows of Opportunity for Privacy Protection." *Villanova Law Review* 51 (4): 921–950.

Boettke, Peter J. 2014. "Entrepreneurship, and the Entrepreneurial Market Process: Israel M. Kirzner and the Two Levels of Analysis in Spontaneous Order Studies." *The Review of Austrian Economics* 27 (3): 233–247.

Bonciani, Dario, and Björn Van Roye. 2016. "Uncertainty Shocks, Banking Frictions and Economic Activity." *Journal of Economic Dynamics and Control* 73 (C): 200–219.

Cottica, Alberto. 2015. "Care by Communities: Greece's Shadow Zero-Cash Health Care System." *Edgeryders*, October 26. https://edgeryders.eu/t/care-by-communities-greeces-shadow-zero-cash-health-care-system/4880.

Coyne, Christopher J., and Peter T. Leeson. 2004. "The Plight of Underdeveloped Countries." *Cato Journal* 24 (3): 235–249.

CJEU [The Court of Justice of the European Union]. 2015. "Case C-362/14: Protection of Individuals with Regard to the Processing of Such Data." *InfoCuria*, October 6. https://curia.europa.eu/juris/document/document.jsf?text=&docid=169195&pageIndex=0&doclang=EN&mode=lst&dir=&occ=first&part=1&cid=7107294.

Deutsche Bundesbank. 2021. "Making Payments in Germany in 2020, the Year of COVID-19: Card-Based and Contactless Payments Trending." *Bundesbank.de*, January 14. https://www.bundesbank.de/en/press/press-releases/making-payments-in-germany-in-2020-the-year-of-covid-19-card-based-and-contactless-payments-trending--858018.

Elahi, Nazima, and Qaisar Ali Malik. 2021. "Assessing the Environmental and Social Obstacles to Women Entrepreneurs: A Case Study of Pakistan." In *Women Empowerment and Well-being for Inclusive Economic Growth*, edited by Shailja Dixit and Sana Moid, 90–105. Hershey, PA: IGI Global.

Elert, Niklas, and Magnus Henrekson. 2014. "Evasive Entrepreneurship and Institutional Change." IFN Working Paper No. 1044, Research Institute of Industrial Economics.

Elert, Niklas, Magnus Henrekson, and Joakim Wernberg. 2016. "Two Sides to the Evasion: The Pirate Bay and the Interdependencies of Evasive Entrepreneurship." *Journal of Entrepreneurship and Public Policy* 5 (2): 176–200.

European Commission. 2022. Regulation EU 2022/1925 of the European Parliament and of the Council of 14 September 2022 on Contestable and Fair Markets in the Digital Sector and Amending Directives (EU) 2019/1937 and (EU) 2020/1828 (Digital Markets Act, DMA). https://eur-lex.europa.eu/legal-content/EN/TXT/?toc=OJ%3AL%3A2022%3A265%3ATOC&uri=uriserv%3AOJ.L_.2022.265.01.0001.01.ENG.

Evlampidou, Iro, and Manolis Kogevinas. 2019. "Solidarity Outpatient Clinics in Greece: A Survey of a Massive Social Movement." *Gaceta Sanitaria* 33 (3): 263–267.
Field, Robert I. 2008. "Why Is Health Care Regulation So Complex?" *Pharmacy and Therapeutics* 33 (10): 607–608.
Geithner, Timothy. 2003. "Fund Assistance for Countries Facing Exogenous Shocks." Policy paper by Policy Development and Review Department, International Monetary Fund. https://www.imf.org/external/np/pdr/sustain/2003/080803.pdf.
Gordeljevic, Vijoleta. 2017. "Austerity vs. the People's Health: How Greeks Built an Alternative Health System (Part I)." *Huffington Post*, December 7. https://www.huffpost.com/entry/how-greeks-built-their-own-health-system_b_8238210.
Hanoteau, Julien, and Virginie Vial. 2020. "Institutional Quality, Conforming and Evasive Entrepreneurship." *Eurasian Business Review* 10 (1): 97–121.
Henrekson, Magnus. 2007. "Entrepreneurship and Institutions." IFN Working Paper, No. 707, Research Institute of Industrial Economics.
Henrekson, Magnus, and Tino Sanandaji. 2011. "The Interaction of Entrepreneurship and Institutions." *Journal of institutional Economics* 7 (1): 47–75.
Henrekson, Magnus, and Tino Sanandaji. 2012. *Institutional Entrepreneurship*. North Hampton, MA: Edward Elgar Publishing.
Jingyao, Wang, and Wei Lai. 2018. "Persistence and Change in the Rural Land System of Contemporary China." *Social Sciences in China* 39 (2): 94–113.
Keep Talking Greece. 2018. "Scandal! Helliniko Project Ousts Metropolitan Social Clinic at Old Athens Airport." *Keep Talking Greece*, June 4. https://www.keeptalkinggreece.com/2018/06/04/metropolitan-community-clinic-hellinikon/.
Kitching, Karen, Raj Mashruwala, and Mikhail Pevzner. 2016. "Culture and Cost Stickiness: A Cross-country Study." *The International Journal of Accounting* 51 (3): 402–417.
Kline, Ronald, and Trevor Pinch. 1996. "Users as Agents of Technological Change: The Social Construction of the Automobile in the Rural United States." *Technology and Culture* 37 (4): 763–795.
Legifrance. 2021. "Conseil d'État, Juge des référés, Case 450163, Inédit au recueil Lebon." *Legifrance*. March 12.
Lewis, James R., and Olav Hammer, eds. 2007. *The Invention of Sacred Tradition*. Cambridge: Cambridge University Press.
Lobel, Orly. 2017. "The Gig Economy & the Future of Employment and Labor Law." *University of San Francisco Law Review* 51 (1): 51–74.
Long, Steven. 2018. "Chowdy: Shutting down a +$110,000/Month Food Startup." *Failory*, October 26. https://www.failory.com/interview/chowdy.
Low, Murray B., and Ian C. MacMillan. 1988. "Entrepreneurship: Past Research and Future Challenges." *Journal of Management* 14 (2): 139–161.
McGrath, Rita Gunther, Ian C. MacMillan, Elena Ai-Yuan Yang, and William Tsai. 1992. "Does Culture Endure, or Is It Malleable? Issues for Entrepreneurial Economic Development." *Journal of Business Venturing* 7 (6): 441–458.
McKinsey & Company. 2021. "New Trends in US Consumer Digital Payments." *McKinsey*, October. https://www.mckinsey.com/~/media/mckinsey/industries/financial%20services/banking%20blog/new%20trends%20in%20us

%20consumer%20digital%20payments/new-trends-in-us-consumer-digital-payments%20-%20final.pdf.

McKinsey & Company. 2021. *eHealth Monitor 2021*. Berlin: McKinsey & Company.

Merriam-Webster Dictionary. 2023. "Tradition." *Merriam-Webster Dictionary*. https://www.merriam-webster.com/dictionary/tradition.

Namenwirth, J. Zvi, and Robert Philip Weber. 1987. *Dynamics of Cultur*e. Boston, MA: Allen and Unwin.

Neuendorf, Ulrike L. 2017. "Surveillance and Control: An Ethnographic Study of the Legacy of the Stasi and Its Impact on Wellbeing." *PhD dissertation*, University College London.

Nielson, Aaron L. 2018. "Sticky Regulations." *University of Chicago Law Review* 85 (1): Article 3.

Ontario Regulation. 1990. "493/17: Food Premises. Ontario Health Protection and Promotion Act, R.S.O. 1990, c. H.7." https://www.ontario.ca/laws/regulation/170493.

Pollman, Elizabeth. 2022. "The Rise of Regulatory Affairs in Innovative Startups." In *The Handbook of Law and Entrepreneurship in the United States*, edited by D. Gordon Smith, Brian J. Broughman, and Christine Hurt, 27–48. Cambridge: Cambridge University Press.

Quadrini, Vincenzo. 2009. "Entrepreneurship in Macroeconomics." *Annals of Finance* 5 (3): 295–311.

Rogers, Brishen. 2015. "The Social Costs of Uber." *University of Chicago Law Review* Online 82 (1): 85–102.

Röglinger, Maximilian, Ralf Plattfaut, Vincent Borghoff, Georgi Kerpedzhiev, Jörg Becker, Daniel Beverungen, Jan vom Brocke et al. 2022. "Exogenous Shocks and Business Process Management." *Business & Information Systems Engineering* 64: 669–687.

Schumpeter, Joseph A. 1934. *The Theory of Economic Development,* translated by Redvers Opie. Cambridge, MA: Harvard University Press.

Smith, Adam. [1776] 1977. *The Wealth of Nations: An Inquiry into the Nature and Causes of the Wealth of Nations*. Chicago, IL: University of Chicago Press.

Smith, J. Walker. 2016. "The Uber-all Economy of the Future." *The Independent Review* 20 (3): 383–390.

Solidarity4all. 2015. "Pitiful Panhellenic Originality: Solidarity Clinics Considered as Illegal Action: Αλληλεγγύη Για Όλους." *Solidarity4all,* April 30.

"Straßenverkehrs-Ordnung (German Road Traffic Act)" of 6. March 2013 (BGBl. I S. 367).

Thierer, Adam. 2020. *Evasive Entrepreneurs and the Future of Governance: How Innovation Improves Economies and Governance*. Washington, DC: Cato Institute.

Ufere, N., and Gaskin, J. 2021. "Evasive Entrepreneurship: Circumventing and Exploiting Institutional Impediments for New Profit Opportunity in an Emerging Market." *PLOS One* 16 (2): p.e0247012.

Wadle, Lisa-Marie, Noemi Martin, and Daniel Ziegler. 2019. "Privacy and Personalization: The Trade-off Between Data Disclosure and Personalization Benefit." In *Adjunct Publication of the 27th Conference on User Modeling, Adaptation and Personalization*, 319–324. New York: AMC.

Chapter 4

Exploring the Persistent Effects of Racial Discrimination on Economic Growth

Olivia Gonzalez

As African Americans began to migrate across the United States following the Civil War, they were not always immediately welcomed (Loewen 2005). Many towns—known as sundown towns—attempted to drive out their Black population by posting signs that warned Blacks to not go out after dark, "or else." Some areas formally passed ordinances barring African Americans from going out after dark or prohibited them from owning or renting property. Other areas didn't have official ordinances, but informally kept out Blacks through harassment and violence.

The emergence of sundown towns corresponds to racially biased attitudes and hostility that grew between 1890 and 1940. In response to what historians have identified as a worsening of race relations during this time, African Americans were forced to make a "Great Retreat" (Bazzi et al. 2022; JLoewen 2005; Quilin 1913; Logan 1954; Woodward 2002). During this retreat, African Americans moved to larger inner cities and a few small towns. Additionally, O'Connell (2019) writes that "The removal of federal expectations left norms of engagement open to local interpretation, and the interaction of Whites and Blacks in new places provided the opportunity for shifts in those interpretations" (O'Connell 2019).

Despite their appalling exclusionary nature, there has been very little research on sundown towns. There has been no comprehensive empirical exploration of how these towns have evolved over time, especially with regard to each area's economy. This chapter is an effort to help fill this gap by connecting the literatures on institutional persistence and the economics of discrimination to the nascent, but growing literature on sundown towns. Utilizing institutional economic theory as a lens, this chapter sets forth on an exercise to better understand how discriminatory policies can shape local communities economically. To aid in this exploration, this chapter also looks at factors that contributed to the emergence of sundown towns and their policies.

Institutional economics emphasizes the importance of rules in society, both formal and informal, for shaping economic interactions and behavior. Some may ask how our ancestors could have been so cruel; how could the inhabitants of towns across America so unabashedly discriminate against African Americans? Surely, no one familiar with U.S. history would be surprised by this fact. Instead of trying to ask how immoral character explains this history, applying the lens of institutional economics to this issue leads us to ask how racist and discriminatory energies filtered through different institutional arrangements can produce different outcomes.

Discriminatory and violent institutions have been shown in many other cases to be detrimental to growth. For the case of sundown towns, I predict that jurisdictions with exclusionary sundown policies will have slower economic growth over time relative to non-sundown areas.

The rest of the chapter proceeds as follows. First, I provide a brief background on sundown towns, cities, and suburbs to orient the reader. Then, I review the emerging literature on the institutional persistence of sundown policies that has been primarily led by sociologists and historians. I also discuss how this literature relates to the larger literature of institutional persistence that has been developed by economic historians.

Next, I analyze the available data, utilizing Illinois as a case study. Not all sundown towns enforced their exclusionary policies the same way. I devote a section outlining the various methods of exclusion that were utilized to expel or keep out African Americans, ranging from violent riots and police bias to sundown ordinances and social ostracism. Before discussing how the effects of sundown policies on growth vary by enforcement mechanism, I explore what factors made certain jurisdictions more predisposed to go sundown. I conclude the chapter with a discussion on discrimination, entrepreneurship, and economic growth.

SUNDOWN JURISDICTIONS: THE NORTHERN RESPONSE TO BLACK MIGRATION

Although most commonly referred to as "sundown towns," sundown policies actually were implemented and enforced at many levels of government: at the city, town, and suburb level. The primary source on this topic consists of a database of confirmed jurisdictions with historical sundown policies across America (Loewen 2005; Loewen and Loewen n.d.). It is helpful to distinguish between "sundown towns" and "sundown suburbs" (Loewen 2005).

The former and their sundown practices grew in prominence between 1890 and 1960 and include jurisdictions legally considered towns or cities, but are referred to as "sundown towns" as shorthand. The "sundown suburbs," on the other hand, grew in prominence between 1900 and 1968 and only include suburbs. The main difference between these two types of sundown areas, other than their time periods of emergence, is that towns largely evolved to become sundown, while suburbs were often incorporated with the intention of being all-white from the start. Sundown towns often had preexisting Black populations and then at some point due to some sort of triggering event decided to expel these residents, often violently.

Moving forward, when referring to sundown towns and suburbs collectively, I will use the term "sundown jurisdictions." I will later explore how these jurisdictions evolved over time as a whole as well as how the towns and suburb dynamics differ. This is important because their institutional origination differ significantly, and this will likely affect how they evolve economically.

The main defining feature of sundown jurisdictions was that for decades they were intentionally all-white by either expulsion or exclusion, particularly when it came to who was allowed within municipal boundaries after dark (Loewen 2005, 3).

The deteriorating race relations of the 1890s laid the groundwork for sundown jurisdictions. The resurfacing of the Ku Klux Klan, the growth in the occurrence of lynchings, and the driving of Blacks from their occupations were three main areas where this manifested. The biased attitudes and norms that intensified in the 1890s interacted with institutional responses of governments when Whites acted to drive out African Americans.

In addition to these deteriorating race relations, Democratic voting majorities, mono-ethnic makeups, and strong labor movements were underlying cultural and social factors that made jurisdictions more predisposed to go sundown (Loewen 2005, 138). Multi-ethnic jurisdictions, or areas with a variety of ethnic groups, were less likely to go sundown (Loewen 2005, 154).

Labor competition played a large role in sundown jurisdiction in- and out-group dynamics. It was a common occurrence for new migrants in towns to break the strikes of pre-existing ethnic groups, as newer immigrants often had little solidarity with pre-existing groups. This often created animosity between ethnic groups. But as Loewen and others document, the animosity was especially strong when African Americans were the strikebreakers. It was much more common for Blacks to be expelled en masse following a labor dispute between Whites and Blacks.

Other than the migration of African Americans directly following the Civil War, the Great Migration period is the other notable widespread migration phenomenon to highlight. At the onset of the Great Migration, nearly 90 percent of the country's Black population lived in Southern rural communities (Loewen 2005). By the height of the Great Migration, Blacks lived in areas all across the United States, most of which were urban. Greater social and economic opportunity was the most prominent driver of this historical exodus (Curtis White et al. 2005; White, Crowder, and Tolnay 2005). As they moved Northward, African Americans tended to migrate to metropolitan areas and central cities.

Migration patterns that emerged both during and following the Great Migration had lasting impacts for the spatial composition of Blacks and their concentration of poverty. White et al. (2005) provide a review of the research in this area and implications for race relations and persistent historical effects. Most notable is research by Blalock (1967) and Lieberson (1980) that suggest that the rapid growth of Black migrants in Northern cities acted as an impetus for an increase in the intensity of discriminatory behavior of native Whites (Blalock 1967, Lieberson 1980). Subsequent research demonstrated how this led to increased efforts to "maintain the residential color line, first through violence and intimidation and later through racial steering and protective covenants" (White et al. 2005, 216). Applied economic research has increased significantly over the years demonstrating various deleterious motivations and effects of such discriminatory policies, including redlining, protective covenants, and zoning, among others (White, Crowder; and Tolnay 2005, 216; Farley, Danziger, and Holzer 2000; Massey and Denton 1993;Philpott 1978; Quillian 2002; Franklin and Hammer 2001; Fischer 2003).

THE INSTITUTIONAL PERSISTENCE OF SUNDOWN POLICIES

Institutional persistence relates to how historical rules and norms in society can have lasting effects, even long after they are officially enforced. Economists have thoroughly documented how extractive historical institutions have negatively influenced long-run economic growth (Acemoglu, Johnson, and Robinson 2001). The theoretical literature argues that cultural norms are powerful in influencing behaviors that persist over time (Bisin and Verdier 2001; Deopke and Zilibotti 2008; Tabellini 2008; Acemoglu and Jackson 2011). The empirical literature is even more developed. Nunn (2008) finds a robust negative relationship between the number of slaves exported from a country and its contemporary economic performance (Nunn 2008). Banerjee and Iyer (2005) examine colonial land revenue institutions established by the British in India and find that differences in historical property rights led to sustained differences in economic outcomes (Banerjee and Iyer 2005).

Other research shows that mortality rates among early European settlers is a strong predictor of whether countries end up with robust institutions that protect private property rights and in turn whether their economies are healthy today (Acemoglu, Johnson, and Robinson 2001). Research also shows that medieval pogroms likely have had persistent effects on antisemitism and Nazi zealotry long after the original occurrence of said pogroms (Voigtländer and Voth 2012).

Williams (2022) finds a link between historical lynchings and contemporary political participation of Blacks, citing the possibility that these anti-black institutions are ultimately a legacy of slavery. The institutional persistence of sundown policies can similarly be traced back to anti-black attitudes that originate from earlier than the beginning of the twentieth century.

It is clear that historical events long ago influence contemporary outcomes today, the manner of which this takes place just varies by context (Alesina, Giuliano, and Nunn 2013; Sokoloff and Engerman 2000). It is important to note what is meant by "institutions" in the context of sundown jurisdictions. The growing sociological literature on sundown jurisdictions focuses on the presence of "sundown histories" and their long-run effects whereas the economic history literature might be more interested in how these histories translate to specific types of or quality of institutions (O'Connell 2019; Crowe 2012; Crowe and Ceresola 2014).

It is helpful to refer to the literature that argues that the presence of lynching in America was a signal of insecure property rights and an explanation of the relative underdevelopment of the postbellum South (Carden 2006). Similarly, Troesken and Walsh (2019) find that segregation laws emerged as an institutional response to a collective action problem (Troesken 2019).

Although much of the research on institutional persistence has been in the field of economic history, much could be gained by connecting the literature with recent work on persistent effects of sundown jurisdictions and their policies. O'Connell (2019), for example, finds a persistent historical link between sundown policies and the spatial patterning of Black-White poverty disparities at the county level. She provides evidence to suggest that counties with towns with sundown histories have lower White poverty rates over time than counties with no historical sundown town presence. It makes sense that policies drafted to favor Whites' race-based preferences would also benefit them in other ways.

O'Connell accounts for industrial composition and economic conditions, but this does not significantly influence her results. Crowe (2012), on the other hand, finds a link between sundown policies and contemporary economic development practices for a random selection of towns in Illinois, Indiana, Ohio, Michigan, Wisconsin, and Iowa. More specifically, of various economic development strategies available to communities, those towns that did not have sundown histories were more likely to employ or engage with more of them.

Crowe's work also highlights several potential mechanisms for how sundown policies could influence economic growth in the long-run. Although she focuses on economic development strategies as the main outcome variable of interest, these strategies have potential to influence economy-wide growth. For example, she points to the location of a large Krispy Kreme factory in Effingham, Illinois, which was also a sundown town. Although Effingham is located on two major interstates which influenced Krispy Kreme's location decision, among other factors, the fact that Effingham was all-white likely also influenced Krispy Kreme's site selection (Loewen 2005). Despite this and other large employer site selections in sundown jurisdictions, these areas saw declining populations over time. Crowe (2010) interviewed community leaders in sundown jurisdictions and discovered that they often purposefully avoided certain economic development strategies due to their likelihood of attracting Latin or African Americans.

As far as Black-White inequality, O'Connell emphasizes local attitudes and segregation as the two primary channels for sundown policies to influence outcomes. O'Connell's work builds on Crowe (2012) and Crowe and Ceresola (2014) who primarily focused on the importance of anti-black attitudes in contributing to the persistent effects of sundown policies (Crowe 2012; Crowe and Ceresola 2014). Loewen (2005) also highlights the racially insulating nature of sundown jurisdictions and how they help perpetuate negative perceptions of Blacks. At the same time, White residents of sundown jurisdictions perpetuate their pro-White perspective when insisting that living in an all-white community is a right.

It is especially important to note that deleterious effects of segregation, and sundown policies, can occur even when individual attitudes do not explicitly wish for them to persist. O'Connell explains how sundown policies promote White economic advantage through the concentration of resources and how this would benefit all Whites living in the area and could occur "without direct expressions of racism" (O'Connell 2019, 315). A somewhat similar theoretical insight is developed by Schelling where he demonstrates that severe racial segregation can result even when the population of a community does not exhibit strong racist preferences (Schelling 1978). This insight implies that when there actually is a strong presence of racist preferences, the segregation and deleterious economic consequences are only more dramatically worsened as a result.

When it comes to sundown policies and their persistence, the original explicit policies are no longer in effect. The removal of sundown signs and formal policies likely took place across most areas during the 1980s and 1990s, if not sooner in some towns due to the shift in race relations promulgated by the civil rights movement. Before that, it is estimated that the peak of sundown jurisdictions took place in 1968 before many started to desegregate (Loewen 2005, 395).

Any remnants of sundown policies that persist are entirely informal. Many towns still record all-white populations in the Census as late as 2000, like Calhoun County of Illinois, for example (Loewen 2005, 360). Zeigler and Johnston City also lacked the presence of any African-American families in the 2000 Census, some sources owing this to reputation for being a former sundown town and the hate crimes that commenced when a Black family tried living in Johnston City for a month in the early 1990s (Loewen 2005, 380). Anna and Villa Grove are other towns with residents holding anti-black attitudes that appear to be remnants of their sundown past. Racist slurs were still common in Anna in as late as 2004. Once it went sundown, Villa Grove had previously started sounding a siren every night at 6:00 p.m. to warn African Americans in the area to leave. It only stopped sounding this siren in 1999. Looking ahead to 2020, we see that many counties still have very low percentages of Blacks in their population. On average, most counties—sundown or not—only had Blacks make up 5 percent of their total population in 2020.[1]

Most of these jurisdictions, however, do have restaurants and hotels that serve African Americans passing through, perhaps not always without glares from locals. The difficulty remains in buying or renting residential property. It has yet to be systematically studied, however, which of these areas are still all-white because they are intentionally excluding African Americans, even if through informal means. What is clear is that sundown histories still play a role in many African Americans' lives when they decide what areas to drive through when traveling (Loewen 2005, 348; Morris 2022; Beagan 2022).

SUNDOWN COUNTIES IN ILLINOIS

This chapter focuses on sundown jurisdictions within Illinois as a representative case study. Illinois has had a strong presence of sundown histories and using Loewen's database on sundown jurisdictions, I identify a sample of relevant 225 sundown jurisdictions within the state.[2] This sample only includes incorporated municipalities in Illinois that have strong recorded evidence of having utilized sundown policies at some point between 1890 and 1968, either supported by oral or written histories.

Figure 4.1 displays the percentage of jurisdictions that were sundown by county in Illinois. The map is displaying a "sundown concentration" variable that is calculated by counting the number of sundown jurisdictions—either city, town, or suburb—within each county and then dividing that number by

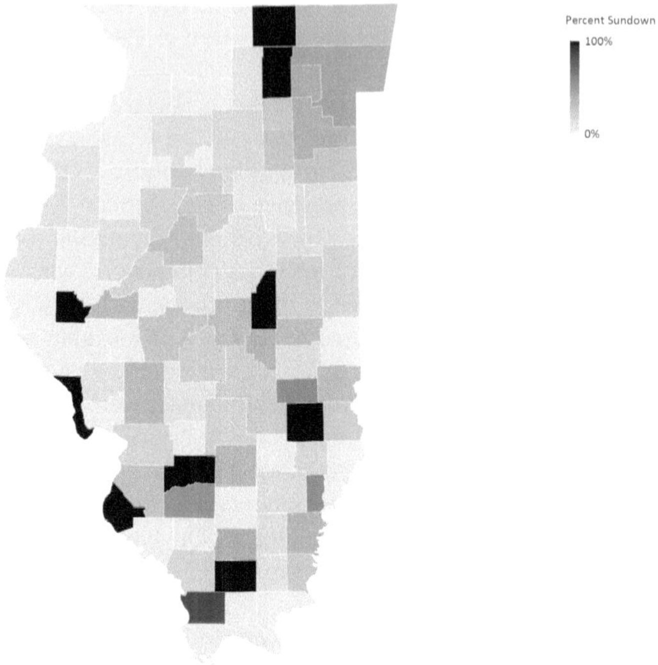

Figure 4.1 Sundown Concentration by Illinois County. Caption: This displays the percentage of each county that had implemented sundown policies at any point between 1890 and 1968. "Sundown concentration" is calculated by dividing the number of jurisdictions—towns, cities, or suburbs—that went sundown by the total number of jurisdictions within each county. Counties that implemented sundown policies at the county level are given a 100% concentration measure. *Source*: Author's calculations using Loewen's database: Loewen, James W. n.d. "Historical Database of Sundown Towns." *History & Social Justice*. Tougaloo, MS: Tougaloo College. https://justice.tougaloo.edu/sundown-towns/using-the-sundown-towns-database/state-map/.

the total number of jurisdictions in the corresponding county. Counties that enacted sundown policies at the county level are automatically given a 100 percent for this sundown town concentration measure.

As figure 4.1 shows, sundown jurisdictions were scattered throughout all of Illinois. The most highly concentrated sundown counties were also spread out through the state. Nine counties were completely sundown; either because the sundown policies were enacted at the county level or because all jurisdictions within the county were sundown, effectively making the whole county unwelcoming to African Americans. Some of these completely sundown counties include McHenry and Kane County in the northeast part of the state. In central Illinois there is Piatt and Brown County. Moving south, there are more sundown counties, including Jasper, Clinton, and Williamson County, among others.

DuPage County, located in Northeast Illinois and the home of West Chicago, was 33 percent sundown, including Western Chicago itself. The rest of Chicago located in Cook County to the east, however, was not officially sundown across the board. The larger area—Cook County—was 37 percent sundown. Previously mentioned Cicero is located in Cook County and went sundown. Alexander County, located in the southwest corner of Illinois, is an example of a county with no sundown towns.

Just north of Alexander County is Union County which is displayed as a primarily sundown county (83 percent). Loewen records Union County as a likely sundown county, all except for the village of Cobden. As discussed earlier, Cobden housed many workers who commuted to the sundown town Anna in the same county in order to work at the hospital there during the day.

Of the 225 jurisdictions that were broadly utilizing sundown policies across Illinois counties, roughly 82 percent were sundown towns—or in other words had previously not been all-white but eventually pushed out their Black populations. Roughly 9 percent were sundown suburbs, or areas that incorporated explicitly to be all-white from the start. Although Loewen's database does not have precise dates for when areas "went sundown," I calculate these rough percentages by counting sundown suburbs as any of the jurisdictions that incorporated after 1910 and sundown towns as any areas that were established before 1900 (White 2012), following the qualitative observations of sundown town and suburb timing made by Loewen. The remaining 9 percent of jurisdictions are harder to classify due to the likely overlap of sundown town and suburb policy emergence between 1900 and 1910.

Methods of Exclusion

Towns, cities, and suburbs across the country used various methods to push out or exclude African Americans. Using Loewen's database, we can calculate the percentage of sundown jurisdictions that are recorded as having utilized each of the approaches. Of the methods confirmed in Illinois, sundown ordinances were the most popular, utilized by 41 percent of sundown jurisdictions in Illinois. The second most popular method of exclusion was the utilization of sundown signs (38 percent of sundown towns). These were then followed by reputational methods of enforcement (12 percent), violence (10 percent), police (6 percent), private bad behavior (4 percent), and official zoning policies (2 percent). These percentages likely underestimate the precise usage rates given that these only account for the practices that have been confirmed by historians. Please note that each of the methods utilized are not mutually exclusive. These figures provide rough estimates primarily to display how sundown enforcement varied widely.

The most popular category—ordinances—was when a jurisdiction passed a local ordinance that either forbade African Americans from being in municipal limits after the sun set or by prohibiting African Americans from owning or renting property. Usually, towns with sundown ordinances rarely had confrontations with African Americans in the same way that jurisdictions that employed violent means to remain all-white. A representative example is the village of De Land located in Piatt County of central Illinois. Due to not being located on a major railroad or highway, it never met an influx of Black migrants.

It is likely that De Land enacted ordinances as a sort of progressive signal; to show that they were up to date with the latest policy trend in treating Blacks as the cause of America's problems (JLoewen 2005, 100). The difficulty with this method of exclusion is that original texts of sundown ordinances were rarely kept. This meant that most ordinances were passed orally at local municipal meetings.

Despite the precedent set by *Buchanan v. Warley* regarding the unconstitutionality of residential segregation ordinances in 1917, many localities ignored this by continuing to pass segregation ordinances even late as the 1950s (Loewen 2005). This constitutional decision clearly had implications for sundown ordinances yet the latter continued to operate illegally in many towns. Part of the lack of enforcement could be attributed to the explicit ignoring of *Buchanan* on a national stage through the federal government's creation of intentionally all-white communities across the nation, including Richland, Washington and Greenbelt, Maryland as examples. Similarly, racially restrictive covenants were required by the Federal Housing Administration before insuring housing loans. Many other cases of the Federal government's explicit disregard of racial equality, especially in the treatment of housing policy, is thoroughly documented by Rothstein's book on how Federal housing policy for decades perpetuated racial segregation (Rothstein 2017).

Sundown signs—the second most common method of exclusion—were often posted in conjunction with one or more of the other methods of exclusion. They usually read something along the lines of "N*****, Don't Let the Sun Go Down On You in ___" or "Whites Only within City Limits After Dark" (Loewen 2005, 223). Some areas that had such signs included Assumption, East Alton, Glen Carbon, and Kenilworth, among many other towns.

The earlier mentioned Villa Grove village in Illinois had municipal support of its siren that it set off each night. Columbia similarly had a whistle sounded each evening at 6 p.m. to warn off African Americans. Even if these policies were never written in official municipal documents, as they often weren't, they were still often backed by governmental officials vocally and enforced by local police. Places like Johnston City believed that their reputation was so prominent as a sundown town that passing an ordinance was superfluous. If a Black person was ever caught trying to move into the area in the 1940s, it was often a police officer that would visit and tell them to leave. Effingham especially had a very strong reputation for anti-black attitudes and prohibited Blacks from going anywhere in town other than the bus and train stations when passing through. This was strictly enforced by police officers (Loewen and Loewen n.d.).

As for violence, the fourth most common method of enforcement in Illinois sundown jurisdictions, incidents ranged from destruction of property to lynchings and riots. A Black woman that attempted living in Elmwood Park ended up leaving town after her car was repeatedly vandalized. There are also reports of crosses being burned on the lawns of other Black families that tried moving into the area. Places like Western Springs effectively kept out African Americans through the threat of violence. Sometimes Black families moved in but didn't stay for long due to the many threats and hostility they faced. Some homes where Blacks were living in Eldorado Illinois were dynamited in the 1920s (Loewen and Loewen n.d.).

It was often smaller towns that were able to get away with violent riots that resulted in the expulsion of Blacks akin to ethnic cleansings. Larger cities that had violent riots—like that of the Springfield riot of 1908—were unsuccessful in their efforts in completely expelling Blacks. However, they often incited more successful expulsions, but on a smaller scale in surrounding towns.

Ku Klux Klan (KKK) presence as a way to exclude African Americans is captured by the "violence," "reputation," and "private bad behavior" categories. There was an active presence of KKK in Lovington with many reported cross-burning incidents. Lexington was another area that had a strong KKK presence that included the mayor and wealthy landowners among its ranks (Loewen and Loewen n.d.).

In 1898, there was a violent incident in Pana between striking White union coal miners and Black newcomers. Records show that some of the Blacks were wounded while none of the White union sustained injuries. The next day state and county warrants were issued for the arrest of all Blacks in the riot, but not the Whites (Loewen and Loewen n.d.). This type of violence was not a rare occurrence in Pana.

Mascoutah in St. Clair County is an example of a town that is documented as having utilized zoning policies to exclude African Americans, but it is not clear or recorded how this was done precisely. Greenup in Cumberland used the combination of zoning policies and police enforcement to prevent African Americans from living in the area (Loewen and Loewen n.d.). Both Bellwood and Arlington Heights are towns that ended up being involved in famous U.S. Supreme Court cases due to discrimination committed by realtors in their areas (Loewen and Loewen n.d.).

Winthrop Harbor, a suburb of North Chicago, is an example of an area that enforced its sundown status through many means. It utilized violent expulsion, the threat of violence, police and other official actions, private behavior, and reputation to keep out African Americans for some time. A large presence of the KKK is recorded as being a driving force behind this (Loewen and Loewen n.d.).

WHY "GO SUNDOWN"?

To better understand why jurisdictions went sundown in Illinois, I utilize the University of Minnesota's IPUMS National Historical Geographic Information System (NHGIS) to extract demographic and economic information on counties, including data on population, religious organizations, literacy, farm production, manufacturing, and other economic activity (Manson et al. 2021). Table 4.1 displays the relevant variables from that dataset and their correlations with each county's sundown concentration.

The goal is to look at the states of counties before the sundown period to see if there are any systematic patterns in counties that had a higher concentration of jurisdictions that went sundown over time. Looking at these variables from the 1860s to 1880s is helpful because they provide a window into how counties compared across these dimensions before the sundown period. The bulk of the variables are from 1870 to 1880. This is important because this follows the end of the Civil War in 1865 and various historical reforms that increased the rights of African Americans, including the passage of the reconstruction amendments. These amendments also made Illinois's previously instated "state sundown law" from the 1848 state constitution obsolete. Following many other states' anti-segregation laws, Illinois passed the Illinois Civil Rights Act of 1885 that forbade discrimination in public places. As described earlier, despite the progress for civil rights following the Civil War, race relations deteriorated significantly starting in 1890. Race riots and lynchings broke out in particular between 1891 and 1915. Data from 1870 to 1880, therefore, is helpful for comparing towns after the divisive period of the Civil War and before recorded racial tensions and discrimination resurfaced. Data from 1860 provides more detail on the historical treatment of Blacks and geographical characteristics across counties.

Table 4.1 Associations between County Characteristics and Sundown Concentration Measures

Variable	*Percent of County that Was Sundown (1890–1968)*	*Percent of County with Sundown Towns (est. before 1900)*	*Percent of County with Sundown Suburbs (est. after 1910)*
Total Population in 1880	0.0332	−0.0013	−0.0233
% Black in 1880	−0.1426***	−0.1324***	−0.0856***
% Indian in 1880	−0.1081***	−0.1023***	−0.0514**
% German in 1880	0.2297***	0.2226***	0.2465***
% Irish in 1880	−0.0458**	−0.0267	0.0285
% Chinese in 1880	−0.0590***	−0.0761***	−0.0627***
% Male in 1880	0.1250***	0.1232***	−0.0098
% Southern migrants in 1880	−0.0626***	−0.0898***	−0.1438***
Family size in 1880	−0.0092	0.0057	−0.0478*
Value of manufacturing products in 1880	0.0597**	0.0212	0.0013
Wages in 1880	0.0588***	0.0207	0.0045
Farm land in acres in 1880	−0.1447***	−0.1083***	−0.1327***
Value of farm products in 1880	−0.1427***	−0.1105***	−0.1084***
% of owned farms in 1880	0.0782***	0.0620***	0.0595***
Assessed valuation of real estate in 1880	0.0138	−0.0146	−0.0254
Water wheels in 1870	0.0619***	0.024	0.0141
Steam engines in 1870	0.0298	−0.0067	−0.0141
Total religious organizations in 1870	−0.024	−0.0395*	−0.0886***
Roman Catholic churches in 1870	0.1546***	0.1400***	0.1364***
Baptist churches in 1870	−0.0241	−0.0606***	−0.0967***
Presbyterian churches in 1870	−0.1951***	−0.1862***	−0.2320***
Count of individuals who did not write in 1870	0.0156	−0.0434**	−0.1126***
Bales of ginned cotton in 1860	0.1860***	0.1381***	0.1781***

(*continued*)

Table 4.1 (Continued)

Variable	*Percent of County that Was Sundown (1890–1968)*	*Percent of County with Sundown Towns (est. before 1900)*	*Percent of County with Sundown Suburbs (est. after 1910)*
Free Blacks in 1860	−0.0057	−0.0226	−0.0588**
Water transport in 1860	−0.0448**	−0.0798***	−0.0446***
Rail transport in 1860	0.0118	0.0098	0.0167
County seat went Sundown	0.2909***	0.3010***	0.2196***

Note: p*** < 0.01, **p < 0.05; p* < 0.10.

Source: Author's calculations using data from various sources. Loewen, James W. n.d. "Historical Database of Sundown Towns." *History & Social Justice*. Tougaloo, MS: Tougaloo College. https://justice.tougaloo.edu/sundown-towns/using-the-sundown-towns-database/state-map/; Manson, Steven, Jonathan Schroeder, David Van Riper, Tracy Kugler, and Steven Ruggles. 2021. *IPUMS National Historical Geographic Information System: Version 16.0 [dataset]*. Minneapolis, MN: IPUMS; Illinois State Library online records.Caption: This displays the pairwise correlation coefficients between characteristics about counties from various sources and each county's sundown concentration measure. Each significant coefficient indicates what characteristics more predisposed to have more sundown policies go into effect over time. The first column shows the correlations with each county's most inclusive measure of sundown concentration; including all confirmed sundown jurisdictions between 1890 and 1968. The second measure of sundown concentration only includes the portion of sundown towns that were established before 1900. The last measure of county sundown concentration only includes sundown suburbs that were established after 1910.

Table 4.1 reports correlation coefficients for three different measures of sundown concentration. The first is the most inclusive measure which takes the total number of jurisdictions with evidence of having sundown policies between 1890 and 1968, and divides this number by each county's total number of jurisdictions. The second measure is a rough measure of only sundown towns because it only includes jurisdictions that were established before 1900. The last measure estimates the percentage of each county's jurisdictions that were sundown suburbs by only including those suburbs that were established after 1910. Separating out results for each of these is important due to how the institutional environment likely differed significantly. Jurisdictions that previously had Black populations and over time went sundown in order to push them out (sundown towns) will look different than jurisdictions that incorporate explicitly to keep out Blacks from the start (sundown suburbs).

For the series of variables on characteristics of counties from 1880, several significant patterns emerge. First, counties that had smaller Black shares of the population in 1880 were more likely to have a higher sundown concentration following 1890. Counties with smaller Indian populations, but larger German populations were also more likely to have more towns go sundown. The associations for Black and Indian shares of the population were slightly smaller for counties with more sundown suburbs. Counties with larger

Chinese populations were less likely to have more jurisdictions of sundown jurisdictions across the board.

The total population of these counties, however, were not significantly different in 1880, for all measures of sundown concentration. Counties that had more jurisdictions go sundown between 1890 and 1968 were more likely to have larger manufacturing industries and higher wages. This association weakens and becomes insignificant for counties with high concentrations of sundown towns and suburbs. Counties with higher sundown concentrations tended to have smaller farming industries, but greater farm ownership.

To capture other characteristics about sundown counties, table 4.1 also displays the associations between counties' sundown concentration measures and variables from 1860 to 1870. Interestingly, the significance of associations varies by the type of religious denomination. Across all three measures of sundown concentration, for example, the presence of more Roman Catholic churches in 1870 is significantly and positively related to the development of sundown policies. On the other hand, counties with more Presbyterian churches in 1870 are less likely to develop sundown policies. This association is especially large for sundown suburbs. Counties with more Baptist churches in 1870 are also less likely to develop sundown policies in sundown towns and suburbs.

Counties that had larger cotton industries in 1860—as measured by bales of ginned cotton—were also more likely to have a larger sundown town concentration over time, with a particularly strong effect in sundown suburbs. Counties that appear to have a more liberal history of allowing for more free Blacks in 1860 are less likely to develop more sundown suburbs.

Some geographic features are also important. Particularly, the number of water wheels that a county has in 1870 is positively related to the likelihood of going sundown later. Water wheels were useful mechanisms for converting the energy developed by moving water in rivers and streams into usable forms of power. This suggests that sundown jurisdictions as a whole were more likely to be placed along a water source and to have the tools to harness its power. It could also suggest that towns that experienced more traffic and migration patterns were also more likely to go sundown. But this effect does not hold when looking specifically at sundown towns and suburbs.

Lastly, institutional capacity and policy diffusion appear to have played a large role. Like mentioned earlier, larger cities were less likely to be able to get away with highly politically visible race riots or violence that led to the expulsion of Blacks. This was because such riots would draw the attention of the state governor and potential state intervention. However, in the cases where the county seat of a county was able to go sundown, the surrounding towns were more likely to go sundown (Loewen 2005, 4). This is captured by the last variable in table 4.1. The county seat variable is calculated from information on what Illinois's county seats were in 1880 (Collins et al. n.d.).

The rest of the variables covered in table 4.1 are not significant. This means aspects like the assessed valuation of real estate, steam engines, and rail transport do not appear to be significant determinants of the likelihood of going sundown, regardless of the sundown concentration measure used.

DISCRIMINATION AND LONG-RUN GROWTH

There is mounting evidence in many other areas that violence and discrimination harms growth (Cunningham, Lee, and Ward 2021) and a smaller, but suggestive literature that this is also at play across many communities with exclusionary sundown histories. Exploring how discrimination, especially when racially motivated, likely influences economic growth at any point of time, requires taking a step back to look at the incentives at play in various institutional environments.

When individuals discriminate against another group of people, they are forgoing the option to trade or do business with that said group. This quite simply limits the number of trades taking place and in turn the extent of the market. When individuals are trading less, then there is a smaller need for the division of labor to help increase efficiency in order to meet high demand. As Smith (1776) has seminally argued, the division of labor is instrumental in influencing why some nations prosper and others don't. This insight is where much of the field of institutional economics cited earlier gains its inspiration.

This is true in cases when the type of discrimination is nonviolent or violent. However, in the former case, economic activity is being forgone by an act of omission, whereas in the latter case harm is explicitly being inflicted upon the property and persons of others. Over time explicit violence in sundown jurisdictions has declined, but the underlying cultural and socioeconomic dynamics are having a lasting effect.

There is a wide array of empirical findings on various types of discrimination and their effect on growth. Esteve-Volart (2006) argues that sex discrimination in the marketplace is an inefficient practice. They find that excluding females from the labor market or excluding them from managerial positions is associated with a reduction in GDP per capita (Esteve-Volart 2006). Gender gaps in education and employment are significantly related to lower economic growth (Klasen and Lamanna 2009). Asli and Gurashvili (2020) find that in the long-run, a 10 percent increase in ethnic discrimination reduces economic growth by about 3 to 4 percent (Asali and Gurashvili 2020). This is just a small sample of the type of empirical work in this area (Lang and Lehmann 2012; Neumark 2018).

Discrimination in the marketplace is ultimately an act of talent misallocation. Absent discrimination, individuals select their occupation based on where they obtain the most utility and on their talents and preferences. This leads occupation choice to be a function of each individual's comparative advantage in the economy. As Hsieh et al. write, there are several forces that prevent individuals from doing this optimally (Hsieh et al. 2019). These forces are labor market discrimination, barriers to forming human capital, and differences in preferences or social norms; three forces that were all at play in preventing Blacks from optimally choosing their occupations during the sundown period of the 1900s.[3]

Discrimination and misallocation of talent on a large scale can have detrimental effects on long-run growth. To demonstrate this in the case of sundown jurisdictions, I provide evidence of a negative relationship between historical sundown policies and contemporary county economic growth.

Using data from the Bureau of Economic Analysis Regional Accounts on county-level gross domestic product (GDP), I calculate annual growth rates of GDP for all counties in Illinois and find that between 2003 and 2020 Illinois counties had on average a growth rate of 0.03 percent. This metric ranged between −0.58 percent and 1.16 percent for all counties over the same time range. These two extremes both took place in the same county—Crawford County—demonstrating some volatility. The counties' relatively high growth rate of 1.16 percent took place in 2012, whereas the lowest rate of –0.58 took place only the year before in 2011. Crawford still demonstrates strength relative to other counties due to it having the strongest 17-year average growth rate of 0.10 percent. Other counties with relatively higher 17-year average growth rates include Cumberland, Hamilton, and Washington County. At the other end of the spectrum, Massac, Randolph, Hardin, and Jasper County have experienced the lowest county-wide growth rates between 2003 and 2020, on average.

The following equation is used to estimate the effect of sundown policies on long-run economic growth:

$$1)\ y_c = \beta_0 + \beta_1\ sundown\ concentration_c + countyseat_{c,1880} + \theta_{c,past} + \mu_t + \varepsilon$$

Where y_c represents the GDP growth rates for county c between 2003 and 2020. This wide sample of years is included in order to identify whether sundown policies have a persistent effect and to avoid the results being disproportionately influenced by any year-specific anomalies.

The independent variables of interest are the sundown concentration measures discussed earlier, each of which provide different ways of measuring the percentage of jurisdictions within each county that went sundown during the 1900s. Whether or not each county's county seat from 1880 ended up

Table 4.2 Regression Results for Sundown Town Concentration and GDP Growth

	Growth Between 2003 and 2020		
	(1)	*(2)*	*(3)*
Percent of county that was sundown (1890–1968)	−0.076*** (0.000)		
Percent of county with sundown towns(est. before 1900)		−1.197*** (0.000)	
Percent of county with sundown suburbs(est. after 1910)			−0.739*** (0.000)
Controls from the past	Y	Y	Y
Vce	cluster	cluster	cluster
County fixed effects	Y	Y	Y
N	1,938	1,938	1,938
R^2	0.027	0.027	0.027

Note: p*** < 0.01, **p < 0.05; p* < 0.10.
Source: Author's calculations using data on sundown jurisdictions and county characteristics from various sources.Caption: Preliminary evidence to suggest a negative association between sundown policies and long-run economic growth in Illinois Counties. The magnitude of the effect is stronger for sundown towns than for sundown suburbs. On "Controls from the past," note that controls for each equation correspond to the coefficients in table 4.1 that are least significant at the p < 0.05 level or lower for each relevant sundown concentration measure. Wherever two variables are highly correlated, one is dropped from the regression to minimize issues of collinearity. For example, controls for equation 1 include the variables from 1880 on %Black, %Indian, %German, %Irish, %Chinese, %Male, %Southern Migrants, value of manufacturing products, wages, % of owned farms, and farmland in acres. Variables from 1870 include Roman Catholic and Presbyterian Churches, and water wheels. 1860 variables include bales of ginned cotton.

going sundown is controlled for in order to account for institutional capacity and policy diffusion. $\theta_{c,past}$ is the mathematical term that represents the series of important variables highlighted earlier in table 4.1. These were the variables that were discovered to be significantly related to the likelihood of counties having greater sundown concentration over time. Lastly, I control for county fixed effects to account for any other county-specific factors that could influence growth over time.

Equation 1 is used to estimate the relationship between sundown policy concentration in counties and long-run economic growth. Table 4.2 displays the results from several specifications of the same equation.

Before controlling for any factors, sundown concentration appears to have an insignificant effect on long-run growth. After taking into consideration the many variables from the past that would bias the results without doing so, I find that sundown concentration actually has a significant negative association with long-run growth.

This association persists across the majority of the specifications, with some slight variation depending on the measures used. Using the most inclusive measure of sundown concentration, equation 1 from table 4.2 demonstrates a significant negative association with long-run county growth. This effect remains significant for equations 2 and 3, but the magnitude differs. Interestingly, long-run economic growth is more drastically hampered in counties with a larger concentration of sundown towns relative to sundown suburbs.

One plausible explanation for the differential effects between sundown town and suburb concentrated areas relates to their historical emergence and relative costs of discrimination. Both areas discriminated against Blacks, but sundown towns in particular had greater occurrences of violence, destruction of property, and violation of the rule of law. In these areas, Black Americans were often once members of the community, but the local institutions failed to protect them from the sundown exclusion that developed over time. Sundown suburbs, on the other hand, did not traditionally exhibit histories as violent. Instead, they incorporated to be all-white from the start and kept Blacks out by primarily reputational means. They had still forgone economic activity with Blacks through an act of omission, but violations of the crucial institutions for economic prosperity were not as rampant.

These results are an important first step in quantifying the long-run effects of sundown policies, but should be interpreted with caution. They provide preliminary evidence of an association between sundown policies and long-run growth, but the data limitations require more work to come to more concrete conclusions about the precise mechanisms at play.

The greater contribution of this chapter is related to how we learn more by improving our measures of what we mean by sundown policies and the precise methods of exclusion. This is highlighted by the differential impact between sundown towns and suburbs that is suggested by table 4.2. Additionally, we can re-estimate the regressions from above, but with different independent variables. Doing so can test how the various methods of exclusion discussed earlier—ordinances, signs, police, reputation, private bad behavior, and zoning—influence long-run growth.

I find that the influence of sundown policies on long-run economic growth can vary by the method of enforcement. The magnitude is the largest, or most negative, for sundown policies enforced primarily through private bad behavior or real estate mechanisms. This is followed by zoning, sundown signs, and police enforcement. All of these enforcement mechanisms appear to have more "bite" in discouraging long-run economic growth relative to the others.

The Discouraging of Productive Entrepreneurship

Well-defined property rights and the rule of law are two key institutions that have a proven track record for being essential to rewarding entrepreneurial energies for producing value and economic growth. When property rights are not well defined, entrepreneurs are discouraged from innovating because it is not clear if they could even benefit from the fruits of their labor. On the other hand, when they are well-defined, there is less uncertainty and entrepreneurs are more encouraged to conduct arbitrage and create better products and services for society. Ensuring that all individuals in society can equally benefit from entrepreneurial energies is also key. When the rule of law is violated—when one group's interests are protected at the cost of another's—this severely damages markets and growth.

A growing body of literature finds a link between these institutions, growth, and discrimination. Carden (2006, 88) makes the link between racial discrimination and growth explicitly.

> The relationship between institutions, social capital, and production is as follows. Institutions can reduce productivity directly by rewarding expropriation rather than production. Institutional uncertainty can reduce productivity by increasing the variance of future income streams. Increasing uncertainty related to whether income will be appropriated will result in lower investment. Weak institutions may also present opportunities to profit by exploiting these weaknesses (e.g., by committing crimes for which one does not expect to be punished) and by diverting resources toward attempting to alter the institutions. Weak or malevolent social capital can be a source of productivity-reducing transaction costs.

Carden tests this by looking at the institutional uncertainty and weak structure of social capital reflected by the history of lynching in the South. Lynchings often took place under the pretext of crime or over disputes related to property rights or contracts. Carden finds that the evidence on lynching suggests that the quality of Southern institutions was a key factor determining labor productivity and productivity growth.

Jaspin (2007) argued that "the greater the number of and adherence to Jim Crow laws, the fewer the encounters between African Americans and Whites and the greater the degree of anxiety, mistrust, and suspicion between the races, which could lead to spontaneous outbreaks of violence."

Cardin's and Jaspin's work both suggest that there are certain institutional environments that discourage productive entrepreneurship. There are some environments that instead incentivize individuals to exert energy to put others down in order to get ahead. The most familiar area, studied extensively by the public choice literature, is that of rent-seeking by large corporations. When large handouts are available for distribution from the government, many companies and individuals will exert their entrepreneurial energies but in unproductive ways: in order to secure rents from the government instead of producing valuable goods or services for consumers.

The case of rent seeking, broadly understood, is when an individual directs unproductive energy toward securing rents within an institutional structure that allows it. The rent seeking process often results in the "favor" of an individual or group of individuals by transferring resources toward them. A less studied form of unproductive entrepreneurship, however, is in the context of discrimination when energies are directed toward changing rules of the game to disfavor one individual or group. Disfavor is when there is "targeted harm that results from a transfer—or the threat of a transfer—of resources or economic surplus away from certain individuals or groups" (Mitchell 2019, 168). The weak institutions in sundown jurisdictions between 1890 and 1968 made room for discriminatory preferences of Whites to be more easily acted upon and impose disfavor upon Blacks as a result.

When individuals discriminate in the marketplace, this leads to higher costs for the individuals discriminating, relative to a situation where exchanges are made solely along the dimension of what is most efficient. This simple yet novel insight was first developed by Gary Becker, considered by many to be the father of the economics of discrimination (Becker 2010). Some discrimination that took place in sundown jurisdictions was a form of what Becker would call taste-based discrimination that increased labor market frictions. This misallocation of talent creates deadweight losses paid by Whites to avoid interactions with Blacks. However, the theoretical context often used in Beckerian models requires that the institutions, or rules of the games, remain constant, and the discrimination takes place within them. In the case of sundown jurisdictions, this was not always the case.

Instead, Whites in sundown jurisdictions exerted energy toward securing their place in the marketplace, and their communities, by competing to change the rules of the games in their favor. This meant passing local ordinances to exclude African Americans. It also meant violating the rule of law and the property rights of African Americans.

When trying to unpack the many entangled factors at play in sundown jurisdictions, it may be helpful to view it as follows. The initial bias of Whites during the sundown period was the first ingredient, the unproductive entrepreneurship they partook in to get ahead and to put their Black neighbors down is the second ingredient common to many localities, and the varying institutions and norms present at the local level was the last ingredient that largely influenced whether unproductive entrepreneurship took place in the form of sundown policies or not. Some of these local institutions came down to a divergence between the formal laws on the national stage and what was treated as the final "law of the land" informally at the local level. The result: a crumbling of social capital between Blacks and Whites and decades of damage.

CONCLUSION

This chapter makes several contributions to our understanding of sundown policies and the economic costs to racial discrimination. First, it adds to the small, but growing literature on the empirical effects of sundown policies. My preliminary application of methods utilized in the literature on institutional persistence provides a ripe area to help inform the development of a more thorough, causal understanding of sundown policies and their effects. It also helps provide preliminary evidence to suggest that these institutions promote racial discrimination and exclusion that persist to influence communities economically.

More specifically, sundown policies appear to have lasting detrimental effects to economic growth. This negative association is especially strong for sundown towns—areas that over time violated the rights of Blacks by destroying their property and pushing them out. Sundown suburbs, or areas that incorporated explicitly to be all-white from their inception also appeared to grow slower than their neighbors, but not as slowly as sundown towns. This chapter also demonstrates that methods of exclusion influence the magnitude of effects on communities over time. This is especially helpful given the common grouping together of sundown and suburbs in prior research, regardless of methods of exclusion.

This chapter is just one step along the journey to encourage more work in this important area. We should not let the difficulty of measuring sundown policies diminish our motivation to study them; that would only perpetuate their historical erasure.

NOTES

1. Note that these calculations do not account for the portion of the population that was in institutional homes like mental health facilities, prisons, or military housing. This suggests that the portion of Black households not in any of these types of homes of the total population may be even smaller.
2. I form this 225 number by first web-scraping all of the sundown jurisdictions listed on Loewen's online database as of November 29, 2019. Then I restrict the sample to just include the incorporated municipalities within Illinois.
3. Although sundown policies were explicitly formed to restrict residential choices of Blacks, they implicitly influenced their occupational choices as well, even if they were technically allowed to work in some sundown towns.

REFERENCES

Acemoglu, Daron, and Matthew O. Jackson. 2011. *History, Expectations, and Leadership in the Evolution of Cooperation.* New York: National Bureau of Economic Research.

Acemoglu, Daron, Simon Johnson, and James A. Robinson. 2001. "The Colonial Origins of Comparative Development: An Empirical Investigation." *American Economic Review* 91 (5): 1369–1401.

———. 2005. "Institutions as a Fundamental Cause of Long-Run Growth." *Handbook of Economic Growth* 1A: 385–472.

Alesina, A., P. Giuliano, and N. Nunn. 2013. "On the Origins of Gender Roles: Women and the Plough." *The Quarterly Journal of Economics* 85 (4): 469–530.

Asali, Muhammad, and Rusudan Gurashvili. 2020. "Labour Market Discrimination and the Macroeconomy." *Economics of Transition and Institutional Change* 28 (3): 515–533.

Banerjee, Abhijit, and Lakshmi Iyer. 2005. "History, Institutions, and Economic Performance: The Legacy Colonial Land Tenure Systems in India." *American Economic Review* 95 (4): 1190–1213.

Barry, Robert J., and Rachel M. McCleary. 2003. "Religion and Economic Growth." NBER Working Paper, National Bureau of Economic Research, Cambridge, MA.

Bazzi, Samuel, Andreas Ferrara, Martin Fiszbein, Thomas Pearson, and Patrick A. Testa. 2022. "Sundown Towns and Racial Exclusion: The Southern White Diaspora and the "Great Retreat." *AEA Papers and Proceedings* 112: 234–238.

Beagan, Ginny. 2022. "What is a 'Sundown Town'? When and Where American Racism Was in Full Public View." *Yahoo News*. June 9.

Beaujot, Ariel. 2018. "Sun Up in a Sundown Town: Public History, Private Memory, and Racism in a Small City." *The Public Historian* 40 (2): 43–68.

Becker, Gary S. 2010. *The Economics of Discrimination*. Chicago, IL: University of Chicago Press.

Bisin, Alberto, and Thierry Verdier. 2001. "The Economics of Cultural Transmission and the Dynamics of Preferences." *Journal of Economic Theory* 97 (2): 298–319.

Blalock, H.M. Jr. 1967. *Toward a Theory of Minority-Group Relations*. New York: John Wiley and Sons.

Boettke, P.J. 2014. "Entrepreneurship, and the Entrepreneurial Market Process: Israel M. Kirzner and the Two Levels of Analysis in Spontaneous Order Studies." *The Review of Austrian Economics* 27 (3): 233–247.

Boettke, P.J., and C.J. Coyne. 2003. "Entrepreneurship and Development: Cause or Consequence?" Emerald Group Publishing Limited, vol. 6.

Boustan, Leah Platt. 2020. *Competition in the Promised Land: Black Migrants in Northern Cities and Labor Markets*. Cambridge, MA: National Bureau of Economic Research Publications.

Brooks, Leah, Jonathan Rose, Daniel Shoag, and Stan Veuger. 2020. "The Long-Run Impact of the 1968 Washington, DC Civil Disturbance." AEI Economics Working Paper 2020-09, American Enterprise Institute, Washington, DC.

Carden, Art. 2006. "Institutions and Southern Development: Lynching as a Signal of Insecure Property Rights." PhD Dissertation, Washington University.

Collins, Raymond, Sandra Fritz, David Johnson, Fancie LaCamera, and Blaine Redemer. n.d. Illinois County Histories at the Illinois State Library. https://www.lib.niu.edu/2000/il000292.html.

Collins, William J., and Robert A. Margo. 2000. "Residential Segregation and Socioeconomic Outcomes: When Did Ghettos Go Bad?" *Economics Letters* 69 (2): 239–243.

Cook, Lisa D., Trevon D. Logan, and John M. Parman. 2018. "Racial Segregation and Southern Lynching." *Social Science History* 42 (4): 635–675.
Cook, Lisa D., Trevon D. Logan, and John M. Parman. 2018. "Rural Segregation and Racial Violence: Historical Effects of Spatial Racism." *American Journal of Economics and Sociology* 77 (3–4): 821–847.
Crowe, Jessica. 2012. "The Influence of Racial Histories on Economic Development Strategies." *Ethnic and Racial Studies* 35 (11): 1955–1973.
Crowe, Jessica, and Ryan Ceresola. 2014. "Racial History, Legacy, and Economic Development." *Patterns of Prejudice* 48 (4): 350–369.
Cunningham, David, Hedwig Lee, and Geoff Ward. 2021. "Legacies of Racial Violence: Clarifying and Addressing the Presence of the Past." *The Annals of the American Academy of Political and Social Science* 694 (1): 8–20.
Curtis White, Katherine J., Kyle Crowder, Stewart E. Tolnay, and Robert M. Adelman. 2005. "Race, Gender, and Marriage: Destination Selection During the Great Migration." *Demography* 42 (2): 215–241.
Curtis, Katherine J., and Heather A. O'Connell. 2017. "Historical Racial Contexts and Contemporary Spatial Differences in Racial Inequality." *Spatial Demography* 5 (2): 73–97.
Cutler, David M., and Edward L. Glaeser. 1997. "Are Ghettos Good or Bad?" *The Quarterly Journal of Economics* 112 (3): 827–872.
Deopke, Matthias, and Fabrizio Zilibotti. 2008. "Occupational Choice and the Spirit of Capitalism." *The Quarterly Journal of Economics* 123 (2): 747–793.
Dippel, Christian, and Stephan Heblich. 2021. "Leadership in Social Movements: Evidence from the 'Forty-Eighters' in the Civil War." *American Economic Review* 111 (2): 1–35.
Dippel, John V.H. 2005. *Race to the Frontier: "White Flight" and the Westward Expansion.* New York: Algora Publishing.
Ellen, Ingrid Gould. 2000. *Sharing America's Neighborhoods.* Cambridge, MA: Havard University Press.
Esteve-Volart, Berta. 2006. "Sex Discrimination and Growth." IMF Working Paper No. 00/84, International Monetary Fund.
Farley, Reynolds, Sheldon Danziger, and Harry J. Holzer. 2000. *Detroit Divided: A Volume of Urban Inequality.* New York: Russell Sage Foundation.
Fearon, James D., and David D. Laitin. 1996. "Explaining Interethnic Cooperation." *American Political Science Review* 90 (4): 715–735.
Ferrara, Andreas, and Price Fishback. 2020. "Discrimination, Migration, and Economic Outcomes: Evidence from World War I." NBER Working Paper 26936, National Bureau of Economic Research, Cambridge, MA.
Fischer, Mary J. 2003. "The Relative Importance of Income and Race in Determining Residential Outcomes in Urban Areas." *Urban Affairs Review* 38 (5): 669–696.
Fishback, Price V., Jessica LaVoie, Allison Shertzer, and Randall Walsh. 2020. "Race, Risk, and the Emergence of Federal Redlining." NBER Working Paper Issue 28146, National Bureau of Economic Research, Cambridge, MA.
Fishback, Price, Jonathan Rose, Kenneth A. Snowden, and Thomas Storrs. 2022. "New Evidence on Redlining by Federal Housing Programs in the 1930s." NBER Working Paper 29244, Journal of Urban Economics.

Franklin, Wilson, D., and Roger B. Hammer. 2001. "Ethnic Residential Segregation and Its Consequences." In *Urban Inequality: Evidence from Four Cities*, edited by A.O. O'Conner, C. Tilly, and L.D. Bobo, 272–303. New York: Russell Sage Foundation.

Frey, William H., and Kao-Lee Liaw. 2005. "Migration Within the United States: Role of Race Ethnicity." *Brookings-Wharton Papers on Urban Affairs* (1): 207–262.

Givel, Michael S. 2021. "Evolution of a Sundown Town and Racial Caste System: Norman, Oklahoma from 1889 to 1967." *Ethnicities* 21 (4): 664–683.

Gregory, James N. 2005. *The Southern Diaspora: How the Great Migrations of Black and White Southerners Transformed America.* Chapel Hill, NC: UNC Press.

Hsieh, Chang-Tai, Erik Hurst, Charles I. Jones, and Peter J. Klenow. 2019. "The Allocation of Talent and U.S. Economic Growth." *Econometrica* 87 (5): 1439–1474.

Jacobs, Jane. 1961. "Chapter 11." In *The Death and Life of Great American Cities*, edited by Jane Jacobs, 189–212. New York: Vintage.

Jaspin, Elliot. 2007. *Buried in the Bitter Waters: The Hidden History of Racial Cleansing in America.* New York: Basic Books.

Jedwab, Remi, Noel D. Johnson, and Mark Koyama. 2019. "Negative Shocks and Mass Persecutions: Evidence from the Black Death." *Journal of Economic Growth* 24 (4): 345–395.

Jha, Saumitra. 2013. "Trade, Complementaries, and Religious Tolerance: Evidence from India." Working Paper No. 2004, Stanford University Graduate School of Business, Stanford, CA.

———. 2013. "Trade, Institutions, and Ethnic Tolerance: Evidence from South Asia." *The American Political Science Review* 107 (4): 806–832.

Johnson, Noel D., and Mark Koyama. 2017. "Jewish Communities and City Growth in Preindustrial Europe." *Journal of Development Economics* 127 (C): 339–354.

King, Ryan D., Steven F. Messner, and Robert D. Baller. 2009. "Contemporary Hate Crimes, Law Enforcement, and the Legacy of Racial Violence." *American Sociological Review* 74 (2): 291–315.

Klasen, Stephan, and Francesca Lamanna. 2009. "The Impact of Gender Inequality in Education and Employment on Economic Growth: New Evidence for a Panel of Countries." *Feminist Economics* 15 (3): 91–132.

Lancaster, Guy, and John A. Kirk. 2014. "Sundown Towns: Racial Cleansing in the Arkansas Delta." In *Race and Ethnicity in Arkansas: New Perspectives*, edited by John A. Kirk, 49–60. Fayetteville, AR: University of Arkansas Press.

Lang, Kevin, and Jee-Yeon K. Lehmann. 2012. "Racial Discrimination in the Labor Market: Theory and Empirics." *Journal of Economic Literature* 50 (4): 959–1006.

Leeson, P.T., and J.R. Subrick. 2006. "Robust Political Economy." *Review of Austrian Economics* 19 (2): 107–111.

Lichter, Daniel T., Domenico Parisi, and Michael C. Taquino. 2015. "Toward a New Macro-Segregation? Deocomposing Segregation within and between Metropolitan Cities and Suburbs." *American Sociological Review* 80 (4): 843–873.

Lieberson, Stanley. 1980. *A Piece of the Pie: Blacks and White Immigrants Since 1880.* Berkeley, CA: University of California Press.

Loewen, James W. 2005. *Sundown Towns: A Hidden Dimension of American Racism.* New York: The New Press.

———. 2009. "Sundown Towns and Counties: Racial Exclusion in the South." *Southern Cultures* 15 (1): 22–47.

Loewen, James W., and Nick Loewen. n.d. *Sundown Towns Database.* Edited by Phil Huckelberry and Stephen Berrey. Matt Cheney and OddBird. justice.tougaloo.edu /sundown-towns/.

Logan, Rayford. 1954. *The Negro in American Life and Thought: The Nadir, 1877–1901.* New York: Dial Press.

Logan, Trevon D., and John M. Parman. 2017. "Segregation and Homeownership in the Early Twentieth Century." *American Economic Review* 107 (5): 410–414.

———. 2017. "The National Rise in Residential Segregation." *The Journal of Economic History* 77 (1): 127–170.

Lucero, Eddie, Ricardo Robles, Lindsey Sanchez, and Jessica Trounstine. 2022. "Political Protection of Privilege: How Land Use Regulations Preserve Exclusivity." Working Paper, Princeton University, NJ.

Manson, Steven, Jonathan Schroeder, David Van Riper, Tracy Kugler, and Steven Ruggles. 2021. *IPUMS National Historical Geographic Information System: Version 16.0 [dataset].* Minneapolis, MN: IPUMS.

Marulanda, Maria. 2010. "Preemption, Patchwork Immigration Laws, and the Potential for Brown Sundown Towns." *Fordham Law Review* 79 (1): 321–368.

Massey, D.S., and N.A. Denton. 1993. *American Apartheid: Segregation and the Making of the Underclass.* Cambridge, MA: Harvard University Press.

McConnell, Eileen Diaz, and Faranak Miraftab. 2009. "Sundown Town to 'Little Mexico': Old-timers and Newcomers in an American Small Town." *Rural Sociology* 74 (4): 605–629.

Messner, Steven F., Robert D. Baller, and Matthew P. Zevenbergen. 2005. "The Legacy of Lynching and Southern Homicide." *American Sociological Review* 70 (4): 633–655.

Mitchell, M.D. 2019. "Uncontestable Favoritism." *Public Choice* 181 (1–2): 167–190.

Morris, Bilal. 2022. "Sundown Towns Black People Should Be Aware of." *Newsone*, June 8. https://newsone.com/4351059/sundown-towns-in-america/.

Musiol, Hanna. 2012. "Sundown and 'Liquid Modernity' in Pawhuska, Oklahoma." *Journal of American Studies* 46 (2): 357–373.

Naidu, Suresh. 2020. "American Slavery and Labour Market Power." *Economic History of Developing Regions* 35 (1): 3–22.

Neumark, David. 2018. "Experimental Research on Labor Market Discrimination." *Journal of Economic Literature* 56 (3): 799–866.

Nunn, Nathan. 2008. "The Long-term Effects of Africa's Slave Trades." *The Quarterly Journal of Economics* 123 (1): 139–176.

O'Connell, Heather A. 2012. "The Impact of Slavery on Racial Inequality in Poverty in the Contemporary U.S. South." *Social Forces* 90 (3): 713–734.

———. 2019. "Historical Shadows: The Links between Sundown Towns and Contemporary Black-White Inequality." *Sociology of Race and Ethnicity* 5 (3): 311–325.

Olzak, Susan. 1992. *The Dynamics of Ethnic Competition and Conflict.* Stanford, CA: Stanford University Press.

Philpott, Thomas L. 1978. *The Slum and the Ghetto: Neighborhood Deterioration and Middle-Class Reform, Chicago, 1880–1930.* New York: Oxford University Press.

Putnam, Robert D. 1994. "Social Capital and Public Affairs." *Bulletin of the American Academy of Arts and Sciences* 47 (8): 5–19.

Quilin, Frank Uriah. 1913. *The Color Line in Ohio: A History of Race Prejudice in a Typical Northern State.* Ann Arbor, MI: G. Wahr.

Quillian, Lincoln. 2002. "Why Is Black-White Residential Segegation So Persistent? Evidence on Three Theories from Migration Data." *Social Science Research* 31 (2): 197–229.

Roscigno, Vincent J., and Marino A. Bruce. 1995. "Racial Inequality and Social Control: Historical and Contemporary Patterns in the U.S. South." *Sociological Spectrum* 15 (3): 323–349.

Rothstein, Richard. 2017. *The Color of Law: A Forgotten History of How Our Government Segregated America.* New York: Liveright Publishing.

Royer, Donald M. 1965. *Indiana's 'Sundown Ordinances' in Nineteen Indiana Towns and Cities.* Indianapolis, IN: Indiana Civil Rights Commission.

Ruef, Martin, and Ben Fletcher. 2003. "Legacies of American Slavery: Status Attainment among Southern Blacks After Emancipation." *Social Forces* 82 (2): 445–480.

Schelling, Thomas. 1978. *Micromotives and Macrobehavior.* New York: WW Norton & Company.

Seneschal, Roberta. 1990. *The Sociogenesis of a Race Riot.* Urbana, IL: University of Illinois Press.

Shertzer, Allison, Tate Twinam, and Randall Walsh. 2022. "Zoning and Segregation in Urban Economic History." *Regional Science and Urban Economics* 94 (C): 103652.

Sherzer, Allison, and Randall P. Walsh. 2019. "Racial Sorting and the Emergence of Segregation in American Cities." *Review of Economics and Statistics* 101 (3): 415–427.

Smith, Adam. 1776. *An Inquiry into the Nature and Causes of the Wealth of Nations: Volume One.* London: Methuen.

Sokoloff, Kenneth L., and Stanley L. Engerman. 2000. "Institutions, Factor Endowments, and Paths of Development in the New World." *Journal of Economic Perspectives* 14 (3): 217–232.

Sood, Aradhya, William Speagle, and Kevin Ehrman-Solberg. 2019. "Long Shadow of Racial Discrimination: Evidence From Housing Covenants in Minneapolis." Working Paper, University of Minnesota.

Tabellini, Guido. 2008. "The Scope of Cooperation: Values and Incentives." *The Quarterly Journal of Economics* 123 (3): 905–950.

Tighe, Rosie J., Megan E. Hatch, and Joseph Mead. 2017. "Source of Income Discrimination and Fair Housing Policy." *Journal of Planning Literature* 32 (1): 3–15.

Troesken, Walsh. 2019. "Collective Action, White Flight, and the Origins of Racial Zoning Laws."*The Journal of Law, Economics, and Organization* 35 (2): 289–318.

Vigdor, Jacob L. 2002. "The Pursuit of Opportunity: Explaining Selective Black Migration." *Journal of Urban Economics* 51 (3): 391–417.

Voigtl'ander, N., and H.J. Voth. 2012. "Persecution Perpetuated: The Medieval Origins of Anti-Semetic Violence in Nazi Germany." *The Quarterly Journal of Economics* 127 (3): 1339–1392.

Von Mises, Ludwig. 1949. *Human Action: A Treatise on Economics.* New Haven, CT: Yale University Press.

Weber, Max. 1930. *The Protestant Ethic and the Spirit of Capitalism.* New York: Talcott Parsons.

White, Jesse. 2012. "Illinois Counties & Incorporated Municipalities." Secretary of State, Illinois, Springfield, IL.

White, Katherine J.C., Kyle Crowder, and Stewart E. Tolnay. 2005. "Race, Gender, and Marriage: Destination Selection During the Great Migration." *Demography* 42 (2): 215–241.

Williams, Jhacova. 2022. "Historical Lynchings and the Contemporary Voting Behavior of Blacks." *American Economic Journal: Applied Economics* 14 (3): 224–253.

Woodward, C.V. 2002. *The Strange Career of Jim Crow.* New York: Oxford University Press.

Section II

ENTREPRENEURSHIP IN CIVIL SOCIETY AND IN RESPONSE TO CRISIS

Chapter 5

"Hot Money"

A Hayekian Process of Polycentric Public Entrepreneurship in Currency Formation in Great Depression North Carolina

Thomas Storrs

Greensboro was broke. With all its commercial banks shuttered in March 1933, commerce in the formerly booming central North Carolina city ground to a halt. The city could not pay its bills, and its residents could not pay their taxes. The nadir of the Great Depression produced a liquidity crisis that threatened to shred the fabric of this textile center. Leading residents across the public and private sectors came together in fits and starts to forge a temporary solution that increased the area's welfare. Tax anticipation note scrip issued by Guilford County emerged as the solution to this entangled political economy and remedied the dearth of dollars. The temporary currency, backed by loans taken by the county against future tax receipts, jumpstarted commerce and helped place Greensboro on an upward economic trajectory. Greensboro was broke, and scrip fixed it.

The entangled political economy framework employed here rejects boundaries between economic and political problems and solutions. The study of entrepreneurial action in the public sector necessarily, if only implicitly, embraces this destruction of boundaries as well. Greensboro in the Depression, a mid-sized southern city in the throes of a crisis, provides a case study for understanding how individuals navigated, slowly but successfully, these entanglements. No great man arrived at any point with a solution and no economic logic invisibly and inevitably propelled the city toward an answer. Instead, a set of actors failed repeatedly until they succeeded. Neither a quantitative economic model nor a formal political theory alone can fully capture this process. Instead, the construction of new rules and new knowledge over several months by actors nominally in both the public and private sectors cleared a variety of economic and political hurdles to emerge at the finish line with an acceptable new framework.

Greensboro was not alone in its struggles. Local issues of scrip blossomed across the United States in the depths of the Great Depression in the early 1930s. Driven by economic collapse and a shortage of physical dollars, these local examples of public entrepreneurship exemplify the resourcefulness born of calamity. Scrip is any substitute for legal tender. During the Depression, scrip took many forms but always fell out of use once sufficient liquidity of dollars returned to local areas. And these solutions were quite local in character. Problems of coordination in launching and facilitating the use of scrip will be explored through a case study of Greensboro, North Carolina, in this section. A tenuous coalition of governments and private sector interests came together in an uncertain environment to grease the wheels of commerce, such that a hard landing was made a little softer and life went on a little more comfortably. The sequencing of events is also important for understanding this as an entangled political economy. The market did not first come to an equilibrium that the government, second, shifted to a new equilibrium. Market and government, through a variety of individuals, interacted simultaneously and inseparably to move between equilibria (Wagner 2007).

Scrip remains relevant today, even if a sudden paucity of physical dollars is not a looming threat. The Federal Reserve has explored creating a Central Bank Digital Currency (CBDC), though they are as yet noncommittal (Board of Governors of the Federal Reserve System 2022). Creating dollar equivalents, or equivalents of any currency, is a goal of many entrepreneurs as well, as seen recently in digital currencies. Sometimes the results are disastrous, such as the May 2022 collapse of TerraUSD, and its companion coin, Luna. TerraUSD sought to peg itself to the dollar and facilitate cryptocurrency transactions. Its failure cost investors $18 billion (Briola et al. 2022). About $150 billion remain in other stablecoins, essentially digital scrip ("Top Stablecoins by Market Cap | CoinCodex" n.d.). An older form of dollar equivalents, the Eurodollar, gained traction in the 1960s. This market dwarfs cryptocurrency and is measured in tens of trillions of dollars (Kreicher, McCauley, and Wooldridge 2014). Other digital uses also make the study of scrip relevant, such as game purchases and online gambling. Disaster preparedness also warrants study of alternative currencies. Exchange beyond barter in the case of extended power outages would quickly exhaust physical currency, and an alternative measure of value, such as scrip, would quickly become essential.

The issuance of scrip by local government officials constitutes public entrepreneurship. The dire setting in which they found themselves impelled them, but they nonetheless had to invent a new way of doing things. These were acts necessary for the survival of their constituencies. They made mistakes, false starts, and did not always tell the whole truth. They also did not, indeed could not, act alone. Private sector actors' consent and support were necessary elements of their strategies. Unbeknownst to the businessmen and public officials in Greensboro, the US economy bottomed out at some point late in 1932 or early in 1933. This bears emphasis because while historians study but one path these actors needed to prepare economic and monetary conditions' getting worse rather than better too. In the progression toward scrip issuance that follows, these actors took in new information each day and assessed their options relative to the goals of their position, but they still did not know the future. They innovated and did things they had not done before. They copied other localities and negotiated with each other. They came together to serve their own interests.

Local public and private institutions placed a billion dollars of scrip in circulation during the Depression (Gatch 2008, 47). Scrip can be used for a variety of purposes: economic and employment stimulus, supporting local businesses against national chains, or a means of local finance (Gatch 2008, 48). All of these goals were present in Greensboro. Additionally, the necessary but not sufficient condition of a lack of currency was present as well. Between those goals and that condition lay the essential step of aligning the interests and capacities of the relevant players between public and private spheres. What follows is a day-by-day account of that process in Greensboro, told mainly through the morning newspaper, the *Greensboro Daily News*. The newspaper held views on scrip that colored its coverage and exploded on its editorial page. It was a pivotal actor, not a dispassionate observer, which makes it an even more interesting, though treacherous, source.

Many Americans sought greater change using scrip beyond just a temporary stopgap in a time of acute crisis. Iowa, in particular, became a hotbed of alternative currency schemes that sought to rejigger the capitalist order, but the end of crisis brought the end to Iowa's nation leading schemes as well (Elvins 2005). Iowans innovated particularly in one area: stamp scrip. Stamp scrip was a scheme that essentially taxed or subsidized the velocity of scrip in that a stamp needed to be applied either each time it was used (tax) or for each week or month of its existence (subsidy). For example, a one-dollar equivalent piece of scrip would need a five-cent stamp applied to it each time it was used or each week. Once the piece of scrip accumulated twenty stamps, it could be redeemed for one dollar funded by the sale of the stamps. For this reason, it was known as "self-liquidating" (Warner 2012). These schemes were suggested for Greensboro, but ultimately other paths were taken.

The tax anticipation scrip that Greensboro, through Guilford County, ultimately settled on was the most successful type of scrip during the Depression. Backed by proceeds from the sale of debt backed by future tax proceeds, this scrip benefited from local government imprimatur. Nearly a hundred local governments across the country implemented tax anticipation scrip during the Depression. Most of these local governments used tax anticipation scrip to pay only a portion of their salaries. Guilford County used the scrip for 100 percent of their salaries because Greensboro's commercial banks had all failed (Gatch 2012).

Scrip currencies were much more common in American history before the Depression than after. The pivotal event was what economist Richard Timberlake called "the abolition of the operational gold standard in the early 1930s." After this point, Franklin Roosevelt devalued the dollar and banned private holdings of gold, making the Federal Reserve the almost exclusive creator of the monetary base (Timberlake 1987, 437). Timberlake wrote on the use of scrip in economically isolated areas, such as timber and mining camps. He makes a few points applicable also to the use of scrip during the Depression. First, while the Constitution states that "No state shall . . . emit bills of credit, [or] make anything but gold and silver coin a tender in payment of debt." So, only the federal government, or its agent the Federal Reserve, can create *legal tender*, but any entity can create *common tender* that acts like the nationally sanctioned currency. Second, only in unique circumstances does the use of scrip make sense. Nonetheless, there were positive-sum benefits for both the issuer and the acceptor in the case of, say, a coal mining company and a miner. The mining company would issue scrip to employees, redeemable only at the company store, between paydays and to be debited from the next paycheck. In this way, the miner received an interest-free loan from the coal mining company while keeping an employee happy and purchasing goods from it. Should the miner wish to buy liquor or other goods and services not sold by the mining company, the scrip could be sold at a discount.

A THEORETICAL SCRIPT FOR SCRIP

The title of this chapter alludes directly to Friedrich Hayek and indirectly to Elinor Ostrom, through polycentrism. This section will outline how the subsequent case study combines these scholars' theories to understand this case, more precisely process, of public entrepreneurship. Two overarching points are crucial. First, the adoption of scrip in Greensboro was a messy process characterized by a multitude of dynamically emerging uncertainties and interests. The final equilibrium was not obvious to participants—they plodded toward it with many detours—and even that crescendo was transitory. Second, the state is not a monolith. Greensboro could not achieve scrip on its own, and the failure was across two dimensions. It needed a coalition of governments including its county and other cities within that county to come together to make scrip work. Also, local private interests played an essential part in Greensboro's adoption of scrip. Many of these local private business leaders also served as elected officials. A myriad of interests needed to converge sufficiently across levels of government and across the porous public-private divide to make scrip a reality in Greensboro.

In his 1945 paper "The Use of Knowledge in Society," Hayek lays out three preconditions for constructing a rational economic order. First, possession of all relevant information. Second, beginning from an established set of preferences. Third, command of total knowledge of the available means (Hayek 1945, 519). In March 1933, when the case study begins, Greensboro found itself scoring zero out of three on the above criteria. Just a few months later, by the summer of 1933, officials in Greensboro had roughly solved all three criteria, and their entrepreneurial solution, in hindsight, was eminently logical and broadly welfare enhancing. As Hayek offers, once those three conditions are satisfied, "the problem which remains is purely one of logic" (Hayek 1945, 519).

The economic crisis in the winter of 1933 has no comparator in subsequent American history. Things were really bad, and the reader should place herself in the shoes of those living through this moment with no assurance that, even though times were tough, better days were ahead. North Carolina Bank and Trust Co., Greensboro's only remaining commercial bank and an essential institution for procuring dollars, was closed with no schedule for reopening. In fact, it never reopened despite hopeful mutterings from its president early in the crisis. The preferences of the community were also unknown. More importantly, the interests of the most important economic leaders did not initially align toward a solution. The relatively more stable industrialists focused primarily in textiles with some tobacco manufacturing, offered some help but proved eventually not to be a core part of the solution. The government of Greensboro proved incapable of reaching a solution on its own without help from other levels of government. The merchants, through whom the scrip would eventually flow, struggled to find a consistent voice and assert their interests.

With these disparate and contradictory interests, the question remains of who is doing the planning, and here lies a seeming contradiction in the notion of public entrepreneurship that this case study aids in solving. As Hayek states, "It is about this question that all the dispute about 'economic planning' centers. This is not a dispute about whether planning is to be done or not. It is a dispute as to whether planning is to be done centrally, by one authority for the whole economic system, or is to be divided among many individuals" (Hayek 1945, 520–521). The answer in Greensboro is that individuals forged a central plan. In Greensboro, individuals, from both the public and private sectors, forged a temporary solution to a crisis. They managed to do so by agreeing to implement a central plan through a tortuous process that required sorting out their individual differences. The answer did not emerge immediately. Haggling and bluster alongside changing circumstances slowly brought forth a solution backed by those individuals with the most to gain and implemented by a central authority, namely Guilford County.

For public entrepreneurs, the Greensboro case study shows that the knowledge problem, as outlined by Hayek, can be surmounted sufficiently but that a process of discovery is first necessary. A crisis, as seen in Greensboro, tugs at both sides of the equilibrium between speed and knowledge acquisition. Move too fast and the solution will fail. Move too slow and the crisis exacerbates. In Greensboro, the check on both too much and too little haste was the consultation and bargaining among and between the affected actors. Viewed narrowly, the solution appears to be centrally planned but when viewed as a process of knowledge aggregation over time Hayek's "many individuals" undergird the final product. Hayek leans heavily on prices as a transmission mechanism for knowledge (Hayek 1945, 526–528). Explicit prices do play a role in Greensboro through interest rates on debt and perhaps revenue levels of public entities and private firms. On the other hand, implicit and unknown prices also play a role. The most conservative and secure interests, the industrialists and the other governments such as the city of High Point and Guilford County, feared the uncertainty of scrip more than the certainty of no scrip. The more change-minded and tenuously situated players, such as the Greensboro elected officials and merchants, fear the status quo more than the hope of scrip. Through the amalgamation of these hopes and fears, an equilibrium solution is found even without explicit, quantitative prices. That process's unfolding is the heart of the case study.

The interdependence of those individuals brings us naturally to the work of Elinor Ostrom on polycentrism, in particular incorporating the Institutional Analysis and Development (IAD) framework. The IAD framework is appropriate for understanding scrip in Greensboro because it allows us to break down and then connect the evolving institutions and individuals' efforts to understand and change them in a method that takes into account how they develop. From the case study, we can see the emergence of a workable coalition for scrip that reflects changes in institutions through the process and constitutes multiple centers of institutional power across the public and private leaders (McGinnis 2011).

And analysis of the changing rules involved in Greensboro's scrip process can be split into public and private with the caveat that the political economy was entangled. On paper, firms and governments as entities funnel into neat boundaries. On the ground, the borders for individual actors between public and private were fungible especially since many individuals operated across the line. Julius Cone, as a formal example, served on the city council and ran the city's largest employer. Other elected officials also spent most of their time in the private sector. Both private and public sector officials communicated through the newspaper and trade organization like the Chamber of Commerce.

The existing institutions, the rules of the game between private and public officials, had been established during a time where Greensboro grew and all sides prospered. The broad crisis of the Great Depression and the immediate crisis of the currency shortage marked a stark turn for Greensboro's leaders after a decade of booming economic growth. After roaring through the 1920s as a growing hub of textiles, tobacco, and transportation, it ground to halt with the Depression and more acutely from its loss of all its commercial banks. It was a city run by and for its white business elite (Kipp 1977). Those elite, by necessity, had to rewrite the rules of their interactions with each other. Greensboro's slightly smaller neighbor High Point shared many characteristics of boom and then bust but did not suffer as acutely from lack of dollars because they had a viable commercial bank through a branch of Wachovia Bank. Guilford County's government, of which High Point was also a part, relied heavily on Greensboro's health for its own viability but also had greater legal options to borrow money and make scrip viable. The county's leaders thus took a keen interest in a viable economy in Greensboro as it was the county government's largest share of revenue and trouble there would reverberate to the rest of the county. Above them, the state of North Carolina, through the legislature and governor, needed to provide permission for some scrip related activities and also instituted the bank holiday that proved to be the death blow for Greensboro's last commercial bank. The US government proved to be a source of hope early in the scrip saga and its actions affected Greensboro's options.

On the private side, Greensboro's firms can roughly be divided into industrials with nationwide, and even international, customer bases and merchants with local customer bases. The former could weather the currency drought more easily and never displayed much enthusiasm for scrip though their leaders went along out of civic duty and the necessity of their workers' being able to live in a community with a functioning economy. The civic norms dictated that the industrial leaders needed to support their hometown even if their livelihoods were not threatened by the crisis. The merchants, though, generally supported scrip vigorously. The lack of dollars translated to a lack of sales. For the merchants like a jeweler, furniture store owner, or a restauranteur, they considered scrip to be essential for their survival as going concerns and thus fought feverishly for its enactment. A last important private institution is the local newspaper the *Greensboro Daily News* as the words that its writers produced, and chose not to produce, shaped the understanding of the crisis. The paper's reporters and editors are both the primary extant source about scrip in Greensboro and an interested party in its development. The paper relied on advertisements from local merchants to pay their salaries and the interests of Greensboro's merchants therefore aligned with the newspaper's employees and leadership. While no truly egregious bias stands out in its coverage, it bears remembering that they had an interest in the results. Largely missing from the discussions over scrip are working class citizens of Greensboro. They are discussed as employees or consumers in relation to other institutions, but their buying into the scrip system was not a concern of either public or private officials. They were policy takers not policy makers.

The analysis of development hinges on an insight gained from Ostrom's work on common-pool resources. As she described it, "Simply allowing communication, or 'cheap talk,' enables participants to reduce overharvesting and increase joint payoffs contrary to game theoretical predictions" (Ostrom 2010, 641). The month of March in 1933 sees a lot of "cheap talk" in Greensboro. A contemporary observer would be excused for thinking the problem intractable. But a solution emerged after various pronouncements of ultimately nonworkable solutions and dueling bluster on unsolvable constraints and fatal flaws. The actors in the development process in polycentric public entrepreneurship share ideas, debate, and eventually work out a solution. It is not obvious that a solution is imminent and that previous seemingly futile engagement was in fact productive and essential.

The last theoretical framework for understanding scrip formation in Greensboro is that of entangled political economy. In this theory "entities must be conceptualized as networks of relationships where individual nodes craft particular connections with other nodes. . . . [M]arket and political actions are undertaken simultaneously, and within an institutional framework that is open to all actors in both arenas" (Smith, Wagner, and Yandle 2011, 47). The relationships, and the new rules that emerge within them, between individual actors in Greensboro located across both the public and private are at the core of this case study. It is neither possible nor productive to delineate the solution into public and private portions. Indeed, the scrip relied on both private and public actors dynamically iterating in order to come to fruition.

CASE STUDY PART ONE: INVISIBLE PROGRESS

What follows is a day-by-day account from the *Greensboro Daily News* of Greensboro and Guilford County's adventure with scrip. Guilford County was one of the largest governing units in the country to resort to scrip during the Great Depression. The story might seem at times rather mundane. But in that mundanity is polycentric entrepreneurialism. In the interest groups' disagreements are the production of knowledge necessary to forge a solution. And the goals and abilities of those different groups are dynamic.

On March 3, 1933, seventy-five members of the Greensboro Merchants Association met to give their approval for the issuance of scrip by the City of Greensboro. With the inauguration as president of Franklin Roosevelt the next day, the dearth of currency, US dollars, in the midsized North Carolina city ground the area's commerce to a halt. N. S. Calhoun, the head of North Carolina Bank and Trust, said the situation was of "considerable moment but may not be alarming." His bank, the only commercial bank left in the city, would never reopen after the Bank Holiday. Julius Cone, the head of the largest denim manufacturer in the world which was based on the edge of town, expressed skepticism that the scrip would be readily accepted. Arnold Schiffman, a local jeweler and past president of the North Carolina Merchants Association, appealed to both the necessity of the city's paying employees in scrip and merchants' civic duty in accepting it as payment. The city attorney and manager Andrew Joyner, Jr. remarked that "a community the size of Greensboro cannot resort to barter and trade and must have some medium of exchange." Joyner informed the merchants that the City Council had informally discussed logistics of a scrip plan, and the merchants went over details as well (*Greensboro Daily News* 1933a).

This group of businessmen and government officials, each driven by his own unique interests with a dollop of civic duty on the side, began to haltingly coalesce around the idea of a local currency to overcome a national emergency. In the deepest depths of the Great Depression, these men made change for dollars that no longer existed. They did not know that things would get better. Indeed, things did not clearly get better for some time to come.

The City Council met again on the evening of the March 3 and some of the merchants already had developed cold feet and differing opinions as to the best way forward. Two plans were proposed, with each centering on the frozen and incalculable assets of the United Bank and Trust, formerly Greensboro's other commercial bank. In one plan, scrip would be issued against a conservative valuation of the bank's assets to depositors and would be redeemable at liquidation of the bank with the depositors maintaining an equity claim over any amount above that level. In the second plan, the scrip would be self-liquidating. Stamps would be applied each time the scrip was used. An issuing corporation would sell the stamps, and the scrip would be redeemable from the liquidated bank's assets once the value of the stamps equaled the value of the scrip. They formed a committee to meet the next day and hash out a plan (*Greensboro Daily News* 1933a). The self-liquidating plan was popularized by economist Irving Fisher. It sought to stimulate commerce while diminishing capital's importance (Fisher and Cohrssen 1933). It became the first of many false starts and dead ends in Greensboro's quest for local liquidity.

On the next day, FDR's inauguration day, Greensboro Mayor Paul Lindley tried to cobble together a plan. He knew that the support of banks, building and loans, and other business enterprises was essential. A new currency that did not generate widespread acceptance would not awaken Greensboro economic activity from its torpor. In meetings between businesses and the City Council, there remained the problem that no one knew the value of the bank deposits. The mayor hoped to iron out the details by the regular council meeting on Tuesday the March 7 so scrip could be issued to city employees on payday the March 15 and as payment for the city's bills. Guilford County, of which Greensboro is the seat, also needed a plan by the March 15. Teachers would be paid in scrip and, in turn, taxes and water bills could be paid in scrip. The merchants sought to seem cooperative while also demanding details on the plan (*Greensboro Daily News* 1933b). These negotiations highlight the various levels of acceptance necessary for a scrip scheme to succeed. The scrip might enter circulation as payment for salaries of government workers. If the workers could not spend that scrip with local businesses, the plan would collapse.

On Sunday, March 5, the plan for scrip expanded to include the governments of Greensboro's neighbor High Point and their common government Guilford County. Officials planned to charter an organization to issue scrip, perhaps a credit corporation as Arnold Schiffman the jeweler proposed and had been suggested by the Greensboro Merchants Association. This plan was adopted by the governments. This larger combination of governments addressed the merchants' concern that all scrip be issued by a central authority so that there would not be competing scrips in circulation. Through this expansion, the proponents of scrip matched the scrip area to the existing marketplace such that they would have a duopoly alongside scarce dollars. Subject to actions by the federal and state governments, the plan envisioned seeking a charter for a non-profit corporation from the state government and management by a board of directors composed of representatives from High Point, Greensboro, Gibsonville, Guilford County, and the merchant associations of High Point and Greensboro. The corporation would then issue scrip redeemable on or before a specific day, redeemable based on collateral deposited with the corporation, and in denominations of \$.25, \$.50, \$1, \$5, and \$10. The merchants bowed to necessity and accepted the plan as well they should because it was their plan, but there remained hope that the federal or state governments would take action nullifying the necessity of the scrip.

N. S. Calhoun, the president of the North Carolina Bank and Trust, explained the different types of scrip and informed the group that Governor Ehringhaus would declare a three-day banking holiday for North Carolina. Calhoun stated that the action was necessary because holidays in other states had increased demand on deposits in North Carolina's formerly relatively healthy banks by those with accounts in multiple states. He offered that his bank had a quarter million dollars in deposits from Greensboro citizens that were subject to withdrawal. This was the previous 5 percent limit on withdrawals and would have been sufficient to cover the currency needs of the community. With the governor's imminent bank holiday, they would no longer be available. Calhoun also disclosed that there was a plan under consideration for the issuance of statewide scrip. He opined that this would be much better than local scrip because North Carolina could get by for a long while trading within its own borders because it was a largely self-contained state (*Greensboro Daily News* 1933c).

On Monday, March 6, Governor Ehringhaus received three wires from Greensboro urging issuance of statewide scrip. Greensboro's mayor, Merchant's Association, and Chamber of Commerce all beseeched the governor. The need for currency was becoming more acute. Meanwhile, plans moved forward for the issuance of Guilford "Money," which the local paper deemed necessary to include in quotation marks (*Greensboro Daily News* 1933d).

On Tuesday, March 7, everyone awaited the federal government's expected action on Thursday. Their plan was at the ready if need be but the merchants especially were optimistic that the national government would relieve them of the necessity. Schiffman's Jewelers ran an advertisement touting their credit program because "MONEY Is Scarce! SCRIP May Be Used For Some Time!" (Schiffman's Jewelers 1933). On Thursday, March 9, no action had been taken by federal or state officials and Greensboro Mayor Lindsay stood ready to take action. All eyes were on Washington (*Greensboro Daily News* 1933e). By Friday, a decision was expected by Monday, and leading businessmen expressed confidence that the scrip would be "sound" money. The corporation would be known as the Guilford Clearing House corporation. Julius Cone, the textile magnate and Greensboro's richest man, was elected president of the as yet nonexistent corporation. He stated that "we have got to get scrip next week" (*Greensboro Daily News* 1933f). The most powerful men in Greensboro lacked the power to control events at higher levels of government. They just had to wait, and their unanimity waned.

On Friday, March 17, the directors voted to table the scrip issue and deemed it unnecessary at that time. The state banking commission had let the committee know that their approval for the issuance of scrip could be obtained whenever the committee wanted to go forward. Overall, the large industrial concerns managed to get sufficient currency to meet their payrolls and the government of High Point also seemed to be in good shape. On the other hand, Greensboro and the county government were less sure of the delay. Most of the merchants clamored for the issuance of scrip as they saw it as a stimulus for commerce with the dual benefits that it would be spent locally and quickly. On the whole, those with sufficient collateral to guarantee the issuance of scrip, the industrials and the High Point government, did not need it. Those who needed or wanted it either did not have or were not yet willing to use collateral. The stalemate hinged on the hope that North Carolina Bank and Trust would soon reopen in Greensboro and the city would once again have a commercial bank. George Stansbury, the representative of the county, thought scrip would be helpful in giving people a method to pay their taxes. In this round, the manufacturers carried the day. Their unwillingness, due to lack of necessity, to put up collateral stymied the efforts (*Greensboro Daily News* 1933g).

The Greensboro Daily News proceeded to continue to editorialize in favor of scrip almost every day. "It has been needed for a month or more and acutely needed for a fortnight," they intoned (*Greensboro Daily News* 1933h). "Business will continue to suffer more, the longer it goes on without this auxiliary currency" (*Greensboro Daily News* 1933i). "Now as to the Greensboro banks, and those who are officially and otherwise engaged in plans with regard to them. Everybody would be glad if, scrip having been decided on, there should be a restoration of bank credit before the issue could be put out" (*Greensboro Daily News* 1933j). Perhaps the newspaper favored scrip out of selfless wisdom, but they also relied on Greensboro's merchants for most of their advertising dollars. Struggling merchants translated into a struggling newspaper. As the primary extant chronicler of Greensboro's scrip saga, it also bears remembering that the paper's enthusiasm for scrip might have seeped out of its editorial pages and into its news coverage.

On Tuesday, March 21, the Greensboro City Council took steps toward authorizing scrip to pay city employees including teachers. They approved an enabling act to be sent to the state legislature for approval. The crux of the act was the use of tax anticipation notes as collateral. These notes were to be of no greater amount than half of the uncollected taxes. After some wrangling, the Council settled on an annual interest rate of 2 percent. Some argued offering interest would increase the likelihood that the scrip traded at par with dollars. The city anticipated being able to place in circulation $50,000 immediately and triple that over time. The scrip would expire in six months from the date of issue. Merchants were excited at the prospect. Greensboro's government was also running out of currency with which to pay its employees and bills. The scrip would doubly solve their problem by giving the means to pay its obligations while also increasing the local supply of currency with which taxpayers could pay the city (*Greensboro Daily News* 1933k). The use of tax anticipation notes, essentially using future tax receipts as the backing for the new scrip, proved to be an essential element in cobbling together the necessary coalition for implementing scrip. The industrialists with ready collateral were unwilling to back the scrip so the county government, for whom the scrip was more of a necessity than for the industrialists, stepped in to back the scrip in a creative manner.

On Thursday, March 23, the executive committee of the Guilford Clearing House association planned to meet in the offices of its president Julius Cone at his Proximity Mill. The city of Greensboro's plan sidestepped the Clearing House, which hoped to serve as a central issuer of scrip. The industrialists, centered around Cone and skeptical from the start, were left out of the implemented plans (*Greensboro Daily News* 1933l). The next day, Friday, March 24, Greensboro moved forward with its plan without the Clearing House. The ability to pay interest to keep the scrip at par seems to have been the deciding factor as this would not be allowed under the Clearing House though this was not explicitly stated. The merchants readily agreed to accept the city's scrip on the condition that it did not result in dollars being taken out of circulation. Proposals to issue scrip with the frozen assets of North Carolina Bank and Trust as collateral were rejected because they would sequester dollars and interfere with the hoped for revivification of the bank. Manufacturers agreed to pay a fixed portion of their salaries in scrip to place it in general circulation. The city planned to pay its local obligations, most pressingly salaries, with the scrip (*Greensboro Daily News* 1933m).

On Friday, March 24, both houses of the North Carolina General Assembly passed Greensboro's proposed scrip issuing enabling act. The city manager-attorney, Andrew Joyner, said his committee would have a proposal for the City Council to approve the next week. Greensboro was now closer to issuing scrip than at any point since 1907 when "the substitute medium was last put into circulation" (*Greensboro Daily News* 1933n). On the same day, Greensboro managed to cobble together funding for the redemption of their scrip by agreeing to sell $50,000 in tax anticipation bonds to local manufacturers at a 6 percent rate. These proceeds could be used to redeem the scrip of merchants who accumulated an excess. The plan was proposed by Julius Cone, who in addition to his textile magnate status was a city councilor. He stated that manufacturers would prefer to just buy the tax anticipation bonds as opposed to the scrip. So, in conjunction with the scrip, the city planned to sell the bonds as well (*Greensboro Daily News* 1933o). The light at the end of the tunnel was not the end but rather an oncoming freight train.

On Monday, March 27, Greensboro gave up. Unable to meet its bills and having scrip in the form of tax anticipation notes, the city changed course. "We'll just have to muddle along and pay [payrolls and local debts] as we get the money," Andrew lamented. The city only collected about $1,000 per day in taxes and sometimes less. Greensboro only paid half of its salaries on March 15. A larger payroll and monthly bills came due on the March 31. Additionally, $72,000 in interest and water bonds was due in New York on April 1. The city had a secured deposit at the shuttered North Carolina Bank and Trust, but no idea on when some portion of that might be available.

The opposition that crippled the plan came in the form of a letter from leading Greensboro merchants. The merchants suggested instead that the city sell tax anticipation notes for the funds necessary to continue operating. In this scenario, the city would skip the scrip part and simply receive cash with which to pay its bills. Joyner took up the suggestion with Julius Cone, the textile magnate and city council member. Cone said that his firm was not in the market for securities but could purchase them out of civic responsibility. Joyner, though, seemed pessimistic that anything could be accomplished, and there were no further meetings scheduled on the topic. The plans for Greensboro's issuing scrip died due to merchants' opposition (*Greensboro Daily News* 1933p). The first efforts and false starts of the early effort to bring scrip to Greensboro seemed to amount to nothing. In fact, they laid a solid foundation for the coalescing of interests that would follow. Knowledge of others' positions was dispersed. The various parties more fully understood their own interests. The situation in the broader nation became clearer. All these parts were necessary preconditions for a successful resolution. In just over a month, Greensboro moved from a hopeful fantasy of scrip to the brink of success though it looked like only a bunch of "cheap talk."

CASE STUDY PART TWO: A VIABLE SCRIP

In this section, dawn breaks. Out of the uncoordinated individuals, a solution emerges that allays their fears, inspires their hopes, and satisfies their interests. The solution meets the basic goal of scrip's initial supporters by creating a dollar substitute to stimulate commerce and stabilize transactions. The details and mechanics of the scrip issuance emerged in a form not discussed in the first part. The issuer was the county rather than the city and the scrip was backed by tax anticipation notes rather than the myriad of other schemes suggested. The actors entanglements formed a sufficiently solid foundation to move forward that had not been dictated by any single one of them.

By Wednesday April 5, progress came but there was no resolution yet. On the commercial banking front, a new national bank sought to raise $200,000 in capital with half coming from the federal government and $66,000 already raised from local sources. City Councilman Fred Taylor led the efforts and claimed to have turned down offers of money from outside the area because they hoped to make it an entirely local effort beyond Uncle Sam's half. A viable commercial bank would both lessen the need for scrip and facilitate its issuance. While the new bank in Greensboro was still many months from opening, its place on the horizon made clear that scrip would only need be temporary.

Guilford County also began to explore the possibility of their issuing scrip via revenue anticipation notes. The county commission discussed issuing as much as $300,000 in scrip though some favored only a third as much. Some local merchants opposed scrip and would not accept it though the commissioners were confident that most would. The county planned to turn over some of the scrip to the High Point and Greensboro boards of education to pay teachers. The commissioners hoped that the scrip would help stimulate local economic activity (*Greensboro Daily News* 1933q). The county commissioners proved to be much more adept in handling scrip politics than the Greensboro city council, but the city's efforts were an important means of establishing a framework for later success.

On Friday, April 14, Guilford County signed a contract with Todd Company of Rochester, New York, for engraving $100,000 in short-term revenue anticipation notes which would be put into circulation the next week. The cost of the notes was $480 and the Todd Company guaranteed against loss through counterfeiting (*Greensboro Daily News* 1933r). On Wednesday, April 19, Guilford County anticipated the arrival of the notes by Tuesday morning. A county officer, whose identity and mode of travel were held in confidence for "obvious reasons," planned to make the trip to Rochester to pick up the notes. The county planned to pay teachers and county employees with the notes and were confident of their ready acceptance by county merchants. High Point merchants were on board and officials expected the same from Greensboro merchants as well. The newspaper also announced that the United States was definitely off the gold standard though there would be purportedly little effect on domestic commerce because gold was only used in settlement of international trade. Cotton and wheat prices rose but experts believed that the dollar would not depreciate too much from free floating as the United States had a strong balance of trade (*Greensboro Daily News* 1933s).

On April 23, the Morrison-Neese furniture company in downtown Greensboro took out a large advertisement to announce that they would accept Guilford County scrip "(when issued) at 100% on the dollar." Undoubtedly, sales of consumer durable goods such as furniture had suffered mightily during the Depression, and they were happy to accept the scrip (Morrison-Neese 1933). On the next day, the board of directors of the Greensboro Merchants Association met with the George Stansbury, the chairman of the board of the county commissioners, and Willis Booth, the county auditor. They explained the forthcoming scrip to the skeptical merchants. The scrip would be redeemable for cash on July 29 with 4 percent annual interest from the date of issuance. The county officials also agreed to make every effort to establish a means of clearing whereby merchants who accumulated excess scrip could exchange it for cash (*Greensboro Daily News* 1933t).

Part of the appeal of scrip was its presumed high velocity. People spent it quickly, and the recipients followed suit in a virtuous cycle that stimulated commerce. The *Daily News* certainly subscribed to this philosophy. As they editorialized, "To the extent to which it gets into general circulation, trade will profit heavily, unless scrip history is to be departed from. The money doctors are saying, what they found out long ago, that prosperity is attended by a swift currency, and conversely a swift currency is the money of prosperity. Scrip has always been a hot money" (*Greensboro Daily News* 1933u). The *Daily News* was taking a victory lap. As the scrip entered circulation, the prominence of their coverage waned, and their advertisers returned. The newspaper continued to report on all things scrip, but the front-page headlines were fewer.

On April 28, the newspaper reported that the scrip was already in circulation and that $40,000 more in scrip would be paid out that day to rural teachers. That the county's credit was completely behind the scrip seemed sufficient to make for its ready acceptance. In an example of its use, a county employee went to a local café and paid with a 50-cent scrip note. Expecting a quarter for change, he instead received a 25-cent scrip note. County officials were gratified at widespread acceptance of their debt anticipation notes. Essentially, they got their employees to loan them money, stimulated local commerce, and increased the ability of their citizens to pay taxes (*Greensboro Daily News* 1933v). In High Point, on the other hand, difficulties emerged. Some locals purchased scrip at discounts of 10 percent and 20 percent though generally, it was circulating at par. County commissioner Joe Hoffman excoriated the discounters as "unpatriotic" (*Greensboro Daily News* 1933w). It is unclear whether those selling their scrip at a discount were simply poorly informed or this in fact represented wider mistrust, and the market price had in fact dipped below par. Nonetheless, reports of scrip trading at less than par to the dollar disappeared, and its widespread acceptance became normal thanks to widespread advertising and the continued scarcity of dollars.

"PUT GUILFORD COUNTY SCRIP TO WORK! Greatest Benefits Will Accrue From Widespread and Rapid Circulation of This Sound Temporary Currency" blared the headline at the bottom of a full-page advertisement in the *Greensboro Daily News* on April 30, 1933. On either side of pictures of the various denominations of the new scrip were listed the various institutions that would accept the new scrip. Car dealerships, dairies, jewelers, clothing and department stores, and even the funeral home all announced their intention to accept the new scrip. The City of Greensboro also jumped on board along with the *Daily News* and its afternoon counterpart *The Greensboro Record*. Interestingly, Gate City Building and Loan Association included its name in the advertisement, while its main competitor, Home Building and Loan Association, did not. Home would soon overtake Gate City as the largest savings and loan company (as buildings and loan would become) in the area. Perhaps, Gate City's eagerness to accept scrip reflected the dire straits it found itself in, but it is also worth noting that its official J. F. Stevens was on the original Greensboro scrip committee, which could also reflect their eagerness for currency of any kind or a greater civic mindedness (*Greensboro Daily News* 1933x).

On May 3, George Stansbury, the chairman of the Guilford County Board of Commissioners, headed to High Point to encourage acceptance of scrip. He was described as "a highly successful missionary in the interest of the recent scrip issue," but High Point proved a tough nut to crack. He arranged for Wachovia Bank to convert scrip for cash in $500 lots and petitioned the High Point city government to accept scrip in payment for municipal obligations (*Greensboro Daily News* 1933y). By May 6, Stansbury's evangelism proved a success as the High Point Merchants Association voted to accept the scrip at par while High Point's city government lifted its cap on the amount of scrip it would accept. Joe Hoffman, a county commissioner living in High Point, seems to have aided in the scrip's acceptance. Also, Hoffman said that arrangement could be made with a local bank to exchange excess scrip for cash (*Greensboro Daily News* 1933z). High Point's initial ambivalence to the scrip scheme is reflected in its merchants showing much more reluctance than Greensboro's in its implementation. As they were both part of Guilford County, High Point had no choice once the decision had been made but some resentment remained at having to go along with scrip to aid its ailing and larger neighbor.

On May 7, Guilford County excitedly announced that they might double or even triple their issuance of scrip because demand was so high. Once again, George Stansbury evangelized. The High Point tax office had taken in $5,000 in a single day. Two leading merchants had approached him about issuing more scrip. Also, people seemed more willing to spend the scrip than dollars, which they were liable to store away. There was also "a lingering suspicion" that the City of Greensboro had made a mistake when they failed to authorize scrip when they had considered it in March after the bank holiday proclamations (*Greensboro Daily News* 1933aa). In hindsight, scrip was obvious to officials in Greensboro, but the initial failures paved the way for a viable solution. Success bred the desire for more scrip.

On May 11, the *Daily News* reported that the county commissioners sought to issue $410,000 in bonds. They had $300,000 in road bonds maturing in 1933. In their current fiscal year, they had already paid off $180,000 in bonds. They had also issued the aforementioned $100,000 in revenue anticipation bonds. George Stansbury stated that the county could also do another round of small denomination revenue anticipation bonds to be used as scrip (*Greensboro Daily News* 1933ab). Viewing the revenue anticipation bonds as a piece of the county's debt puzzle illuminates the incentives that the county faced in using them to finance their debts.

At the commissioners' meeting on Friday, May 12, the issue of debt was delayed. They decided to meet again in a week. Resistance came from the

Greensboro Merchants Association. While the existing amount of scrip could be handled, they contended that additional scrip risked "clogging" commercial channels. Tax collections by the county had dropped off by $100,000 since the banks had closed, that is, over the past couple months. Stansbury argued that the scrip did the county no good unless it remained in circulation and that half of the initial $100,000 had come back to the county. Stansbury also reported that "one large concern would take the entire $410,000 bond issue if it was in small denominations." The board did not think this was a good idea and left the details to the committee meeting the next Friday (*Greensboro Daily News* 1933ac). Stansbury seems to be arguing that the scrip does not do the county much good as a means of borrowing if the county had to "pay" it back sooner as acceptance of taxes having been paid. On the other hand, if the county were in possession of the scrip at expiration, then they could just pay the interest to themselves and the loan would be costless beyond the cost of printing the scrip.

On May 16 in its weekly bulletin, the Greensboro Merchants association encouraged people to keep scrip in circulation. Merchants were redeeming scrip in $500 lots at the Home Industrial Bank faster than anticipated. The association encouraged its merchants to use the scrip first to pay employees then local bills and, lastly, to save it. The request from the merchants emphasized the tenuous financial situation of the county. "As a means of working with the county and for whatever benefit may accrue from stimulation of trade and improved collections, businesspeople are asked to exert themselves to use and keep scrip circulating" (*Greensboro Daily News* 1933ad).

CASE STUDY PART THREE: RETIRING, A SECOND ROUND, AND FORGERY

In this final section of the case study, Guilford County redeems the first round of scrip and begins the second. After the fractious and uncertain early days, scrip becomes routine and unremarkable while also being subject to a variety of mechanical hiccups. Minor forgery proves to be a persistent problem, but this does not prevent another round of scrip's approval. Indeed, the equal parts stimulative and stabilizing success of the first round shifts toward stimulative goals in the second round. The placid redemption and second life of scrip in Guilford County speaks to its success and the refiguration of institutions.

On July 19, the county prepared to retire its scrip that it issued on April 16. The retirement process would continue until July 29. The county offered to let citizens pay off their delinquent 1932 taxes with the scrip or prepay their 1933 taxes with a 2.5 percent discount. This prepayment amounted, if done with scrip, to a 3.5 percent discount. Essentially, the county got its money almost nine months early at a cost of 3.5 percent as taxes are late on the first day of the year after (*Greensboro Daily News* 1933ae).

On July 22, Guilford County began consideration of a second round of scrip. George Stansbury claimed to have been approached by several businessmen interested in another round after the retirement of the earlier block. Stansbury said that the county did not need to issue another round as its finances were in good shape but would give it consideration if there was sufficient demand from businesses. Full cooperation of merchants would be essential both for accepting the scrip as payment and as it would need to be put in circulation through them because the county's payroll needs were not as high with the teachers out for the summer. Stansbury also stated that his preference was an entirely new issue of scrip rather than a recycling of the old paper because it was worn out. He thought the denominations could change from the original $0.25, $0.50, $1, and $5 denominations and be for a longer period. The maximum length would be about a year because the county could not issue short-term obligations for longer than thirty days beyond the current fiscal year, which began on July 1 (*Greensboro Daily News* 1933af).

Forgery proved to be a problem with the scrip as well. R. M. Moser, a cement worker, paid for his 10-cent café bill with a $.25 piece of scrip that had been doctored to be appear as a $5 piece of scrip, receiving $4.90 in change. The "2" in ".25" had been marked out. Moser claimed to not remember where he received the scrip and apologized for the mishap. He was acquitted on the charges brought by the café owner when he could not be tracked down (*Greensboro Daily News* 1933ah).

On Saturday, citizens continued to redeem scrip on the maturity day. $.25 pieces received no interest as it was less than half a cent. $.50 and $1 pieces received 1 cent. $5 pieces received six cents. This was 4 percent interest over less than four months. County officials stated that holders of scrip could turn it in at a later date, presumably at no additional interest, or keep it as a souvenir (*Greensboro Daily News* 1933ag, 30). While the scrip mostly circulated in Guilford County, one piece made it all the way across the country. A man in Seattle, Washington, by the name of Max Shell returned a $.25 piece. He said he found it in Seattle (*Greensboro Daily News* 1933ai).

On August 16, the Guilford County Board of Commissioners authorized a new issue of $100,000 in scrip or revenue anticipation notes. The money received would be used for debt requirements and routine matters. It does not seem to have been a move of desperation, but there is also no mention of clamoring by merchants for the issue (*Greensboro Daily News* 1933aj). The county commissioners once again left the matter of a new issue of script up to business interests. Chairman George Stansbury was left in charge of surveying them to see if they could handle another issue. They requested that a method for disposing of large amounts of scrip be available. Stansbury confirmed that the Home Industrial Bank would be available in the same manner as the previous issue and that the soon-to-be open Guaranty Bank could probably function in the same manner. Generally, the merchants seemed willing to accept a new issue of scrip, but not with enthusiasm (*Greensboro Daily News* 1933ak).

By August 18, most but not all of the first issue of county scrip had been returned. Indeed, about $91,000 had been returned, leaving $9,000 unaccounted for. Three weeks after the notes had matured, the county looked likely to turn a nice profit thanks to these missing notes. There was no profit in holding onto them because they stopped accruing interest at the date of maturity. The county planned to keep them on their books indefinitely as unpaid indebtedness, though (*Greensboro Daily News* 1933ag, 30).

On Wednesday August 23, Guilford County decided to put out another $100,000 in scrip. The commissioners had been assured that the scrip "will be circulated without any trouble." The notes would bear interest of 4 percent with a start date of September 1 and a maturity date of January 15. The September 1 date was the last possible day that the commissioners could issue the notes with facsimiles of their signatures as opposed to individually signing each of what was approximately 100,000 notes. This new issue would also have a $10 note. The mix of business and professional interests that spoke in favor of the new issue is interesting. The furniture stores and automobile dealers remained in support as with the first round. In addition, Dr. R. A. Schoonover spoke in favor as president of the Guilford County Medical society, and Dr. J. L. Kernodle spoke in favor as a representative of the local dentists. Kernodle said that collections by local dentists were 50 percent higher after the issuance of the first round of scrip. The commissioners, in seeking bids for the new round of scrip, decided to seek out a better quality paper to preserve the texture. A portion of the notes would be used for county payroll and bills while some would be sold to business houses that had expressed interest in them (*Greensboro Daily News* 1933).

On September 6, the new scrip, the second round, went into circulation. Banks in both Greensboro, the Home Industrial Bank and Guilford Depository, and High Point, Wachovia Bank and Trust and Hood System Industrial Bank, agreed to exchange large amounts of the scrip for dollars. The county also distributed scrip to the cities of Greensboro and High Point to pay their employees. Businesses were encouraged by the county to accept the scrip with emphasis on using them for payroll to keep them in circulation. For purposes of understanding the size of Guilford County's government, it is worth noting that it announced on this same day that it had collected $986,031 in taxes for the previous fiscal year which ended on July 1 (*Greensboro Daily News* 1933am; *Greensboro Daily News* 1933an).

In the month since the second issue of scrip went live $79,000 of the $100,000 had been placed in circulation. $7,000 had been returned to the county for redemption. Most of the issue had been used for government payrolls and bills. There is no mention of businesses buying any but their support is mentioned, and it is stated that the second issue came at their request (*Greensboro Daily News* 1933ao). On January 15, 1934, Guilford County Treasurer WC Coble placed an advertisement in the *Daily News* reminding readers that the second round of scrip could be redeemed the next day. The revenue anticipation notes, "commonly called scrip," would no longer accrue interest after that date (Guilford County 1934).

As the second round of scrip was cashed, a number of counterfeit $5 notes were found. The sheriff notified the Secret Service Bureau in Charlotte, and the suspect notes were sent to the printers of the notes, the Security Bank Note company of Philadelphia, for examination. The fraudulent notes seemed to have entered circulation about ten days before the redemption date. A careful comparison by the printers brought forth a litany of differences between the actual and imitation notes. About twenty-five of them were found by the county (*Greensboro Daily News* 1934a). A few days later after the discovery of the counterfeits, the county urged merchants to stop accepting scrip altogether. About $94,000 of the $100,000 in notes had been returned, but over $350 of the counterfeit notes that had been found were turned into the county treasurer. The Sheriff continued to investigate but without "developments" thus far (*Greensboro Daily News* 1934b).

CONCLUSION

Simply put, Greensboro was broke, and scrip fixed it. But the road to "hot money" was not straightforward. On the way, there was a lot of "cheap talk." The process of knowledge dispersion and acquisition looked like they were spinning their tires. Large groups, even with seemingly overlapping interests, require time to understand each other and get to, what is in retrospect, the obvious solution.

Case studies are messy, and Greensboro's Great Depression scrip episode fits that script. Nonetheless, it offers clear lessons to inform scholars of theory and contemporary entrepreneurs endeavoring to create new alternative currencies. First, the process of knowledge creation and dissemination is awkward and opaque. The results are imperfect and incomplete. Grasping and responding to the varied fears, hopes, and interests of merchants, residents, and elected officials presents a difficult problem for all the individuals affected in this case study. Success required open communication and a willingness to work across boundaries and innovate in the creation of new rules for commerce during a currency crisis. What looks like failure might soon prove to be the path to success. Second and relatedly, polycentric solutions are emergent phenomena as actors from different spheres learn to communicate and coordinate under both informal and formal rules. The crisis of disappearing dollars that arrived in Greensboro required public entrepreneurship to meet the challenge, but multiple local governmental bodies had to coordinate alongside fractious private interests. Success arrived only after seeming failure.

REFERENCES

Board of Governors of the Federal Reserve System. 2022. "Money and Payments: The U.S. Dollar in the Age of Digital Transformation." https://www.federalreserve.gov/publications/files/money-and-payments-20220120.pdf.

Briola, Antonio, David Vidal-Tomás, Yuanrong Wang, and Tomaso Aste. 2022. "Anatomy of a Stablecoin's Failure: The Terra-Luna Case." *Finance Research Letters* 51: 103358.

Elvins, Sarah. 2005. "Scrip Money and Slump Cures: Iowa's Experiments with Alternative Currency During the Great Depression." *The Annals of Iowa* 64 (3): 221–245.

Fisher, Irving, and Hans RL Cohrssen. 1933. *Stamp Scrip*. New York: Adelphi.

Gatch, Loren. 2008. "Local Money in the United States During the Great Depression." *Essays in Economic & Business History* 26 (1): 47–62.

———. 2012. "Tax Anticipation Scrip as a Form of Local Currency in the USA During the 1930s." *International Journal of Community Currency Research* 16 (D): 22–35.

Greensboro Daily News. 1933a. "Issuance of Scrip by City Is Given Approval at Merchants' Meeting." March 4, 1933.

———. 1933b. "Calling Meeting Today to Discuss Scrip Issue." March 5, 1933.

———. 1933c. "Plans Are Tentatively Made for Countywide Authorization of Scrip." March 6, 1933.

———. 1933d. "Statewide Scrip Issue Urged upon Governor by 3 Local Sources." March 7, 1933.

———. 1933e. "Organization Is Ready to Pass on Scrip Issue If That Is Necessary." March 10, 1933.

———. 1933f. "Matter of Scrip Issue Here Will Very Likely Be Decided Monday; Corporation Formed to Handle It." March 11, 1933.

———. 1933g. "Scrip Issue Is Held Unnecessary Because of Improved Conditions; Organization to Remain Intact." March 17, 1933.

———. 1933h. "We Want Scrip (Editorial)." March 19, 1933.

———. 1933i. "We Want Scrip (Editorial)." March 20, 1933.

———. 1933j. "We Want Scrip (Editorial)." March 21, 1933.

———. 1933k. "Preliminary Steps Are Taken by City Council for Issuance of Scrip." March 22, 1933.

———. 1933l. "Scrip Committee to Meet This Morning." March 23, 1933.
———. 1933m. "Scrip Issue Is Nearer as City Gets Promises That It Will Be Used." March 24, 1933.
———. 1933n. "City Authorized to Put Out Scrip Issue." March 25, 1933.
———. 1933o. "Revenue from Sale of Tax Anticipation Notes Can Be Used in Retirement of Scrip." March 26, 1933.
———. 1933p. "Is Now Doubtful That City Can Meet Its Bills April 1." March 28, 1933.
———. 1933q. "County Asks Ruling on Legality of Scrip." April 6, 1933.
———. 1933r. "Contract Is Signed for County's 'Scrip'." April 15, 1933.
———. 1933s. "County 'Scrip' Will Be Ready by Middle of Coming Week." April 20, 1933.
———. 1933t. "Notes Are Explained to Merchants Board." April 26, 1933.
———. 1933u. "Provisional Currency (Editorial)." April 27, 1933.
———. 1933v. "Guilford County 'Scrip' Is Being Put Into Circulation." April 28, 1933.
———. 1933w. "Practice of Discounting County's Scrip Scored." April 29, 1933.
———. 1933x. "Scrip Is Acceptable (Advertisement)." April 30, 1933.
———. 1933y. "High Point Merchants Will Discuss Scrip Acceptance." May 4, 1933.
———. 1933z. "Merchants to Take Guilford's Scrip." May 6, 1933.
———. 1933aa. "May Greatly Enlarge Scrip Issue." May 8, 1933.
———. 1933ab. "Board to Work Out Bond Details Friday." May 11, 1933.
———. 1933ac. "Postpone Action on County Bond Issue." May 13, 1933.
———. 1933ad. "People Are Urged to Keep County Scrip in Circulation." May 17, 1933.
———. 1933ae. "County Gets Ready to Retire Its Scrip." July 19, 1933.
———. 1933af. "New Issue of Scrip By County Is Sought." July 23, 1933.
———. 1933ag. "Near $30,000 Woth of Scrip Cancelled." July 28, 1933.
———. 1933ah. "Moser Is Cleared of Passing Bogus Scrip." July 30, 1933.
———. 1933ai. "Piece of Guilford Scrip Redeemed by Seattle Man." August 8, 1933.
———. 1933aj. "County to Borrow to Meet Debt Needs." August 17, 1933.
———. 1933ak. "Scrip Issue Put Up To Business People." August 18, 1933.
———. 1933al. "County Board Decides to Put Out Another $100,000 Scrip Issue." August 24, 1933.
———. 1933am. "$986,031 Collected by County Tax Office." September 6, 1933.
———. 1933an. "County's Scrip Issue to Be Received Today." September 6, 1933.
———. 1933ao. "$79,000 Of County Scrip in Circulation." October 10, 1933.
———. 1934a. "Counterfeit Notes Found Among Scrip." January 16, 1934.
———. 1934b. "People Urged Not To Take Scrip." January 18, 1934.
Guilford County. 1934. "Scrip (Advertisement)." *Greensboro Daily News*, January 14.
Hayek, F.A. 1945. "The Use of Knowledge in Society." *The American Economic Review* 35 (4): 519–530.

Kipp, Samuel M., III. 1977. "Old Notables and Newcomers: The Economic and Political Elite of Greensboro, North Carolina, 1880–1920." *The Journal of Southern History* 43 (3): 373–394.

Kreicher, Lawrence, Robert N. McCauley, and Philip D. Wooldridge. 2014. "Benchmark Tipping in the Global Bond Market." BIS Working Papers, No. 466. Basel, Switzerland: Bank for International Settlements.

McGinnis, Michael D. 2011. "An Introduction to IAD and the Language of the Ostrom Workshop: A Simple Guide to a Complex Framework." *Policy Studies Journal* 39 (1): 169–183.

Morrison-Neese. 1933. "We Will Accept Guilford County Scrip (Advertisement)." *Greensboro Daily News*, April 23, 1933.

Ostrom, Elinor. 2010. "Beyond Markets and States: Polycentric Governance of Complex Economic Systems." *American Economic Review* 100 (3): 641–672.

Schiffman's Jewelers. 1933. "Money Is Scarce! (Advertisement)." *Greensboro Daily News*, March 8, 1933.

Smith, Adam, Richard E. Wagner, and Bruce Yandle. 2011. "A Theory of Entangled Political Economy, with Application to TARP and NRA." *Public Choice* 148 (1): 45–66.

Timberlake, Richard H. 1987. "Private Production of Scrip-Money in the Isolated Community." *Journal of Money, Credit and Banking* 19 (4): 437–447.

"Top Stablecoins by Market Cap | CoinCodex." n.d. Accessed November 6, 2022. https://coincodex.com/cryptocurrencies/sector/stablecoins/.

Wagner, Richard E. 2007. *Fiscal Sociology and the Theory of Public Finance: An Exploratory Essay*. Cheltenham: Edward Elgar Publishing.

Warner, Jonathan. 2012. "Iowa Stamp Scrip: Economic Experimentation in Iowa Communities during the Great Depression." *The Annals of Iowa* 71 (1): 1–38.

Chapter 6

Sub-innovation

The Case of Fraccionamiento *in Mexico*

Carlos Noyola

Fraccionamiento is a type of settlement, common in Latin America, characterized by being an enclosed neighborhood with access restricted to those living inside and those granted permission by them (e.g., a plumber coming to repair something, friends coming to visit). This restriction is enforced by automated doors that only those with an electronic key (usually pasted in the windshield) can open and security guards in charge of asking permission from residents to allow a visitor in and registering their basic information. The purpose of this chapter is to provide an economic analysis of Fraccionamiento from the perspective of Constitutional Political Economy, which focuses on how individuals create rules and live with them.

To understand Fraccionamientos, it is important to distinguish between government and governance. The former refers to the State (a monopoly of force over a given territory), while the latter refers to the process by which society (or a given group within society) is governed. My definition of governance is based on the work of R. A. W. Rhodes, who characterizes governance as a process in which (1) non-state actors are included, (2) there is constant interaction among members of the group, (3) interactions are regulated by rules but rooted in trust, and (4) there is a significant degree of autonomy from the State (Rhodes 2007, 1246).

According to this definition of governance, we can think of Fraccionamientos as places where a particular type of governance occurs. Fraccionamientos include non-state actors (the citizens who inhabit them), and those citizens constantly interact. Their interaction is regulated by the rules of the Fraccionamiento but is ultimately rooted in trust since they became members of the Fraccionamiento voluntarily, and their autonomy from the State is shown in their ability to establish and change the rules that regulate their interactions.

Well-defined property rights and the rule of law are the two essential institutions for encouraging entrepreneurship (Boettke and Coyne 2003). The key feature of the Fraccionamiento can be seen as a response to the absence of state-provision of the rule of law. Based on Buchanan's argument, along with Boettke and Coyne's argument, I will argue that Fraccionamientos (using a Fraccionamiento in Puebla, Mexico, as a case study) are an entrepreneurial activity that represents sub-innovation, in the sense that citizens are providing for themselves something (i.e., security) that was supposed to be provided by the institutional setting they are already living in (i.e., the Mexican law).

Following the idea that "entrepreneurship manifests itself differently across alternative institutional regimes and some of these manifestations are consistent with economic development, while others are not" (Boettke and Coyne 2003, 69), I will show that the Fraccionamiento settlement is intended to overcome an institutional regime that is not consistent with economic development. By being forced to provide for themselves the preconditions for innovation, citizens in countries such as Mexico with high levels of violence are not innovating to their full potential.

In the English-speaking world, some studies have paid attention to the phenomena of gated communities. Most prominently, *Fortress America: Gated Communities in the United States* (Blakely and Snyder 1997), published at the end of the twentieth century, looked at enclosed neighborhoods across the United States and focused not only on those created for security concerns but also for status and lifestyle reasons. Building up on their research, other studies have tried to characterize the physical characteristics of gated communities (Grant and Mittelsteadt 2004) and emphasize the similarities between the creation of gated communities and segregation dynamics (Vesselinov 2008), but they overlook the reasons for their creation and contexts foreign to the United States.

In the Spanish-speaking world, although only in recent years, some researchers have turned their attention to Fraccionamientos in particular. Some have looked at large-scale Fraccionamiento developments (Chen), others at the values of those who inhabit Fraccionamientos and the symbolism of their architecture (Camus 2019; Castillo Rodríguez 2016), and still others at the effects of Fraccionamientos that already exist (Galaviz Mosqueda et al. 2014; Enríquez Acosta 2006). However, none of them has taken an economic approach to the issue, and they have not paid attention to the rationale behind their existence.

From previous studies three things stand out. First, none analyzes Fraccionamientos from an economic perspective. All the researchers belong to other disciplines, such as architecture, urbanism, and sociology. Second, there is a general trend to conduct the analysis based on the assumption that free market solutions are not good, that privatization is undesirable (at least with negative connotations), and that Fraccionamientos are completely detrimental to life. Third, they all focus either on the differences between Fraccionamientos and other settlements, how they became generalized, or different effects that Fraccionamientos have. However, none of them looks at the motivations behind the creation of Fraccionamientos.

Before continuing, it is important to define Constitutional Political Economy as well as the term "constitution." Constitutional Political Economy is a program of "inquiry to the working properties of rules, and institutions within which individuals interact, and the processes through which these rules and institutions are chosen or come into being" (Buchanan 1999, 377). The focus of this research program is on the choice among constraints. By constitution (with lowercase "c"), in this chapter, I refer to a set of rules governing a group of people, larger than one unit but smaller than the entire polity. For instance, in contrast with U.S. Constitution (with a capital "C"), the set of rules governing the conduct of the members of the University of Notre Dame (students, faculty, and staff), commonly known as Code of Conduct, will be the constitution of the University of Notre Dame (with lowercase "c").

This chapter contributes to the literature in three ways. First, it is the first study of Fraccionamientos in Puebla, a city of over 3 million people, that, even though is the fourth largest city of the country, has received no attention when it comes to understand enclosed neighborhoods. By comparing the results of my research with studies done in other cities, we will be better able to draw conclusions. Second, to the best of my knowledge, this is the first attempt to analyze the phenomenon of enclosed neighborhoods in Latin America from an economic perspective. Previous studies have looked at Fraccionamientos from architectural, sociological, anthropological, and even historical perspectives, but I will examine the incentives at play in their formation and operation. Lastly, in contrast with previous studies, which focused on comparisons between Fraccionamientos and other settlements or the effects of Fraccionamientos, my research, without romanticizing life in society, concentrates on the reasons driving their development. By understanding why Fraccionamientos come to be in first place, policymakers will be better equipped to identify the problems that spurred their emergence.

This chapter proceeds as follows. The second section provides a history of Fraccionamientos in the Mexican context. The third section provides a theoretical framework for analyzing the rules that govern a certain community. The fourth section studies the rules that govern Fraccionamiento Residencial San Martinito in Puebla, Mexico. The final section concludes.

HISTORY OF FRACCIONAMIENTOS

Closed neighborhoods are very common in Mexico. Living locked up in a fort seems, to many Mexicans, to be the order that things should follow. But it is not. If we are to understand Fraccionamientos we should understand their place in Mexican history.

The history of enclosed neighborhoods in Mexico goes as far back as the arrival of Spaniards to America and the conquest of Mesoamerica. In 1521, after the Spaniards finally subjugated the capital of the Aztec empire, Tenochtitlan, Hernán Cortés, who oversaw the mission, created the first enclosed neighborhood by reserving the center of the city exclusively for the Spaniards while the rest, the surroundings, was to be occupied by Mesoamericans. Mesoamericans and Spaniards had different laws, courts, and authorities (civil and ecclesiastical). The division was not only spatial but also judicial and political: there were two republics.

To ensure that the center was reserved for the Spaniards, they built their houses in the form of forts. Spatial segregation had a racist component, but it was also based on preoccupations of survival. Newly conquered, Mesoamericans could revolt at any moment. The subjugated empire was a constant threat to the Spanish minority. Right from the start, in this proto-Fraccionamiento, we can distinguish a clear motivation for the enclosed form set up by the Spaniards that lies within the pre-constitutional moment pointed out by Buchanan, that is, providing a safe environment to live before they can undertake any other enterprise.

In the sixteenth and seventeenth centuries, the segregation trend started in the early days of the new colony was reversed. There was integration of different social groups—partly because the Mesoamerican population was decimated (it no longer seemed so much of a threat to the Spanish conquerors), partly because erecting walls was incompatible with the principles of Catholicism (that the Spaniards sought to spread), and partly because many of the children of Spaniards lacked the fortune of their parents—so they found themselves forced to live among Mesoamericans.

Integration, however, did not last long. The Spanish crown was worried about losing control of its colony and forcefully tried to reinforce it throughout the eighteenth century. They did so by implementing a series of reforms, known as Bourbon Reforms, both economic and political, including a significant restructuring of the ways in which New Spain was administered by local authorities. One of its main purposes, of course, was to increase the dependency of local authorities from the Spanish Monarchy. The Bourbon Reforms resulted in a new spatial order, where the lower classes did not mix with the upper classes. The change not only affected the relationship between social classes but also between members of the same class. The idea of the nuclear family gained strength, and the society of New Spain of the late eighteenth century was divided into smaller units, each one responsible for its own future.

With the economic growth during the Díaz dictatorship—in the nineteenth century—the limits of the cities significantly expanded, turning rural areas into residential ones. The expansion followed the French bourgeoisie as a model of refinement and good taste. Once the Díaz regime was overthrown during the Mexican Revolution in the first decades of the twentieth century, violent conflicts catalyzed migration to the suburbs because people wanted a quiet place to live. This movement created the breeding ground for the contemporary form of the Fraccionamiento.

One of the pioneers of Fraccionamientos was Lomas de Chapultepec, built in the 1930s, promoted as the "first garden city" and which—according to Diana Sheinbaum (2008)—imitated the Saxon model developed by Ebenezer Howard at the end of the nineteenth century. However, the first Fraccionamiento as we understand it today did not come until the fifties, designed by none other than one of the most important Mexican architects of the twentieth century, Luis Barragán. It was named Jardines del Pedregal. Its characteristics, with the limitations of the moment, are the characteristics of the twenty-first century Fraccionamiento: plots of land with more or less of the same sized green areas for the exclusive use of the Fraccionamiento's inhabitants—and controlled access, reinforced by a street design based on cul-de-sacs. In 1958, the Mexican government approved the first Fraccionamiento Law, granting this type of settlement official recognition.

Jardines del Pedregal was promoted as "the ideal place to live," but Fraccionamientos have drawbacks. The neighbors of a street will never know those of the street behind if that other street belongs to another Fraccionamiento. Fraccionamientos may increase fear of the other since the habit of segregation reinforces the idea that we are only safe when we are quartered (Galaviz Mosqueda et al. 2014). To make matters worse, Fraccionamientos are expensive (like any product of insecurity): citizens have to pay for private guards, administrative staff, surveillance cameras, and maintenance of access-controlled entrances and be willing to waste time: people have to wait in line to undergo the necessary revision before being allowed inside the Fraccionamiento to visit a friend. If some Mexicans are willing to live under such conditions, it must be because the benefits of doing so surpass the costs.

FRAMEWORK

Before we start the analysis, it is useful to remember the foundations of Constitutional Political Economy. This begins with what Buchanan calls methodological individualism, which holds that "the autonomous individual is a sine que non for any initiation of serious inquiry in the research program" (Buchanan 1999, 390). Citizens living inside a Fraccionamiento are assumed to be able to make their own decisions, voluntarily opting to become part of an enclosed community because they are convinced that the benefits derived from the limitations that a Fraccionamiento imposes on others' behavior are greater than the costs associated with the constraints imposed on their own behavior.

Starting with autonomous individuals, it is important to remember that those individuals are "either already organized or potentially organizable in a political unit" (Buchanan 1999, 393). In the case of Fraccionamientos already established and recognized by the State, we are dealing with individuals already organized into a political unit. One last thing to note is that in this chapter, Fraccionamientos are considered a type of technology, understood as "the application of organized knowledge to practical tasks" (Barbour 1993, 44). Collectively, citizens are applying their knowledge pertaining to the threats of lawlessness in their city to solve it. In this sense, we can think of citizens creating Fraccionamientos as engaging in a particular type of entrepreneurial activity.

We should also stress why it is possible to study the emergence of constraints within the realm of Constitutional Political Economy without having to use another approach (or moving to another discipline). Buchanan reminds us that "the individual who joins in a collective decision to impose a generally applied constitutional rule is not, at base, acting differently from observed behavior in a setting that involves giving up one desired good, apples, for another desired good, oranges" (Buchanan 1999, 381). The analogy, at first, may not seem obvious. The reason is that:

> in the latter example, we can, without violating the meaning of words, say that the individual chooses to constrain, or to limit, the potential consumption of apples in exchange for the expanded opportunity to consume oranges. Expressed in this way, all that is required is that we classify the restrictions on others' actions as goods in the individual 's preference function along with the more natural classification of restrictions on his (her) own actions as bads. (Buchanan 1999, 381)

In other words, the individual chooses to limit his liberties of behavior (accepts restrictions) in exchange for the restrictions on others' actions. Therefore, the creation of rules is not an extension of Constitutional Political Economy but a particular case of it.

My study looks at how entrepreneurial activity tries to solve the problem of crime. According to Boettke and Coyne (2003), there are two essential institutions for encouraging entrepreneurship: well-defined property rights and the rule of law. Without any of these two necessary conditions society will incur a cost in the form of lost opportunities for entrepreneurial activity. However, the rule of law has been shown not to be necessary in certain contexts to engage in market activity. Therefore, it is important to look at how the situation of Fraccionamientos is different and makes the rule of law necessary.

One of the challenges of living within a society in which the State is absent is the constant abuse of weak citizens by those who are stronger. Leeson (2014) studies the case of west-central Africa in the last decades of the nineteenth century, in particular the relationship between African producers and Caravans of middlemen employed by settlers to collect goods. While communities of African producers were for the most part stationary, caravans, by definition, were highly mobile. On top of that, caravans of middlemen were more powerful than the producers, mainly due to the modern weaponry they possessed. Taken together, the lack of weaponry and low mobility made communities of producers an ideal target for banditry. Middlemen could simply use their appalling force to get everything they wanted from African producers, without having to engage in any peaceful form of exchange.

However, as Leeson explains, trade constantly took place between the caravans of middlemen and communities of producers. Even though weaker, African producers used two mechanisms to ensure that caravans engaged in peaceful trade with them. First, they exchanged with middlemen on credit, asking for payments and promising to give the goods that the middlemen were looking for at some point in the future. In this way, middlemen were not tempted to steal from producers (since the products did not exist yet, there was nothing to steal) and producers got paid.

Leeson, framing the transaction as a game, shows that for sufficiently patient middlemen the best strategy is to trade peacefully with producers. Besides, exchanging on credit incentivized middlemen to care about the wellbeing of producers so that they would be able to deliver the goods owed to them on time. Secondly, communities often asked for a tribute before letting middlemen into the community. Moreover, particularly in communities whose wealth mainly consisted of livestock, "community headmen were gatekeepers to their community's producers and required middlemen to meet their tribute demands before they would consummate trade relations" (Leeson 2014, 71). This tribute worked as a tax paid by patient middlemen, compensating for the losses incurred due to the banditry of impatient middlemen.

Like communities of producers in west-central Africa, Mexican citizens represent communities with low mobility, whereas criminals who are a threat to their security, like the caravans of middlemen, are mobile (at least in relative terms) and are in possession of weaponry that citizens lack and therefore able to plunder them. However, unlike communities of producers, citizens are not trying to engage in trade with robbers. Likewise, trade is not a feasible option for robbers. First, because even if they wanted to, often those things they are looking for their owners are unwilling to sell (i.e., jewelry, TVs, computers), and more importantly, robbers simply want to get those goods for free.

Therefore, citizens cannot use boycott as a strategy for dealing with the threat nor use credits or tribute as producers in nineteenth century Africa. Since trade is not an option, the rule of law is necessary, and if the government does not enforce laws, citizens facing the threat of robbers have to find a way to protect themselves using force. In fact, Leeson acknowledges this option, even though he does not examine it in detail: "One possible solution to this problem is for physically weaker persons to invest in becoming stronger" (Leeson 2014, 58). Citizens might invest in becoming stronger individually, but they may also organize themselves in order to invest to become stronger as a collective unit.

According to Sherman (1983), crime control can either take the form of "watching," "walling," or "wariness." These three are investments in becoming stronger. Watching refers to constant observation of people and places that are possible criminal targets in order to capture criminals red-handed. On the other hand, walling refers to any action whose purpose is to prevent criminal activities, including (but not restricted to) installing locks, fences, and security cameras and building walls. Lastly, wariness consists of behavior strategies to avoid crime, ranging from self-defense classes and possession of firearms to staying at home at night and not walking alone.

Even where there is a State in place, that does not automatically protect people from criminal activities. The State should adequately enforce rules to guarantee the protection of individual rights. Stringham (2015) studied the case of San Francisco which, during the 1850s, suffered severely from a public safety problem, even though there were institutions in place in charge of providing security for citizens. There were few policemen—most were poorly trained and many were corrupt. The citizens of San Francisco reacted by creating private police units to ensure their security. Usually, people living in a given building would collectively provide the funds necessary to pay for guards.

To understand the magnitude of the problem, Stringham explains that San Francisco "had more than one thousand Special Police Officers in different firms at the beginning of the twentieth century, and for perspective that means San Francisco had more private police than 99.5 percent of jurisdictions today have government police" (Stringham 2015, 120). Citizens were so worried about the criminal threats to their security that ended up with a level of protection not even enjoyed by cities nowadays.

Stringham makes the interpretation very clear: "using security hired by the entity managing the property, as opposed to government . . . means that customers of a physical space have opted into a security structure that they prefer" (Stringham 2015, 130). It is due to the inefficient delivery of security from the government that citizens opt for another option.

Economists have looked constantly at how individuals faced with restrictions make their decisions, the best example of which may be the basic maximization problem of a utility function subject to a budget constraint stating that the income of the individual must be greater or equal than the total amount of spending in goods and services. However, Buchanan explains that "the inclusive domain of constitutional economics also includes the derivation, analysis of, and justificatory argument for rules that constrain both individual and collective behavior in a wide array of membership groupings, larger than the one-unit limit but smaller than the all-inclusive limit of the whole polity" (Buchanan 1999, 384). That is, we should also study why the constraints that individuals are subject to exist in the first place and why precisely those rules and not others.

We may be tempted to restrict our analysis to a state, county, or municipality, but groups larger than one unit and smaller than the whole polity include other groups within our society that have their own set of constraints, even though they may not be governed by laws in the strict sense that we refer to when we speak of the laws of a country (a capital "C" Constitution). Buchanan makes this explicit: "Clubs, trade unions, corporations, parties, universities, associations—these, and many more, exist and operate under constitutions that are amenable to scientific inquiry" (Buchanan 1999, 384).

Buchanan makes an analogy between citizens as members of an organized political body and poker players. He explains that during the game, "individuals, as players, abide by the rules that exist and that define the game itself" (Buchanan 1999, 369). The strategies players employ to win work within the rules already established, but this does not mean players cannot reflect upon the rules themselves. "At the same time, however," says Buchanan, "the same persons may evaluate the rules themselves, and they may enter into side discussions about possible changes in the rules, so as to make for a 'better' game" (Buchanan 1999, 369). Changes in rules are not automatic, but "if, as a result of such discussion, agreement is reached, then rules are changed and the regime shifts. A new constitution emerges" (Buchanan 1999, 369). For Buchanan this shows that "the individual player may, but need not, enter into the dialogue and discussion about changes in the rules" (Buchanan 1999, 369).

The objection to Buchanan's analogy comes from two sides. The first is that a poker game, no matter how complex, cannot involve more than fourteen players, and it usually involves less than ten. That is, poker games are very small. The second one is that people are not forced into playing poker: if anyone happens to be seated at a poker table wondering what to play next, it is exclusively because the person wants to be there. Playing poker is voluntary.

The political game, if we may call it that, differs from poker in both ways. First, it is usually comprised of large numbers of people (hundreds of millions in many countries today), and citizens do not voluntarily choose to become part of it. They are in it, and they cannot opt out if it.

The consequence of having millions of participants in the game, Buchanan explains, is that "there may exist little or no incentive for any single player to participate actively in any serious evaluation of rules" (Buchanan 1999, 370). But why would citizens choose not to engage in the evaluation of rules even if they think they could benefit from modifying them? The reason is simple enough: because citizens do not think they can actually modify them. Buchanan puts it this way: "the individual player may not consider himself or herself influential in controlling the ultimate selection among sets of rules; hence, the fully rational player may well refrain from participating in the choice among regimes" (Buchanan 1999, 370).

As for the second objection, that the political game is not optional, the result is that individually "we cannot exercise even residual influence over the rules through an effective exit option" (Buchanan 1999, 370). In a small game, like poker, one player threatening to quit the game may exert enough pressure for the group to consider a change in rules, but in a country like Mexico, with more than 120 million people, it would be absurd to try to exert any pressure on fellow citizens by leaving the political game (viz., moving permanently to another country). For Buchanan the conclusion is very clear: "if the individual cannot ultimately influence the choice among regimes, it is not rational to participate actively in any discussion of constitutional change or to become informed about constitutional alternatives" (Buchanan 1999, 370).

THE FOUNDATIONS OF RESIDENCIAL SAN MARTINITO

Fraccionamiento Residencial San Martinito is located in the southwest of Puebla, the fourth largest city in Mexico. The area where it is located is the fastest growing area of the city and newest one. It is located a few meters away from Bulevard Atlixcáyotl, the most important avenue of Puebla and around which the financial and commercial center of the city is located. No plot of land can be less than 300 square meters, and there are no apartment complexes inside. The first houses began to be built in 2004, but as of October 2022, there are still a few plots of land without any house. Since many properties have been sold since 2004, the Assembly of the Fraccionamiento decided to reestablish the Fraccionamiento in May 2021. Therefore, I will base my analysis on the constitution of the Fraccionamiento approved in May 2021.

The rules of Fraccionamiento Residencial San Martinito are legitimized by Mexican law. In fact, the first article of the document states that "these regulations are created in compliance with Article 1120 of the Civil Code of the State of Puebla." These rules are the product of autonomous individuals voluntarily deciding to become part of the enclosed community, as a response to the high levels of violence in the country. In Article 3, Fraccionamiento Residencial San Martinito is defined as an association of proprietors of a plot of land or a house built in one of the plots of land located in one of three streets. Since the rules of the Fraccionamiento have official status, and following Buchanan's terminology referred earlier of constitutions under which groupings within a society operate, from now on I will refer to the set of rules regulating Fraccionamiento Residencial San Martinito as its constitution.

Those who are proprietors, as well as tenants (while their contract is in place), are considered associates of the Fraccionamiento. There are spaces within the Fraccionamiento that belong to all associates, a kind of public good whose access is restricted to members of the Fraccionamiento.

There is an executive board of the Fraccionamiento, and the Executive Board is in charge of designating an administrator of the Fraccionamiento. The administrator is always subject to the orders of the Executive Board, that is, the Executive Board of the Fraccionamiento is the governing body. It serves for two-year periods and is comprised of the president, a secretary, a treasurer, and a substitute, the latter in charge of taking the role of any member of the Executive Board in case he/she is unable to serve anymore. All members of the Board must be associates of the Fraccionamiento. Decisions regarding the Fraccionamiento, therefore, are made using the knowledge of those closest to the problems (i.e., the residents).

The creation of a subgovernment within an organized political body that already has its own government (i.e., the government of the State of Puebla, which in turn is subject to the federal government of Mexico) should make us wonder the reason for such subgovernment. It is a voluntary action since no one is required to live inside a Fraccionamiento in Mexico. Up until now, the association has nothing remarkably particular, and it could well be that the Executive Board serves to organize recreational activities. Later on, it will be clear that the creation of this governing body directly responds to a necessity, but for now suffice it to say that the creation of a subgovernment is not an idle matter.

Article 3 states that every owner is subject to the rules stated in the constitution of the Fraccionamiento. This constitution can only be modified by the majority vote of the assembly, but the executive board, as well as any group of members that accounts to 25 percent of the assembly is entitled to make modification proposals. This is consistent with our methodological individualism approach, since "collective choice is factored down into the participatory behavior of individual members" (Buchanan 1999, 383). Here we also have evidence of one important reason for citizens to become part of the Fraccionamiento. Considering Robert Dahl and Charles Lindblom's assertion that individuals do not get to choose among the grand organizational alternatives in a society but only among the options available within the organizational regime currently in place (or given), James Buchanan makes the case that not getting involved in choosing among sets of rules is not the same as not being able to.

Article 3 of the constitution of Fraccionamiento Residencial San Martinito faces the two challenges to Buchanan's analogy and, by doing so, provides an incentive for citizens to become part of it. Since the constitution of the Fraccionamiento can only be modified by a majority vote, and right now the assembly is now comprised of 100 members, at least 51 have to vote in favor of any modification. Such a number is small for any individual to influence the choice among rules, and therefore there is an incentive for everyone to be informed about the alternatives they are facing.

Furthermore, as little as twenty-five votes are required to propose a modification of the constitution, which means that anyone with an interest in changing a rule has a real possibility of bringing his proposal to the whole assembly. All he has to do is convince twenty-four other members that such a change would also benefit them. This gives us a first important reason why a Fraccionamiento comes into existence. By creating a small community with its own government within the larger polity, the Fraccionamiento gives its members a real possibility of defining the rules under which they live (at least those rules that can be defined by the Executive Board of the Fraccionamiento), motivating them to be informed about the constitution of the Fraccionamiento and engaging them in discussions about possible changes to it.

Article 4 gives us a good reason to think residents of the Fraccionamiento have the incentives to comply with the rules. It establishes that in order to build a house in the Fraccionamiento, the owner of the plot of land must first get an official letter of approval from the Executive Board. Importantly, this letter is required by the government of the municipality to grant government approval for the construction. This means that, for instance, if the owner refuses to sign the constitution of the Fraccionamiento (meaning he is unwilling to make a compromise to abide by it), he will not be able to build his house.

Article 5 establishes that no house inside the Fraccionamiento can be used for a purpose other than housing. No businesses, no offices, and no corporate headquarters are allowed. Owners can only use their land to live there or to rent it to someone else who will live there. This is an important constraint on the freedom of any owner, since they are not allowed to set up a business within their property. Moreover, the constraints do not end up there. Part c of Article 11 establishes that any type of advertising other than advertising the sale of that property is strictly forbidden. Owners cannot use their property for business nor to advertise their business somewhere else.

Even the ways in which a house can be built are limited. The floor plan of every house must first be approved by the administrator (designated by the Executive Board) so as to make sure that it complies with certain specifications, such as the maximum height of the walls, that the construction will be completely contained within the limits of the owner's property, and that all entrances are exclusively located at the front of the house. During the construction of the house, all workers must be registered with an official ID, and they are allowed to work only from 8 a.m. to 5 p.m. from Monday through Friday and Saturdays only until 2 p.m.

On top of all the abovementioned restrictions, owners are obliged to pay a monthly fee, established in Article 29. The assembly must approve the annual fee every year and is entitled to approve extraordinary fees when necessary. For the period 2021–2022, the monthly fee for an inhabited house in the Fraccionamiento was 1,350 Mexican pesos (70 USD), 550 Mexican pesos (30 USD) for a plot of land without a house, and 1,150 Mexican pesos (60 USD) for either a house under construction or a finished but uninhabited house. The assembly also approved by unanimity an extraordinary fee of 4,000 Mexican pesos (200 USD) for every owner, for the purpose of repairing perimetral fences, providing adequate maintenance to the well that serves the Fraccionamiento, and the technology system under which the automatic doors for residents operate. Although the entire concept of Fraccionamiento can be seen as an example of "walling," one of the ways in which citizens can control crime according to Sherman (1983), this particular fee makes it explicit. If a proprietor fails to pay the monthly fee within the first five days of every month, Article 30 establishes that he will have to pay an extra 5 percent for every month or fraction of a month that the payment is delayed.

With all these restrictions on their behavior, it may be surprising that citizens are not only willing, but actively try to live inside a Fraccionamiento such as this. And given that they do want to live in such an association, there must be a good reason for it. As Buchanan explains, "a necessary condition for cooperation in social interaction is the prospect for positive expected gains by all parties, or, in the gainer-loser terminology, the prospect that there be no net losers" (Buchanan 1999, 386). The problem found in society at large, in general, is that "at a first descriptive cut, this condition seems to be foreign to the whole political enterprise" (Buchanan 1999, 386). In this case, since people are voluntarily associating to form the Fraccionamiento without anyone forcing them to acquire land inside of it, and having other options outside of Fraccionamientos without restrictions, the situation must be different. We should now examine how is the situation different.

Up until now, it seems like residents of Fraccionamiento Residencial San Martinito are giving up many liberties and subjecting themselves to the orders of the Executive Board without getting anything in return. However, Buchanan makes clear that "in agreeing to be governed, explicitly or implicitly, the individual exchanges his own liberty with others who similarly give up liberties in exchange for the benefits offered by a regime characterized by behavioral limits" (Buchanan 1999, 389). Let's us turn to examine the limits that the constitution of the Fraccionamiento imposes on others.

Article 36 establishes that the Executive Board, through the administration, will hire as many private security guards as necessary according to the number of residents (although without specifying the ratio of guards to residents). There will be a guardhouse at the entrance, and guards in duty at the guardhouse are in charge of taking an official ID from every visitor and calling the owner who is inviting him to get his explicit permission to let the visitor in. Article 37 establishes that visitor's ID is retained in the guardhouse until he leaves, and, in exchange, he is given a card that he must keep visible all the time inside the vehicle crediting him as an authorized visitor. Proprietors and tenants have a special decal on the front window of the vehicle that allows them to open the door of the Fraccionamiento without having to wait for any of the guards to open it.

To understand the relevance of these restrictions we should understand the Mexican context. Mexico has been suffering from increased levels of violence since the beginning of the century, but the situation dramatically worsened in 2006.[1] Felipe Calderón won the presidency in a very close election that sparked accusations of fraud by the opposition. A few days after taking office, on December 10, 2006, Calderón announced Michoacán Joint Operation, consisting on mobilizing more than 6,600 elements of the public forces (including soldiers, police, and marines) to recover areas of the southern state of Michoacán that were under control of criminal groups. A month later—dressed in military clothing—Calderón referred to the mobilizations against organized crime as "war," thus baptizing the since-then-infamous War on Drugs.

Although there are discrepancies in the numbers, thousands have died since then. For instance, even though Calderón's government did not recognize the 84,000 deaths reported by newspaper Semanario Zeta during his term, the official death toll rose to 64,000 people. During that period, even if the official figures are taken, the National Institute of Statistics, Geography, and Informatics (INEGI) placed the homicide rate at 18 per hundred thousand inhabitants, above African countries plagued by civil conflicts such as South Sudan and the Democratic Republic of Congo.

The discontent caused by the increased violence and militarization of the country was one of the reasons why the National Action Party (to which Calderón belonged) lost the presidency in the 2012 elections. Unfortunately, with opposition candidate Enrique Peña Nieto, things in terms of security not only did not improve but worsened. In total, intentional homicides increased 14 percent during Peña Nieto's six-year term, reaching 156,000 murders. In some cases, according to Human Rights Watch, even state forces perpetrated human rights violations (Human Rights Watch 2018). Mexico, with an impunity index of 94.8 percent[2] (i.e., 94.8 percent of cases reported to authorities are never solved) and with a rate of almost thirty homicides per hundred thousand inhabitants,[3] today is number thirteen on the list of the most violent countries in the world.

With such high levels of violence, it is not hard to understand anymore the benefits that an enclosed neighborhood like a Fraccionamiento represents for Mexican citizens. Paying a monthly fee, even when the house is uninhabited or the plot of land empty, making the house plan abide by the construction rules, restricting the use of one's property exclusively for living purposes without advertisements, and in general subjugating one to yet another organized body of people (i.e., the Executive Board), these are all less costly for many Mexican citizens than going through the unfortunate event of having people break into their houses to steal their property or having a gun pointed at their heads right outside their door. As Buchanan explains using apples and oranges, those living in Fraccionamiento Residencial San Martinito are willing to accept many restrictions to their behavior in exchange for strict control of those who can get to the vicinity of their house since the risk of being robbed is high. In light of this, the voluntary organization of an enclosed neighborhood with its own government becomes an entrepreneurial activity since citizens identified a problem (lack of security) and are trying to solve it by living inside a Fraccionamiento.

There are no official statistics regarding Fraccionamientos. Therefore, it is not possible to make any assertion regarding their success in terms of reduced crime levels within them. Nonetheless, given the Mexican context, the fact that citizens are acquiring plots of land and building their homes within these gated communities indicates that a primary concern for them is their security. Having walls all around them, guards controlling entrances, security cameras all over the place, and having to wait a few extra minutes every time a visitor comes so that he completes the registration process is a way of reducing the probability of becoming the victim of crime.

The last two articles, Articles 41 and 42, refer to the resolution of conflicts that may arise. The former establishes that before starting a judicial process, any discontent among proprietors or between an owner and the governing body of the Fraccionamiento must first undergo at least one conciliatory talk moderated by a Public Notary and witnessed by at least two other members of the Fraccionamiento. After thirty days without reaching an agreement, the parties can proceed to the court. In this way associates of the Fraccionamiento have an alternative way of solving their conflicts without having to appeal to a judge. Given the impunity level of over 90 percent referred to before, this is another benefit of living inside the Fraccionamiento. The last article establishes that ultimately, in case of controversy, the judicial authority of the municipality is in charge of interpreting the rules of the Fraccionamiento, again, backing the rules of the enclosed community with the force of the State.

Now that we have analyzed the rationale for the rules governing the Fraccionamiento, it is relevant to analyze the impact of living in such an enclosed neighborhood. Once again, since there is a complete lack of data regarding these settlements in Mexico, it is nearly impossible to adequately measure the opportunity cost of Fraccionamiento Residencial San Martinito for its inhabitants. However, a small calculation will be illustrative. A household will pay 1,040 USD a year in fees (including the extraordinary maintenance fee approved by the assembly). Since, according to World Bank, GDP per capita in Mexico was 9,926 USD in 2021, the cost of living in Fraccionamiento Residencial San Martinito represents at least 10 percent of Mexican GDP per capita. This is without taking into consideration the fact that living in Fraccionamientos usually increases transportation costs since many are located in the suburbs of the city and the opportunity cost of longer waiting times to meet with people since often there are lines of visitors and delivery services waiting to complete the registration process before they can get into the Fraccionamiento. Therefore, there is clearly a waste of resources in the sense of lost opportunities for those Mexican citizens who are investing in private security in the form of living within a Fraccionamiento simply because the government is not providing security for citizens.

The main obstacle for the study of the modern phenomena of Fraccionamientos is the lack of data. The study of the rationale of the establishment of Fraccionamientos (to which this research contributes) can be approached analyzing what I have called their constitutions, and the context in which citizens opt out of normal neighborhoods to live in gated communities where they have to pay extra fees for private security, apart from being subject to another governing body capable of fining them in case of non-compliance, but is not enough to have an accurate picture of the success of this type of gated communities.

One possibility is that private guards hired by people are corrupt or not good enough, such that criminals still manage to break into houses inside, or criminals simply opt to rob citizens outside of Fraccionamientos, such that the increased security is a perception effect rather than an actual benefit. Moreover, the governing body of the Fraccionamiento, far from solving problems, could become just another inefficient bureaucratic entity that is not only an obstacle but creates more problems. Since the Executive Board is not paid, even though its members are associates of the Fraccionamiento, if, for example, they own plots of land but are still not living there, their incentives could be misaligned with those of the tenants and owners who are living there. Measures of the amount of police reports filed by people living in a Fraccionamiento, as opposed to those living outside would be very helpful in assessing their success.

CONCLUSION

Economists have traditionally focused on how individuals make decisions within a set of constraints they cannot change in any way. Based on the ideas of James Buchanan within the research program of Constitutional Political Economy and the rule of law as a crucial institution for the flourishing of entrepreneurial activity, I have undertaken the study of a fairly overlooked contemporary phenomenon from an economic perspective: the enclosed neighborhood known in Mexico as Fraccionamiento, characterized by citizens organized to lock themselves by building walls and hiring private security to control entrances. By analyzing the rules of a particular case, Fraccionamiento Residencial San Martinito in Puebla, Mexico and showing that citizens come to live inside of it due to security concerns, we have more evidence that "institutions, defined broadly, are variables subject . . . to explicit choice" (Buchanan 1999, 384), and, on the other hand, we are better able to understand the Fraccionamiento as an entrepreneurial activity that citizens undertake to provide for themselves the necessary conditions to engage in other market activities.

NOTES

1. A more detailed history of the Mexican War on Drugs can be found at https://www.chicagotribune.com/hoy/ct-hoy-8766718-la-guerra-contra-el-narco-en-mexico-costosa-cara-y-mortal-story.html.
2. The figure comes from the 2021 report of the Mexican based think tank México Evalúa, and can be found here: https://www.mexicoevalua.org/mexicoevalua/wp-content/uploads/2022/10/hallazgos2021vf-4oct.pdf.
3. The figure comes from the National Institute of Statistics, Geography and Informatics (INEGI) and can be found here: https://www.inegi.org.mx/contenidos/saladeprensa/boletines/2022/DH/DH2021.pdf.

REFERENCES

Asociación de Propietarios del Fraccionamiento Residencial San Martinito A.C. 2021. "Reglamento de la Asociación de Propietarios del Fraccionamiento Residencial San Martinito A.C. de la ciudad de San Andrés Cholula, estado de Puebla." Puebla: Asociación de Propietarios del Fraccionamiento Residencial San Martinito A.C., May 3.

Barbour, Ian. 1993. *Ethics in an Age of Technology*. New York: Harper One.

Blakely, Edward J., and Mary Gail Snyder. 1997. *Fortress America: Gated Communities in the United States*. Washington, DC: Brookings Institution Press.

Boettke, Peter J., and Christopher J. Coyne. 2003. "Entrepreneurship and Development: Cause or Consequence?" In *Advances in Austrian Economics, Volume 6: Austrian Economics and Entrepreneurial*, edited by Roger Koppl, 67–87. New York: Elsevier Science.

Buchanan, James M. 1999. *The Logical Foundations of Constitutional Liberty*. The Collected Works of James M. Buchanan, Vol. 1 Indianapolis, IN: Liberty Fund.

Camus, Manuela. 2019. "Habitar el privilegio: relaciones sociales en los fraccionamientos cerrados en Guadalajara." *Desacatos* 59 (1): 32–49.

Castillo Rodríguez, Ana Paola. 2016. "Los fraccionamientos cerrados en México, una expresión de 'anticiudad.'" Escuela técnica superior de arquitectura. Grado en Fundamentos de la Arquitectura. Valladolid: Universidad de Valladolid, July.

Chen, Yu. n.d. *What is Unique about Fraccionamientos?* Austin: University of Texas, Austin.

Enríquez Acosta, Jesús Ángel. 2007. "Ciudades de muros. Los fraccionamientos cerrados en la frontera noroeste de México." *Revista Electrónica de Geografía y Ciencias Sociales* 11 (230): 229–255.

Galaviz Mosqueda, Ana Isabel, Reyna Valladares Anguiano, and Martha Chávez. 2014. "Fraccionamientos cerrados residenciales, productores de inseguridad urbana subjetiva." *Cuadernos de Vivienda y Urbanismo* 7 (13): 50–67.

Grant, Jill, and Lindsey Mittelsteadt. 2004. "Types of Gated Communities." *Environment and Planning B: Urban Analytics and City Science* 31(6): 913–930.

Human Rights Watch. 2018. *Informe mundial 2018: México*. New York: Human Rights Watch.

Leeson, Peter T. 2014. *Anarchy Unbound*. New York: Cambridge University Press.

Rhodes, R. A. W. 2007. "Understanding Governance: Ten Years On." *Organization Studies* 28 (8): 1243–1264.

Sheinbaum, Diana. 2008. "Gated Communities in Mexico City: An Historical Perspective." *Urban Design International* 13 (4): 241–252.

Sherman, Lawerence W. 1983. "Patrol Strategies for Police." In *Crime and Public Policy*, edited by James Q. Wilson, 145–163. New Brunswick, NJ: Institute for Contemporary Studies Press.

Stringham, Edward Peter. 2015. *Private Governance: Creating Order in Economic and Social Life*. Oxford, UK: Oxford University Press.

Vesselinov, Elena. 2008. "Members Only: Gated Communities and Residential Segregation in the Metropolitan United States." *Sociological Forum* 23 (3): 536–555.

Section III

PUBLIC POLICY ENTREPRENEURSHIP WITHIN THE ADMINISTRATIVE STATE

Chapter 7

Exploring the Interplay of Taxation and Regulation in Institutional Arrangements

Dallin Overstreet

Institutional arrangements are an important factor to consider when making cross-country comparisons. The rules that determine what a state can and cannot do have an impact on how they govern and the tools they use to do so. The differences between countries with respect to their institutional arrangements can have implications for economic performance and social welfare within those states. Thus, any analysis of cross-country differences should take into account the institutional differences between the countries being compared.

Institutional economists often use the concept of institutional environment or institutional framework to describe the set of formal and informal rules that shape economic behavior and outcomes in a country (Ostrom 1986). This can include factors such as the legal system, the political system, the property rights regime, and the social norms and customs that govern economic interactions. By comparing the institutional environment of different countries, we can gain a better understanding of the factors that contribute to differences in economic performance and social welfare. Additionally, this kind of analysis can also identify best practices and potential areas for institutional reform that could improve economic performance and social welfare.

Taxation and regulation are both powers of government that are commonly utilized in governance. However, the rules controlling their usage as tools by governing authorities vary by country. Both of these interventions allow a government to intervene in an economy to pursue some goal in the interest of the public. While each has its specific function that it is used for, there are both positive and negative consequences for the general welfare of society from its usage as well as for the welfare of the public official who uses the method.

One of the main purposes, if not the purpose of taxation, is to generate financial resources for governments. However, in some cases, such as with a Pigouvian tax, taxation can serve as a close substitute for regulation while still generating tax revenues. With these resources, the government can provide public goods and services. The types of public goods and services provided through tax revenues include things like public education, emergency services, public roads and transportation, water, and public parks. Without these tax revenues, governments and the state actors who administer public goods and services would have little to no budget with which to produce. An efficient and well-designed tax system would minimize distortions to economic behavior in society while aligning tax revenues with public spending priorities and preferences (Auerbach and Hines 2002).

Alternatively, regulation is used by government officials to impose limitations on the behavior of organizations and individuals. Regulations are a more direct intervention in society as opposed to the indirect nature of taxation, with specific actions or behaviors being curtailed or outright banned. The constraints can be implemented to correct market failures, improve social welfare, or achieve some societal goal. The regulatory process in the United States is a complicated mixture of legislative and quasi-legislative action taken by Congress and the bureaucracy, respectively. When Congress passes a law, bureaucrats take up the task of putting the law to work. This involves setting specific requirements, or regulations, on actions that individuals affected by the law can make, implementing the new regulation, and adjudicating any issues with applying the rules and precedents that may occur with individual cases. The power to regulate gives government wide-ranging authority on many issues that affect the day-to-day activities of individuals and organizations in the United States. Similar to an efficient and well-designed tax system, an efficient and well-designed regulatory regime would minimize distortions to economic behavior in society while maximizing public welfare based on the preferences and desires of the individuals who live within a society (Noll 1989).

While the powers to tax and regulate are often considered inherently different and analyzed independently, this chapter argues that when both of these powers are held by a single authority, the power to tax could serve as an additional constraint on the power to regulate. While this may not be the only constraint public officials face, it may be an extremely relevant variable to consider when trying to understand differences in regulatory burdens across countries. This check on the power to regulate may disincentivize the creation and implementation of regulations that could be harmful to the economy, increasing GDP and tax revenues for the governing authority. Additionally, the creation of regulations that are beneficial to the economy and increase GDP may be incentivized. This constraint is likely moderated by the percentage of GDP the state extracts in tax revenue, with the idea being that governments are increasingly interested in the size of GDP as the percentage it extracts rises.

This relationship between the powers to tax and regulate may be of importance when designing government institutions. Affording a governing body, the power to regulate without the power to tax may be detrimental to society, be it at the Federal, state, or local level, such as has been done in the European Union (EU; European Union n.d.). Such a design may incentivize regulators to rely more heavily on intrusive regulations without the same regard for the detrimental effects on the economy. Given the increasingly interconnected nature of the world economies and the collective action problems the world faces, such as climate change, this relationship may be an important consideration when designing international governing bodies to solve these issues.

This theory may explain why EU member states experience higher levels of regulation compared to similarly sized economies. Additionally, this theory may help to explain why relatively low-GDP member states of the EU may be subject to more burdensome regulations than their high-GDP counterparts. Thus, the institutional design of states and governing bodies with respect to the powers to tax and regulate is essential to understanding the differences between countries and the regulatory burdens their citizens face.

The chapter will first present a literature review of relevant work, discussing the Public Choice and institutional design considerations that influence the decision-making of state actors in relation to this analysis. Next, it will examine different institutional designs for governments regarding the power to tax and regulate. This chapter will then delve into the incentives faced by state actors in these institutional designs, showing how the ability to tax constituents can act as a check on regulatory power within government institutions. The substitutability and complementarity of these two policy tools will be discussed in order to understand more fully how the state determines to employ these two tools at its discretion. An example of the relevant institutional designs will be given to further illustrate these arguments, largely focusing on the tax-regulatory regime present in the EU. Empirical evidence will be given to help support these arguments. A discussion of the implications of the theory and examples will follow.

LITERATURE REVIEW

The relationship between the power to tax and the power to regulate, while not heavily researched, may be understood more clearly by examining the field of Public Administration and through the lens of Public Choice economics. Early in the field of Public Administration, scholars tended to view public officials as individuals removed from politics and self-interest, solely motivated in pursuing the public interest (Wilson 1887). Many debates have occurred over the years regarding the tension between the efficiency of government and the accountability of government officials to the public, with one side advocating to leave expert government officials alone to pursue the public interest in the most efficient manner possible while the other advocated for more democratic control (Friedrich 1940; Finer 1941).

Buchanan and Tullock (1965), Ostrom (1973), and other Public Choice theorists sought to change the then-dominant perception of public officials as agents who solely acted in the interest of the public. Instead, they applied economic principles to the study of the behavior of government officials. Bucking the "romantic view" of politics, they favored viewing public officials as self-interested, utility-maximizing agents. This view of government officials as self-interested economic actors helped fuel Niskanen's (1968) portrayal of bureaucrats as budget-maximizing individuals seeking to secure prestige and power for themselves. Niskanen's model of bureaucrats leads to an explanation of why bureaucracy is consistently inefficient and overproduces public goods and services. Thus, in essence, Niskanen showed that, like all other humans, government officials respond to incentives.

This does not suggest that government officials are inherently malicious, but rather that they act rationally and respond to incentives, often prioritizing their own interests or those of their constituents over the broader interests of society. This self-interested behavior can lead to suboptimal policy decisions. In the context of fiscal and regulatory policy, public officials may seek to increase their budgets through higher tax revenue or exert their influence on the economy or society through regulations in order to maximize their own utility. This perspective, known as Public Choice theory, highlights the potential for government actors to use their powers to pursue their own aims and goals.

There is significant evidence of self-interested behavior among public officials in the making of fiscal and regulatory policy. This behavior can result in suboptimal policy designs, as demonstrated by the New Public Management movement within the field of Public Administration, which aimed to improve efficiency in government by introducing market principles to government administration and increasing competition (Hood 1991; Boyne 1998). Public Choice theory also highlights how political costs and benefits, as well as the desire for political stability and maintaining power, can influence policy decisions (Niskanen 1968; Holcombe 1998). This can be seen in the case of tax policy, as public officials may prioritize revenue-enhancing measures that increase their own budget and power, subject to political constraints (Brennan and Kliemt 2008). Similarly, the state and its actors may prioritize revenue-enhancing measures in order to increase their own resources (Niskanen 1971).

Self-interested behavior and the incentives that drive it in the realm of regulatory policy exist as well. Regulatory capture is a phenomenon that occurs when regulatory agencies become controlled by the industries they are supposed to be regulating, leading to outcomes that benefit the regulated industries and the public officials involved rather than the public interest, such as instituting barriers to entry (Stigler 1971; Overstreet 2020). This self-interested behavior can be driven by a variety of factors, including the desire for campaign contributions, favorable media coverage, or other personal or political benefits. In comparison to taxation, it may be relatively harder to detect and identify regulatory capture, making it difficult to punish regulators who become captured (Carpenter and Moss 2013). While several paths exist for a regulator to become captured, in most cases, a regulation (or non-regulation) that is in some private interest is instituted (or not instituted) disregarding what is in the public interest (Dal Bo 2006). The private interest in favor of such actions benefits from favorable regulatory action and rewards the regulator, while public welfare diminishes.

While the political costs associated with self-interested behavior on the part of public officials may work to persuade them to work in the public interest, it is not always capable of ensuring "good" behavior. Oftentimes, the institutional structures of government may not align the incentives of public officials with the public interest, causing a disconnect between what voters want and what policymakers, bureaucrats, or elected officials do. For example, in the United States as well as in other countries, bureaucrats ultimately are the individuals who carry out and administer the services of the government to the public. Bureaucrats are enlisted by elected officials to provide government goods and services to society, as well as regulate its activities under the purview of those elected officials. Gordon Tullock (1965) explained how bureaucrats may be able to take advantage of the communication breakdown that occurs between these two parties, arguing that politicians in this principal-agent problem face issues in communicating their desires to the bureaucracy as well as seeing that they are carried out, empowering bureaucracy to function without much oversight. While this argument is logical, Weingast and Moran (1983) disputed the idea that bureaucracy operates largely independently of Congress and that monitoring, interest groups, and ex-post sanctions may be effective in checking the actions of the bureaucracy. However, it is worth noting that without these interventions by Congress, the institutional design of the administration of the government would lead to misaligned incentives. Tullock (1959) added additional insight into this puzzle by discussing the phenomenon of logrolling. According to Tullock, logrolling occurs when many voters are asked to decide several complex societal issues, like deciding which political party to put in power or several policy decisions in a referendum vote. Politicians offer up a complex mix of policies in order to attract support, knowing that voters may be interested enough in the outcome of one issue that they will ignore the outcomes of the others which they (the voters) oppose. Politicians may essentially be able to "sneak" suboptimal policies into action by forcing voters to approve them through logrolling.

These issues of incentive misalignment due to institutional features are of particular importance to this chapter. Many scholars have focused on the importance of good institutions to society, with institutions often being defined as the "rules of the game" (North 1990). Good institutions are important for economic development because they provide a stable and predictable environment in which businesses can operate and grow. They protect property rights, enforce contracts, and ensure that there is a level playing field for all economic actors. They also provide the necessary infrastructure and public goods that are essential for a functioning market economy (Ostrom 1986). Additionally, good institutions can promote transparency, accountability, and the rule of law, which can help to reduce corruption and improve the efficiency of the economy. All of these factors can create an environment that is conducive to investment, innovation, and economic growth. Conversely, bad institutional design can lead to many issues concerning the efficient functioning of government, as was mentioned before with the misalignment of incentives. Thus, good institutional design can serve as a check on the self-interested behavior of public officials where political consequences fail to do so.

INSTITUTIONAL DESIGNS OF TAX-REGULATORY REGIMES

This section will explore the different institutional designs that may exist when examining states or governments with respect to their ability to tax and regulate. An examination of the different incentives present in each design will follow, demonstrating why affording a government institution the ability to regulate but not tax may produce suboptimal regulatory policy. As a point of clarification, the terms public official, politician, and state actor will be used interchangeably often in the remainder of this chapter. These terms are meant to represent the high-level public officials who have the power to make decisions on behalf of the state itself, as the state itself is incapable of making decisions.

A two-by-two matrix can illustrate the four possible combinations of having or not having the powers to tax and regulate. Two of these combinations are of relevance to this analysis. Table 7.1 shows the four possible combinations of having or not having the powers to tax and regulate.

Table 7.1 Potential Institutional Designs of Tax-Regulatory Regimes

	Power to Regulate	
Power to Tax	Yes	No
Yes	A	B
No	C	D

Source: Table created by Dallin Overstreet.

The distinction between the different combinations is important, with particular concern for the differences in incentives created by regimes A (institutions with both the power to regulate and tax) and C (institutions with the power to regulate but not to tax). This analysis will focus on these two different regimes and the differences between them, as well as touch on the incentives driving behavior in regime B (institutions with the power to tax but not to regulate). As has been alluded to before, endowing a central authority with the power to regulate but not the power to tax may introduce incentives into the decision-making process of public officials that may not exist when the central authority possesses both powers.

Incentives faced by public officials can be influenced by the combination of powers held by a central authority. It is important to note, as referenced before, that public officials are rational actors who seek to maximize their own utility given the constraints they face. The rules of the game, or institutional framework, under which these actors operate can affect their behavior. Regimes A and C represent different institutional frameworks, with different rules and incentives, which may lead to different behaviors by public officials. With this economic way of thinking, I will discuss the incentives these institutions create.

The use of regulation could be considered a tool governing authorities use to effectively govern. A government regulation is a rule or order that has the force of law and is issued by a government agency in order to control or influence the behavior of citizens or businesses. Regulations can take many forms, such as laws, ordinances, rules, standards, or orders, and they can be issued at any level of government, including federal, state, and local levels. Regulations are often used to protect the public, the environment, and other interests, and to ensure that certain activities are conducted in a manner satisfactory to the governing body. They can cover a wide range of areas, including environmental protection, health and safety, financial markets, food and drug safety, transportation, and many others.

Taxation is also a tool used by governments to govern by generating revenue which is used to fund public goods and services such as education, emergency services, transportation, water, and parks. Public goods and services are those that are non-excludable and non-rival in consumption, meaning that they cannot be withheld from individuals and one person's consumption does not reduce the availability of the good or service for others. These goods and services are typically provided by the government because the private sector may not have sufficient incentive to produce them. Without tax revenues, governments would not have the necessary funds to provide these important goods and services to the public. Thus, the ability to regulate and tax are powerful tools in the hands of governing authorities to effectively govern.

Employing the methodology of the many Public Choice scholars discussed prior, public officials that govern using the tools of regulation and taxation are rational, self-interested individuals seeking to maximize their utility. As Niskanen (1971) argued, the utility functions which these governing officials attempt to maximize may consist of a number of variables, including salary, perquisites of the office, public reputation, power, patronage, output, ease of making changes, and ease of governing. In a very real sense, public officials with the power to regulate or tax, or both, are interested in expanding their influence and power, with regulations and taxes as their method for doing so.

ANALYZING THE POWER TO TAX AND REGULATE SEPARATELY

Analyzed separately, as would be the case in regimes B and C, obvious incentives emerge from the institutional design. In the case of taxation, the Laffer Curve can largely explain the decision-making process of a public official tasked with solely considering the effects of taxes. The Laffer Curve is a graphical representation of the relationship between government tax revenue and the rate of taxation. It suggests that there is an optimal rate of taxation at which the government can maximize its revenue (Laffer 2004). The curve is named after economist Arthur Laffer, who popularized the concept in the 1970s. According to the curve, as the tax rate increases from 0 percent, the government will initially see an increase in tax revenue. However, at some point, the tax rate becomes so high that it discourages economic activity and results in a decline in tax revenue. The idea is that there is a point at which the tax rate is too high and further increases will result in less tax revenue, rather than more. Thus, a rational, self-interested public official seeking to maximize his budget, power, and influence would be incentivized to pick the tax rate that maximizes the tax revenue collected at this optimal point on the Laffer Curve.

The amount of tax revenue collected however would not be the only variable such a public official would be interested in. As described before, politicians and bureaucrats alike are subject to political constraints. These can include things like the preferences of voters or constituents, the influence of special interests or lobby groups, the media, and the broader political climate.

For example, a public official may be constrained by the need to appeal to voters or constituents in order to get re-elected. This could influence the official's decision-making by leading them to prioritize tax policies that are popular with the public, potentially at the expense of their ability to maximize tax revenues.

Political constraints can also come from special interests or lobby groups, which may seek to influence the policy-making process in order to benefit their own interests. For example, a lobby group representing a particular interest may seek to have tax cuts implemented. Because the official's preference is to stay in power and maximize his power and influence, he may be forced to oblige. Thus, political constraints may work to limit the self-interested behaviors of state actors.

The concept of the Laffer Curve can be extended to the government's use of regulations in a similar way that it applies to taxation. Just as the Laffer Curve suggests that there is an optimal tax rate at which the government can maximize its revenue, it could be argued that there is also an optimal level of regulation at which the government can maximize public welfare. In this context, the curve might suggest that as the government increases the number or stringency of regulations, it will initially see a positive impact on the outcomes it is trying to achieve. But at some point, the level of regulation becomes so burdensome that it discourages economic activity and innovation, and ultimately undermines the very objectives the regulations were intended to achieve. Indeed, the World Bank has published extensively about the negative effects of excessive regulation and regularly publishes a dataset tracking the regulatory environment of nations around the world with respect to business regulations (World Bank 2020). Many scholars have explored the causes and effects of inefficient regulatory decisions (Stigler 1975; Laffont and Tirole 1991). However, while the "Regulatory Laffer Curve" seems to make intuitive sense, it is not likely that a rational, self-interested regulator would limit the level of regulation to this optimal point on the curve. This may be due to several reasons.

First, as opposed to taxation, it may be difficult for regulators to accurately estimate the optimal level of intervention, as it can depend on a range of complex and changing factors, such as the state of the economy, technological advances, and the preferences of consumers and businesses. With taxation, while it may still be somewhat difficult to find the optimal point on the Laffer Curve, it is far easier to quantify and measure changes in the economy and tax revenue due to changes in the tax rate.

Second, regulators may face political pressures or incentives that lead them to err on the side of caution and set the level of regulation higher than what is optimal. Public officials may be incentivized to act as opposed to doing nothing in an attempt to please their constituents. For example, regulators may be more likely to impose stricter regulations in order to protect public health or safety, even if those regulations impose significant costs on businesses or consumers. While political pressures certainly exist that tend to push tax rates and the level of regulation downward, again, it is much easier to quantify and measure the effects of tax changes than it is for regulations.

Third, regulators may have their own interests or agendas that are not aligned with the broader public interest. For example, they may be more inclined to favor certain industries or special interests at the expense of others, or to pursue regulations that serve their own interests rather than the public good. For a regulator interested in maximizing his power and influence, his own interests may come at the expense of the public interest. And yet again, because it is difficult to quantify the effects of regulation, regulators may be able to "sneak" through suboptimal regulations that benefit themselves at the expense of the public. Thus, while the Regulatory Laffer Curve certainly may exist, the utility-maximizing location on the curve for such a regulator most likely lies beyond the optimal level of regulation for a society where the regulator does not possess the power to tax. This would imply that governing bodies endowed with the power to regulate, but not tax, may tend to overregulate.

In summary, the Laffer Curve can be used to understand the decision-making process of a public official in charge of setting tax rates or implementing regulations. It illustrates that there is an optimal tax rate or level of regulation at which the government can maximize its revenue or public welfare, but that increasing beyond this point will ultimately decrease tax revenue and diminish public welfare, leading to reduced economic activity. While the incentives for tax rates to be set optimally are clear, estimating the optimal level of regulations, navigating political pressures, and succumbing to special interests or their own self-interest can create challenges for regulators. When the power to tax is denied to the regulating authority, this may incentivize excessive regulation.

ANALYZING THE POWER TO TAX AND REGULATE TOGETHER

Analyzing the power to tax and regulate together, as would be the case in regime A, new incentives emerge. While the political constraints that play a large part in containing the self-interested behavior of public officials in regimes B and C still exist in regime A, a new institutional constraint is introduced into the equation when both powers become available for use. This new constraint may be able to push the level of regulation set back toward the optimal point on the Regulatory Laffer Curve.

The objective of the public officials involved remains the same in this case; however, their methods have now potentially changed. The rational, self-interested official still seeks to maximize his influence, power, and budget, but now he must consider the effects of his usage of one tool on his ability to use the other tool to govern effectively. This constraint may come from the need to balance the use of these powers in order to achieve policy objectives and maximize revenue. For example, if a public official has the power to both tax and regulate, they may be incentivized to consider the trade-offs between these two tools and choose the one that will be most effective and efficient in achieving their goal of utility maximization. This may involve setting the tax rate at the optimal point on the Laffer Curve while also considering the costs and benefits of different regulatory approaches. Or it may involve some optimal combination of a tax rate and a level of regulation that maximizes the public official's utility.

In this scenario in which the regulator also levies taxes directly, the incentives that previously pushed the regulator to implement regulations beyond the optimal point will be tamed by the new institutional setting in which he operates. If the regulator pushes beyond the optimal point, the negative consequences of excessive regulatory burdens will be internalized and absorbed by the governing body, which will be reflected in decreased tax revenue collected by the governing body. In this scenario, the revenue lost from implementing excessively costly regulation can no longer be used to further the goals of the regulator. As a result, regulators who also have the power to levy and distribute tax revenue will consider the fact that their regulatory decisions may reduce the size of the resources they can control, ultimately decreasing the benefit they receive from their actions.

This effect will likely be moderated by the tax rate itself that is set. Because public officials are concerned about the amount of tax revenue they control, they will be aware of the negative effects of excessive regulation. Higher tax rates might make this scrutiny more intense, as governments with high tax rates may rely more heavily on tax revenue to fund public goods and services. With higher tax rates, these negative effects of excessive regulation are felt more intensely by those relying on the revenues created by the tax. Therefore, they may be more cautious about implementing excessive regulation that might have a negative impact on economic growth and tax revenues.

As noted in the prior section, it may be difficult for the regulator to know exactly when he has reached the optimal level of regulatory burden. In a simple model with only one bureau enforcing all regulations on an economy, it might be fairly easy to see the marginal economic impact of overly burdensome regulations. A regulator with the power to tax could isolate the marginal effect of regulatory action on its tax revenue, indicating a need to scale back on additional regulations or use alternative methods. However, in the much more complex real world, it becomes increasingly difficult to isolate the marginal effect of a regulation. In this case, regulatory accumulation becomes a problem, where the collection of regulations builds over time, creating a regulatory burden which is greater than the sum of its parts (McLaughlin and Williams, 2014). This creates additional difficulty in determining the marginal effect of an additional regulatory burden. However, recent work on regulatory budgeting may be quite helpful in improving the ability of regulators and governments to determine the marginal impact of additional regulations (Jones and McLaughlin 2022).

The Complementarity and Substitutability of Taxation and Regulation

Taxation and regulation have often been used as complements and substitutes for one another. At times, officials with both tools at their discretion may combine their usage to obtain their objectives. Similarly, these officials may substitute these tools for one another based on political or efficiency constraints placed on them.

Taxation and Regulation as Complements

Regulators may be incentivized to create rules that increase GDP, and subsequently, the amount of tax revenue collected. In this sense, regulatory powers may be seen as a potential complement to taxation powers, providing the governing body with an additional tool with which they can maximize the power and influence they can exert. The government can use the combination of both regulatory powers and taxation powers to achieve its objectives, such as promoting economic growth, redistributing income, and providing public goods and services. An example of such a regulation that has the ability to increase social welfare, address a market failure, and help spur economic growth is the patent system. Joseph Schumpeter stressed the importance of entrepreneurship in an economy. Using the term "creative destruction", Schumpeter described the dismantling of old practices to usher in new technologies, products, methods of production, and means of distribution (Schumpeter 2010). The creation of new developments to replace old ways of doing things lead to efficiency gains and welfare increases, not only for those who create them but for society in general as well.

However, without the protection of intellectual property rights like those Schumpeter deemed as necessary for economic growth, the incentive to innovate may not exist or may not be great enough for much innovation to occur, potentially resulting in a suboptimal production of innovation in society. When no protections for new ideas exist, an entrepreneur may not find it worth his time to develop a new innovation. Without the ability to keep it secret and exclusive to himself, the financial reward of employing new technology or practices will be limited or non-existent. Competitors would simply copy the new ideas and any competitive edge gained by the innovator would quickly vanish, decreasing the incentive for entrepreneurs to innovate. However, instituting intellectual property rights has been shown to alleviate this market failure that leads to lower than socially desired levels of innovation (Gould and Gruben 1997; Park and Ginarte 1997; Kanwar and Evenson 2003; Kanwar 2006).

Apart from intellectual property rights, other regulations or institutions can also spur economic growth and increase tax revenues. Property rights in general have been shown to increase economic growth (Goldsmith 1995; Besley and Ghatak 2010). Other regulations or policy actions that could contribute to economic growth could include those surrounding education, bankruptcy, and loans, among many others (Armour and Cumming 2008; Ferdousi 2015). Thus, in some cases, regulation and taxation can act as complements.

However, the regulator must act prudently when using these tools, balancing their usage of regulation and taxation to achieve their purposes. This implies a trade-off, as too much regulation or taxes can discourage economic activity and reduce GDP growth and tax revenue. Therefore, the regulator must find an optimal balance between these tools, taking into account their effects on economic growth, investment, and revenue collection, while also considering the welfare of the citizens and the overall fairness of the system.

Taxation and Regulation as Substitutes

This calculus is further complicated when considering the ability of the public official to use regulation and taxation as substitutes for one another. Indeed, regulation by taxation is not an uncommon practice. In some cases, rather than employing a tax as a means of raising revenue, it can be used as a means of accomplishing a specific regulatory end (Barnett and Yandle 2004). A common example is a carbon tax, used to reduce the emission of carbon dioxide by polluters. Such a Pigouvian tax is a tax on a market activity that creates a negative externality. Because the social cost of a negative externality created by market activity is not included in the private cost of the activity, a tax is set to correct the inefficiency. The government sets the tax equal to the external marginal cost of the negative externality, causing those in the market to internalize the social cost.

Taxation by regulation, while less obvious, is used by governments as well, though to a lesser degree and less effectively. A government, especially local governments, may generate significant revenues through the regulation of businesses by enforcing occupational licensing (Chambers et al. 2019). Similarly, fines and fees enforced by police departments have been shown to be a significant revenue source for local and municipal governments, regulating the behavior of their residents in a manner that can be highly profitable for the government (Mughan 2021). While not the explicit purpose of the regulation at times, revenue generation can become an important factor for the continuance of such a regulation.

While each interventional approach has its specific applications for which it may be better suited in terms of its ability to regulate behavior, there are pros and cons to each. A command-and-control approach may make it easier to explicitly prohibit certain behavior found to be immoral or unwanted by society compared to a tax (Sandel and Anne 2005). Regulation may also lead to more certain outcomes, due to the explicit targets created by the rules enforced. Regulation might also be more flexible than a tax, allowing for specific guidelines to be created for individuals and businesses.

On the other hand, Pigouvian taxes may be more efficient and less costly for society compared to command-and-control regulation (Masur and Posner 2015) and more politically feasible. In contrast, regulation is more restrictive and inflexible compared to taxation (Alesina and Passarelli 2014). For example, setting specific targets for carbon emissions through regulation would not consider the costs of achieving those targets, while a fiscal approach like a carbon tax allows for a more refined assessment of the costs and effects of the intervention. A carbon tax that is uniform across all emitters can also allow for better adaptation and reduction in emissions (Brennan and Kliemt 2008). Implementing a regulation to directly control carbon emissions requires much more information (Jagers and Hammar 2009), including the marginal social benefit of reducing emissions and the marginal cost, including lost output and tax revenue. Thus, the public official may be able to substitute one for the other in order to achieve the optimal utility-maximizing outcome.

In summary, under regime A where the powers to tax and regulate are centralized, new institutional constraints may force public officials to alter their decision-making in comparison to those under regimes B and C. Rational utility-maximizing individuals in this regime will be forced to consider the effects of his actions with respect to his regulatory powers on the tax revenues collected. This effect may be magnified the higher the tax rates are set. The official may be able to use both tools to his advantage, leading to higher tax revenues and subsequently more power for himself. Additionally, he may be able to use them as substitutes for one another, using the best tool for his specific purposes. While such public officials are still beholden to the same political constraints faced by those in regimes B and C, he is now subject to this additional institutional constraint. This may lead regulators to rely less heavily on overly burdensome regulations in an attempt to maximize the power and influence he possesses in his position of power. Thus, in comparison to C, it is reasonable to expect governing bodies modeled after regime A to be subject to less burdensome regulations.

TAX-REGULATORY REGIME OF THE EUROPEAN UNION

In order to paint this picture more clearly, considering an example may help to clarify certain points. Several states or government organizations may fit into the tax-regulatory regime represented by regimes A and C. Juxtaposing these two regimes begins to help identify the misalignment of incentives that exist in such a scenario.

A prime example of a state or government organization that fits this description of possessing the power to regulate but not tax is the EU. The EU is a political and economic union of twenty-seven member states in Europe. The European Commission (EC) operates within the EU, with an administrative body of about 32,000 civil servants (European Commission n.d.(a)). The EC has been given the power by the EU and member states to draft, propose, implement, monitor, and enforce laws and regulations that are binding on the member states of the EU. As such, the EU can exert significant influence over the economies of its member states.

While member states of the EU do have the power to regulate within their own jurisdictions, the EU holds exclusive rights to legislate and regulate in specific areas. These include customs union, competition rules for the single market, monetary policy for the eurozone countries, trade and international agreements, and common fisheries policy (European Commission n.d.(b)). Additionally, the EU and member states have joint authority to legislate and regulate in a long list of additional areas, but member countries are only able to do so if the EU has not proposed laws or has decided that it won't do so. This list includes areas such as employment and social affairs, economic, social and territorial cohesion, agriculture, environment, consumer protection, transport, energy, justice and fundamental rights, migration and home affairs, public health, and humanitarian aid.

This power to regulate, however, is not accompanied by the ability to levy taxes. Instead, the EU relies on member states to contribute funds to its budget, which is then used to implement the policies and regulations set forth by the EC (European Union n.d.). Since the creation of the EU, scholars have argued that the European community has been hesitant to give their centralized institutions the power to tax, as they fear that this could lead to increased centralization of power in Brussels, away from the member states themselves (Brennan and Kliemt 2008). They do, however, seem willing to grant central EU institutions a significant amount of power to regulate.

As discussed in the prior section, this lack of direct taxation power can create a misalignment of incentives for the EU. Because the EU's link to its funding source is indirect, it could lead regulators to rely heavily on regulations to govern. Compared to a state with the power to tax, the EU can more freely regulate without the concern of losing tax revenues. Additionally, as it may be more inclined to propose regulations that favor specific member states rather than considering the individual costs and benefits to each member state. This could potentially lead to resentment and pushback from member states that bear a disproportionate cost for the regulations. Similarly, the EU's reliance on member state contributions for funding can also create an incentive for it to prioritize the interests of the larger, more financially influential member states over those of the smaller ones. Thus, the lack of taxation power within the EU's institutional design can lead to challenges in effectively balancing the needs and interests of all member states within the organization.

Empirical Evidence

Empirical evidence may show some of these incentives at work. The Fraser Institute publishes an annual index of various measures of "economic freedom," attempting to show how free various economies around the world are (Gwartney et al. 2022). This index contains measures of various indicators of economic freedom, including scores for the size of government, legal system and property rights, sound money, freedom to trade internationally, and regulation. The indexes range from zero to ten, with a zero indicating extremely unfree economies and a ten indicating extremely free economies.

The data seems to support the theory in question in that EU member states are more heavily regulated than many similarly sized non-EU economies. These similarly sized non-EU economies fall more clearly into the tax-regulatory regime depicted by regime A, with the ultimate authority of governance residing in their national or federal governments. This list includes several countries, such as the United States, Canada, New Zealand, Australia, and Japan, as well as several others. Figure 7.1 shows this comparison.

In this index, the average EU member state scored a 7.34 for the measurement of regulatory burdens in the economy, compared to an average of 7.72 in similarly sized non-EU economies. This indicates that EU countries are more heavily regulated in comparison to similarly sized non-EU economies. While this difference in scores is not enormous, there is still a noticeable gap between EU and non-EU countries. As said before, this could be driven by the misalignment of incentives due to the EU's inability to tax their member states directly.

The United Kingdom's recent exit from the European Union (EU) may provide an additional example of the negative consequences of the EU's policy-making process. Many UK citizens who voted in favor of leaving the EU expressed concerns about the ability of non-elected officials to make laws and regulations for countries they did not reside in (Clarke, Goodwin, and

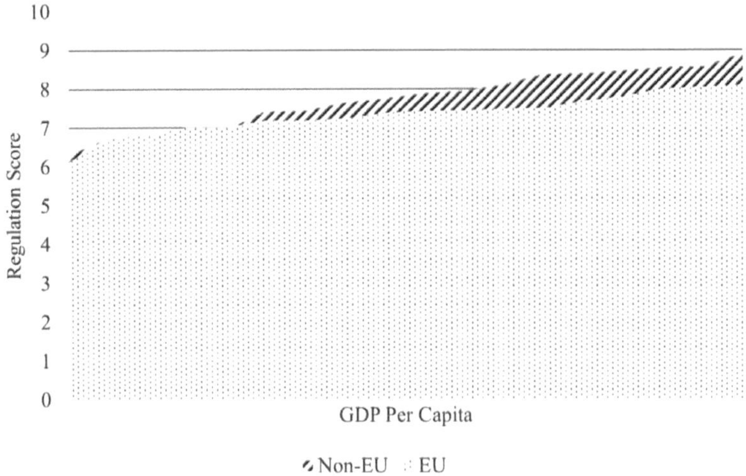

Figure 7.1 Regulation Scores for EU and non-EU Economies. *Source*: Figure made by Dallin Overstreet using data from Gwartney et al. 2022.

Whiteley 2017). In particular, there was a fear that elites in Brussels would exert too much control over the decisions of individuals and businesses in the United Kingdom (Taylor 2017). While more research is needed to fully understand the motivations behind the decision of the United Kingdom to leave the EU, it is worth noting that EU member states do tend to experience higher levels of regulatory burdens, which may support the idea that the EU's policy-making process is not always aligned with the needs and preferences of its member states.

The inability of the EU to tax their member states directly may also explain why lower-GDP member states experience higher levels of regulation than their higher-GDP neighbors. An interesting form of regulatory capture could occur, with the EU becoming somewhat beholden to higher-GDP countries. Because the EU relies indirectly on member states for their budget, the EU may be incentivized to regulate high-GDP countries more favorably than low-GDP countries. Regulators seeking to maximize their power and influence through regulations would prefer to continue regulating up to the point where their political constraints allow them. Graphically, this would be evident if a positive correlation exists between the GDP and Regulation Score of EU countries. Figure 7.2 shows this positive correlation does indeed exist.

While this relationship does indeed exist, this may not be the only explanation for the positive correlation. As was mentioned before, high-GDP countries in general tend to have greater economic freedom, not only in the EU. The effect that this inability to tax directly may be less potent than pictured

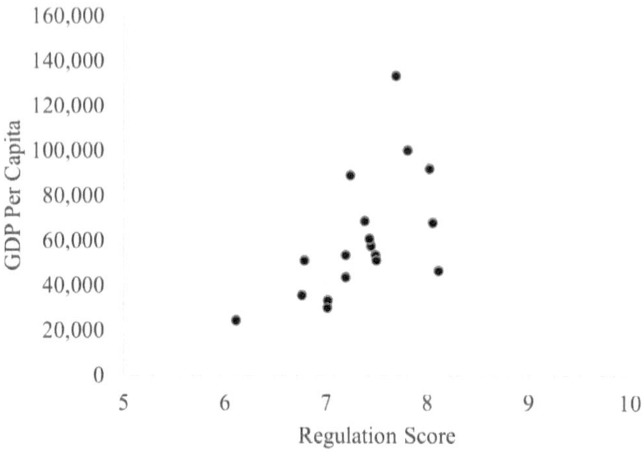

Figure 7.2 GDP and Regulation Scores of EU Countries. *Source*: Figure made by Dallin Overstreet using data from Gwartney et al. 2022.

here graphically. However, paired with the evidence in Figure 7.1, these incentives do seem to possibly be at play in the EU.

Other scholars have hypothesized similarly about favoritism playing a role in the politics of EU policy. Hooghe and Keating (1994) argued that competition policies might tend to favor more productive regions of the EU due to the political nature of the policy process in the EU. While these authors did not attempt to tie this behavior to the specific institutional design discussed in this chapter, it is a plausible explanation for this previously observed phenomenon. Similarly, several other scholars have argued that due to the political structure of the EU, territorial interests tend to dominate the functional interests of the EU as a whole, leading to suboptimal policies due to favoritism and regulatory capture (De Haan and Sturm 1994; Borzel and Hosli 2003). It is possible that the incentives discussed before present in the EU institutional design may be driving this behavior, leading to suboptimal policies and overregulation.

As a final empirical example, the relationship between tax rates and regulatory burdens is examined. The data collected by the Fraser Institute, however, may present a challenge when attempting to demonstrate this correlation. As previously stated, governments and the public officials in charge of them are motivated to maximize their budgets. This suggests that public officials who have both the authority to regulate and the authority to tax would exercise greater caution when implementing regulations than officials who only have the power to regulate. Additionally, this would imply that countries with higher tax rates may be more attuned to the detrimental effects of excessive regulations, compared to countries with lower tax rates, all other factors being

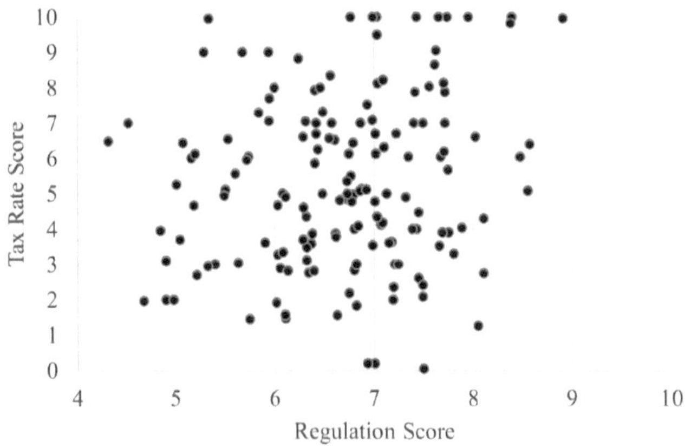

Figure 7.3 Tax Rate and Regulation Scores for Non-EU Countries. *Source*: Figure made by Dallin Overstreet using data from Gwartney et al. 2022.

equal. This relationship, however, is not evident in the data. Figure 7.3 shows the correlation for non-EU countries between their tax rate and regulation scores.

Figure 7.3 shows a weak positive relationship between tax rate scores and regulatory burden scores, indicating that countries with lower tax rates tend to have fewer regulatory burdens. However, it is important to note that this relationship is likely more complex than it appears. There may be other underlying factors that affect the relationship between these two variables, such as government ideology, culture, or the need to address certain societal issues unique to the country. Controlling for these factors may show the hypothesized relationship between tax rates and regulatory burdens for economies that fit into tax-regulatory regime A.

DISCUSSION AND CONCLUSION

In summary, the main emphasis of this chapter is on the significance of examining the institutional frameworks and limitations of states regarding their ability to tax and regulate. Adopting the perspective of many scholars in Public Choice, this chapter aims to demonstrate that states and the officials heading them are rational actors who strive to maximize their utility. While political constraints may help tame the self-interested behavior of public officials, they may not always be sufficient. In these cases, focusing on the institutional design may be helpful.

This chapter attempts to show that when a state or governing body possesses solely the power to tax, they will attempt to maximize the amount of tax revenue drawn in by setting the optimal tax rate as described by the Laffer Curve, subject to political constraints. In contrast, when a state or governing body possesses solely the power to regulate, they may tend to push beyond the optimal point on the Regulatory Laffer Curve and overregulate. This may be due to three causes: the complex nature of determining the optimal amount of regulation, political pressures for the state to 'do something' as opposed to nothing, and self-interest enabled by the difficulty of quantifying the effects of regulation as compared to taxation.

In the case of regulation, political constraints may not be sufficient in taming the self-interested behavior of the state and public officials. However, considering the institutional design of various countries with respect to their ability to tax and regulate simultaneously is helpful in solving these negative consequences of self-interested behavior. Granting the state the ability to both tax and regulate forces the internalization of the negative effects of excessive regulation, creating the incentive for the state to be prudent in how they regulate. This constraint may be magnified in high-tax states where the negative effect of excessive regulation is felt more intensely.

Some of the empirical evidence presented helps to support this theory. The evidence presented is simply correlational and cannot be ruled as causal in this analysis, though future studies may be able to find such evidence. Additionally, there may be additional heterogeneity between EU states with respect to sovereignty and tax policy, blurring the true effect we are interested in observing. As implied by this theory, states that fit more closely resemble the tax-regulatory regime C likely will experience higher regulatory burdens than those that resemble A. Looking at similarly sized economies to those of the EU, member states of the EU do tend to be more heavily regulated. This theory also implies a difference between the regulatory burdens within governing bodies that resemble the EU, based on its inability to raise its own tax revenue while still being able to regulate. This difference was observed in the data as well, with higher-GDP member states having lower regulatory burdens than their lower-GDP counterparts. As mentioned before, while this theory predicts this phenomenon, it may not be the only explanation for its occurrence. High-GDP countries in general tend to have fewer regulatory burdens and this phenomenon is not unique to the EU. But as was shown, the explanation given here may contribute to the overall effect observed, especially given the prior research on this specific relationship. Finally, this theory implies that countries that both tax and regulate with higher tax rates should be more sensitive to the negative consequences of burdensome regulation. This correlation was not observed in the data, but this may be due to the complex nature of the relationship. The true relationship between tax rates and regulatory burdens may be distorted by various mediating factors, such as the political ideology of each country, their culture and opinions on government intervention, and unique issues within each country that would require them to stray from the optimally efficient point.

These findings are relevant not only to the EU but also to the international community at large. Many international organizations exist with the purpose of achieving international goals and improving public welfare. These could include groups such as the World Trade Organization, the International Monetary Fund, the World Health Organization, and the United Nations Framework Convention on Climate Change, among many others. To the best of my knowledge, none of these organizations is capable of directly imposing taxes on their members or their citizens. They rely on contributions from their members determined by a political process. With the recent COVID-19 pandemic, as well as the international push to coordinate on other international crises more effectively such as climate change, the implications of this theory may be important in designing such governing bodies that aim to address these issues. The institutional design of such structures may need to be created so as to internalize the negative effects of excessive regulation in the budgets of the governing bodies themselves, allowing public officials the ability to substitute their method of governance between the two tools as well as taming their self-interested behavior more effectively.

While this chapter focused on higher-level governing bodies such as countries and a political-economic union, it is possible that this theory could be relevant for government agencies or state and local governments. While state and local governments generally have both the power to tax and regulate, many bureaucratic agencies that create and enforce regulations do not. Their budgets are indirectly created through tax revenues imposed and controlled by politicians. Although this scenario is quite different in character, as well as especially difficult to find a counterfactual, it may be worthwhile to examine the incentive structures of federal and state regulatory agencies.

Finally, a word of caution is in order with respect to the analytical methodology used in this analysis. While in some cases, it may be convenient analytically to view the state as a single entity that can act unilaterally and optimize its actions, this framework may not be beneficial in understanding the true nature of government and the individuals that wield its power. Given the often decentralized and polycentric nature of states around the world, especially in the United States, viewing states in this manner is often not realistic. The state in actuality is a collection of individual actors constrained by specific institutional characteristics behaving in rationally self-interested manners, resulting in emergent behavior that we observe at the macro level. The analytical methodology in this chapter focuses on the behavior of states and their high-level public officials who make regulatory and tax decisions. Of course, in actuality, this process of decision-making is much more complex. Opening this box of complexity may be beneficial in future studies on this topic to understand how these macro-level relationships are generated by the complex decision-making processes of states around the world.

In conclusion, a variable often neglected but essential to understanding the differences between the regulatory environments of states is their institutional design with respect to the power to tax and regulate. The additional institutional constraint placed on public officials in regulatory bodies that also have the power to tax forces state actors to internalize the negative effects of overly burdensome regulation. Further research could add to the understanding of how these incentives and constraints work.

REFERENCES

Alesina, Alberto F., and Francesco Passarelli. 2014. "Regulation Versus Taxation." *Journal of Public Economics* 110: 147–156.

Armour, John, and Douglas Cumming. 2008. "Bankruptcy Law and Entrepreneurship." *American Law and Economics Review* 10 (2): 303–350.

Auerbach, Alan J., and James R. Hines, Jr. 2002. "Taxation and Economic Efficiency." In *Handbook of Public Economics*, Vol. 3, edited by Alan J. Auerbach, and Martin Feldstein, 1347–1421. Amsterdam, Netherlands: Elsevier.

Barnett, Andy H., and Bruce Yandle. 2004. "Regulation by Taxation." In *Handbook of Public Finance*, edited by Jürgen Backhaus, and Richard E. Wagner, 217–236. Boston, MA: Springer.

Besley, Timothy, and Maitreesh Ghatak. 2010. "Property Rights and Economic Development." In *Handbook of Development Economics*, Vol. 5, edited by Dani Rodrik, and Mark Rosenzweig, 4525–4595. Amsterdam, Netherlands: Elsevier.

Börzel, Tanja A., and Madeleine O. Hosli. 2003. "Brussels Between Bern and Berlin: Comparative Federalism Meets the European Union." *Governance* 16 (2): 179–202.

Boyne, George A. 1998. "Bureaucratic Theory Meets Reality: Public Choice and Service Contracting in US Local Government." *Public Administration Review* 58 (6): 474–484.

Brennan, Geoffrey, and Hartmut Kliemt. 2008. "Regulation and Revenue." *Constitutional Political Economy* 19 (3): 249–260.

Buchanan, James M., and Gordon Tullock. 1965. *The Calculus of Consent: Logical Foundations of Constitutional Democracy*. Ann Arbor, MI: University of Michigan Press.

Carpenter, Daniel, and David A. Moss. 2013. *Preventing Regulatory Capture: Special Interest Influence and How to Limit It*. Cambridge: Cambridge University Press.

Chambers, Dustin, Patrick A. McLaughlin, and Laura Stanley. 2019. "Barriers to Prosperity: the Harmful Impact of Entry Regulations on Income Inequality." *Public Choice* 180 (1/2): 165–190.

Clarke, Harold D., Matthew Goodwin, and Paul Whiteley. 2017. "Why Britain Voted for Brexit: An Individual-Level Analysis of the 2016 Referendum Vote." *Parliamentary Affairs* 70 (3): 439–464.

Dal Bó, E. 2006. "Regulatory Capture: A Review." *Oxford Review of Economic Policy* 22 (2): 203–225.

De Haan, Jacob, and Jan-Egbert Sturm. 1994. "Political and Institutional Determinants of Fiscal Policy in the European Community." *Public Choice* 80 (1/2): 157–172.

European Commission. n.d.(a). "How the Commission Is Organised." https://ec.europa.eu/info/about-european-commission/organisational-structure/how-commission-organised_en.

European Commission. n.d.(b). "Areas of EU Action." https://commission.europa.eu/about-european-commission/what-european-commission-does/law/areas-eu-action_en.

European Union. n.d. "Taxation." https://european-union.europa.eu/priorities-and-actions/actions-topic/taxation_en.

Ferdousi, Farhana. 2015. "Impact of Microfinance on Sustainable Entrepreneurship Development." *Development Studies Research* 2 (1): 51–63.

Finer, Herman. 1941. "Administrative Responsibility in Democratic Government." *Public Administration Review* 1 (4): 335–350.

Friedrich, Carl J. 1940. "Public Policy and the Nature of Administrative Responsibility." *Public Policy* 1: 1–20.

Gould, David M., and William C. Gruben. 1997. "The Role of Intellectual Property Rights in Economic Growth." In *Dynamics of Globalization and Development*, edited by Satya Dev Gupta, and Nanda K. Choudhry, 209–241. Boston, MA: Springer.

Goldsmith, Arthur A. 1995. "Democracy, Property Rights and Economic Growth." *The Journal of Development Studies* 32 (2): 157–174.

Gwartney, James, Robert Lawson, Joshua Hall, and Ryan Murphy. 2022. *Economic Freedom of the World: 2022 Annual Report*. Fraser Institute.

Holcombe, Randall G. 1998. "Tax Policy from a Public Choice Perspective." *National Tax Journal* 51 (2): 359–371.

Hood, Christopher. 1991. "A Public Management for All Seasons?" *Public Administration* 69 (1): 3–19.

Hooghe, Liesbet, and Michael Keating. 1994. "The Politics of European Union Regional Policy." *Journal of European Public Policy* 1 (3): 367–393.

Jagers, Sverker C., and Henrik Hammar. 2009. "Environmental Taxation for Good and for Bad: the Efficiency and Legitimacy of Sweden's Carbon Tax." *Environmental Politics* 18 (2): 218–237.

Jones, Laura, and Patrick A. McLaughlin. 2022. "Measurement Options for Regulatory Budgeting." *Harvard Journal of Law & Public Policy Per Curiam* 1 (25): 43–60.

Kanwar, Sunil 2006. "Innovation and Intellectual Property Rights." Working Paper No. 142, Centre for Development Economics, Delhi School of Economics.
Kanwar, Sunil, and Robert Evenson. 2003. "Does Intellectual Property Protection Spur Technological Change?" *Oxford Economic Papers* 55 (2): 235–264.
Laffer, Arthur B. 2004. "The Laffer Curve: Past, Present, and Future." *Backgrounder* 1765 (1): 1–16.
Laffont, Jean-Jacques, and Jean Tirole. 1991. "The Politics of Government Decision-Making: A Theory of Regulatory Capture." *The Quarterly Journal of Economics* 106 (4): 1089–1127.
Masur, Jonathan S., and Eric A. Posner. 2015. "Toward a Pigouvian State." *University of Pennsylvania Law Review* 164 (1): 93–147.
McLaughlin, Patrick A., and Richard A. Williams. 2014. "The Consequences of Regulatory Accumulation and a Proposed Solution." Working Paper No. 14-03, Mercatus Center at George Mason University.
Mughan, Siân. 2021. "Municipal Reliance on Fine and Fee Revenues: How Local Courts Contribute to Extractive Revenue Practices in US Cities." *Public Budgeting and Finance* 41 (2): 22–44.
Noll, Roger G. 1989. "Economic Perspectives on the Politics of Regulation." In *Handbook of Industrial Organization*, Vol. 2, edited by Richard Schmalensee, and Robert Willig, 1253–1287. Amsterdam, Netherlands: Elsevier.
Niskanen, William A. 1968. "The Peculiar Economics of Bureaucracy." *The American Economic Review* 58 (2): 293–305.
Niskanen, William A. 1971. *Bureaucracy and Representative Government* (1st ed.). New York: Routledge.
North, Douglass C. 1990. *Institutions, Institutional Change and Economic Performance*. Cambridge: Cambridge University Press.
Ostrom, Elinor. 1986. "An Agenda for the Study of Institutions." *Public Choice* 48 (1): 3–25.
Ostrom, Vincent. 1973. *The Intellectual Crisis in American Public Administration*. Tuscaloosa, AL: University of Alabama Press.
Overstreet, Dallin. 2020. "The Negative Impact of Barriers to Entry on Income Inequality." *Economic Affairs* 40 (3): 344–357.
Park, Walter G., and Juan Carlos Ginarte. 1997. "Intellectual Property Rights and Economic Growth." *Contemporary Economic Policy* 15 (3): 51–61.
Sandel, Michael J. and2005. *Public Philosophy: Essays on Morality in Politics*. Cambridge, MA: Harvard University Press.
Schumpeter, Joseph A., and Joseph Stiglitz. 2010. *Capitalism, Socialism and Democracy*. London: Routledge.
Stigler, George J. 1971. "The Theory of Economic Regulation." *The Bell Journal of Economics and Management Science* 2 (1): 3–21.
Stigler, George J. 1975. *The Citizen and the State: Essays on Regulation*. Chicago, IL: University of Chicago Press.
Taylor, Graham. 2017. *Understanding Brexit: Why Britain Voted to Leave the European Union*. Bingley: Emerald Group Publishing.

Tullock, Gordon. 1959. "Problems of Majority Voting." *Journal of Political Economy* 67 (6): 571–579.

Tullock, Gordon. 1965. *The Politics of Bureaucracy*. New York: Public Affairs Press.

Weingast, Barry R., and Mark J. Moran. 1983. "Bureaucratic Discretion or Congressional Control? Regulatory Policymaking by the Federal Trade Commission." *Journal of Political Economy* 91 (5): 765–800.

Wilson, Woodrow. 1887. "The Study of Administration." *Political Science Quarterly* 2 (2): 197–222.

World Bank. 2020. "Doing Business Legacy." https://www.worldbank.org/en/programs/business-enabling-environment/doing-business-legacy.

Chapter 8

Representation, Taxation, and Policy Entrepreneurship

Natalia Pushkareva

This chapter analyzes the ways in which limited access to international tax policymaking has encouraged policy entrepreneurship among developing and lower-income countries on tax policy matters, both "within" and "over" the rules of the game. It proceeds as follows:

First, it provides an overview of the barriers faced by developing countries when participating in international tax policymaking on the global level, concluding that due to an existing influence gap between them and developed nations, their opportunities to partake in shaping rules of international taxation are often limited.

The chapter then reflects on the experiences countries, even "developed" ones, have during regional tax policy negotiations, concluding that they are not immune to the issue of overlooking interests of relatively lower-income countries either.

I then argue that, having limited opportunities to reflect their interests in international tax standards, developing and lower-income countries can extract significant value from exploring policy entrepreneurship opportunities "within the rules of the game," exploring an example of introducing the Global Minimum Tax (GMT).

Originally, taxation was a strictly national matter and a key component of national sovereignty. This meant that countries were completely free to design their tax systems as they pleased, and no external actor could affect such decisions. However, globalization and digitalization of the economy have made both businesses and individuals significantly more mobile than before. The hyper-mobility of capital, as well as people, allowed countries to quickly realize that taxation is an important factor considered by multinational corporations when structuring their businesses, as well as by high-net-worth individuals when making residency decisions. Jurisdictions saw an opportunity to attract valuable taxpayers and investment and engaged in tax policy entrepreneurship, designing their tax systems in ways that would make them most competitive for taxpayers they aspired to attract. However, it soon became clear that features of one jurisdiction's tax system can have effects that spread well beyond that country's borders. Feeling the pressure to compete for residency of multinational corporations and high net-worth individuals, countries found themselves offering unsustainably low effective tax rates, and thus under-collecting tax revenues required for funding public services for their citizens. As the international community was becoming increasingly concerned about the issue, curbing harmful tax competition became one of the key international tax policies goals.

In recent years we have witnessed an increasing "globalization" of tax policies in an attempt to address the issue, with leading policy institutions such as the Organisation for Economic Co-operation and Development (OECD) arguing that intensified "internationalization" of tax policies and setting international standards is key to the prosperity and stability of the global community.[1] Other key international organizations such as the United Nations also referred to a need for "solidarity" and cooperation on international taxation issues and "stronger global cooperation to promote financial integrity" (UN 2021, 54). This approach makes sense. Indeed, to improve the health of the global financial system and reduce illicit financial flows (IFFs) including tax evasion, the cooperation of all the countries engaging in such practices, or enabling them will be required, as in the presence of defecting ones the IFFs would just move there. However, such full cooperation seems unlikely from a practical perspective since the presence of defecting countries significantly reduces the potential value of cooperation. Some countries receive their main income from hosting shell companies and hidden money of wealthy individuals, and in the absence of mechanisms of effective international enforcement of cooperation and transparency standards, changing their behavior seems like a demanding task due to lack of motivation to do so.

At the same time, even among countries that are not traditionally associated with large-scale tax avoidance, we see more and more lower-income jurisdictions refusing to cooperate or adapt "global" tax policies, and implementing unilateral solutions instead (Pushkareva 2020). Many of them have claimed that international tax policy fora fail to properly include them in decision-making processes and represent their financial interests adequately (Christensen, Hearson, and Randriamanalina 2020, 12), which lead to some of these countries refusing to follow the international tax standards promoted by such organization and finding other ways to protect their tax base.

Globalization and digitalization of the past decades led to increased interconnectedness of sovereign nations. However, tax policy choices of different jurisdictions still differ significantly due to variations in the size and structure of their economies, their geographical location, the role they play in Multinational Enterprises' (MNEs') supply chains, political, and many other factors. Recent research shows that the existing global tax policy institutions are indeed systematically biased toward protecting the financial interests of large, industrialized, capital-exporting countries. At the same time, "developing" countries are still experiencing an "influence gap" when it comes to international tax policymaking, meaning it is much harder for them to protect their interests at such organizations (Christensen, Hearson, and Randriamanalina 2020, 12). Feeling underrepresented in international policy making, many of such jurisdictions ended up exploring the potential of various unilateral measures to protect their financial and political interests where possible instead of complying with the international standards that do not really benefit them. Where the room to maneuver was limited, countries engaged in policy entrepreneurship within the tax policy standards they were pushed to accept.

It is known for a long time that equitable policymaking is important not only from the point of view of international equity but also from an efficiency point of view. According to Rustomjee,

> a system of decision making that makes it almost impossible for one segment of the membership to achieve an outcome on any matter at all that, on balance, favors its interests above those of the rest of the membership is alienating to that group. In practice, because decisions are always seen to be arrived at based, at best, on a consensus centered on the interests of creditor members, there has been a growing sense of loss of ownership by the developing countries. (Rustomjee 2004, 22)

While democratic governance is generally associated with increased redistribution and reduced inequality in theory, in practice it is not necessarily so (Acemoglu, Naidu, Restrepo, and Robinson 2015, 1895). When it comes to international organizations involved in policy work, we see that many of them struggle to effectively include developing and lower-income countries in policymaking processes, and granting a formally equal access to the forum for developed and developing economies does not always ensure that they enjoy equal policy influence opportunities (Hoffman 2012; Christensen, Hearson and Randriamanalina 2020, 13). Unequal access to policymaking results in overlooking the interests of developing and lower-income states as well as efficiency losses (Burton-MacLeod and Chaulia 2011, 9; Christensen, Hearson, and Randriamanalina 2020, 12).

THE THEORETICAL FRAMEWORK

The term "policy entrepreneur" was first used by John Kingdon in his fundamental work "Agendas, Alternatives and Public Policies" in 1984 to describe actors engaging in strategic behaviors to sell ideas based on their deep understanding of the policy process to improve policy outcomes for themselves or others (Kingdon 1984, 21, 104). They are not necessary politicians, but certainly those possessing creativity, courage, and a gift of persuasion allowing them to identify opportunities for effective policy interventions in areas of interest, reframe complex policy challenges and push for innovative solutions. Such actors can include bureaucrats, policy think tanks, non-governmental organizations, private political consultants or researchers, among others.

The theoretical framework on which this chapter is based is an adapted version of the framework suggested by Mintrom (1997, 738–770), and can be summarized as follows.

Lack of representation and the influence gaps faced by underprivileged actors lead to a lack of trust and cooperation on their side, as well as increased resentment to policy solutions designed by and pushed for by institutions suffering from inclusivity issues. Thus, demand for innovation is created as underrepresented actors are seeking to improve their outcomes.

Then, innovative policy tools and reforms are proposed to meet such demand for a change.

Finally, strategic behaviors are used to ensure that the policy innovation is placed on the global agenda.

Policy outcomes are understood broadly and include not only policies and legislation themselves, but also de-facto outcomes resulting from application of policies or laws by governments, other involved bodies, local traditions, customs, and so on.

POLICY ENTREPRENEURSHIP "OVER THE RULES OF THE GAME": THE FIGHT FOR INCLUSIVE TAX POLICY MAKING

The problem of ensuring a truly inclusive policymaking process is not unfamiliar to most international organizations. The following summarizes recent attempts of the OECD to improve the representation of lower-income jurisdictions and explores opportunities that developing and lower-income countries have for policy entrepreneurship *over the rules of the game*.

The Global Level: OECD Inclusive Framework on BEPS

The OECD is an international institution that works to build "better policies for better lives."[2] Its mission is to shape policies that foster prosperity, equality, opportunity, and well-being for all. According to their website, "together with governments, policy makers and citizens, we [the OECD] establish evidence-based international standards and find solutions to a range of social, economic and environmental challenges" and "provide a unique forum and knowledge hub for data and analysis, exchange of experiences, best-practice sharing, and advice on public policies."[3]

Over the past several decades, the OECD, being historically a union of thirty-eight rich—mostly European—countries, became an undoubted leader in setting international tax standards, shifting leadership away from the United Nations and G20. The organization has been working on issues of international taxation for decades. For example, The OECD Model Tax Convention, which aims to reduce double taxation and forms the basis of over 3,000 bilateral tax treaties, has been a fundamental part of the international tax architecture for more than fifty years.

The OECD has been working on issues related to tax avoidance and evasion for many years. Since 2013, it has been working on the BEPS (Base Erosion and Profit Shifting) project, an initiative aimed at aligning taxation of international transactions with actual value creation and stopping tax avoidance and evasion by multinational corporations. The ambitious undertaking aims to adjust the international tax system to the realities of the globalized and digitalized economy, and reduce opportunities for using differences and gaps in tax and accounting systems of different countries for tax avoidance and hiding wealth. While the project is of significant importance and long overdue, it was severely criticized by tax practitioners and academics alike for being designed primarily by developed countries and biased toward protecting their financial interests rather than supporting international equity (Christians 2018, 17).

Responding to such criticism, in 2016, the OECD created an Inclusive Framework on BEPS, an initiative that allows interested non-member countries and jurisdictions to work with OECD and G20 members on developing standards on BEPS-related issues, as well as review and monitor the implementation of the BEPS Package. Quite quickly, the Inclusive Framework grew from initial eighty-two member states to an impressive 142 members it has today, and currently has a truly "global membership, including about 70% of non-OECD and non-G20 countries from all geographic regions."[4] It claims to give a seat at the negotiating table over international tax matters not only to developed but also to developing jurisdictions, praising itself as representing all its members "on an equal footing." But does it really live up to this promise? A short answer to this question is not quite.

Indeed, solid evidence in form of academic articles, policy reports, interviews of tax policy professionals and press publications provide convincing proof that the OECD is facing challenges in making the organization and its BEPS Inclusive Framework truly inclusive (a good summary of the issue is given in Christensen, Hearson, and Randriamanalina 2020, 12). While there are multiple reasons for this, key issues can be summarized as follows.

OECD meetings are held physically and in Paris, which is an important issue on several levels. It is much more expensive for representatives of developing countries to come to Paris, even in nominal terms, ignoring the fact that developing countries have significantly less resources available to them than developed ones to start with. The travel costs associated with attending multiple OECD meetings are seen as a barrier for participation in international tax policy making by many jurisdictions, as a result of which such countries only participate in a required minimum of such meetings, while developed countries can easily afford active participation in every step of the international tax policymaking process.

When developing countries do manage to attend OECD meetings, they mostly attend plenary meetings which mainly approve policies designed by working groups, which in turn are mostly attended by representatives of developed economies. The plenary itself rarely provides participants with an opportunity to have a say on policy design—policies that make it to this stage are effectively already "pre-approved" and are very likely to be adopted as they are. This is confirmed by analysis that revealed that the attendance rate for meetings of the Steering Group, the body that prepares and guides the future work of the Global Forum, is 50 percent for OECD member states while the corresponding number for lower-income countries is only 12.5 percent. For Working Parties, where most of technical work regarding shaping tax policies takes place, such numbers are 77.4 percent versus 5.4 percent for developed and lower income countries, respectively (Christensen, Hearson, and Randriamanalina 2020, 12). It is hard to imagine equal involvement of OECD member states and lower income countries in the conversation about global tax standards when, in most cases, developing countries cannot even afford having a "seat at the table."

Traveling to Paris for a rather long period of time also presents significant opportunity costs for developing countries' civil servants. Not only does it mean a long absence of some of the most qualified tax policy professionals in a country, but also the fact that much fewer people are involved in international tax policy matters in developing countries in general makes such person's absence even more critical. There is evidence that many representatives of developing economies simply cannot afford stopping their "home" work while physically in Paris and have to parallel it with their Inclusive Framework commitments. The OECD tax policy documentation is already voluminous and complex, and combining its proper analysis with attempts to voice one's position at a global forum while continuing to be involved in work at home seems hardly possible.

Another issue is that the OECD's Inclusive Framework moves really fast. Its work is so dynamic that developing jurisdictions often face problems with allocating enough time to analyze or comment on policies within such a limited period of time. In fact, many representatives of lower income jurisdictions shared that they feel pressured by the OECD to not slow down the policy process, which often stops them from voicing or discussing their concerns and makes them more likely to stay silent. While the desire to achieve maximum results in the shortest time can be understood from a political point of view, it inevitably leads to policies being less inclusive and the OECD being less multilateral after all.

The international tax policies developed by the OECD are increasingly complex, it can be argued that sometimes unnecessarily so. They are designed with the capacity of developed countries with an army of highly qualified accountants and tax professionals in mind, which is very far from the reality faced by most developing economies. Sometimes, acting in conditions of incomplete and imperfect information, developing jurisdictions are having trouble even estimating the potential effects of OECD tax policies on their economies before they commit to implement them, which should not be the case.

Finally, when designing international tax policies, the OECD is still paying a disproportionate amount of attention to tax issues that are specific to or especially important for large, industrialized, capital exporting developed countries. In fact, many developing countries confess that the issues considered by the OECD are so irrelevant to them that the net effect of participating in the Inclusive Framework for many developing and lower-income jurisdictions is negative, and that they joined the Framework, and remain part of it, solely because of reputational risks of not doing so and potential issues with accessing EU funding.

Thus, evidence shows that the formal—quite impressive—increase in a number of Inclusive Framework members did not quite result in a quality change in policymaking processes and tax policy design that would take developing countries' interests into account. As of now, it is pretty clear that the OECD is still significantly biased toward protecting the financial interests of developed countries, often ignoring those of developing economies even though. Due to higher reliance on corporate income tax, they are often affected by BEPS-related issues disproportionately heavily. Low-income economies were given a seat at the table, but that appeared to not be enough to effectively include them in the decision-making process and make the policies produced by the OECD more just or fair to them. Doing so will take time and require significant effort, as well as organizational—and cultural—changes.

Understanding the limited opportunities for affecting international tax policies' content, some countries made a decision to implement unilateral measures instead, such as Digital Services Tax, for instance. At the same time as dealing with the current tax challenges, the institutional problem of a bias toward developed economies in international tax policy making has been addressed on a more fundamental level. Understanding that the OECD, having inherited the "rich countries' club" legacy, is still disproportionately benefiting the large, industrialized economies and the United States in particular. A union of African countries named Africa Group made a resolution (UN 2022) in November 2022 demanding a shift of the institutional tax center of international tax policy making from the OECD to the United Nations system which is more likely to produce development-oriented outcomes.

The Regional Level: Introducing Global Minimum Tax in the European Union (EU)

The discussion about developing countries' underrepresentation at global economic policy fora and the influence gap that follows has been going on for quite some time, and many researchers and policy professionals across the world acknowledge the existence of the problem. However, it seems like it is not exclusively the developing countries' issue anymore.

In June 2022, Hungary, which has the lowest in Europe corporate income tax rate of 9 percent and whose currency is the weakest in the European area, and one of the weakest in the world, has blocked an EU directive that would impose a 15 percent minimum tax on large multinational corporations. EU regulations require unanimity of member states on tax policy matters, and after initial consent, Hungary voted against introduction of the global 15 percent minimum tax, and blocked the entire deal in the EU as not serving Hungary's national interests.

In particular, the Hungarian government was concerned that the levy would kill competitiveness of Hungarian firms, and thus endanger tens of thousands of domestic jobs and increase inflation. Another voiced concern was the competitiveness of Europe as a region. According to the country's Foreign Minister Péter Szijjártó, "Europe is in deep enough trouble without the global minimum tax" (Liboreiro 2022). He also openly admitted experiencing significant political pressure to accept the proposal. Hungary's finance minister, Mihály Varga, agreed and expressed an opinion that passing the minimum tax at this time would only worsen the economic challenges the country is currently facing. According to him, "interest rates and inflation are rapidly increasing, supply chains are also disrupted. . . . All these unfavourable developments call for significant losses for businesses and households. Under such circumstances, introducing the global minimum tax at such an early stage would cause serious damage to the European economies" (Deloitte 2022).

The collective West reacted quite negatively to Hungary's attempts to protect its own interests: given that the European Commission has still been holding back billions of euros in COVID-19 relief funds in a dispute over the rule of law at the time, which meant that the Hungarian government was already in a difficult financial position, the country's stance against introduction of the global minimum tax lead to the United States terminating a 1979 US-Hungary tax treaty, which in turn has contributed to pressure on the forint, making it drop to record lows despite significant increase in the central bank rate.

The French finance minister, Bruno Le Maire, made a statement claiming that "minimum taxation will be implemented in the coming months without or with Hungary," adding that he and colleagues are working "on alternative solutions which would allow countries which are willing to adopt a European text . . . without Hungary" (Leali 2022). At the same time, the European Parliament highlighted in its statement that "unanimity decision making in the EU requires a very high level of responsibility, in line with the principle of sincere cooperation, as set out in the EU Treaty. For the longer term, member states should consider the benefit of transitioning to qualified majority voting, and the Commission should relaunch the idea to gradually introduce majority voting on tax matters" (European Parliament 2022).

Major EU jurisdictions, namely France, Germany, Italy, Spain, and the Netherlands, have been considering the so-called "enhanced cooperation" mechanism, which would allow member countries to go ahead without having securing unanimity, which is usually required for tax policy matters. A minimum of nine EU jurisdictions would need to reach a consensus on the tax bill in the presence of the procedure, while other EU countries can decide to abandon the legislative initiative if they wish.

As a response, Hungary's Economic Affairs Panel adopted a political declaration to parliament titled "About the rejection of political pressure against the protection of Hungary's economic interests," in which it convinced the European Parliament to put excessive pressure on EU members opposing the introduction of the global minimum tax, which is in conflict with their interests: "Clearly overstepping its authority, the European Parliament would force Hungary to surrender its economic interests," the document said (Szakacs 2022).

Even though the core values on which the EU is based include freedom, democracy, and equality, we can see that even EU member states can be subject to political pressure, borderline blackmail, and sanctions if they make a decision to protect their national interests in crisis times rather than comply with regulations that benefit predominantly the richest members of the group.

In the case of Hungary, many made the argument that the real reason behind the country's objection to the global minimum tax has nothing to do with protection of its national interests, firms, or jobs. In fact, at the beginning of the entire discussion, Hungary was supportive of the reform. The actual reason the country opposed introduction of the global minimum tax at the EU level by exercising its veto right, many reasonably believe, is using the unanimity requirement for adopting tax policy reforms in the EU to gain political leverage for getting its way in other policy areas.

Nevertheless, whatever the reasons behind the Hungarian veto in this particular case were, it is hard to argue with the view that the member states should have the freedom to disagree with an EU-level tax proposal where they have legitimate reasons to do so. Otherwise, if we accept the Union's right to go ahead with a policy proposal nevertheless, the value of such Union, especially for its more vulnerable members, is rather questionable. If the Union, whose goal is to promote its members' well-being, is vested with coercive powers which it can use for implementation of initiatives that are likely to damage some of its members, what is such union's nature? And also, can such behavior be really considered as "sincere cooperation" on behalf of other union member states? What makes one member state, or a group thereof, entitled to advancing their economic interests at the expense of the other, often smaller, lower-income and more vulnerable members of the group?

While it is true that membership in an international organization or a union comes with both benefits and costs, it is often the case that large, industrialized economies benefit disproportionately more from tax policies adopted at the international level, while lower-income countries benefit *somewhat* at best, which contributes to a rise of inequality, discontent, conflicts, and increases the risk of unilateral actions and non-cooperation in the long run. These consequences are not quite in line with ideas of solidarity and enhanced collaboration the EU has been built on, and demonstrated that even within the EU, member states can face issues of representation and chose unilateral measures instead.

TAX POLICY ENTREPRENEURSHIP *WITHIN THE RULES OF THE GAME*: A CHALLENGE AND AN OPPORTUNITY

As many developing and lower-country jurisdictions observe "cooperation" on international tax matters falling apart and realize that their opportunities to influence the rules of international taxation are quite limited, they unavoidably start exploring opportunities for policy entrepreneurship within the rules that are imposed on them. As of now, it is fair to say that the "losers" of the international tax policies produced by global economic policy fora in recent years are mainly developing, low-income jurisdictions. A big part of the problem is that in many cases, they face multiple barriers when participating in the tax policymaking process or are unable to participate at all, which means that their opportunities to influence the content of international tax policies and protect their interests but entrepreneurship *over the rules of the game* are very limited: that has become the rich countries' domain. Developed countries have had a chance to use their economic and political power to influence the content of tax policies designed at international institutions, as well as to reframe the procedures of decision making, sometimes to the point of allowing them to ignore interests of "lower-income" jurisdictions completely. Not unexpectedly, feeling powerless in their attempts to change the rules of international taxation to their benefit, many developing countries moved to entrepreneurship *within the rules of the game* they had to face instead.

Case Study: Introducing the Global Minimum Tax

Since at least 2019, the OECD has been working on designing a Global Minimum Tax proposal that would help countries end harmful international tax competition by providing them with an incentive to tax the largest multinational corporations more effectively. After multiple discussions and public consultations, the Global Anti-Base Erosion Model Rules (Pillar Two) were released in 2021 (OECD 2021). In simple terms, the rules suggested that countries ensure that the income of multinational enterprises with an annual turnover of over 750 million euros operating in their jurisdiction is taxed at an effective rate of at least 15 percent. In the case where this condition is not met, other countries where such corporations operate can collect revenues on the "untaxed income." The idea behind the mechanism is eliminating tax competition by entitling jurisdictions that were not able to tax such MNEs effectively before or felt pressured to provide generous tax benefits to collect more revenues from the largest multinationals, because if they do not choose to do so, the global income of the corporation will be simply taxed at another jurisdiction that imposed such tax. Thus, the multinationals are to accept the new effective tax rate that they have to apply to their global income, and the only question left is what jurisdiction(s) will collect the tax. The OECD assessed the additional annual revenues to be collected thanks to implementation of the Global Minimum Tax at $220 billion (OECD 2023a). The question of who will be able to access these benefits, however, remains unanswered.

Both the OECD and the African Tax Administration Forum (hereafter, ATAF) have designed recommendations for the implementation of the Global Minimum Tax—the ones developed by ATAF being more focused on implementation of the reform in developing countries' realities. Essentially, countries have at least five options of reacting to the introduction of the global minimum tax:

Introduce a Qualified Domestic Minimum Top-Up Tax in accordance with the GLoBE Rules and OECD Administrative Guidance on the Global Anti-Base Erosion Model Rules (Pillar Two)

Some developing countries with a significant MNEs' presence can collect material additional revenues should they chose to introduce a Qualified Domestic Minimum Top-Up Tax (hereafter, QDMTT). In a set up where if they do not collect such revenues, they will be collected by the jurisdiction of the company's headquarters, and low-tax developing countries have a direct incentive to implement QDMTT and tax MNEs more heavily. It is also the most obvious response to the reform. With administrative guidelines in place from both the OECD and the African Tax Administration Forum (OECD 2023b; ATAF 2023) on both designing and implementing the tax, it is relatively easy to introduce QDMTT and ensure the requirements of Pillar Two are met. However, for some countries, especially those finding tax administration and enforcement of tax rules challenging, introducing the QDMTT might present a significant commitment as administrating the tax may require significant resources. To make an informed and balanced decision, it is advisable for developing and lower-income countries to track the implementation of the GMT by other countries and the impact it has on the MNEs operating in one's jurisdiction, which, again, requires significant technical expertise and analytical capacity.

Introduce General Tax Provisions which Fulfil Conditions of GLoBE (i.e., Ensure an Effective Corporate Tax Rate of at Least 15 percent on the Largest MNEs)

Countries do not have to implement a separate QDMTT that specifically follows tax design suggested by the OECD. General corporate tax provisions might achieve exactly the same results, given they are included within the definition of Adjusted Covered Taxes and, thus, in the calculation of the MNEs' global effective tax rate. To make sure that the domestic tax is considered to be achieving the same results as GLoBE, where such tax is imposed on a tax base different from general income, for instance, turnover, it will need to be positioned as a tax "imposed in lieu of a generally applicable corporate income tax," and thus pass as a "Covered Tax" in under Article 4.2.1(c)) of GloBE.

Review the System of Tax Incentives as its Effectiveness is Likely to Be Affected by Implementation of Pillar Two

For a long time, many developing countries used generous systems of tax incentives for foreign investors to attract the FDI.[5] It has also been argued that such benefits need to be revised as they often leave developing countries in a vulnerable, unfavorable position, especially where such incentives concern the mining sector in developing countries rich in non-renewable natural resources. Plus, in many cases, it is not clear if such incentives are an effective instrument for attracting foreign direct investment in the country at all (see, for instance, Blomström and Kokko, 2003).

As the provisions of Pillar Two require an effective corporate tax rate of 15 percent to be applied to MNEs generating profits of a certain amount, they directly affect the effectiveness of tax incentive systems in many countries (OECD 2022). Tax benefits, whether they are offered by the general tax legislation or in investment contracts, form an integral part of the tax regime of a particular taxpayer and directly affect the effective tax rate they are facing. Thus, the introduction of the global minimum tax will require not only reviewing statutory corporate tax rates but also the system of tax incentives they work together with, which is often complex and fragmented (World Bank 2021).

What is even less obvious is that a thoughtful implementation of GLoBE rules might require developing countries to go even further and analyze aspects of their tax systems not directly relevant to the reform but affecting MNE's effective corporate tax rate, for instance, Controlled Foreign Company (CFC) rules. When calculating an MNE's effective tax rate, GLoBE rules allocate CFC tax back to the "controlled foreign entity" itself, in which case the need for introducing a domestic top-up tax might be reduced or eliminated at all.

A thoughtful assessment of Pillar Two's impact on a jurisdiction will require analysis not only of the domestic tax landscape but also of the impact of taxes applied by other jurisdictions on in-scope MNEs operating in the country. As GLoBE empowers jurisdictions where MNE's subsidiaries are located to tax the group's income that is undertaxed in the jurisdiction of MNE's headquarters, analysis of tax incentives provided by that state, especially for companies headquartered there, is important for assessing the benefits of this strategy.

Respond with Changes in Other Policy Areas and Attempt Moving Competition away from Taxation

Countries can also choose to not respond with any changes in the tax policy domain and instead strategically compete in other policy areas, such as labor regulation, education, immigration rules, the quality of the legal framework, law enforcement in general, and so on. It must be mentioned that both payroll and tangible assets are important factors taken into account when calculating how much tax a country should collect in accordance with the GLoBE rules, and so countries have direct incentives to do what is in their control to attract both. Developing and lower-income countries can use this opportunity to their advantage. Both factors vary by industry significantly, so it may be worth it focusing on meeting the needs of specific sectors.

Not to Respond to the Reform at All

Not every country needs to actively respond to the challenge presented by the implementation of the Global Minimum Tax. Some countries will not be significantly affected as MNEs' role in their economies is not that significant. Others already meet the requirement of the GMT—in fact, in many developing countries the tax rates faced by MNEs are already 15 percent or higher.

Obviously, there is no "universal" correct answer to what response to the introduction of the Global Minimum Tax will deliver maximum value to a developing or lower-income country. Economies are different, and the context differs significantly from one jurisdiction to another, including the intensity of MNE presence, access to technical expertise and data required for policy formulation, as well as other resources, quality of institutions, the legal framework, and so on. However, encouraging developing and lower-income countries to explore potential opportunities they have within the tax standards imposed on them in a set up where they face difficulties affecting content of such rules and can be significantly affected by other countries' tax policy choices can be empowering and enable developing countries to significantly improve their outcomes.

One of the most effective interventions to close the "influence gap" between developed and developing countries in international tax policy making is by providing technical assistance on tax policy matters (Christensen, Hearson, and Randriamanalina, 2020, 26). The African Tax Administration Forum has been especially effective in helping African countries accumulate and share their expertise with each other and empowering them to come up with creative tax policy options protecting their financial interests. For instance, ATAF issued guidance on designing a strong ICT tax system, together with the Inter-Governmental Forum on Mining, Minerals, Metals and Sustainable Development. Regional cooperation of countries with similar interests proved to improve outcomes for many developing economies.

Joining forces in policy advocacy efforts has also been a crucial component of success for many developing countries. While the relative "weight" of many developing countries in the global economy is insignificant, accumulating economic and political powers has helped them in making their voices heard. In particular, the resolution demanding an unprecedented change in tax policymaking and moving the center of international tax standards setting from the OECD to the United Nations, was plead by the Africa Group, a union of African countries, rather than by one jurisdiction alone. It also helped that it was championed by Nigeria, the largest economy on the continent.

CONCLUSION

Over the last several years, we have had a chance to observe the OECD arguing in favor of enhancing cooperation and coordination in international tax policymaking, as well as the organization's first steps toward becoming more diverse and multilateral. While it did increase the formal number of the Inclusive Framework significantly, at the moment, it is hard to say that the organization represents "interests of developed and developing countries on equal footing." Multiple changes will be needed to achieve this goal, with the main changes being related to institutional design, which affects the content of the policies developed by the OECD significantly.

At the moment, developing countries are still facing multiple structural barriers when trying to join tax discussions at the OECD, which is, unfortunately, a common problem faced by many international economic policy institutions. This means that lower-income economies have fewer chances to effectively participate in setting international tax standards, and, thus, define the rules of the game. However, they can often improve their outcomes by either acting entrepreneurially over the rules of the game and choosing to adopt unilateral policies where possible, or acting entrepreneurially within the rules of the game where such rules are imposed on them and they have to face their consequences. Both options require creativity and technical expertise but may benefit developing countries significantly. In the international tax policy context, entrepreneurship "within" given rules of the game may look like focusing on other but related tax policy areas, focusing on other policy domains or waiting it out and not responding with any policy changes at all. If grounded in the local context, such responses can benefit developing countries by helping them to minimize the risks associated with the implementation of tax reforms imposed on them.

Among the most empowering factors allowing lower-income economies to protect their financial interests when it comes to international tax policy design are technical assistance or technical tax policy expertise, collaboration with other actors facing similar issues, and effective advocacy and communication strategies.

NOTES

1. The G 20 countries started putting tax policy high on their agenda in the aftermath of the 2008 financial crisis when it became obvious that the international tax system is part of the problem and mismatches and gaps in it, together with bank secrecy and refusal of some countries to cooperate and exchange information on suspicious financial transactions, are contributing to fragility of the system of

international finance. More on this available at: https://www.oecd.org/corruption/beatingthecrisistheroleoftheoecdandg20.htm.

2. OECD website.
3. Ibid.
4. Ibid.
5. Foreign Direct Investment

REFERENCES

Acemoglu, Daron, Suresh Naidu, Pascual Restrepo, and James Robinson. 2015. "Democracy, Redistribution, and Inequality." In *Handbook of Income Distribution*, Vol. 2B, edited by Anthony B. Atkinson, and F. François Bourguignon, 1885–1966. Oxford: North-Holland.

African Tax Administration Forum. 2023. "ATAF Suggested Approach to Drafting Domestic Minimum Top-Up Tax Legislation." https://www.orbitax.com/news/archive.php/ATAF-Releases-Suggested-Approa-51930.

Blomström, Magnus, and Ari Kokko. 2003. "The Economics of Foreign Direct Investment Incentives." NBER Working Paper No. 9489. JEL No. J23, O12.

Burton-MacLeod, Jonathan A., and Sreeram Chaulia. 2011. "*Rethinking International Institutions: A Global South Agenda.*" Jindal Global Legal Research Paper No. 1/2011.

Christensen, Rasmus Corlin, Martin Hearson, and Tovony Randriamanalina. 2020. "At the Table, Off the Menu? Assessing the Participation of Lower-Income Countries in Global Tax Negotiations." ICTD Working Paper 115.

Christians, Allison, and Laurens van Apeldoorn. 2018. "The OECD Inclusive Framework." *Bulletin for International Taxation* 72 (4/5): 226–233.

European Parliament. 2022. "As Hungary Blocks Global Tax Deal, MEPs Denounce National Vetoes." Press release, November 7. https://www.europarl.europa.eu/news/en/press-room/20220701IPR34359/as-hungary-blocks-global-tax-deal-meps-denounce-national-vetoes.

de la Feria, Rita. 2022. "The Perceived (Un)Fairness of the Global Minimum Corporate Tax Rate." Forthcoming in *The Pillar 2 Global Minimum Tax*, edited by Haslehner et al. https://papers.ssrn.com/sol3/papers.cfm?abstract_id=4205720.

Kingdon, John W. 1984. *Agendas, Alternatives and Public Policies*. Boston, MA: Little, Brown and Company.

Leali, Giorgio. 2022. "EU Can Cut Hungary Out of Minimum Tax Rate Deal, Bruno Le Maire Says." *POLITICO*. 30 June. https://www.politico.eu/article/eu-to-implement-minimum-tax-rate-without-hungary-le-maire-says/.

Liboreiro, Jorge. 2022. "Hungary Blocks EU Deal on 15% Minimum Corporate Tax." *Euronews*. June 17. https://www.euronews.com/my-europe/2022/06/17/hungary-blocks-eu-deal-on-15-minimum-corporate-tax.

OECD. 2021. *Tax Challenges Arising from Digitalisation of the Economy—Global Anti-Base Erosion Model Rules (Pillar Two): Inclusive Framework on BEPS*. Paris, France: OECD Publishing.

OECD. 2022. *Tax incentives and the Global Minimum Corporate Tax: Reconsidering Tax Incentives After the GloBE Rules.* Paris: OECD Publishing.
OECD. 2023a. "Revenue Impact of International Tax Reform Better Than Expected." *OECD.* January 18. https://www.oecd.org/newsroom/revenue-impact-of-international-tax-reform-better-than-expected.htm.
OECD. 2023b. *Tax Challenges Arising from the Digitalisation of the Economy—Administrative Guidance on the Global Anti-Base Erosion Model Rules (Pillar Two).* Paris, France: OECD Publishing.
Pushkareva, Natalia. 2020. "Can't Wait: 'Google Tax' Marching the World While the OECD Is Finalizing the Unified Approach." *Global Tax Governance Blog*, January 29. https://globtaxgov.weblog.leidenuniv.nl/2020/01/29/cant-wait-google-tax-marching-the-world-while-the-oecd-is-finalizing-the-unified-approach/.
Rustomjee, Cyrus. 2004. "Why Developing Countries Need a Stronger Voice." *International Monetary Fund.* September. https://www.imf.org/external/pubs/ft/fandd/2004/09/pdf/rustomje.pdf
United Nations. 2021. *Our Common Agenda—Report of the Secretary-General.* New York: United Nations. https://www.un.org/en/content/common-agenda-report/assets/pdf/Common_Agenda_Report_English.pdf.
United Nations. 2022. "Promotion of International Cooperation to Combat Illicit Financial Flows and Strengthen Good Practices on Assets Return to Foster Sustainable Development." *United Nations General Assembly*, October 10. Resolution A/C.2/77/L.8. https://documents-dds-ny.un.org/doc/UNDOC/LTD/N22/621/90/PDF/N2262190.pdf.
World Bank. 2021. *The Global Minimum Tax: from Agreement to Implementation [Overview booklet]. Information and Communications for Development.* Washington, DC: The World Bank Group. https://www.worldbank.org/en/programs/the-global-tax-program/knowledge-center.

Chapter 9

Knowledge and the Efficacy of Energy Efficiency Programs

Arthur R. Wardle

Global climate change poses a major problem with a broad suite of potential remedies, most of which come along with substantial upfront costs.[1] New zero-carbon energy generation, disaster mitigation infrastructure, and transitions to less energy intense forms of transportation, agricultural production, and manufacturing are all commonly included in climate strategies. Developing and deploying these types of technologies with any speed is likely to require government mandates or subsidies, given that most will fail a private cost-benefit test in the absence of carbon pricing.

By contrast, energy efficiency programs are commonly touted as a rare "hundred-dollar bill lying on the ground"—capable of paying for themselves even before considering the avoided costs of environmental externalities. The supposed promise of energy efficiency programs is perhaps best illustrated in the famous "McKinsey curve," a graphic produced by management consulting firm McKinsey & Company showing potential sources of carbon abatement and their associated costs (Creyts et al. 2007). The McKinsey curve shows that roughly 1.3 gigatons per year of CO_2 equivalent greenhouse gas emissions can be avoided with *negative* net cost (i.e., projects with a positive return on investment before considering the carbon benefits), and almost all of this is made up of efficiency improvements to lighting, heating, electronics, and transportation fuel economy.

Advocates of government energy efficiency incentives name a number of factors that may stop households and firms from undertaking efficiency improvements even with positive returns. Some of these are behavioral, like the possibility that consumers are myopic or uneducated regarding the efficiency characteristics of appliances that they buy and therefore make consistently suboptimal decisions about the best appliances for their needs. Others are institutional, such as that in rental properties, appliances are generally purchased and maintained by property owners, while lower energy bills accrue to renters. This incentive incompatibility might stymie adoption.

The severity of each of these causes is hotly debated, and each likely plays some role in the observed purchasing patterns of energy-efficient goods. But another, more important reason repeatedly rears its head in retrospective analysis of existing energy efficiency programs: engineering estimates of potential energy savings, the estimates that form the basis of the McKinsey curve and other similar analyses, are simply wrong when applied outside the doors of a controlled laboratory.

Engineering estimates of energy savings are determined in controlled settings by expert installers under ideal conditions. This generates an easy-to-understand, articulate form of scientific knowledge that is simple to incorporate into program evaluation. But when programs are rolled out, unexpected consumer behavior, improper installation, and more can dramatically reduce the value of efficiency improvements well below the level where the investment makes ex ante financial sense.

Better projections are possible. Rather than relying on engineering estimates, government agencies could adopt the use of randomized controlled trials (RCTs) using real-world households and installers to assess the scope for cost-justified efficiency improvements on the ground. RCTs are often the tool used in the academic literature that call major efficiency programs into question; formally incorporating these as part of agencies' own program evaluation protocols would help to identify wasteful programs before they expend large sums of scarce government funds.

But better methods for generating estimates of energy savings solve only one small piece of the problem. First, there are limitations to what RCTs can teach, even when well-designed. Second, even where academic research has identified monumental economic losses from poorly designed efficiency programs, those programs often continue unabated and continue to rely on faulty engineering analyses for regulatory assessments. This points to deeper underlying problems with the organization of energy efficiency program development and the incentives facing program bureaucrats.

In short, bureaucrats overseeing energy efficiency programs dramatically overrate their own ability to assess the rationality of consumer choices and to predict how their programs will affect energy efficiency outcomes. The problem is twofold. First, the success of an energy efficiency intervention will depend in large part on variables that are difficult or impossible for regulators to measure and are therefore often ignored in initial analyses. This is a *knowledge* problem that would hinder even the most well-intentioned bureaucrat. Second, bureaucrats face very little incentive to get it right and ensure they consider potential pitfalls in their regulatory analyses. However, bureaucrats stand to gain when efficiency programs are evaluated positively and receive more funding. This is an *incentive* problem that ensures that any ambiguity is resolved in favor of the bureaucrat's preferred outcome.

This chapter will begin by explaining the energy efficiency gap and how its existence is established. It will proceed by reviewing the performance of the Weatherization Assistance Program and Corporate Average Fuel Economy standards, two major pieces of federal energy efficiency legislation, and discuss why these programs initially seemed promising but ultimately delivered lackluster results. I will discuss why the knowledge that government agencies collected before implementation failed to concord with their actual efficiency gains. I will then offer suggestions for how government agencies could substantially improve their projections of possible energy improvements by conducting randomized controlled trials (RCTs) of energy efficiency programs before program roll-out, the limitations of RCTs in this area, and why these measures are not and likely will not be undertaken. I conclude with a broader discussion of the political economy of energy efficiency program analysis and a plea for greater humility in the design of efficiency programs.

THE ENERGY EFFICIENCY GAP

With rising costs of climate change looming on the horizon, government officials across the world are interested in identifying cost-effective strategies for managing greenhouse gas emissions. In most jurisdictions, carbon emissions themselves are completely unpriced, meaning firms and consumers have little incentive to curb emissions absent "carrots" in the forms of subsidies or "sticks" in the form of bans and mandates. Any carrot or stick promulgated by a government comes along with an implicit cost of carbon—the cost that a ton of carbon would need to impose on society in order for the policy to break even in a benefit/cost analysis. The implicit costs of carbon for existing climate policies are wildly variable, and frequently well beyond the range of cost estimates calculated by environmental economists.

Energy efficiency programs, unlike most other carbon mitigation policies, are often justified based on their negative net cost. In other words, even if carbon emissions imposed no social costs at all, these policies supposedly pass a benefit-cost analysis due to direct energy cost savings alone. This calculation is based on engineering estimates of the energy savings from efficient technologies. Using those estimates, program advocates argue that consumers and firms around the world are missing many opportunities to simultaneously cut their energy usage and save money.

Numerous organizations assessing greenhouse gas mitigation scenarios offer rosy views of the potential savings from negative-cost efficiency improvements. The International Energy Agency, an offshoot of the OECD that advises many countries on energy policy, argues that worldwide adoption of already-existing negative-cost energy-efficient technologies *alone* would be enough to peak emissions by 2040 and deliver more than 40 percent of the cuts necessary to comply with the Paris Agreement (International Energy Agency 2019).

As a result of these analyses and other political factors, energy efficiency programs now constitute a major portion of many jurisdictions' climate strategies. Among these are many recognizable policies including the Weatherization Assistance Program, Corporate Average Fuel Economy standards, Cash for Clunkers, and EnergyStar certification.[2] State and local governments and regulated utilities also oversee numerous codes and standards, rebates, and tax credits that seek to promote energy-efficient technology adoption.

All these programs justified by a "free lunch"—the opportunity to cut emissions and energy costs simultaneously—raise a major question: if these cost savings are so widely available, why aren't firms and consumers availing themselves of these investments already? Consumers are generally attentive to their budgets and firms are attentive to their profits. What would cause a systematic failure to enjoy the same or higher levels of energy consumption at lower cost?

Before answering this question, it is important to be clear about how the existence of an energy efficiency gap is established. In general, the claim is based on data describing purchases of durable appliances or products (light bulbs, refrigerators, cars, etc.), including their prices and energy consumption attributes. The energy efficiency of the products is typically based on some rigorous engineering test, in which the appliance is used under controlled conditions designed to be comparable across products. This is, in Hayek's terminology, a highly scientific form of knowledge about the efficiency attributes of products that "limits the facts which are to be admitted as possible causes of the events which occur in the real world" (Hayek [1974] 2014, 363). This "observable and measurable" knowledge is readily interpretable and amenable for use by bureaucrats (and economists!) in policymaking and research but ignores the "tacit knowledge" of how real-world installers and consumers use the products.

In a comparison between an efficient appliance with a comparatively higher upfront cost and a cheaper, less efficient alternative, the neoclassical theory of discounting implies that consumer decisions about which appliance to buy will be dictated by their discount rate. A discount rate dictates how much less a consumer values a dollar received in the future compared to a dollar today. For example, a person who would rather have $100 today than $105 a year from today must have a discount rate above 5 percent; any lower and they would have preferred to wait and take the $105. Because the benefit of an efficient air conditioner with a higher upfront cost is accrued over many years, the discount rate plays a central role in determining consumer choices over durable appliances. The "energy efficiency gap" result, found for many products across multiple decades by academics and energy efficiency advocates alike, is that the discount rates necessary to rationalize actual consumer purchasing decisions are suspiciously high. In other words, though it is unsurprising that a consumer would be willing to purchase a less efficient appliance when it is cheaper, purchasing data seems to show that people are willing to take major efficiency hits for comparatively minuscule upfront price savings.

Economists have identified a number of potential explanations for these results. Consumers may lack information on which appliances are more efficient or lack the background necessary to interpret the relevant information even when it is presented to them. Landlords, being unable to fully pass through the costs of more efficient appliances into rental prices, may fail to update appliances even when renters desire them to do so (Davis 2010). For poorer consumers or in developing countries, an inability to access cheap credit may preclude worthwhile efficiency investments (Berkouwer and Dean 2022). Each of these explanations is consistent with neoclassical economics but reflects frictions missing from the basic model.

Moving away from the realm of neoclassical economics, numerous behavioral explanations have been proposed, including a role for "present biases," since failure to invest in efficient appliances is not unlike the problems of failing to save for retirement or adhere to a healthy lifestyle (Tietenberg 2009). A complete review of explanations for the efficiency gap is beyond the scope of this chapter; a number of such reviews are available elsewhere (e.g., Allcott and Greenstone 2012; Gillingham and Palmer 2014; Gerarden, Newell, and Stavins 2017). Here, it suffices to say that most of these explanations have been convincingly shown to play some role in at least some contexts, and each is plausibly a contributor to low take-up rates.

However, a growing body of empirical evidence demonstrates that a major (and perhaps the single biggest) contributor to the "energy efficiency gap" is mismeasurement of the relevant efficiency attributes of appliances. The following sections describe two cases where idealized scientific efficiency measures proved woefully inadequate for measuring the potential for on-the-ground deployment of efficiency improvements.

THE WEATHERIZATION ASSISTANCE PROGRAM

The United States's federal Weatherization Assistance Program pays for energy audits and weatherization improvements for low-income households across the country. The federal government spends billions on the program, which is supplemented by contributions from states and regulated utilities.

The program assists with a wide variety of weatherization improvements, including repair or replacement of furnaces and water heaters, ducting, insulation, air sealing, window replacement, and more. Since its inception in 1976, the Weatherization Assistance Program has paid for weatherization improvements to more than seven million low-income households.

Each participating household undergoes an energy audit, which collects intensive data about characteristics of the house. This is then fed into a complex engineering model that returns the incremental savings (calculated with a 3 percent discount rate) that would accompany each potential weatherization improvement. The model takes local weather, details of the house, and fuel costs into consideration. Only improvements which incrementally provide net positive savings, according to the output of this model, can be funded by the program. In other words, it is the explicit goal of the program that *only* investments making independent financial sense should be funded, regardless of their potential benefits to climate mitigation or other goals.

The Department of Energy boasts of major returns from this program, claiming that every dollar invested returns $1.76 in energy benefits. These estimates are based on the engineering model outputs for funded investments. Recipient households enjoy the weatherization for no out-of-pocket cost but must undergo an intense and bureaucratic sign-up procedure to qualify.

Pioneering work by Fowlie, Greenstone, and Wolfram (2018) sought to assess how these projected savings compared to actual reductions in energy costs. Doing this well can be tricky; simply looking at how energy consumption changed for program participants can lead to misleading results because of selection effects (people more interested in cutting energy consumption sign up for the program) and other confounding factors. To circumvent these issues, Fowlie, Greenstone, and Wolfram (2018) implemented a form of randomized controlled trial (RCT) called a randomized encouragement design. Because the Weatherization Assistance Program is an ongoing federal program, researchers cannot experimentally vary eligibility or enrollment. Under randomized encouragement, researchers identify a pool of eligible households, split that pool randomly into treatment and control groups, and then offer verbal encouragement as well as administrative assistance in the application process to only the treatment group. Randomization assures that the only reason program take-up should be higher among the treatment group (on average) is due to the study's encouragement. By examining how energy consumption among treated households changed after weatherization and comparing that to changes in energy consumption in non-treated households, this design provides causal (rather than merely correlational) evidence of how participation in the Weatherization Assistance Program affected energy consumption.

What Fowlie, Greenstone, and Wolfram (2018) found is that the engineering models dramatically overstate efficiency improvements. The ex-ante predictions provided by engineering models projected a ten-year private return of 7 percent.[3] The randomized encouragement design estimated a –10.6 percent return over the same time horizon. The cost of carbon necessary to make these investments break would even be $322 at a 3 percent discount rate, beyond even the highest estimates of the social cost of carbon as calculated by the United States Interagency Working Group on the Social Cost of Greenhouse Gases. The full social rate of return, which takes into account the fact that avoided electricity bills will in part be covered by other utility ratepayers to cover the utility's fixed costs, yields an incredible –17.8 percent return. Note that none of these calculations include the non-monetary costs and hassles of participating in the program, which are so substantial that very few targeted households agreed to participate, resulting in an implementation cost of $1,000 to the research team per encouraged weatherization (Fowlie, Greenstone, and Wolfram 2015).

Their analysis proceeds to rule out some potential explanations for the poor performance of the engineering model, including rebound effects (energy efficiency inducing additional energy consumption), inflated installation costs, and abnormally poor contractor quality. They are left to conclude that the engineering estimates are simply wrong, noting that "this is not an industry where there is a culture of objective ex post evaluation and that contracts are not written with penalties for a failure to deliver promised returns."

In separate research, Christensen et al. (2023) dig deeper into why the Weatherization Assistance Program's engineering models perform so poorly. They find that the engineering models are substantially biased for particular technologies like wall insulation, perhaps because small errors in installation can dramatically reduce the efficiency benefits of these measures. They also uncover substantial heterogeneity in contractor quality, which weighs against the savings for households employing worse contractors.

It is difficult to design a laboratory protocol for comparing appliances that properly accounts for idiosyncratic factors like errors in installation, but these factors matter a great deal for the on-the-ground performance of weatherization upgrades. The difficulty or impossibility of measuring these determinants of efficiency outcomes leads to them being ignored by technocratic regulators. Even when a policy is designed to be cost effective and includes explicit limitations on spending designed to guarantee only positive-return investments get made, ignoring human determinants of outcomes leads to sizable losses.

CORPORATE AVERAGE FUEL ECONOMY STANDARDS

The United States's Corporate Average Fuel Economy (CAFE) program requires automobile manufacturers' fleets to meet minimum fuel efficiency standards. Unlike the Weatherization Assistance Program, CAFE is not justified solely based on fuel cost savings; the program explicitly considers and targets the externalities generated by vehicle exhaust. However, resolving the "energy efficiency gap" as it applies to consumer vehicle purchases still factors into agency analyses and influences the level of stringency that the regulatory agencies decide to target.

CAFE standards are periodically updated, and, from 2016 to 2018, the agencies administering the standards undertook a "midterm evaluation" to assess whether regulations previously slated to take hold for 2022–25 remained appropriate. As part of that process, the Environmental Protection Agency, National Highway Traffic Safety Administration, and California Air Resources Board jointly put together a massive technical assessment report reviewing everything from recent technological developments in fuel-efficient engine design to economic evidence on consumer vehicle purchasing behavior. The report sought to cover anything related to the "wide range of technical issues relevant to GHG emissions and augural CAFE standards for MY2022-2025" (TAR, ES-1).[4] In the final determination of that process (deciding to move forward with previously determined standards), the U.S. Environmental Protection Agency determined that the program's "fuel savings exceed the costs even without considering any other benefits" (Environmental Protection Agency 2017).

Compliance with CAFE standards is determined based on controlled emissions tests, which yield miles per gallon (MPG) estimates dramatically different than what is actually experienced on the road by actual drivers. Though the EPA recognizes this and adjusts their regulatory analysis and the MPG ratings displayed to consumers to more accurately reflect actual emissions, their adjustment is admittedly imperfect and not updated over time (TAR 10-1-2). Though this may lead to some inaccuracy, the bigger issue in CAFE regulatory analysis is its treatment of consumer behavior.

Though the final determination would make it sound like the EPA has robust evidence of an energy efficiency gap to be filled by policy, the technical assessment report is far less straightforward. The report notes that an EPA review found "as many studies with undervaluation of fuel economy as there were studies with about-right or overvaluation" (TAR 6-6). In particular, some of the best and most recent research (e.g., Sallee, West, and Fan 2016) finds no efficiency gap at all. Research released after the EPA report's publication experimentally intercepted new car buyers and walked them through detailed information about the fuel economy of the cars they were considering and found that the information had no discernible effect on vehicle purchasing behavior (Allcott and Knittel 2019). Though the EPA report provides no reason to distrust the results finding no gap, they do point out that hidden costs of efficiency technologies (due to, e.g., reduced performance or aesthetic appeal) may be affecting the results that do find a gap. In spite of all this, the administering agencies continue to discuss CAFE standards as if they solve a consumer behavior problem.

The technical assessment also underestimates or completely ignores unintended economic consequences of mandated increases in fuel economy that work against the emissions reductions the policy seeks to bring about. In particular, the report underestimates the rebound effect and purposefully ignores the Gruenspecht effect; I will describe each of these in turn.

Consumers who move from a less-efficient to a more-efficient product will use that product comparatively more due to the lower cost of its use; this is the rebound effect. As applied to vehicles, this means an effective CAFE standard will increase the number of miles that people travel on average. Though the CAFE standards should mean that any given mile of travel will emit fewer emissions than they would have without the standards, the additional miles traveled eat into the emissions savings from the program. To be clear, this effect is not dramatic enough to completely eliminate the emissions benefits of the policy, only to reduce them. An appropriate cost-benefit analysis would need to appropriately deflate the benefit side to account for the rebound.

The technical assessment report settles on using a rebound effect estimate of 10 percent (TAR 10-20). The interpretation of this is that if fuel efficiency increases by, say, 20 percent, vehicle miles traveled will increase by 10 percent of *that* (i.e., 2 percent). To be fair to the agencies that drafted the report, there are a wide range of rebound effect estimates in the academic literature, but by the report's own admission, 10 percent is "on the low end of the range reported in previous research." While this itself may not be too concerning, it is worth digging deeper into what explains the differences between various rebound effect estimates.

Most estimates of the rebound effect do not actually use variation in fuel efficiency; instead, they make use of the fact that what consumers actually care about is the fuel cost for a trip and that this is jointly determined by fuel efficiency and fuel prices. In the short run, doubling your fuel efficiency has the same effect on your wallet as leaving your fuel efficiency unchanged and halving the price of fuel. This provides much more useful variation to researchers, as fuel prices are highly volatile. The problem is that this is only true in the short run. While a reduction in gasoline prices may induce people to take a few more trips than they otherwise would have, they are unlikely to make permanent changes like moving to a house that requires a longer commute due to such a fleeting change in per-mile fuel costs. A permanent upgrade to fuel efficiency, however, may push people at the margin to take on more permanent shifts in average weekly mileage. Clearly, estimates tailored toward measuring this long-run effect are better suited to understanding the effects of CAFE.

Dimitropoulos, Oueslati, and Sintek (2018) do the hard work of assembling 1,120 estimates of the rebound effect from seventy-four studies to comprehensively understand what drives their differences. They find an unweighted average of the rebound effect estimates with respect to fuel efficiency of 24.3 percent with a good deal of dispersion, which roughly concurs with the report's analysis that 10 percent is at the low end of reported results but still within a reasonable range. When explicitly focusing on estimates tailored to long-run rebound effects, however, that average jumps substantially to 35.1 percent. The massive literature of short-run estimates is the source of most <10 percent estimates and seriously drags down the unweighted whole-literature average. If the 35.1 percent estimate is roughly correct, that means the report uses a rebound effect estimate 40 percent as big as it should be. That would imply that the emissions benefits calculated in the report are pretty dramatically overstated.

The only serious justification offered for selecting 10 percent in the TAR is that the rebound effect decreases with higher incomes and that income levels are expected to continue rising in the United States (TAR 10-20). Though that statement is true in isolation, even the highest income settings examined by Dimitropoulos, Oueslati, and Sintek (2018) still have long-run rebounds higher than 10 percent. In addition, Dimitropoulos, Oueslati, and Sintek (2018) find that the rebound effect increases with higher fuel prices, which are also expected to continue rising in the United States.

Unlike the rebound effect, the Gruenspecht effect is not even considered in the CAFE standard evaluation. The Gruenspecht effect describes the phenomenon that when modern versions of a vehicle class become more expensive (due to, say, complying with stricter efficiency standards), owners of older models of that same class tend to hold onto them longer before being scrapped. Given that older models are generally less fuel efficient, this also works against the emissions benefits of CAFE. Like the rebound effect, the Gruenspecht effect is only strong enough to undermine, not completely reverse, the emissions benefits of the CAFE program.

The Gruenspecht effect has received less scholarly attention than the rebound effect, but a seminal paper by Jacobsen and van Benthem (2015) estimates that 13–16 percent of the emissions benefits of CAFE leak away through extending the lifetime of older, less efficient vehicles, a magnitude comparable to the rebound effect. How does the technical assessment report handle this finding? It dedicates a single paragraph to this point, reproduced in its entirety here:

> Jacobsen and van Bentham (2015) look at the effect of fuel prices and fuel standards on the used vehicle market. They argue that the increased price of new vehicles subject to the standards will decrease new vehicle sales, and increase sales and prices in the used vehicle market. As people switch to used vehicles, the greenhouse gas benefits of more efficient new vehicles will be reduced. Their results depend on the standards depressing new vehicle sales. As discussed in Chapter 6.2, we have not identified ways to estimate the effects of the standards on new vehicle sales. (TAR 6-17, citations and footnotes removed)

The dismissal of the result is hardly satisfying; the report details the added manufacturing costs involved in CAFE compliance in great detail. It would be quite shocking if those costs did not result in higher prices and therefore lower sales of new vehicles. Estimating the precise magnitude of these price and sale changes would admittedly be difficult, but that does not justify simply pretending the effect does not exist.

The CAFE program demonstrates two points relevant to this chapter. First, even when agencies do their own research finding little existence of an energy efficiency gap, they will continue to maintain that gap exists and justifies their chosen policy outcomes. Second, even with a great deal of analysis of compliance pathways for fuel efficiency regulation (over 500 pages of the technical assessment report), the difficulty of comprehensively accounting for unintended economic consequences can undermine ex-ante predictions of emissions savings. Where ambiguity exists, it will be exaggerated and used to stack the deck in favor of regulators' favored actions.

THE POTENTIAL AND PITFALLS OF USING RCTS TO IMPROVE EFFICIENCY PROGRAMS

If government agencies are to continue implementing energy efficiency programs without relying on engineering estimates, they'll need an alternative for identifying worthwhile investments. An immediately apparent alternative is to do what Fowlie, Greenstone, and Wolfram (2018) did: pilot the program with an RCT and use empirical performance measures to design programs. While Fowlie, Greenstone, and Wolfram (2015) demonstrate that recruiting for such an RCT can be quite costly, they're certainly less costly than proceeding to roll out flawed programs. In fact, difficulty in recruiting can be an early sign that a program may not have much promise. If the Weatherization Assistance Program had been subjected to such a test in the 1970s, the federal government could have saved billions of dollars.

For a neatly tailored program, for example, a subsidy for an efficient appliance, RCTs are an ideal assessment tool. When designed according to best practices, an RCT can naturally accommodate the many behavioral responses that derail engineering estimates, including human errors in installation or usage and rebound effects. They give a much clearer picture of how efficiency upgrades will perform when installed by actual installers and used by actual consumers (Gandhi et al. 2016).

That being said, RCTs are not a panacea. For one, they are not feasible for assessing policies with major general equilibrium effects, like Corporate Average Fuel Economy standards. An RCT may do better than engineering tests at capturing the fact that vehicle owners with more efficient cars will drive more (the rebound effect), but would still miss the delay in scrappage (the Gruenspecht effect), which occurs only due to the economy-wide change in prices driven by the policy.

Even beyond this, RCT methods do not escape the problem of coercing scientific knowledge out of a fundamentally complex environment; an RCT pilot conducted during unseasonable weather or among an unrepresentative set of participants could have questionable external validity. For this reason, RCTs do not offer an opportunity to turn our brains off and "let the data speak" when assessing policy (Mitchell and Boettke 2017). They are only another tool—but often, I argue, the best existing tool—for quantifying the efficiency gains theorized to be achievable under a program.

THE POLITICAL ECONOMY OF WASTEFUL EFFICIENCY PROGRAMS

The first portion of this chapter established that the "energy efficiency gap" widely used to justify energy efficiency programs is often an illusion generated by inaccurate projections of potential energy savings and that broader use of RCTs could improve those projections to devise better policy. If RCTs are feasible and stand to improve policy, why aren't they already being used?

Answering this question requires understanding the incentives at play in regulatory analysis. One would hope that a desire to deliver real energy efficiency improvements is a key motivator for energy efficiency program bureaucrats, and I don't deny that this is the case. However, this motivator will inevitably be mixed with the more pedestrian incentives of salary, career advancement, reputation, or patronage (Niskanen 1971, 38–39), none of which is likely to be advanced by shooting down the agency's proposed programs with rigorous tests of efficacy.

Why should an agency bureaucrat seek to improve program assessments in ways that pose a real risk of killing programs and jeopardizing their funding? Bureaucrats and agencies are not the residual claimants to savings generated by shutting down failing efficiency programs but do enjoy benefits from their continuation in the form of larger budgets. Agitation for a more rigorous analysis of efficiency policy is unlikely to arise from within this institutional environment. Indeed, bureaucratic assessments tend to stack the deck in favor of the programs they are funded to administer, regardless of their actual merits (Gayer and Viscuci 2013; Sutter 2017). The influence of domestic appliance manufacturers, whose products tend to be both more expensive and more efficient than foreign alternatives, may also play some role.

One may hope that the efficiency programs of private utilities would fare better, given their profit incentives and the costs they incur to run the programs. Here too, however, incentives that would encourage careful financial analysis are muted. In the United States, electric utilities occupy a middle-ground between government agency and private company. They are generally investor-owned (rather than publicly owned) and many aspects of their management are governed privately by their investors. However, many of their most important management decisions (such as what price to set and what infrastructure to construct) are directly overseen and governed by state Public Utility Commissions. This is the "regulated monopoly" setup—in exchange for a state-approved territorial monopoly, the utility's key business decisions are subjected to approval by a state regulatory body. That body is supposed to prevent the utility from charging monopoly prices; in reality, this means the regulatory body is tasked with determining an electricity price that fully recovers costs while generating a predetermined rate of return for the private investors.

What this means is that investment decisions for the regulated utility are based primarily on whether the utility can justify to the regulator that the costs ought to be included in the "recoverable costs" that determine its rates. If the goal is to get the monopolist to offer the same prices that would prevail under strong utility competition, the regulator lacks both the knowledge and the incentive to assess these investments properly. So long as the utility's cost of capital is lower than its regulated rate of return, this pushes the utility to get as many capital investments approved as possible to maximize returns. As a result, there is little reason for a utility facing these incentives to pursue efficiency projects; in fact, they should be actively hostile to the idea.

Recognizing this (and at the active behest of the regulated utilities themselves), states across the country allow utilities to propose efficiency programs whose costs are included in recoverable costs (Joskow 1995), the idea being that investing in reducing consumption should be treated equivalently to investing in increasing production and transmission. In many states, utilities are additionally allowed to profit from energy efficiency programs either through the ability to earn the regulated rate of return on these programs or otherwise receive financial incentives for implementing them.

SCIENTIFIC KNOWLEDGE, ANCILLARY COSTS, AND EPISTEMIC HUMILITY

The previous discussion focuses heavily on whether the energy savings of efficiency programs justified their cost, the methodologies agencies use to assess that question, and alternative methodologies that could provide more reliable answers. With regard to the Weatherization Assistance Program, I noted that neither government nor academic benefit-cost analyses attempted to include the onerous application process in their calculations. This is just one example of a broader phenomenon in which costs that are difficult to objectively measure are ignored entirely.

Many regulatory analyses presume that the efficient and inefficient versions of a product are otherwise equivalent, at least controlling for a number of easily observable characteristics like size or horsepower. In reality, consumers have idiosyncratic preferences for all sorts of attributes that are difficult to capture quantitatively. Washing machine standards make a great case for this point. Analysis of front-loading washing machines, preferred by the Department of Energy due to their superior energy efficiency, failed to account for their higher mold prevalence, more frequent leaks, and shorter lifespan, not to mention the added difficulty of their use in most household laundry room layouts (Fraas and Miller 2020). In many cases, these factors are important enough to consumers that differences in energy efficiency are too small to sway their choices (Sallee 2014). Observing that consumers continue to purchase less efficient products without observing the qualitative differences that drive those choices can easily lead researchers to erroneously attribute purchasing behavior to the energy efficiency gap. In Hayek's words, because a great multitude of relevant product characteristics are those that "we cannot measure and on which indeed we have only some very imprecise and general information," "those sworn to admit only what they regard as scientific evidence [. . .] happily proceed on the fiction that the factors which they can measure are the only ones that are relevant" (Hayek [1974] 2014, 363).

Nothing in this chapter is intended to suggest that the energy efficiency gap does not exist at all or that none of its causes could be resolved by government policy. What I do hope to convey is that there are severe limitations to what government agencies do know, some of which are and some of which are not surmountable with better measurement. A claim that bureaucrats are better situated to select the best product for a consumer than consumers themselves should demand a high standard of proof, certainly higher than is currently common in regulatory analysis of efficiency programs (Gayer and Viscuci 2013; Mannix and Dudley 2015).

CONCLUSION

Energy efficiency subsidies, mandates, and standards are often justified on the theory that consumers fail to maximize their own utility when purchasing energy-intensive products. Evidence for that theory is based on engineering estimates of the efficiency of available products and data demonstrating that many consumers purchase cheaper, less efficient products when more efficient ones would save them money in the long run. When these policies are implemented, however, missing knowledge and poor bureaucratic incentives yield programs with disappointing efficiency gains.

First, engineering estimates undergirding efficiency policies are often flawed because they fail to capture the way efficient products are installed and used by real people. They fail to account for mistakes in installation or use as well as behavioral responses to the availability of a more efficient technology. Future programs could benefit by conducting randomized controlled trials, which would provide a more rigorous assessment of the efficiency properties of supported products.

Even with randomized controlled trials, however, regulators should adopt more humility before declaring that consumers are mistaken in their purchasing decisions. Besides mismeasuring the efficiency gains of these products, regulatory analyses also inevitably miss important costs. Often these costs are difficult to quantify, like added difficulty of use and worse performance of efficient products or the hassle costs of participating in the government program. Meanwhile, bureaucrats lack both the information and incentives to appropriately decide which products are best for each and every consumer.

In sum, energy efficiency programs of the future should be based on clear theories of why consumers are misoptimizing and backed by credible empirical demonstrations that the expected energy savings are achievable outside of a lab. RCTs can help with that mission, but better energy policy will ultimately require humility among regulators and a presumption of consumer reasonability.

NOTES

1. This research was funded by the Mercatus Center as part of the Frédéric Bastiat Fellowship Program. I thank the organizers and participants of the 2021–2022 Frédéric Bastiat Fellowship Program for helpful comments and suggestions. All errors are the author's.

2. Not all these policies were necessarily claimed to have negative net cost.

3. All rates of return compare the financial costs incurred by the program to the energy savings of the funded investments. They do not include time or hassle costs to the participating household incurred as part of participation.

4. To avoid repeating the lengthy in-text citation Environmental Protection Agency, National Highway Traffic Safety Administration, and California Air Resourced Board (2016), I will instead cite the abbreviated TAR (for Technical Assessment Report) alongside the page numbers used in that report, which are counted separately for each chapter.

REFERENCES

Allcott, Hunt, and Michael Greenstone. 2012. "Is There an Energy Efficiency Gap?" *Journal of Economic Perspectives* 26 (1): 3–28.

Allcott, Hunt, and Christopher Knittel. 2019. "Are Consumers Poorly Informed About Fuel Economy? Evidence from Two Experiments." *American Economic Journal: Economic Policy* 11 (1): 1–37.

Berkouwer, Susanna B., and Joshua T. Dean. 2022. "Credit, Attention, and Externalities in the Adoption of Energy Efficient Technologies by Low-Income Households." *American Economic Review* 112 (10): 3291–3330.

Christensen, Peter, Paul Francisco, Erica Myers, and Mateus Souza. 2021. "Decomposing the Wedge Between Projected and Realized Returns in Energy Efficiency Programs." *Review of Economics and Statistics* 105 (4): 1–20.

Creyts, Jon, Anton Derkach, Scott Nyquist, Ken Ostrowski, and Jack Stephenson. 2007. *Reducing U.S. Greenhouse Gas Emissions: How Much at What Cost?* Washington, DC: McKinsey & Company.

Davis, Lucas W. 2010. "Evaluating the Slow Adoption of Energy Efficient Investments: Are Renters Less Likely to Have Energy Efficient Appliances?" In *The Design & Implementation of US Climate Policy*, edited by Don Fullerton, and Catherine Wolfram, 301–318. National Bureau Chicago, IL: University of Chicago Press.

Dimitropoulos, Alexandros, Walid Oueslati, and Christina Sintek. 2018. "The Rebound Effect in Road Transport: A Meta-Analysis of Empirical Studies." *Energy Economics* 75: 163–179.

Environmental Protection Agency. 2017. "Final Determination on the Appropriateness of the Model Year 2022–2025 Light-Duty Vehicle Greenhouse Gas Emissions Standards Under the Midterm Evaluation." EPA-420-R-17-001.

Environmental Protection Agency, National Highway Traffic Safety Administration, and California Air Resources Board. 2016. "Draft Technical Assessment Report: Midterm Evaluation of Light-Duty Vehicle Greenhouse Gas Emission Standards and Corporate Average Fuel Economy Standards for Model Years 2022–2025." EPA-420-D-16-900.

Fowlie, Meredith, Michael Greenstone, and Catherine Wolfram. 2015. "Are the Non-Monetary Costs of Energy Efficiency Investments Large? Understanding Low Take-up of a Free Energy Efficiency Program." *American Economic Review* 105 (5): 201–204.

———. 2018. "Do Energy Efficiency Investments Deliver? Evidence from the Weatherization Assistance Program." *Quarterly Journal of Economics* 133 (3): 1597–1644.

Fraas, Art, and Sofie E. Miller. 2020. "Measuring Energy Efficiency: Accounting for the Hidden Costs of Product Failure." *Economics of Energy & Environmental Policy* 9 (2): 181–198.

Gandhi, Raina, Christopher R. Knittel, Paula Pedro, and Catherine Wolfram. 2016. "Running Randomized Field Experiments for Energy Efficiency Programs: A Practitioner's Guide." *Economics of Energy & Environmental Policy* 5 (2): 7–26.

Gayer, Ted, and W. Kip Viscuci. 2013. "Overriding Consumer Preferences with Energy Regulations." *Journal of Regulatory Economics* 13: 248–64.

Gerarden, Todd D., Richard G. Newell, and Robert N. Stavins. 2017. "Assessing the Energy-Efficiency Gap." *Journal of Economic Literature* 55 (4): 1486–1525.

Gillingham, Kenneth, and Karen Palmer. 2014. "Bridging the Energy Efficiency Gap: Policy Insights from Economic Theory and Empirical Evidence." *Review of Environmental Economics and Policy* 8 (1): 18–38.

Hayek, Friedrich A. [1974] 2014. "The Pretense of Knowledge." In *The Market and Other Orders*, edited by Bruce Caldwell, 362–372. Chicago, IL: University of Chicago Press.

International Energy Agency. 2019. "Multiple Benefits of Energy Efficiency." Paris, France: IEA. https://www.iea.org/reports/multiple-benefits-of-energy-efficiency/emissions-savings.

Jacobsen, Mark R., and Arthur A. van Benthem. 2015. "Vehicle Scrappage and Gasoline Policy." *American Economic Review* 105 (3): 1312–1338.

Joskow, Paul L. 1995. "Utility-Subsidized Energy-Efficiency Programs." *Annual Reviews of Energy and the Environment* 20 (1): 526–534.

Mannix, Brian F., and Susan E. Dudley. 2015. "The Limits of Irrationality as a Rationale for Regulation." *Journal of Policy Analysis and Management* 34 (3): 705–712.

Mitchell, Matthew D., and Peter J. Boettke. 2016. *Applied Mainline Economics: Bridging the Gap Between Theory and Public Policy*. Arlington, VA: Mercatus Center at George Mason University.

Niskanen, William A. 1971. *Bureaucracy and Representative Government*. Chicago, IL: Aldine Atherton.

Sallee, James M. 2014. "Rational Inattention and Energy Efficiency." *Journal of Law and Economics* 57 (3): 781–820.

Sallee, James M., Sarah E. West, and Wei Fan. 2016. "Do Consumers Recognize the Value of Fuel Economy? Evidence from Used Car Prices and Gasoline Price Fluctuations." *Journal of Public Economics* 135: 61–73.

Sutter, Daniel. 2017. "Propagandistic Research and the U.S. Department of Energy: Energy Efficiency in Ordinary Life and Renewables in Electricity Production." *Econ Journal Watch* 14 (1): 103–20.

Tietenberg, Tom. 2009. "Reflections–Energy Efficiency Policy: Pipe Dream or Pipeline to the Future?" *Review of Environmental Economics and Policy* 3 (2): 304–320.

Chapter 10

Majority Opinions and the Entrepreneurial Pursuit of Judicial Power

Christian McGuire

We don't usually think of judges as entrepreneurs. The stereotypical judge is learned, impartial, and careful. The stereotypical entrepreneur is a college drop-out, passionate, and willing to take risks.

This chapter argues that we should. Given our preconceived notions, it is not surprising that few scholars have studied the intersection between judging and entrepreneurship. But doing so can help us understand how and why jurists make the decisions that they do.

It helps to give an example, so this chapter illustrates its point by examining the early Supreme Court's decision to eschew seriatim opinions in favor of a singular "Opinion of the Court." A "seriatim opinion" is the work of a single judge that explains why she is voting to resolve a case in a certain way. Traditionally, common law judges on multi-member courts would decide disputes using seriatim opinions. An "Opinion of the Court" is a document forged by the consensus of the majority of the court, explaining the decision of the court rather than the votes of the individual judges. These can also be called "majority opinions."

This episode can help us understand what judicial entrepreneurship looks like. By switching to majority opinions, the Court adopted a relatively new method. Yet entrepreneurs are not simply people who do new things; they innovate with a purpose in mind. Therefore, this chapter considers what might incentivize a judge to innovate. It then explores how the switch to majority opinions was, or wasn't, consistent with those incentives.

A single case study does not prove a theory, of course. And, this chapter does not purport to read the minds of early American judges to uncover their subjective intentions. Therefore, it cannot prove that judicial actions are often entrepreneurial, or that the judges considered in this chapter innovated because of the incentives it discusses.

The point of the chapter is instead to suggest a new avenue for the analysis of judicial decisions. Judges are not staid automatons that mechanically apply preexisting norms to new situations. Nor are they impervious to the inducements that affect other actors. Judges are human. They change and create. They respond to incentives. The aim of this chapter is to illustrate these facts and to help future scholars think rigorously about them.

It does so in three parts. First, it reviews the literature on seriatim opinions and entrepreneurship. In so doing, it (a) gives a historical introduction to Anglo-American opinion-writing practices and (b) gives a composite sketch of what it means to be an *entrepreneur* generally, more specifically a *public entrepreneur*, and most specifically a *judicial entrepreneur*. Second, it considers what might incentivize judges to innovate and whether each incentive is consistent with the decision to abandon seriatim opinions. Third, it asks whether the decision benefitted the consumers of legal services.

The conclusion offers the following takeaways. First, the early Supreme Court belongs to the pantheon of judicial entrepreneurs, if for no other reason than its decision to adopt majority opinions. Second, in legal systems like to the United States, some incentives affect judges more than others. One of the most important incentives is power, which judges can pursue through their decisions. Third, the decision to adopt majority opinions is consistent with a pursuit of judicial power. Fourth, it is unclear whether that decision benefited other stakeholders. There are strong arguments in each direction, and what one believes may depend on what one values most in a legal system.

BACKGROUND AND LITERATURE

Seriatim and Majority Opinions

At the outset, it might help to explain why this chapter uses the example of seriatim opinions. There are three reasons. First, it is a defining moment in early American history that has received surprisingly little attention. This chapter argues that it changed the nature of the American judiciary, yet few scholars have devoted much attention to the subject. Second, most people do not have strong ideological convictions about the decision. That makes it easier to set aside the partisan feelings that often spring up with regard to more recent decisions. Third, there is widespread consensus that the Court has the discretion to write majority opinions or seriatim opinions (Hochschild 2000). This is important because the aim of this chapter is to establish that judges can act as entrepreneurs without abandoning their proper role as judges. The two roles are not necessarily in conflict with one another. In sum, it is an important, little-understood decision that can be studied without a large risk of ideological bias or the accusation that the Court abused its power.

It is also useful to know a little more about judicial opinion-writing. When judges decide a legal issue, they often accompany their decision with a written opinion. This opinion serves many purposes. It gives litigants an explanation as to why they won or lost. It informs third parties about how the judge who wrote the opinion interprets the relevant law and how that judge is likely to rule in the future. If the decision is appealed to a higher court, the opinion written by the lower court judge provides a starting point for both sides' arguments; generally, the petitioner will argue that the opinion was legally flawed, and the respondent will defend the lower court's reasoning.

If multiple judges preside over a case, there are two approaches to judicial opinion-writing. The first is familiar to Americans: a majority of the judges sign onto an opinion for the court. At the outset, the judges will take a vote as to which party should prevail. In the simplest set of circumstances, one judge will pen a majority opinion, which will be endorsed by each judge in the majority. If there is a minority view, one or more members of that minority will write a dissent. Of course, there are many variants and complications to this model. In civil law countries, for instance, opinions are unsigned and open dissent is not permitted. In the United States, a majority of judges might agree on who won the case but might want to offer additional thoughts, which will often lead to opinions called "concurrences." Sometimes multiple judges work together to write the majority opinion. But in each of these variations, there is still a single written opinion backed by an outright majority of the judges that heard the case. This means that the court has staked out an institutional stance. The opinion no longer represents the beliefs of a particular judge, but of the court as a whole.

The other option is to write seriatim. The judges will still vote on who won the case and return a judgment for that party. But rather than cobble together a majority, each judge will explain their own vote in separate opinions. They are traditionally given in order of seniority—thus the name "seriatim," which means "in a series; one after another in regular order" (Collins English Dictionary). While writing seriatim is rare in modern America, it is not quite extinct. A mutant form of seriatim is borne when a majority of the court cannot agree on a majority opinion, leading to numerous concurrences and dissents, none of which are the opinion of the court (e.g., *Bush v. Gore*). In such cases, lower courts generally treat one of the opinions as the "controlling" opinion—although deciding *which* opinion controls can be a matter of intense debate (Toepfer 2021).[1] But even when one opinion is treated as controlling, mutant seriatim opinions remind us that courts do not always act as a single, unified entity.

Seriatim opinions are the older approach. They were originally given orally, although it later became custom to write them down. The practice originated in the English common law so long ago that it is not clear when it began (Henderson 2007). But by the time of the American War for Independence, seriatim opinions were well-established.

By comparison, majority opinions are of recent vintage. Their earliest practitioner was Lord Mansfield, a judicial giant who was Lord Chief Justice of the King's Bench from 1756 to 1788. To put it mildly, Lord Mansfield was not content with the state of the English common law when he arrived on the bench (Lowry 1973). Of his numerous attempts to reform English law and legal procedures, one of the most important was his modernization of mercantile law, where he sought to create uniform and easy-to-utilize rules. It is possible that he found seriatim opinions to be poor vehicles for such a project and jettisoned them in favor of a single "Opinion of the Court" that could clearly and efficiently communicate the new legal standards that he sought to promulgate (Henderson 2007). Regardless of his motives, Lord Mansfield's influence over British law proved more enduring than his influence over British opinion writing. After his tenure, the King's Bench reverted to its old practice of seriatim opinion writing. Only in recent years have UK courts begun to experiment again with majority opinions (Henderson 2007).

Founding-era America might have seemed like an unlikely place for majority opinions to take root. After all, Lord Mansfield's reformist approach to the law seemed at odds with American notions of judicial power. According to the Federalist Papers, the federal judiciary would be the "least dangerous" branch. What modern observers would call "policymaking" was completely outside the realm of judicial power; the Supreme Court was built to exercise "neither FORCE nor WILL, but merely judgment" (Federalist No. 71, 464). While some of the Anti-Federalists warned that the Supreme Court would come to exercise unbound influence, they failed to convince the state ratifying conventions (Brutus XV).

Immediately after ratification, the Supreme Court gave few signs of the political power it would later come to wield. Stuck in the basement of the Capitol, the Supreme Court rarely stepped into the limelight. The main exception—a decision in a case called *Chisholm v. Georgia*—was almost immediately repudiated via constitutional amendment. And the early Supreme Court had a good reason to stay out of political controversies: it was unclear whether the other branches would respect its decisions. Indeed, one of the main dilemmas facing the Court in *Marbury v. Madison* was that no one knew if Madison would obey the Supreme Court if it delivered a verdict that he disagreed with. The job of Supreme Court Justice quickly became downright undesirable. John Jay refused the position of chief justice when offered to him in 1800 on the grounds that the Court lacked prestige or power. Congress often made the jobs of federal judges even harder: it canceled Supreme Court terms, forced the Justices to ride across the nation in punishingly difficult circuits, and assigned it administrative duties unconnected with its judicial function.

The transition away from seriatim opinions was slow and difficult. In cases involving easy issues where the Court was unanimous, the Justices were quick to adopt a single written statement for the whole court. But these documents could hardly be characterized as "opinions," since they rarely gave any details as to the Court's reasoning (Kelsh 1999). When the case was complicated, the Justices almost always delivered seriatim opinions (Kelsh 1999). Chief Justice Ellsworth was the first leader of the Court to actively campaign for majority opinions, but his attempt at reform was met with two obstacles. The first was ambivalence among his colleagues. The other Justices agreed to sign on to a few majority opinions during Ellsworth's tenure, but immediately went back to their old ways when he retired (Rotunda 2017). The second was opposition from outside the Court. Prominent statesmen such as James Madison and Thomas Jefferson strongly preferred seriatim opinions, which they believed kept all the Justices honest by forcing them to articulate their reasoning in tough cases (Madison 1819; Kelsh 1999). Only through the remarkable efforts of Chief Justice Ellsworth's successor, John Marshall, did the Court surmount these barriers. Never once during Marshall's tenure did the Justices revert to seriatim opinions, and after his death, the Court continued the practice of majority opinions (Rotunda 2017).

So why did a beleaguered Supreme Court invest the time and effort necessary to adopt majority opinions? Few scholars have taken up this question. In fact, this facet of American history is so little studied that academic literature commonly assumes that Marshall, not Ellsworth, was the first chief justice to write majority opinions (Hochschild 2000). Todd Henderson (2007) is the only scholar to date who has attempted a theoretical explanation for the Court's decision. He argues that there is no intrinsically superior method of opinion writing, but that different courts adopt different approaches in order to define—or redefine—their role. Henderson concludes that the early Supreme Court moved to majority opinions to enhance its importance. He further concludes the pursuit of power typifies Anglo-American courts' decisions regarding opinion writing.

Entrepreneurs Generally

The literature on entrepreneurship is vast, contentious, and difficult to characterize (Schneider, Teske, and Mintrom 1995; Pozen 2008). One cause for this state of affairs, or perhaps effect, is that there is no agreed-upon definition of an entrepreneur. Indeed, some modes of analysis—notably the neoclassical model of economics—lack a definition of the entrepreneur altogether (Baumol 1968). Rather than adopt any single economist's definition, this chapter relies on three scholars to draw a composite sketch of the entrepreneur.

One of the first and most influential economists to rigorously analyze the entrepreneur, Joseph Schumpeter (1939) emphasized two aspects of her role. She is first and foremost an innovator. She does not merely meddle with economic inputs or outputs—she changes the factors of production that transform inputs into outputs. Second, she champions a product or service. The product must be aggressively marketed to consumers, even at a loss. Others will not see the economic opportunity, but an entrepreneur understands and seizes the zeitgeist. Timing is of the essence (Schumpeter 1949; Shannon 2016).

Economist Israel Kirzner (1973; 1997) saw the entrepreneur as an innovative participant in private markets. In his view, entrepreneurship is the taking advantage of "available (but hitherto overlooked) opportunities" for profit (Kirzner 1997, 72). Their role is essentially dynamic. The key feature is alertness to potential profit opportunities. Entrepreneurial actions lead to the "systematic tendency toward that succession of wholesome surprises which must constitute the equilibrative process" (Kirzner 1997, 72).

Paul Drucker, an authority on entrepreneurship in the context of management, took a broader view. According to him, an entrepreneur's actions need not be unprecedented. Instead, he or she may creatively imitate the ideas of others. What differentiates the entrepreneur is not her ideas but her execution. Many useful ideas languish in obscurity because they lack some essential quality—additional product features, segmentation of the product for different markets, and proper marketing are a few of the examples he offers (Drucker 2001). This, too, can be part of the entrepreneurial process.

While Schumpter, Kirzner, and Drucker portrayed entrepreneurs in different lights, there are also some significant similarities. In each portrayal, the entrepreneur's role in society is largely benign—and, in many cases, beneficial. He or she ushers people toward something new; in some sense, progress is achieved through the entrepreneur. And the entrepreneur seems to possess a special insight, or else a will to pursue that insight that others lack.

This chapter draws upon all three views to formulate a working definition of entrepreneurship: a person who moves his or her society in a new direction through an insight or idea. Importantly, under this definition, the *idea* need not be novel—only the direction that society takes as a result of the idea. The entrepreneur is the point of contact between the world of ideas and the world of lived experience; he or she transforms the potential into the actual.

Public Entrepreneurs

Terms like "public entrepreneurship" are controversial.[2] As some scholars have noted, analogizing a market concept to a non-market context is a fraught endeavor (Pozen 2008). And as said earlier, scholars such as Kirzner defined entrepreneurship explicitly in terms of markets (Kirzner 1973; 1997).

Nevertheless, there is a reason that so many have seized on the analogy. A huge literature describes how individuals in government or non-profits innovate to further their aims (Pozen 2008). Terms like "public entrepreneurship" denote the unfolding of this process within an arm of the state, whether it be legislative, executive, or judicial.

The role of the market entrepreneur is generally seen as beneficial, but the influence of public entrepreneurs may be less salutary (DiLorenzo 1988; Shockley, Frank, and Stough 2006). Rather than seek market profits, public entrepreneurs may seek new ways to increase their influence or resources—even at the cost of the common good (Holcombe 2002). Indeed, the tendencies of government officials to alter their behavior to maximize power or resources have been well-studied since at least the 1970s (Niskansen 1971).

Not all scholars see public entrepreneurs in a skeptical light, however. John Kingdon (1984) portrayed "policy entrepreneurs" in a neutral fashion, seeing them as individuals who seize upon narrow windows for change in the policy process. Kingdon conceived of three important entrepreneurial qualities. In the first place, the entrepreneur must have a claim to a hearing, such as being an expert or being in an authoritative decision-making position. Second, to achieve his agenda, he must possess strong negotiating skills and political savvy. Third, and most important, he must be persistent. This characterization sets aside the question of whether the entrepreneur damages or benefits the polity; he is identifiable solely through his methods, not his effects.

Other scholars are even more optimistic. Schneider, Teske, and Mintrom (1995) extend the market analogy in an unusual fashion by positing a market for *public* entrepreneurs. They argue that this market "not only produces opportunities and rewards for individual entrepreneurs, this market also produces benefits for society" (Schneider, Teske, and Mintrom 1995, 7). Nevertheless, they acknowledge that individual public entrepreneurs may have less-than-pure motives. "Public entrepreneurs have utility functions that must include the desire for power, prestige, and popularity, the desire to influence policy, and other factors in addition to any monetary income derived from their political activities" (Schneider, Teske and Mintrom 1995, 13).

This chapter's definition of a "public entrepreneur" is "a person who moves his or her society in a new direction through an insight or idea, *using the organs of the state.*" This sidesteps the question of whether such entrepreneurship is salutary. Nevertheless, the question of what might tend to motivate public officials, and the ramifications of those motives for society, is an important theme.

Judicial Entrepreneurs

The possibility that judges might act as public entrepreneurs has received little attention. Prominent American jurists often seem to push back against this line of thinking. Chief Justice Roberts's opening statement during his nomination is typical: "Judges are like umpires. Umpires don't make the rules, they apply them" (Roberts 2005). The belief that judges should apply preexisting norms, rather than change them, stands in tension with the notion that judges could be entrepreneurial in the confines of their role.

But figures like Judge Posner force the question. One of the most cited and revered jurists of all time, Judge Posner openly admitted to sidestepping old rules he disagreed with. An interview with the *New York Times* after his resignation from the bench is illuminating:

> "I pay very little attention to legal rules, statutes, constitutional provisions," Judge Posner said. "A case is just a dispute. The first thing you do is ask yourself—forget about the law—what is a sensible resolution of this dispute?" The next thing, he said, was to see if a recent Supreme Court precedent or some other legal obstacle stood in the way of ruling in favor of that sensible resolution. "And the answer is that's actually rarely the case," he said. "When you have a Supreme Court case or something similar, they're often extremely easy to get around." (Liptak 2017)

It is hard to dispute that Judge Posner's view of his role led him to engage in a number of entrepreneurial pursuits. Indeed, Shannon (2016) provides one of the fullest accounts yet of judicial entrepreneurship by using Judge Posner as a guiding example.

Judge Posner stands out for his remarkably candid admission to innovation, but he isn't the only example that scholars have studied. Crowe (2007) characterizes Chief Justice Taft's early actions to enhance the independence of the judiciary as an episode of political entrepreneurship. Pothula (2015) draws a link between Kingdon's concept of the policy entrepreneur and judicial decisions in India regarding euthanasia. McIntosh and Cates (1997) treat the ideas of numerous jurists, from Jerome Frank to Sandra Day O'Connor, as examples of intellectual entrepreneurship. And Frederickson and Johnston (1999) note the possibility that judges can wield their power to enact innovative public policy reforms.

For my purposes, the definition of a "judicial entrepreneur" is simply "a person who moves his or her society in a new direction through an insight or idea, using the organs of the state, *in the judicial role*." This definition implies that judicial entrepreneurs share important qualities with public entrepreneurs. Nevertheless, as we shall see, there are of course some aspects of the judicial role that differentiate it from other public offices.

INCENTIVES

With this background established, we can consider the incentives that might have nudged the Supreme Court toward majority opinions. Public officials face a variety of incentives when making important decisions; judges are no exception. Recognizing that such ulterior motives exist does not demean the many—perhaps most—judges whose overriding ambition is the public good. On the contrary, recognizing that such incentives exist makes it more impressive when judges forego such temptations. Therefore, it is no disservice to the judiciary to recognize that judges are human, susceptible to the same motives as any other person. Legal observers have identified at least four kinds of incentives that merit mention here: money, reputation, power, and position.

Finances

Financial incentives can affect how judges do their job. These financial incentives can be baked into judges' official compensation. For example, English jurists in the 1700s were often paid by the case. It's possible that this system encouraged Lord Mansfield to modernize English commercial law, so that his court could capture a larger market share of commercial cases (Henderson 2007).

But judges can also financially benefit from their position in a less official capacity. The examples range from benign to corrupt. Judges can (and do) cash in on their prestige by writing books and collecting speaking fees. This gives them a financial stake in their own reputation, or at least their own notoriety. Sometimes, judges are faced with a case that might affect their own financial interests. Developed nations generally enforce conflict-of-interest rules to avoid this quandary. And, like other public officials, some judges become corrupt and accept bribes. However, in countries with a strong rule of law, bribes are deterred by a significant risk of legal punishment, negating much of the incentive. And many judges care too much about their legacy and reputation—not to even mention their own sense of morality—to hazard outright corruption.

Reputation

Judges are motivated by reputation. Ginsburg and Garoupa (2009) persuasively distinguish two types of judicial reputation—group reputation and individual reputation. Historically, common law systems have heavily rewarded judges' individual reputation. This phenomenon is much rarer in civil law countries, where judges tend to be fairly anonymous. By comparison, a well-educated observer of American politics can be expected to know most, if not all, of the justices on the Supreme Court. Anglophone judges often use their written opinions to establish individual reputations. For many judges, an important aspect of individual reputation is avoiding reversal by higher courts (Smith 2006).

Group reputation refers to how a court—or even the judiciary of a nation as a whole—is perceived. Some countries boast high group reputations for their judiciary, even where there is low individual reputation. Non-corrupt civil law systems usually fall into this category (Ginsburg and Garoupa 2009).

The key is to leverage these two types of reputation to solve a group production problem (Ginsburg and Garoupa 2009). Judges should be sufficiently incentivized by their own personal reputation that they are motivated to each work hard and contribute individually. But they should also be able to think of the reputation of the judiciary as a whole and recognize when efforts to advance their own individual reputation will degrade the credibility of the institution. In other words, judges should ideally see themselves as part of a larger group effort. However, there is also a danger in only thinking of the judiciary's reputation in a group—low incentives for any individual to contribute because they cannot distinguish themselves.

Power

In addition to reputation, judges are motivated by power. This is a fact that the Framers would have well understood—indeed, they were counting on it. In their idealized constitutional order, "[a]mbition must be made to counteract ambition" (Federalist No. 51, 319). They believed that human nature necessarily means that figures in authority will seek to increase their own power.

This doesn't necessarily bespeak villainous intent. Judges usually desire the optimal outcome in a given case—by "power," one can simply mean, "the ability to reach X optimal outcome." Judge Posner has already afforded us an example of this quest for optimal outcomes. Other judges are a little less forward, but not less obvious, in desiring the means necessary to achieve their preferred ends. When the Texas legislature exploited the Supreme Court's precedents to craft an abortion bill that would evade injunctions from federal courts, Justice Kagan decried the fact that "some geniuses came up with a way to evade the commands of" the Supreme Court (Oral Argument Transcript 2021, 57). She voted to enjoin the Texas law despite the procedural limits on the Court's power.

When a judge acts in a way that tests the limits of her power, other judges will often emulate her actions. Thus, the exercise of power by one judge can set a precedent for others. This can occur even where the goals of the different judges diverge radically. One example of this phenomenon is the rise of nationwide injunctions, a remedy whereby a single judge can issue orders that must be obeyed throughout the nation. Scholars debate whether such remedies are legal. Nevertheless, nationwide injunctions have proliferated in the past two decades, going from rarity to commonplace (Lampe 2021). Due to this phenomenon, judges now have more opportunities than ever to change national policy.

Position

Judges also change their behavior to angle for certain jobs. This can be part of an attempt at promotion, or an effort to retain an existing judicial office. At the state level, judges infamously alter their decisions when they are up for re-election (Berry 2015). On the federal level, judges don't need to worry about re-election. However, many legal commentators have speculated that judges will design their opinions to increase their chances of being appointed to a more influential judgeship.[3] This is particularly true where judges write separately, either in dissent or concurrence, rather than silently sign on to majority opinions. These separate writings can signal that the judge holds views that are too controversial to include in a majority opinion but are nevertheless popular with the politicians who could one day have the power to fill an important job vacancy.

One final coda. Obviously, the categories we are discussing overlap. More prestigious judges probably have more influence over their colleagues, as well as legal thought generally, which would mean that they have more power. And when the judiciary is especially powerful, as it is in the United States, that can provide a boost to individual reputation: consider the aforementioned fact that American judges are far more famous than their less powerful civil-law counterparts. And holding important judicial positions gives individuals both power and prestige.

THE TRANSITION

Having discussed these incentives in general terms, it is possible to consider them in the context of the Supreme Court's decision to adopt majority opinions. By outlining how the incentives—especially power—intersect with that decision, it also becomes clear that the decision was an example of judicial entrepreneurship. The chief justices moved their society in a new direction (a direction that increased the power of the judiciary) through an insight or idea (the relatively new "technology" of majority opinions), using the organs of the state (specifically, the Supreme Court), in the judicial role.

For starters, it is safe to say that two incentives likely played no role. The justices had nothing to gain financially from the decision. And as lifetime appointees to the highest court in the nation, it is unlikely that they were angling for a job. Besides, for much of the transition, pro-seriatim presidents (Thomas Jefferson and James Madison) controlled appointments to plum federal jobs. The two more likely possibilities are reputation and power.

Reputation

Seriatim opinions are quintessentially oriented toward individual reputation. One can distinguish oneself with a particularly well-written and well-reasoned opinion, so there are high incentives to get the individual opinion right, as Jefferson and Madison repeatedly argued. However, there are low incentives to make the collection of seriatim opinions that will be issued in a particular case understandable as a whole. For this reason, seriatim opinions are often deeply confusing to new students of the law.

At least in the opinion of Chief Justice Roberts, separate writings also diminish the group reputation of the court (Henderson 2007). This theory accords with Ginsburg and Garoupa's (2009) characterization of the unanimous and anonymous opinions usually written in civil law countries. On the other hand, since no individual reputational benefits accrue from issuing such opinions, there is probably less incentive to think through alternative arguments. For the sake of unanimity, judges might be tempted to sign on to the opinion of the court even if they don't agree with everything said in the opinion.

The current practice of the Supreme Court is somewhere in the middle. It still follows the basic model of a majority opinion, but several features separate it from the extremely group-oriented nature of civil law opinions. The identity of the justice who wrote the majority opinion is usually public. Dissent is allowed, and therefore justices are incentivized to carefully think through opposing arguments in controversial cases.

But one should not assume that merely because a practice is in the middle of two extremes, and thus shares some of the benefits of each approach, it is necessarily a superior approach. The current practice also shares in the vices of both extremes. Majority opinions afford fewer individual incentives than seriatim opinions and fewer incentives to think of group reputation than unanimous, anonymous majority opinions. Some dissents, such as the one in *Dobbs v. Jackson Women's Health Organization*, explicitly argue that the majority opinion undermines the legitimacy of the Court. This arguably erodes group reputation, even though it probably furthers other important interests, such as forcing the majority to grapple with inconvenient arguments and informing the public where the dissenting justices think the Court has gone astray.

Nevertheless, one defense of the current system along these lines is advanced by Henderson (2007). He argues that there is no one "right" way to write an opinion. Instead, different situations necessitate different styles of opinions. And one of the strengths of the current system of judicial opinion writing is that it is fairly adaptable. Where issues are fairly clear-cut, the Supreme Court can issue short, anonymous majority opinions called "per curiam" opinions to dispose of the case. Where a case is especially controversial, the opinions may start to look more like seriatim—where many different positions are staked out, none of which commands a majority by itself. This variability means that different judicial needs are met at different times.

In sum, there are reputational pluses and minuses to writing separately. Overall, seriatim opinions were probably attractive to judges who valued their individual reputations over their group reputations. The reverse was also true.

Power

The most obvious advantage to majority opinions is that they increase the reach of judicial authority. Many of the powers that are presently associated with the Supreme Court exist only because of majority opinions. Their adoption, then, was a critical influence on the future of American jurisprudence and American society writ large.

To understand how the abandonment of seriatim writing would have affected the Court's power, it's important to review what the powers of the Supreme Court actually are. There are at least four ways to conceptualize the Court's power, each somewhat more controversial than the one before it.

The first account of the Court's power is the least controversial. This is its ability to assign legal rights and duties to the parties before it. Article III of the Constitution vests the Supreme Court with the power to decide the "cases and controversies" that come before it. But to come before the court, a case must fall in one of two categories. First, a case might be part of the Supreme Court's original jurisdiction. If so, the parties can appear before the Supreme Court immediately, without having to first litigate their cases in lower courts. Only a narrow set of cases fall under the Court's original jurisdiction, such as suits between states or suits involving ambassadors. As decided in *Marbury v. Madison*, Congress does not have the power to expand the original jurisdiction of the Court as set forth in the Constitution.

The second category is the Court's appellate jurisdiction. Almost all legally significant decisions come from this part of the court's docket. As the name suggests, the Court takes these cases on appeal from other courts—generally, either lower federal courts or state supreme courts. Usually, the Court does so to resolve one or more disputed questions of federal law. Big-ticket constitutional questions are decided here, as are many issues of statutory construction. Sometimes the appeal is on one simple question. This fact belies the complexity of the average case, which often starts with many disputed facts and questions of law. But most of these issues are decided by the trial court and affirmed or reversed by lower courts of appeals. By the time a case is appealed to the Supreme Court, only the closest, most difficult issues in a case are still in dispute. Further, if the Supreme Court is not interested in one of the legal questions still present in the case, it can simply refuse to take that "question presented," effectively affirming the court below on everything except the question that the Supreme Court grants. The Supreme Court can even alter the wording of the question presented by the parties. Once it has pruned an acceptable question, the Supreme Court can give its preferred answer.

But what effect does the Supreme Court's decision have in these instances? The most directly impacted are the parties before the Court. In the most basic theoretical model, this is the function of a court; it exists to resolve a dispute by assigning legal rights and duties to each party. While the Court's orders to the parties technically rely on enforcement from the executive branch, the executive has generally followed the decisions of the Court. However, it is unclear whether the executive can refuse to enforce Supreme Court decisions—some scholars, as well as some presidents, have thought otherwise (Paulsen 2018).

There's a certain symmetry to this belief. After all, presidents often exercise prosecutorial discretion when deciding whether to enforce acts of Congress; consider recent administrations' refusal to enforce federal marijuana policy in states that have legalized the drug. These sorts of actions often get pushback but are not anywhere near as controversial as refusing to enforce judicial decisions. Yet the separation-of-powers principle is the same: the legislature and the judiciary can both assign legal rights or duties, but the executive decides whether to enforce them.

The second model of the Supreme Court's power emphasizes its ability to use a decision in one case to signal to other courts that it will rule the same way again if presented with a similar case. Lower courts pay close attention to the decisions of the Supreme Court. Most judges do not want to be reversed. Independent of the desire to avoid the negative reputational effects of reversal, though, most judges consider themselves bound to follow Supreme Court precedent, although what that means and the justifications for why that is the case differs somewhat, depending on judicial philosophy, what kind of court, and what kind of case is under discussion. Federal lower courts are explicitly called "inferior" courts in Article III, which seems to reasonably imply that they should derive their rules of decision from Supreme Court precedent. However, even this is subject to some back-and-forth. In cases where the Supreme Court has made decisions that are deeply unpopular in lower courts, some literature has questioned whether that Supreme Court precedent is applied faithfully (Ghosh 2012).

The situation is slightly less clear with regard to state courts. After all, states did not entirely give up their sovereignty when ratifying the Constitution. And as the entities that ratified the Constitution, they originally argued that they had a co-equal role in deciding the meaning of the Constitution. The Supreme Court put this argument to rest in *Martin v. Hunter's Lessee* (1816), concluding that its interpretation of the Constitution was final over state court judgments.

In other words, the Supreme Court, according to Article III, holds the judicial power of the United States. This certainly means that the Supreme Court can decide cases on appeal from state courts, and that their resolution of that particular dispute is final. But it also is generally understood to mean that state courts have a duty, in future cases, to decide in a way that reflects the precedent set down by the Supreme Court. The second option is less conceptually obvious but is generally assumed. It is also symmetrical, since matters of state law are finally decided by state Supreme Courts—federal courts can, at best, guess as to what a state court would rule in a gray area of state law. It makes sense, then, that the Supreme Court would have the same final decision-making authority over federal law.

Even so, there is some debate at present as to what it means to faithfully apply Supreme Court precedent (Blackman 2022). There is widespread agreement that a skilled judge can create an artificial reason why one case is different from the case before it. But there is also the opposite danger: extending Supreme Court precedent to situations where it genuinely ought not apply.

In sum, although there is some room for debate at the edges, the Supreme Court can not only overrule other courts as regards the particular case, but also force other courts to use a similar rule of decision in similar cases. Therefore, every party whose case might one day fall under the Supreme Court's jurisdiction (or under the jurisdiction of a court that will faithfully apply Supreme Court precedent) has to change their behavior if they wish to avoid an unfavorable ruling. True, an adverse Supreme Court ruling might not matter much in the hypothetical case where the executive refused to put the decision in force, but that situation has not arisen in the modern era. Therefore, litigants have every reason to abide by Supreme Court precedent.

The third account of the Supreme Court's power is hotly contested. This is the ability to settle not only how other courts will apply the law but the objective meaning of the law itself. In this model, not only courts and litigants but also other branches of government must interpret the law in a manner consistent with Supreme Court rulings. This view is known as judicial supremacy. This "judicial supremacy" is often associated with the Court's ruling in *Aaron v. Cooper*. Court decisions are not just the *judiciary's* final word on what federal law means, but *the* final word on what federal law means. *Aaron v. Cooper*'s sweeping language was meant to end the back-and-forth between state governments and the Supreme Court in the aftermath of *Brown v. Board of Education*. Some argue that this decision was implied in the precedents set by the Marshall Court. And it is true that John Marshall sometimes struck this tone. "It is emphatically the role of the judiciary to say what the laws are" (*Marbury v. Madison* 1803). Since the advent of judicial review, the Supreme Court has declared the acts of other branches unconstitutional. One might be tempted to conclude that this is synonymous with judicial supremacy.

This docs not seem to have been the consistent view of the Founders. In early American history, each branch of government often took up the task of interpreting the Constitution. Congress decided whether it was constitutional to let the executive determine where postal roads were built (Mortenson 2021). President Washington solicited interpretations of the Necessary and Proper Clause from his cabinet (Holloway 2016).[4] The view that each branch of government had an independent duty to interpret the Constitution is called "departmentalism," and it was popular during much of the 1800s. President Jackson famously endorsed the theory during his tussle with the Second Bank of the United States. So did President Lincoln in the wake of the *Dred Scott* decision (Whittington 2002).

However, judicial supremacy finds a great deal of support in twentiethcentury philosophical jurisprudence. Arguably the most important philosopher of law in that century, H. L. A. Hart (1961, 141) is illustrative: "A supreme tribunal has the last word in saying what the law is and, when it has said it, the statement that the court was 'wrong' has no consequences within the system: no one's rights or duties are thereby altered." Karl Llewellyn strikes a similar note: "what these officials do about disputes is, to my mind, the law itself" (2012, 13). This view might seem correct where, in systems such as ours, the executive routinely enforces judicial decisions. As long as that continues to be the case, and the state maintains its monopoly on force, no other actor can trump the judiciary if a suit is brought. And, in almost all cases where a legal right or duty is at stake, a suit will likely be brought.

A departmentalist would object. Rather than simply align legislative and executive actions with the judiciary's interpretation of federal law, these branches might adopt varying interpretations of the Constitution by using their own powers. Say, for example, that the Supreme Court has decided a case and stated that regulating X is unconstitutional. The legislature might simply disagree, and pass a law that nevertheless bans X. Will those laws be enforceable? Probably not. It will not be possible to prosecute the violator in court, and the executive cannot punish them without a judicial decree. Doing so would itself usually trigger a lawsuit based on the Fifth Amendment's (or the Fourteenth Amendment's) Due Process Clause. But, importantly, even unenforced laws remain on the books. They are not erased merely because the courts prevent anyone from enforcing them. Ergo, to say that courts can "strike down" a law is technically inaccurate (Mitchell 2018). This is part of why Texas's fetal heartbeat law was able to dissuade abortions even before *Roe v. Wade* was overturned. The Court can opine that a law is unconstitutional, but those opinions do not technically repeal a law. Courts need a particular case to come before them, and the Texas law used federal courts doctrines to prevent the abortion clinics from bringing pre-enforcement challenges to block the application of the law.

Departmentalists are sometimes characterized as playing constitutional hardball, but legislatures can use less confrontational approaches to undermine the Supreme Court's interpretation of the law. During the Reconstruction, Congress stripped the Supreme Court of jurisdiction over a habeas corpus suit while the case was pending before the Court (*Ex parte McCardle* 1869). This effectively prevented the Court from issuing an opinion that might have undermined the Reconstruction.

The executive is similarly empowered to check the Supreme Court's interpretation of the law. Consider President Jackson's Bank Veto. Congress had previously passed similar statutes, and the Supreme Court had already recognized those laws as constitutional in *McCulloch v. Maryland* (1819). Nevertheless, President Jackson vetoed the bill on the grounds that it was unconstitutional. If the Supreme Court has the final word on the meaning of the law, then President Jackson's veto was wrongly exercised. Nevertheless, it took legal effect, and the Second Bank of the United States passed out of existence.

Presidential vetoes are not the only way in which the executive can supplant the Court's interpretation of the law with the executive's. All three branches could agree that a law is constitutional: Congress could pass a law, the president could sign it, and the Supreme Court could rule it is constitutional. Even so, the president could later change his or her mind, or a new president could be elected who thought the law was unconstitutional. Accordingly, the president could refuse to prosecute anyone under the law, and pardon everyone who was previously convicted. Once again, the president's opinion of the law's constitutionality would be given legal effect. The prosecutorial discretion and pardons would be legally valid.

As a descriptive matter, then, the judicial supremacy view is at least sometimes wrong. It may emphatically be within the province of the judiciary to say what the law is, but it is also within the province of the executive and the legislative branches. The debate between departmentalism and judicial supremacy rages on, and the fact that many people see the Supreme Court's opinions as settling the meaning of the law demonstrates just how much power the Court has.

The fourth and final account of the Court's power is usually rejected, even by the Court itself. This is the view that the Supreme Court can simply make law. Judges and scholars usually regard this as a violation of the Constitution, which vests all legislative power in Congress. In fact, the Supreme Court disclaimed the ability even to develop common law—a body of law that is widely regarded as judge-made—in *Erie Railroad Co. v. Tompkins* (1938). There are a few exceptions to this principle; for example, the Court engaged in a limited common law analysis when dealing with the Alien Tort Statute in *Sosa v. Alvarez-Machain* (2004). But usually, the Court expresses discomfort at the thought that it is making law rather than interpreting it.

Yet there is some evidence to support this view. David Strauss (1996) argues that the Supreme Court's constitutional jurisprudence can best be explained as following a common-law model. Over time, the Court creates precedents that build out the meaning of the Constitution, creating law where none previously existed. And some Supreme Court rulings do appear quite law-like. *Roe v. Wade* (1973), for example, set out a detailed trimester framework that is hard to characterize as merely the result of constitutional interpretation, rather than active lawmaking.

The Court has tried to dispel this notion, though it continues to live on. Justices often give speeches that frame the Court as a neutral arbiter. Nevertheless, because of the extreme importance of Supreme Court precedent, many people treat majority opinions as if they are the law. In response, in the recent case of *Brown v. Davenport* (2022), the majority opinion took the unusual and somewhat paradoxical step of rebuking parties for taking the language of past majority opinions too seriously.

These accounts of the Supreme Court's power are listed from most modest to greatest. But obviously, they overlap to some degree. The power to settle individual disputes means that courts at least have to treat those parties in a manner consistent with the Supreme Court's ruling, so (1) always impacts (2) on some level. The fact that the Supreme Court can get all other courts to use its rules of decision means that other branches are not operating in a vacuum, and probably align their approaches to the law in a way that more closely reflects Supreme Court precedent——they can't rely solely on the fact it is highly unlikely that the Supreme Court will ever hear their case. So (2) impacts (3). And it is notoriously difficult to differentiate category (3) from category (4), such that many courts that claim to be merely interpreting the law are accused of making it. In sum, then, there are several flavors of judicial power that SCOTUS currently exercises to some degree or another. (1) It has control over the litigants before it. (2) It can usually command all other courts to adopt the same rules of decision that it announces—and therefore control anyone who wishes to be a litigant before any court. (3) It can declare the meaning of the law for any and all purposes, binding even co-equal branches in their interpretations. And (4) it can make law.

What does all of this have to do with seriatim opinions, and how is it linked to judicial entrepreneurship? Think about it this way. How many modern accounts of judicial authority only work with the assumption that there is a majority opinion? If most accounts rely on majority opinions, then the Supreme Court moved society in a new direction by transitioning their approach to opinion-writing—in other words, they acted as judicial entrepreneurs. Further, if most accounts of judicial power rely on majority opinions, that would have been a powerful incentive in favor of the Supreme Court's transition.

The first power is unaffected. Courts can still resolve individual cases and controversies, whether they do so by issuing a majority opinion, seriatim opinions, or no opinion at all.

However, seriatim opinions reduce the power of the Court to supply rules of decision to other courts, federal or state. If there is no "opinion of the court," there can be no single interpretation of the Constitution from the Court, except insofar as the justices agree on a point of law. And often, different seriatim opinions will emphasize different reasons why they arrived at their conclusion. Controlling lower federal courts probably was not a big concern for Marshall—after all, justices at the time also helped compose circuit courts. However, as the case of *Martin v. Hunter's Lessee* demonstrated, it was a huge issue for state courts, which were inclined to issue their own independent interpretations of federal law. Without majority opinions, it might have been impossible to force the state courts to coalesce around a single interpretation of the Constitution.

Likewise, judicial supremacy is difficult to imagine in a world without majority opinions. In lieu of a majority opinion, many of the problems that arise in corralling state courts would have presented themselves with equal or greater urgency in the context of the other branches of the federal government. Suddenly, Supreme Court decisions would look more like legislative debates wherein multiple views as to the meaning of a law are expressed. Those opinions might still have some weight, but it would probably depend on the length of the practice and the unanimity of interpretation.

Finally, seriatim opinions make it practically impossible to make law. This is for the simple reason that there is no single text that future parties can read as a prospective rule. While precedent played an important part in the system of English common law, it was mostly appealed to by analogy—that is, X case was decided in X way, so a similar Y case should be dealt with in the same manner as X. Parties had considerable leeway to argue that the analogy should or should not hold; one could not appeal to any individual seriatim opinion as giving a prospective rule that all parties should follow. Rules gradually arise from decentralized knowledge, rather than being announced from on high. By contrast, the adoption of the majority opinion showed that a majority of the Court agreed, not only on the way in which a particular case should be disposed of but also on the reasoning behind why the case was resolved in that way. This led to the possibility that the Court could lay out prospective rules for future parties. The public was essentially put on notice: abide by the letter of the majority opinion, or the courts will dispose of your case unfavorably. The Court was no longer simply dealing with the "cases or controversies" that came before it. Instead, it resembled a legislature: the agreement of a majority of the body on some rule resulted in that rule being applied to all future parties.

Seriatim opinions, then, significantly diminish the various real and perceived powers of the Supreme Court. They are left with the core power—disposing of the individual case and controversy before them. But more extensive claims are difficult to defend.

Now reconsider the position of the early Supreme Court. Chief Justices Marshall and Ellsworth held office in a time when the Supreme Court had a strong need for group reputation and power. In between their two terms, John Jay refused the position of chief justice on the grounds that the Court lacked "energy, weight, and dignity" (Bomboy 2016). Even their core power—the ability to dispose of particular cases—was somewhat under fire. As stated earlier, the Court had reason to fear that hostile government officials such as James Madison would simply refuse to obey its orders.

It was in the context of a lack of group reputation and power that the transition occurred. Furthermore, Marshall managed the transition in such a way that his individual reputation as a jurist was bolstered rather than degraded by the move toward majority opinions. Again, even now many scholars simply assume that he was the first jurist to introduce majority opinions at the Supreme Court. Historians speak of many of the decisions of the Supreme Court from that time as Marshall's handiwork, and for good reason: it's widely known that he penned many of the decisions. Indeed, one of Jefferson's biggest complaints about majority opinions was that the system made the other justices less likely to pay close attention to the cases before them.

Of course, none of this establishes the private motives of any of the justices. All it does is establish that the adoption of majority opinions was consistent with—and to a large degree, necessary for—the Court to enhance its power and group reputation. Suddenly, the Court was able to lay claim to a role in American public life that had once been out of reach.

EFFECTS

Now we can consider how the change impacted the consumers of legal services. Recall that entrepreneurship in the private sphere, according to Schumpeter, tends to push markets toward equilibrium. There are no such promises with regard to public entrepreneurship.

One important argument in favor of majority opinions is that they facilitate clear prospective rules from the court. Many ostensibly market-oriented judges strive to craft just such rules. These judges have often emphasized the predictability that brightline rules afford market actors. Judge Robert Bork, the preeminent force behind modern antitrust law, was of this mind (Heyer 2016). Justice Scalia favored the same approach (Bloom and Walker 2021). Early in his career, so did Judge Posner (Baker 2001). This is a serious objection, but two facts should be kept in mind.

First, although majority opinions make the stance of the Court clearer in the moment, they may destabilize the law in the long term. That is because the Court will occasionally find it necessary to overrule a prior decision's prospective rule. A rule adopted by a majority of the Court can be later discarded, as the recent history of the Court has shown. This is particularly likely if a justice signs on to majority opinions that they do not fully agree with by way of compromise, meaning that the justice's vote in a later case can come as a surprise to litigants. This is especially true in cases where the facts at hand differ in an unanticipated but important way from the facts involved in a prior decision. In such cases, a seriatim approach might have led to better outcomes, since there would not be an overbroad rule that would dictate an undesirable result. True, the Court's ability to overturn itself keeps this problem from being permanent, but the many cases disposed of in the interim—and the many more cases that were never even brought because of the rule—are lasting and often irreversible negative effects of the current approach.

In a court that adheres to the older common law model, this problem does not arise; two cases have been decided in different ways, but over the long term the tension will tend to resolve and a solution will emerge. The different points on the graph will plot a through-line. But if the Court seeks to lay out a prospective rule right away, then any change of course is intrinsically disruptive. The Court attempts to control for this effect by accounting for "reliance interests" in its stare decisis doctrines (*Planned Parenthood v. Casey* 1992). But judges have a limited ability to analyze or predict the effects of switching from one prospective rule to another.

Second, there is a question of *who* is competent to draw brightline rules. Courts have limited fact-finding abilities outside of the record of the particular dispute at hand. Introducing facts not contained in the record is discouraged. By contrast, legislatures have enormous resources to survey the conditions of the entire society and deduce what rules would best govern the population. By supplying their own brightline rules, it may well be that courts disincentivize legislators from doing the hard work of fixing vague areas of the law themselves. Prominent formalists such as Justice Scalia have often advanced this line of argument (Scalia 1997).

Majority opinions sacrificed one of the common law's strengths. Judicial rules in common law could arise only after numerous, relatively similar cases were decided. In each decision, the court could focus on what it knew best—the facts of the individual case before it. On those facts, the court could assess whether a certain application of the law was appropriate or not. This process arguably reflects the decentralized nature of knowledge and the difficulty of laying down one prospective rule for a wide variety of cases in a single decision. Over time, a large number of highly specific decisions could begin to plot the course of a broader rule, relying on distinctions that might not be obvious at the first glance but become more obvious when the many individual cases are considered. This approach might be especially preferable because the judiciary is not always the most qualified branch to announce top-down. Institutional competence questions become especially great when judges start intruding on specialty areas like the demographic challenges posed by redistricting cases or the economic problems inherent in antitrust. This critique sets aside entirely the formalist complaint that judges were simply not granted the authority to craft prospective rules by the Constitution.

CONCLUSION

The argument given earlier has several takeaways. First, the efforts of Chief Justices Ellsworth and Marshall to adopt majority opinions belong to the growing list of examples of judicial entrepreneurship given in the literature. These historical figures indubitably moved their society in a new direction through an insight or idea, using the organs of the state, in the judicial role. Although neither chief justice originated the idea of majority opinions, they creatively utilized Lord Mansfield's to alter the American legal landscape. Moreover, they perceived that majority opinions presented an opportunity to enhance the Court's stature—an insight that many of their colleagues seem to have missed. Eventually, their "product"—majority opinions—came to dominate the American "market" for judicial decisions, leading to the status quo of today where seriatim opinions are all but forgotten.

Second, many of the tensions and pitfalls identified by the scholarship on public entrepreneurship recur in the specific context of judicial entrepreneurship. Indeed, although it is not cast in these terms, scholarly research on what motivates judicial behavior has flagged some of the same incentives found in the literature on public entrepreneurship. Power and resources are particularly important in both contexts. Nevertheless, there are some interesting differences. For example, the literature on judges places a particular premium on reputation, a factor that is less prevalent in other public choice accounts.

Third, robust accounts of judicial power—at least in the modern American context—are reliant on the existence of majority opinions. As stated in the introduction, it is not the goal of this chapter to investigate the subjective, psychological intent of early American judges. But it is significant that the changes they introduced to the opinion-writing process enabled an expansive view of the judicial role. This enabled the Supreme Court to exercise the legal and political authority that it often lacked under the seriatim system.

Fourth and finally, the expansion of the judicial role may or may not improve the aggregate welfare of the policy. The conclusion is not that seriatim opinions are better than majority opinions, or vice versa. This chapter does not establish either proposition. Instead, it is that judicial entrepreneurship can be motivated by concerns that diverge from the common good. Some of these incentives, such as judicial power, are particularly potent. And the decision to adopt majority opinions is consistent with a pursuit of judicial power.

NOTES

1. Of course, in true seriatim opinion-writing, there is no controlling opinion—that would just be giving one justice's vote the power of the majority.

2. There are a number of names for people who engage in entrepreneur-like activities in the public sphere. They are often called political entrepreneurs, social entrepreneurs, or policy entrepreneurs, although these terms tend to describe somewhat different groups (Pozen, 2008; Holcombe 2002). When not directly discussing other academic literature, this chapter uses the rarer—although not unheard of—term "public entrepreneur" (Roberts and King, 1989). It does so to avoid casting the aspersion that judges who engage in entrepreneurial activities are motivated by an ulterior political, social, or policy goal.

3. Two recent examples that commentators have identified: then-Judge Gorsuch's self-concurrence on the legality of *Chevron* deference (Doerfler, 2022) and Judge Walker's district court opinion dealing with the intersection of COVID restrictions and the freedom of religion (Millhiser, 2020). While she was not accused of "auditioning" for a promotion as Justice Gorsuch and Judge Walker were, Justice Jackson's opinions for the D.C. Circuit were also closely watched by the media in connection with her possible elevation to the Supreme Court (Stern, 2022).

4. This finds some parallel in the current practice of the Department of Justice, which generates legal opinions for the executive branch.

REFERENCES

Baker, Jonathan B. 2002. "Horizontal Merger Analysis Grows Up: A Review of Chapter 5 of Richard Posner's Antitrust Law." *The Antitrust Source*, January. https://www.americanbar.org/content/dam/aba/publishing/antitrust-magazine-online/01_02.pdf.

Berry, Kate. 2015. "How Judicial Elections Impact Criminal Cases." Brennan Center for Justice. https://www.brennancenter.org/sites/default/files/publications/How_Judicial_Elections_Impact_Criminal_Cases.pdf.

Blackman, Josh. 2022. "Originalism and Stare Decisis in the Lower Courts." Lecture at The Heritage Foundation, May 12. https://www.heritage.org/the-constitution/lecture/originalism-and-stare-decisis-the-lower-courts#:~:text=Originalism%20operates%20differently%20on%20the,how%20flawed%20those%20cases%20are.

Bloom, Robert M., and Eliza S. Walker. 2021. "Rules and Standards in Justice Scalia's Fourth Amendment." *University of Richmond Law Review* 55 (3): 713–763.

Bomboy, Scott. 2016. "Drama, Controversy Marked the First Supreme Court Justices." The National Constitution Center, September 24. Blog post. https://constitutioncenter.org/blog/drama-controversy-marked-the-first-supreme-court-justices.

Brutus. 2003. *The Anti-Federalist Papers and the Constitutional Convention Debates*. New York: Signet.

Crowe, Justin. 2007. "The Forging of Judicial Autonomy: Political Entrepreneurship and the Reforms of William Howard Taft." *The Journal of Politics* 69 (1): 73–87.

DiLorenzo, and J. Thomas. 1988. "Competition and Political Entrepreneurship: Austrian Insights into Public-Choice Theory." *Review of Austrian Economics* 2 (1): 59–71.

Doerfler, Ryan D. 2022. "Late-Stage Textualism." *The Supreme Court Review* 2021 (1): 267–313.

Frederickson, H. George, and Jocelyn M. Johnston. 1999. *Public Management Reform and Innovation: Research, Theory, and Application*. Tuscaloosa, AL: University of Alabama Press.

Ghosh, Saurav. 2012. "Boumediene Applied Badly: The Extraterritorial Constitution After *Al Maqaleh v. Gates*." *Stanford Law Review* 64 (2): 507–534.

Ginsburg, Tom, and Nuno Garoupa. 2009. "Judicial Audiences and Reputation: Perspectives from Comparative Law." *Columbia Journal of Transnational Law* 47: 451–489.

Hamilton, Alexander, James Madison, and John Jay. 2012. *The Federalist Papers*. New York: Dutton/Signet.

Hart, H. L. A. 1961. *The Concept of Law*. Oxford: Clarendon Press.

Henderson, M. Todd. 2007. "From Seriatim to Consensus and Back Again: A Theory of Dissent." John M. Olin Program in Law and Economics. Working Paper No. 363.

Heyer, Kenneth. 2014. "Consumer Welfare and the Legacy of Robert Bork." *Journal of Law and Economics* 57: S19–S32.

Hochschild, Adam S. 2000. "The Modern Problem of Supreme Court Plurality Decision: Interpretation in Historical Perspective." *Washington University Journal of Law and Policy* 4: 261–287.

Holcombe, Randall G. 2002. "Political Entrepreneurship and the Democratic Allocation of Economic Resources." *The Review of Austrian Economics* 15: 143–159.

Holloway, Carson. 2016. "The National Bank: An Early Lesson in Constitutional Fidelity." *Public Discourse*, March 18.

Kelsh, John P. 1999. "The Opinion Delivery Practices of the United States Supreme Court 1790-1945." *Washington University Law Review* 77 (1): 137–182.

Kingdon, John. 1984. *Agendas, Alternatives and Public Policies*. New York: Harper Collins.

Kirzner, Israel M. 1973. *Competition and Entrepreneurship*. Chicago, IL: University of Chicago Press.

Kirzner, Israel M. 1997. "Entrepreneurial Discovery and the Competitive Market Process: An Austrian Approach." *Journal of Economic Literature* 35 (1): 60–85.

Lampe, Joanna R. 2021. "*Nationwide Injunctions: Law, History, and Proposals for Reform*." Congressional Research Service Report R46902.

Liptak, Adam. 2017. *An Exit Interview with Richard Posner, Judicial Provocateur*. New York City: The New York Times.

Llewellyn, Karl N. 2012. *The Bramble Bush: On Our Law and Its Study*. New Orleans, LA: Quid Pro Books.

Lowry, Todd. 1973. "Lord Mansfield and the Law Merchant: Law and Economics in the Eighteenth Century." *Journal of Economic Issues* 7 (4): 605–622.

McIntosh, Wayne V., and Cynthia L. Cates. 1997. *Judicial Entrepreneurship: The Role of the Judge in the Marketplace of Ideas*. Westport, CT: Greenwood Press.

Millhiser, Ian. 2020. "The Controversy Over a Trump Judge's Oddly Partisan 'Religious Liberty' Opinion, Explained." Vox.

Mitchell, Jonathan F. 2018. "The Writ-Of-Erasure Fallacy." *Virginia Law Review* 104 (5): 933–1019.

Mortenson, Julian Davis, and Nicholas Bagley. 2021. "Delegation at the Founding." *Columbia Law Review* 121 (2): 277–368.

Official Reporters. 2021. "Oral Argument Transcript, *Whole Woman's Health v. Jackson*." Washington, DC: Heritage Reporting Corporation.

Paulsen, Michael Stokes. 2018. "The President and the Myth of Judicial Supremacy." *University of St. Thomas Law Journal* 14 (3): 602–626.

Pothula, Aishwarya. 2016. *Euthanasia as a Case of Judicial Entrepreneurship in India? Analysing the Role of the Supreme Court in the Policy Process of Euthanasia*. The Hague, Netherlands: International Institute of Social Studies.

Pozen, David E. 2008. "We Are All Entrepreneurs Now." *Wake Forest Law Review* 43: 283–340.

Roberts, John G. 2005. "Chief Justice Roberts Statement—Nomination Process, Excerpted from 'Confirmation Hearing on the Nomination of John G. Roberts, Jr. to be Chief Justice of the United States.'" Committee on the Judiciary, United States Senate, 109th Congress 55–56. Washington, DC: U.S. Government Printing Office.

Roberts, Nancy Charlotte, and Paula King. 1989. "Public Entrepreneurship: A Typology." Naval Postgraduate School (U.S.). Dept. of National Security Affairs. Report Number NPS-56-89-018.

Scalia, Antonin et al. 1997. *A Matter of Interpretation: Federal Courts and the Law*. Princeton, NJ: Princeton University Press.

Schneider, Mark, and Paul Teske with Michael Mintrom. 1995. *Public Entrepreneurs: Agents for Change in American Government*. Princeton, NJ: Princeton University Press.

Schneider, Mark, and Paul Teske with Michael Mintrom. 2011. *Public Entrepreneurs: Identifying Agents for Change in the Local Market for Public Goods*. Princeton, NJ: Princeton University Press.

Schumpeter, Joseph A. 1939. *Business Cycles: A Theoretical, Historical and Statistical Analysis of the Capitalist Process*. New York: McGraw-Hill Book Company.

Schumpeter, Joseph A. 1949. *The Theory of Economic Development*. Cambridge, MA: Harvard University Press.

Shannon, Sean J. 2016. "Richard A. Posner: A Study in Judicial Entrepreneurship." PhD diss. The City University of New York.

Shockley, Gordon E., Peter M. Frank, and Roger R. Stough. 2006. "Towards a Theory of Public Sector Entrepreneurship." *International Journal of Entrepreneurship and Innovation Management* 6 (3): 205–223.

Smith, Joseph L. 2006. "Patterns and Consequences of Judicial Reversals: Theoretical Considerations and Data from a District Court." *The Justice System Journal* 27 (1): 28–46.

Stern, Mark Joseph. 2022. "What We Learned from Ketanji Brown Jackson's First Appeals Court Opinion." *Slate*, February 25. https://slate.com/news-and-politics/2022/02/ketanji-brown-jackson-supreme-court-nominee-opinions-rulings.html.

Strauss, David A. 1996. "Common Law Constitutional Interpretation." *University of Chicago Law Review* 63: 877–935.

Toepfer, Owen P. 2021. "June Medical and the Marks Rule." *Notre Dame Law Review* 96 (4): 1725–1754.

Whittington, Keith E. 2002. "Extrajudicial Constitutional Interpretation: Three Objections and Responses." *North Carolina Law Review* 80: 773–852.

Chapter 11

Urban Deindustrialization and Its Discontents

A Commentary on the Social Policy Education of President Barack Obama

Michael Lachanski

Starting in the early 1960s the US federal government undertook a set of policies that roughly doubled the fraction of GDP allocated to anti-poverty social programming (Peterson 1991, 619–620).[1] Against the widely held expectations of the Democratic and academic establishments, this social policy revolution preceded an unprecedented decline in productivity growth, stagflation, and record-breaking increases in violent crime (Lavoie [1985] 2016; Jencks 1992; Wilson [1987] 2012; Latzer 2016). Social policy academics were so puzzled by the rise in Black urban poverty after the deployment and expansion of so many government programs aimed at its alleviation that a literature devoted to the so-called "paradox of continuing poverty" emerged (Peterson 1991, 618). Many of the 1960s and 1970s policy changes were justified based on their potential to reduce Black-White inequalities, which have remained at about the same level in relative wage terms from 1980 to the present (Hurst, Rubinstein, and Shimizu 2021, 1). The dashed hopes of that era yielded to silence and counternarratives increasingly disconnected with the reality of Black urban immiseration on the left and increasing cynicism toward the civil rights movement on the right (Wilson [1987] 2012, 20–22, 149–151; Peterson 1991).

In this era of rising unrest, on an island thousands of miles away from the turmoil, a future president came of age in Honolulu, Hawaii. A member of the "choom gang," known for the quality of its marijuana, Barack Obama would fondly reflect on his "idyllic sort of childhood" and later adolescence spent playing basketball, philosophizing with friends, and publishing poetry in the school newspaper (Garrow 2017, 57, 84, 93–96). Although it had the odd "desolate" neighborhood and "panhandler," Honolulu gave Obama little first-hand experience with the economic, social, and political problems afflicting urban America in the later 1960s and 1970s (92, 116, 119). Garrow's encyclopedic biography revealed only hints of policy interest in Obama's pre-college life, for example, Obama achieved an A− in an "exceptionally demanding class" on "Law and Society" in his senior year of high school (100). The only nonfiction book Obama read prior to college, *The Autobiography of Malcolm X,* might have pointed to precocious radicalism in another student, but Garrow was unable to document any activism by the future president until his arrival at Occidental College (88).

Obama's sophomore-year roommate, a committed Marxist, quickly converted Obama to the faith. Subsequently, one classmate identified him as "some species of GQ Marxist," and another recalled an argument in which Barack Obama advocated for "a simple-minded version of Marxist theory" (Garrow 2017, 120–121, 123, 127–129). As a senior at Columbia University, Obama attended the "inaugural Socialist Scholars Conference" in 1983 (158). Obama found his off-campus political footing as a community organizer for the Calumet Community Religious Conference which was founded in part to pressure the federal government to bail out the collapsing Chicago steel industry (Garrow 2017, chap. 4). He tersely summarized his business editing career prior to community organizing as teaching him about the "coldness of capitalism" (180). In his first campaign for elected office in 1996, Obama would share a stage with the "quietly Marxisant" sociologist William Julius Wilson at a Chicago meeting of the Democratic Socialists of America (Sugrue 2010, 74). Wilson ([1987] 2012), arguably Obama's most important pre-presidency domestic policy influence, advocated national economic planning (NEP hereafter) policies and a jobs guarantee to solve the social problems associated with urban deindustrialization.

Given this background, how did Obama come to believe, as reported by Leonhardt (2008), "There is a connection between the freedom of the marketplace and freedom more generally" and "The market is the best mechanism ever invented for efficiently allocating resources to maximize production?" Prior to Garrow (2017), journalistic accounts and scholarship speculated that Obama's encounters with Austan Goolsbee and Cass Sunstein during his lectureship at the University of Chicago Law School (UCLS hereafter) moved him toward skepticism of government-directed "structural economic transformation" (Sugrue 2010, 70–71; Leonhardt 2008; Peters 2012). Sugrue (2010, 57, 70–72) holds that former President Obama's studies at Harvard Law School (HLS hereafter) had essentially no consequences for his understanding of urban socioeconomic problems. In what follows, I argue that neither claim is plausible in light of a close reading of Barack Obama's policy writings as a third-year law student (3L hereafter), originally drafted in 1991 with his friend and law school classmate Robert M. Fisher, also a 3L, as chapters for an unpublished policy manifesto.

The manuscripts (the HLS manuscript(s) hereafter) remained obscure until their popularization by Shenk (2022a, b) in a *New York Times* op-ed and book. I obtained a copy of the HLS manuscripts, which I digitized and closely read. They consist of the following four documents:

1. A marked-up book outline, called "OUTLINE–TRANSFORMATIVE POLITICS" (Fisher and Obama 1991a hereafter)
2. A tentative chapter titled "PLANT CLOSINGS: CREATIVE DESTRUCTION AND THE VIABILITY OF THE REGULATED MARKET" (Fisher and Obama 1991b hereafter).
3. A tentative chapter titled "RACE AND RIGHTS RHETORIC" (Fisher and Obama 1991c hereafter)
4. Minow's (1991) comments on the above three documents.[2]

Contra Sugrue (2010, 70; Leonhardt 2008; Peters 2012), Obama had mastered a particular set of arguments for a more market-oriented approach *before* he arrived at UCLS. Obama and Fisher's pro-market arguments derived primarily from two sources: (1) an empirical reckoning with the political and economic failures of planning in the Soviet Union and (2) then-recent innovations in the philosophy of science as well as the broader Austrian school of economics, a circle of classical liberal economists that emerged in late nineteenth-century Vienna who were later distinguished by their skepticism of econometrics and mathematical economics.

Garrow (2017, 416) first discovered the manifesto, which "unquestionably represented an analytical and political capstone of Barack and Rob's three years of intellectually intense policy debates." In his summary of the manuscripts, Garrow (2017, 416) notes that Fisher and Obama (1991b) "examined plant closings," that is, local deindustrialization, "from neoclassical, Keynesian, and Austrian school economic perspectives." Specifically, Garrow notes that the analysis in Fisher and Obama (1991b), which borrows (and cites) Schumpeter's idea of creative destruction, suggests a degree of skepticism about the feasibility of reindustrialization. Fisher and Obama (1991b) also include arguments against NEPs in general which appear borrowed from Hayek ([1944] 2014; 1948), albeit without citation. Those arguments, if taken seriously, would have led Obama not only to skepticism of reindustrialization but also to recognize "the apparent successes of laissez-faire economics" (Leonhardt 2008) and to ignore much of the advice of his intellectual lodestar Wilson when it came to urban social policy.

This chapter develops the ideas I have discussed earlier across three parts and then concludes. In the next part, I discuss the historical "structural economic transformations" that preoccupied urban social policy analysts of the early 1980s and 1990s (Jargowsky 1997, 117). I review prior evidence showing that Obama essentially accepted Wilson's ([1987] 2012) diagnosis of what was ailing America's cities (Obama 1988; Sugrue 2010; Shenk 2022b). I conclude the first part by contrasting Wilson's policy recommendations with those put forth by the 1980s Austrian school of economics as represented in economist Donald Lavoie's ([1985] 2016) book *National Economic Planning: What Is Left?* (NEPWIL hereafter).

Wilson ([1987] 2012) and Lavoie ([1985] 2016), both originally published between Obama's graduation from Columbia University and start at HLS, set the stage for the second part of this chapter, in which I describe and comment on the HLS manuscripts. Despite a shared concern for racial equality and urban deindustrialization's harms, Fisher and Obama ignored many of Wilson's ([1987] 2012) most radical social policy recommendations and condemned NEPs outright. Lavoie's criticism of contemporary planning proposals and the political deductions arising from that criticism prefigure the conclusions that Fisher and Obama (1991a, b, c) drew several years later, but neither read Lavoie directly.[3] Rather, I argue through their shared reading of similar sources, for example, Hayek ([1944] 2014; 1948) and philosophers of science, particularly Lakatos (1970) and Popper (1972), Fisher and Obama came to the same conclusions as Lavoie about the infeasibility of NEPs and made astonishingly similar political calculations.

In the third part of this chapter, I argue that Fisher and Obama's HLS manuscripts exemplify an emerging neoliberal consensus. In this consensus, policy elites with explicitly leftist commitments accepted Hayekian anti-planning arguments while rejecting laissez-faire because of the latter's potentially antiegalitarian consequences. Obama's engagement with ideas from the philosophy of science and broader Austrian school of economics provides a case study in how political leaders' academic experiences pointed a way forward for the post-Soviet political left but simultaneously limited the range of potential policy responses to long-term socioeconomic dislocations.

ECONOMIC AND SOCIOLOGICAL PERSPECTIVES ON DEINDUSTRIALIZATION AND NEPs

Garrison (1979, 175) found in a set of surveys that at least a quarter of all men graduating high school in the 1970s aspired to work as machine operators (operatives), skilled manual laborers, or unskilled manual laborers. A teenager aspiring to complete high school to obtain work in the local trades or local factory might inspire only a quizzical look today, when the most desired occupation is YouTuber, but throughout the twentieth century substantial fractions of the less educated US male population might expect to spend some time working as operatives or laborers in manufacturing (Goldin 1998, 351–353). This occupational system began to unwind in the mid-1970s after the global oil cartel OPEC suddenly quadrupled oil prices (Bluestone and Harrison 1982; Wilson [1987] 2012, 44). Bluestone and Harrison (1982) argued that outsourcing, foreign trade, automation, and capital mobility would eventually permanently deindustrialize America and consequently disadvantage less-educated male workers even absent future oil shocks.

Urban Deindustrialization as a Historical Structural Economic Transition

Figure 11.1 presents data on the historical urban deindustrialization in the 1970s and 1980s that captured so many analysts' attention. I graph levels of total male manufacturing employment for fifteen historically important metro areas' inner cities in the top part of Panel A, total male manufacturing employment outside of these areas at the bottom part of Panel A, and poverty rates for both areas in Panel B. The United States underwent a sustained deindustrialization in its historical inner-city, losing around 1,000,000 male manufacturing jobs. This corresponded to a sustained increase in the poverty rate for households containing at least one male of around 5 percentage points in the same areas over the entire period.[4] Areas outside of the historical inner-city only shed around 200,000 male manufacturing jobs over the whole period. In these areas, male manufacturing jobs actually increased until 1981. Poverty rates outside of the historical inner-city fell in the 1970s, rose in the mid-1980s, and then fell again to about the same rate as in the early 1970s. A natural interpretation of Figure 11.1 is that urban deindustrialization substantially contributed to the sustained rise in inner-city poverty rates.

The US's historical urban cores were by no means the only areas to lose manufacturing jobs in this time period. For instance, deindustrialization starting in the 1970s in some smaller cities like Youngstown, Ohio contributed to an uninterrupted depopulation that has continued to the present day (Raymond 2021). I focus on deindustrialization in America's historical urban cores because this phenomenon played a critical role in the thought of Obama's mentor Wilson ([1987] 2012). In particular, Wilson argued that urban deindustrialization created a persistent mismatch between recent Black male migrants to the North who had relatively little formal schooling, and the actual jobs available near them, which often required postsecondary education. Just as this mismatch started, the Black middle-class began to move out of the inner-city, geographically segregating the Black community by class (Pattillo [1999] 2013). Deprived of a social "buffer," an isolated, inner-city jobless "underclass" began to form without exposure to mainstream mores or functional institutions. Wilson ([1987] 2012, chap. 2, 103) argues that 1970s and 1980s urban pathologies like rising substance abuse, household collapse,

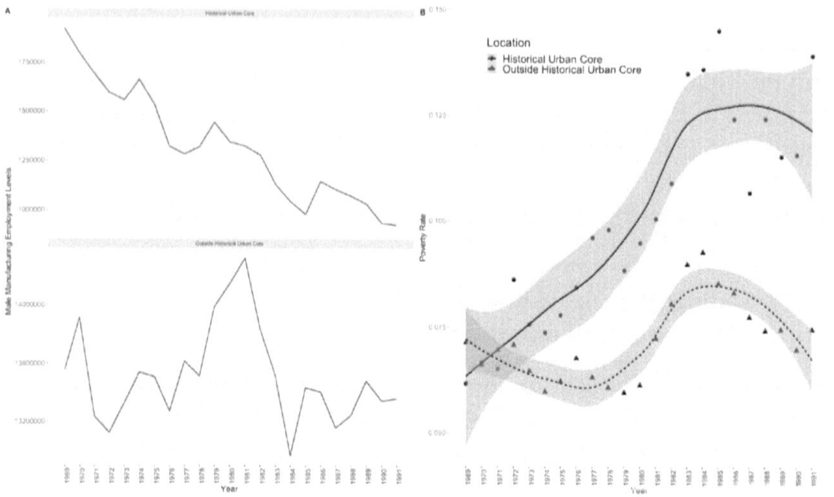

Figure 11.1 Historical Urban Deindustrialization Coincided with the Rise in Inner-City Poverty. Caption: This figure shows the number of prime-aged (19–65) White and Black males working in the manufacturing sector by region from 1969 to 1991. The top part of Panel A shows the number for the US's historical urban core, consisting of inner-city metro areas for Baltimore, Bloomington, Buffalo-Niagara Falls, Chicago, Cleveland, Detroit, Houston, Los Angeles, Minneapolis, New York, Philadelphia, Pittsburgh, St. Louis, San Francisco, and Washington, D.C. The bottom part of Panel A shows the count for the rest of the United States. Around 1,000,000 fewer prime-age White and Black males in the US's historical urban core worked in manufacturing from in 1991 than in 1969. However, over the same period for the same sample population, everywhere outside these historical urban cores only around 300,000 fewer people worked in manufacturing jobs. Panel B presents data on household poverty rates for the same sample population over the same areas. Poverty levels in the historical urban cores of the United States were similar to poverty levels outside of those areas in the late 1960s and early 1970s, but rapidly and substantially diverged over the next two decades. Household poverty rates increased by nearly 5 percentage points in the US's historical urban cores from 1969 to 1991. Poverty rates remained more stable outside these areas, falling during the late 1970s, rising in the mid-1980s and falling again from 1986 to 1991 so that it wound up at nearly the same level as in the late 1960s. In Panel B, 95 percent confidence bands with a loess smoother are traced. *Source*: Michael Lachanski, using data from Flood et al. 2022.

and welfare dependence were driven by *concentration effects* that arose from pockets of jobless young men who were isolated from mainstream institutions and ultimately, social control.

Wilson: NEPs Can Solve Urban Social Problems

What could end America's long urban crisis? Wilson ([1987] 2012, 158) dismissed self-help as a solution for problems in inner-city Black communities because "[P]roblems such as joblessness are so overwhelming and require such a massive effort to restabilize institutions and create a social and economic milieu necessary to sustain such institutions . . . that it is surprising that advocates of black self-help have received so much serious attention from the media and policymakers." Instead, Wilson ([1987] 2012, 152) says that a necessary but not sufficient set of programs would focus on "macroeconomic policy, labor market strategies, and manpower training programs." The latter policy recommendation represents a break from many early 1980s planning advocates like Bluestone and Harrison (1982), Harrington (1982), and Rohatyn (1983), who were skeptical of human capital policies. Wilson ([1987] 2012, 121) ultimately proposed, "[L]ong-term planning to promote both economic growth and sustained full employment, not only in higher-income areas but in areas where the poor are concentrated as well. Such a policy would be designed to promote wage and price stability, favorable employment conditions, and the development and integration of manpower training programs with educational programs." Wilson ([1987] 2012, 155) leaves no doubt about what he means by favorably citing, "Bayard Rustin's plea during the early 1960s that blacks ought to recognize the importance of . . . a system of national economic planning along with education, manpower, and public works programs to help reach full employment."

Wilson's ([1987] 2012, 155) NEP proposal was the centerpiece of his "hidden agenda" strategy "to improve the life chances of truly disadvantaged groups such as the ghetto underclass by emphasizing programs to which the more advantaged groups of all races and class backgrounds can positively relate." Wilson (128) negatively assesses slogans calling for "reparations," or "black control of institutions serving the black community" as derailing more politically robust universal programs that effectively redistribute resources to members of disadvantaged racial, ethnic, and class groupings. Wilson (156) saw the concentration of power that an NEP entails as an opportunity to achieve "a universal program of reform including policies that could effectively address inner-city social dislocations," and à la Rohatyn (1983, 275–276) believed that "a national bargaining structure" could be erected to "achieve sufficient consensus on the program of reform" that he described earlier. Wilson ([1987] 2012, 211n28) wanted the planning process to be insulated from the political process, criticizing those who wanted "governmental involvement in economic reform without stipulating the need for 'rational' intervention, i.e., systematic long-term planning. Most current planning, whether undertaken by the executive branch, by Congress, or by the Federal Reserve, looks no further than the next election. The results speak for themselves."

The Social Science Education of a Future President

Sugrue (2010, 72–80, 84) and Shenk (2022b) argue that William Julius Wilson had a substantial impact on Obama's analysis of urban social problems, but to read Obama's memoirs and Wilson's reflections on his career (Gates 2009; Wilson 2011), neither made a conscious impression on the other. Wilson is neither cited directly nor mentioned by name in Obama's autobiographical trilogy.[5] Wilson planned to provide policy guidance (and presumably vote) for Hillary Clinton in the 2008 Democratic Primary until Barack Obama won the Iowa caucuses (Gates 2009, 15). A dearth of textual evidence on Obama's pre-Senate intellectual life outside of sympathetic journalistic accounts, unsympathetic sources making incredible (and often unverifiable) claims, and autobiography continues to challenge academic historians.

Much of the evidence for Wilson's influence on Obama in Sugrue (2010) comes from Sugrue's interpretation of Obama's semifictional recollections.[6] In Obama's ([1995] 2007, 283) first memoir, Obama wryly has his pastor Reverend Jeremiah Wright denounce Wilson (though unnamed in-text) for the latter's concern about class divisions within the Black community:

> "Some people say," I interrupted, "that the church is too upwardly mobile.
>
> The reverend's smile faded. "That's a lot of bull," he said sharply. "People who talk that mess reflect their own confusion. They've bought into the whole business of class that keeps us from working together. Half of 'em think that any black man with an education or a job, or any church that respects scholarship, is somehow suspect.
>
> "We don't buy into these false divisions here. It's not about income, Barack. Cops don't check my bank account when they pull me over and make me spread-eagle against the car. These miseducated brothers, like that sociologist at the University of Chicago, talking about 'the declining significance of race.' Now, what country is he living in?

Wilson ([1978] 2012), referred to indirectly by the title of his book *The Declining Significance of Race*, claimed that family class inheritance was becoming more determinative of people's life chances than race as such.[7] Despite condemning Wilson's (1978; [1987] 2012) ideas, Wilson's concern about Black geographic and social isolation was clearly shared by Obama's rendering of Reverend Wright, who in this passage and elsewhere exhorted his parishioners to maintain racial solidarity across class lines (Obama [1995] 2007, 284–285). In another irony, just before the aforementioned meeting with Reverend Wright, Obama ([1995] 2007, 281) provides another example of the increasing within-race class segregation that concerned Wilson:[8]

> Tracy, one of Reverend Wright's assistants . . . asked if I wanted some coffee. As I followed her back into a kitchen toward the rear of the church, we began to chat. . . . It had been a difficult year, she said: Her husband had recently died, and in just a few weeks she'd be moving out to the suburbs. She had wrestled long and hard with the decision, for she had lived most of her life in the city. But she had decided the move would be best for her teenage son . . . there were a lot more black families in the suburbs these days; how her son would be free to walk down the street without getting harassed; how the school he'd be attending had music courses, a full band, free instruments and uniforms.

As these passages indicate, Obama accepted Wilson's key diagnosis that class segregation was an important phenomenon and a driver of the Black community's problems in the 1980s.

Sugrue (2010, 76) gives the now standard history of Wilson's influence on Obama: "Using black Chicago as a case study, Wilson highlighted the devastating impact of deindustrialization, offering evidence that jibed with Obama's hands on experience." Sugrue (2010, 80) infers that Obama accepted Wilson's hypothesis that urban deindustrialization was a key driver of declining relative Black fortunes in America from the economic policy and race chapters of Obama's (2006, 245) second memoir. Subsequent events and materials that Sugrue did not have access to at the time of his writing suggest that, if anything, he understated the influence of Wilson on Obama.

For instance, in Obama's (2020) most recent memoir, he argues that the "changes that were sweeping not just Chicago but cities across the country" arose from "the decline of manufacturing" and "the rise of a discrete and disconnected underclass." Garrow (2017, 286) discovered that Obama first spoke to Wilson during a Q&A session at a Harvard Divinity School conference at which Wilson was the "lunchtime speaker" called "The Disadvantaged Among the Disadvantaged."[9] While ambling in Cambridge after the conference's conclusion, Obama told his boss, Jerry Kellman, that he was planning on leaving community organizing essentially because he had been convinced by both Wilson and his own experience that "community organizing was not an effective means for attaining large-scale change" and "problems like joblessness and bad public schools were 'citywide issues, statewide issues, national issues.'"[10] Indeed, Obama's Chicago community organizing career coincided with a project to match employers with employees that "failed to find work for even one applicant" (Garrow 2017, 207–208, 223, 286), suggesting a deficit of jobs for less-educated workers rather than a matching problem that could be solved by a third party. Garrow's account is supported by a leaked typescript of Obama ([1995] 2004), titled *Claims of Inheritance* ([1993?], 352–353), in which Obama's extremely negative assessment of his own community organizing essentially takes Wilson's explanation of why local problems were insurmountable by community-level self-help for granted:

> The sun was now slipping behind a cloud. . . . I'd been feeling run down for some time now. More than run down: I felt defeated. I knew that not much had changed in the neighborhood on account of my presence; that those changes that I had helped bring about were always too partial, too localized, too little too late. . . . We found a job for one youth, only to find another ten-thousand in need of the same. We'd had no effect on . . . foreign trade policy or middle-class flight from the city.

Although Wilson's analysis was based on a close study of Chicago, he also concluded that since deindustrialization in America's historical urban cores was a national-level phenomenon, only national or state-level policy changes could reverse the local social problems that manufacturing job losses and class segregation were engendering. As Obama rose in the world, his relationship with Wilson changed from devotee to acquaintance and colleague. Obama and Wilson would continue to discuss these issues at Harvard University's "Saguaro Seminars" hosted by Robert Putnam throughout the 1990s. These seminars were intended to bring together academics, activists, columnists, and politicians for policy discussion. Before Obama's election to the Senate in 2004, it is also not difficult to find more casual contacts between Obama and Wilson at mutual friends' parties and conferences (Garrow 2017, 563, 592, 620, 632–633).[11]

As we have shown, Obama essentially accepted Wilson's diagnosis of America's urban pathologies and persistent social problems. He also rejected self-help and nongovernmental solutions to inner-city social problems. Still, in his pre-presidential political career he evinced little interest in NEPs, job guarantees, or reindustrialization policies. Unsurprisingly, his rise was viciously condemned by left-wing poverty scholars. For example, Marxist scholar Adolph Reed Jr. ([1996] 2000) lambasted Obama as "a smooth Harvard lawyer with impeccable do-good credentials and vacuous-to-repressive neoliberal politics" after his 1996 election to the state Senate. Given his background, why did Obama not see reindustrialization or Wilson's preferred solution, an NEP, as viable in either his public writings or pre-presidential political career (Obama 2006, chap. 5–7)? To understand the case against reindustrialization and NEPs circa the 1980s, I turn to Lavoie ([1985] 2016).

Lavoie ([1985] 2016) on Planning Problems and the Irrelevance of Deindustrialization

Although not a direct influence on Obama, Lavoie ([1985] 2016, 1) aimed to influence leftist policymakers' responses to deindustrialization in particular and their assessments of planning in general. Lavoie ([1985] 2016, xv) described NEPWIL as a synthesis and application of ideas from earlier Austrian school economists Mises ([1922] 1981) and Hayek ([1944] 2014; 1948) to then contemporary planning proposals. Lavoie ([1985] 2016, 2) defines economic planning as "[P]olicy measures that involve concentrating power to shape the economy in a special government agency" ranging from "Japan's Ministry of International Trade and Industry (MITI)" to "an ambitious socialist attempt to run the whole economy." Planning "is not distinguished from" impersonal markets or the traditional, hunter-gathering and peasant forms of economy "by the presence of rational planning of some kind, which is found in all human societies, but by its intention of subsuming the whole of social production under a single rational plan" (29). Originally, planning entailed "the complete abolition not only of private ownership of the means of production, but also markets, prices, and even money. These institutions were all to be replaced by . . . administrative control of the whole production process by a single hierarchical agency" (3–4). Lavoie (3–4, 228) notes that nearly all NEP proposals and implementations had abandoned this ambition after catastrophic attempts to do so in the early Soviet Union, but goes on to argue that even more limited NEPs, for example, industrial policy, will suffer from the same flaws that doomed the Soviet experiment.[12]

Lavoie ([1985] 2016, chap. 5–6) argues that any NEP will suffer from three weaknesses compared to the market process as a resource allocation mechanism. The first weakness is that the concentration of political power entailed in a NEP creates opportunities for government abuse. Lavoie ([1985] 2016, 20, 44–45, 99) calls this the "totalitarian problem." An entity with authority over all resources could eliminate any known internal opposition by preventing them from consuming resources until they died. Even an entity with coercive authority over only some resources at its creation may not be "able in practice to avoid degenerating into political tyranny" (7, 140, 156). An initially uncorrupt planning authority would prove an irresistible target for capture and eventual corruption by entities outside of it (20–3, 44, 99, 140). Lavoie ([1985] 2016, 4, 21, 24, 44) points out that the totalitarian problem was generally recognized since at least Hayek ([1944] 2014).

The second weakness, relative to markets, is that NEPs are wasteful. The knowledge required for individual rational planning in a market process is often inarticulate, and only revealed through impersonal exchange; it cannot be extracted by a third party, for example, a planner (Lavoie [1985] 2016, chap. 2–3, esp. 5). Attempts to plan prove "utterly disastrous" because any "central planning board, even if very well intentioned, would lack the knowledge to combine resources in a way that is economic enough to sustain modern technology" (20, 52). Even limited attempts by a planning agency to "steer the Market toward particular outcomes are really blind and dangerous obstructions of the very source of that knowledge," the competitive process between entrepreneurs, "which is essential to rational economic decision-making" (Lavoie [1985] 2016, 56–57). This is the "knowledge problem." Since ex-ante "no single agent can be trusted to be able to identify consistently particular instances of . . . where government planning is known to be able to do better," NEPs cannot allocate resources more effectively than the market (74). As Obama concluded in his interview with Leonhardt (2008), government control over economic activity can never be justified on ex-ante productivity grounds.

Lavoie cites advances in the philosophy of science by Lakatos (1970) and Popper (1972) to argue that the knowledge required for rational planning is "tacit" and "personal," so "the data" required by a hypothetical well intentioned central planning board "do not exist" in an exploitable form (Lavoie [1985] 2016, 55–59). Lavoie argues by analogy: just as scientists conjecture, experiment, and reason to discover what is true, and then communicate their findings at conferences, entrepreneurs coordinate production in the society through competitive bidding on goods and services.[13] Prices set by competition communicate entrepreneurial discoveries about the multiple potential productive uses (and relative scarcity) of resources to the rest of the society. Attempting to render all scientific knowledge legible by a bureaucracy would shut down the scientific process because much of what scientists know is "inarticulate" (Lavoie [1985] 2016, 78, 80, 83).

Lavoie ([1985] 2016, 1 2, 12, 232–236, 239–241) also argues that NEPs are incompatible with the aims of the political left, insofar as it is a movement dedicated to human emancipation and solving "such difficult human problems as poverty, disease, and environmental decay," reducing "escalating crime and taxes," and increasing "tolerance of nontraditional life-styles." Lavoie (52) finds that the "knowledge problem" and "totalitarian problem" are so deleterious as to rule out achieving these goals. I call this third weakness the "sociopolitical problem" as Lavoie does not name it in the book. Clearly, the existence and insolubility of the sociopolitical problem hinge on Lavoie's definition of leftism. Indeed, Lavoie (1–2, 52) explicitly rules out an egalitarian distribution of wealth as a policy objective for the left, interpreting attempts to abolish "gross inequalities of wealth and income . . . as popular means favored for their presumed ability to achieve other more fundamental ends."[14]

Most of the concrete NEPs challenged in NEPWIL were motivated by (then mostly urban) U.S. deindustrialization.[15] Whether consisting of reindustrialization policies, guaranteed employment schemes, wage and price controls, or national bargaining proposals, Lavoie assessed the NEPs he reviewed as so "utterly counterproductive that literally doing nothing and preserving—but at least not aggravating–all our current problems would be preferable" (201). Lavoie singles out Rohatyn's (1983) case for reindustrialization based on the benefits that such policies generate for cities as a clear case of "special pleading" especially worthy of criticism (183). Lavoie counters Rohatyn: the apparent decline of cities in the Northeast arising from urban deindustrialization may not be harmful to the overall economy as capital is redeployed elsewhere. Deindustrialization has no special economic significance.

The sharp divergence between how Lavoie and Wilson saw deindustrialization and NEPs was probably shaped in large part by how the fields of economics and sociology see the world. In a 2020 email, Wilson confirmed that no arguments or events changed his mind about NEPs. Rather, he stopped advocating NEPs because private discussions with mainstream economists at Harvard University and the University of Chicago convinced him that they would be difficult to publicly defend. Similarly, Lavoie and Wilson's visions for the political left were opposed. Particularly illustrative of their clashing visions is their conflicting analysis of the 1960s federal welfare payment expansion. Wilson ([1987] 2012, 150–152, 185–186) finds no strong negative effects of the 1960s welfare payments' expansion in his literature review. Wilson concludes that transfer payments should be preserved and even expanded on this basis. Lavoie ([1985] 2016, 148, 153) argues that no strong positive effects of the welfare transfer programs have been documented, and (one infers) they should be disfavored on this basis.[16]

ON THE SOCIAL POLICY EDUCATION OF A FUTURE PRESIDENT

Perhaps because Obama has not revealed his undergraduate transcripts and publicly downplayed the importance of his legal education, journalistic and scholarly accounts prior to Garrow (2017) uniformly neglected the role of Obama's pre-UCLS educational and work experiences in forming his pro-market outlook (Sugrue 2010; McClelland 2010; Garrow 2017, 155–156, 416–417, 532). Instead, absent textual evidence, many journalists and researchers naturally guessed that Obama's market-oriented turn arose from his experiences at UCLS, which had a reputation for hiring and fostering market-friendly scholars. Sugrue (2010, 70–72) summarizes the conventional wisdom:

> For three years, Obama had been cloistered at Harvard, and there is no indication that his legal education there was formative for his understanding of urban inequality and poverty. But his new intellectual home, the University of Chicago, would be. . . . His closest colleague was law professor Cass Sunstein, a prominent advocate of "judicial minimalism" (focusing on a narrow reading of cases, unencumbered by sweeping legal principles) . . . Obama befriended his future economic policy adviser Austan Goolsbee, an MIT-educated scholar of taxation and regulation, whose version of neoclassical economics was well within the mainstream of the profession. . . . Neither Sunstein nor Goolsbee had

much to say about race and public policy, though it is likely that their regulatory gradualism (emphasizing incremental policies over sweeping legal change or structural economic transformation) influenced Obama.

Peters (2012, 4) connects Obama's experience as "a professor (lecturer and senior lecturer) in the Law School at Chicago" to his purported embrace of "the ethos of the free market." He goes on to report that "some commentators have indicated" that Obama "is sympathetic to the Chicago school [*sic*] economics as a result of his days at the University of Chicago." If true, this would explain Obama's rejection of reindustrialization and NEPs, as the Chicago school of economics had a well-developed set of critiques of these policies. The problem with narratives that center UCLS faculty networks as the source of Obama's market-friendly turn is simply a lack of any concrete evidence. Obama published no scholarly work while at UCLS. Kantor (2008) summarizes her reporting on Obama's career at UCLS as follows: "[I]f teaching alongside some of the most formidable conservative minds in the country had any impact on Mr. Obama, no one can quite point to it."[17]

Garrow's (2017) comprehensive research into Obama's educational and work history uncovered no hidden connection between his experiences as a faculty member at UCLS and his opinions on NEPs, reindustrialization, or urban policy, but made a number of discoveries relevant for understanding Obama's turn away from his youthful embrace of Marxism. For instance, Obama's last class at Columbia University was on "State Socialist Societies" by sociologist Andrew Walder. Walder, who was described by one student as "anything but a Marxist," taught that actually existing socialist societies were plagued by arbitrary inequalities, political repression, and high mortality rates (154–155). Unfortunately, little of Obama's academic writing from either that class or his undergraduate education has been retained. This makes it difficult to verify Obama's public account to Leonhardt (2008) of his intellectual development, in which he emphasized that he tried "to synthesize approaches" of "both sides" of the "ideological competition between a social-democratic or even socialist agenda and a free-market, Milton Friedman agenda." For instance, no external evidence supports Obama's 2008 claim to *Time*, recounted in Garrow (2017, 1049) that he "was reading Milton Friedman and Friedrich Hayek" as an undergraduate. In a heated presidential race, Obama would have had strong incentives to make claims like this as an olive branch to right-of-center voters who might otherwise have been hesitant to vote for a presidential nominee with a genuine (though perhaps weakly held) Marxist pedigree.

Given the evidential gaps in Obama's intellectual trajectory, it is startling that Garrow's (2017, 432–434, 449–453) discovery of Fisher and Obama's drafts for a never-published book attracted almost no academic attention prior to Shenk (2022a; 2022b). Garrow (2017, 452, 432) assesses Fisher and Obama's proposal, which Fisher described as "very much a product of both of our minds," as providing "significant insight into how more than two years' worth of almost daily debates had shaped" their "thinking about a great many social and political questions." The HLS manuscripts constitute the most intense written pre-presidency engagement by Obama with both the social science of his time and public policy outside of his heavily edited autobiographies (Shenk 2022a; 2022b).

Robert Fisher, a Ph.D. economist from Duke University obtaining a second advanced degree, and Barack Obama had become fast friends from their first class as 1Ls, bonding over their relatively advanced age and worldliness as well as a shared love of basketball (Garrow 2017, 331–332, 338). Prior to attending HLS, Fisher (1986) published a well-received volume arguing that Lakatos's (1976) philosophy of science, originally applied to physics, also explained progress in economics. Fisher was familiar with the Austrian school of economics because he specialized in the history of economic thought and comparative economic systems at Duke. For instance, Fisher cited Mises's ([1962] 2012) final monograph in his 1986 book because he assessed it as a comparatively recent work developing the approach to marginal analysis pioneered by Menger, c.f. Jaffé (1976).

As Fisher and Obama entered their third year of law school, they used their coursework in a seminar on "Civil Society" taught by Mary Ann Glendon, Martha Minow, and Todd Rakoff to "pursue an idea they had been discussing for more than a year: to coauthor an intensely analytical book examining several present-day policy problems and critiquing overly ideological approaches to them" (Garrow 2017, 425). Closely supervised by then-Professor Martha Minow, over the course of 1991, Obama and Fisher drafted hundreds of pages for what "they hoped could become a coauthored book" tentatively titled "Transformative Politics" or "Promises of Democracy: Hopeful Critiques of American Ideology" (432, 454, 466).

By the time he graduated, Obama and his closest friend had in hand at least two long chapters and an outline for a book on America's economic, political, and social problems. The economic surplus generated by the end of the Cold War and the renewed enthusiasm for anti-poverty policy generated by Wilson ([1987] 2012) created entrepreneurial opportunities for social policy analysts (Wacquant 2022). As he was graduating HLS, Obama was contacted by Douglas Baird, a professor at UCLS, to work as a fellow on a book tackling "race-related issues such as voting rights" and civil rights, broadly construed (Garrow 2017, 454–455). That book would never see publication. After accepting Baird's offer to take a "Law and Government" Fellowship at UCLS, Obama later "perplexed" his colleagues by using his time there to instead work on his first memoir (Garrow 2017, 454, 466). Fisher, on the other hand, would go on to have a demanding and successful career as an economist and lawyer in the civil service. The HLS manuscripts would remain undiscovered in Fisher's family home for decades as Obama rose. In a 2020 email correspondence, Garrow stated that the manuscripts were found by Fisher's mother sometime between 2013 and 2014.

What Obama Learned at Harvard

In the HLS manuscripts Fisher and Obama (1991b) argue the following: (i) NEPs are both incompatible with political liberalism and generally wasteful, (ii) the process of creative destruction generates enormous general benefits and concentrated (but usually smaller in the aggregate) costs, (iii) the problems of racial inequality can be ameliorated without top-down economic planning and (iv) NEPs are not a viable policy for a resurgent left. The manuscript arguments (i) and (ii) imply that Fisher and Obama did not believe the reindustrialization policies were efficient and thought that NEPs were unlikely to achieve their objectives at a reasonable cost. Because they were drafted in the Spring of 1991, these manuscripts confirm that Obama's market-friendly turn occurred before he arrived at UCLS.

Fisher and Obama on the Importance of Deindustrialization

As shown in Figure 11.1, male manufacturing employment had changed little from the late 1960s outside of the US's historical urban cores, albeit with some wild swings along the way. Fisher and Obama (1991b, 1–3) interpret this data as showing Bluestone and Harrison's (1982) reports on the death of American manufacturing were greatly exaggerated. Manufacturing, both in terms of total output and as a fraction of GDP, had increased from its 1982 trough. On an annualized basis, the manufacturing employment decline for the nation as a whole was small.

Fisher and Obama (1991b, 4–5) nonetheless agree with Wilson's analysis when they write that "Economic, social, and health problems appeared to worsen considerably in areas of concentrated poverty, particularly in the inner cities" and, like Wilson, they ask what "periods of economic transition teach us about social policy more generally?" Section VII of Fisher and Obama (1991b, 42), devoted to "The Negative Externalities of Plant Closings," discusses how community-level disruption arising from manufacturing shutdowns can trigger a "downward spiral" of "labor flight," "social unrest," and "growing crime." Still, Fisher and Obama (1991b) do not seriously consider NEPs, nationalization, or bailouts as recommended in Bluestone and Harrison (1982, 248), Bowles, Gordon, and Weisskopf (1983), who they favorably cite, or Wilson ([1987] 2012).

Fisher and Obama (1991b, 12–13) did not explain why these are not viable options, but it is not difficult for the reader to infer why they would be skeptical of government-directed reindustrialization from their summary of the Austrian school's analysis of plant closings:

> Those who myopically focus upon the destruction entailed by the closing of a plant avert their gaze from the creative half of the story. . . . But one plant's closing is another's opening as capital is redeployed to other places and other sectors of the economy. Undoubtedly communities that lose a plant have a narrowly-conceived incentive to oppose the mobility of that capital, but that same community has been and continues to be the beneficiary of the mobility maintained in the rest of the economy. . . . Even though one community may lose relative to the others, they are all clear gainers relative to the impoverished, feudal world we would inhabit if we lacked resource mobility.

In other words, federal policy to achieve urban (or regional) reindustrialization constitutes "special pleading" as argued years earlier by Lavoie ([1985] 2016, 183). In Fisher and Obama's (1991b) telling, plant closings are a regional problem. Recall that for Wilson, the concentrated poverty induced by urban deindustrialization explained the subsequent and persistent rise in inner-city poverty and motivated increasing government control of the economy. Figure 11.1's Panels A and B represent a causal relationship offering an opportunity for policy intervention. For Lavoie, by contrast, there is no necessary connection between the data presented in Panels A and B in Figure 11.1. Even if they were connected, this could simply represent the market process generating value elsewhere in the economy. Fisher and Obama split the difference: they recognize the disruptiveness of community-level deindustrialization à la Wilson while agreeing with Lavoie that local deindustrialization might also be generating value elsewhere in the economy.

Economic and Political Problems with NEPs as a Policy Solution for Social Problems

All three of NEPWIL's arguments against NEPs—the sociopolitical problem, totalitarian problem, and knowledge problem—are presented in Fisher and Obama (1991b). It is easiest to start with the conclusion. Fisher and Obama (1991b, 84) conclude that "markets are not only necessary, but in fact must be more consciously employed to serve the needs of the people." They implore "the left" to "grasp the historical situation" so it can once again become a catalyst "of social progress." Like Lavoie, they find that "There is nothing intrinsically conservative about recognizing the powers of the market and putting them to use to better serve the community. In fact, nothing could be more radical." On the final page of the chapter, Fisher and Obama (1991b, 99) conclude that "if the Left could understand and embrace this harsh economic constraint on our collective freedom" then leftists could focus their "energy on the real social battleground . . . to the benefit of all." Why did Fisher and Obama come to agree with Lavoie on the insolubility of the sociopolitical problem? They come to this conclusion because they also agree with Lavoie's analysis of the totalitarian problem and knowledge problem. I cover each in turn.

Fisher and Obama (1991b, 92–93) argue for the egalitarianism of the market system compared to planning because "rationing techniques other than the market" prevent "the socially disadvantaged" from purchasing the goods they want. Central planning's "nondemocratic nature" requires the "brutal repression of any dissent" (Fisher and Obama 1991b, 84, 90). As noted by Lavoie ([1985] 2016, 4), even advocates of NEPs were sometimes aware of the challenges they posed to liberal democratic political systems because of their tendency to concentrate power. Fisher and Obama's (1991b, c) recognition of the totalitarian problem is thus routine rather than noteworthy.

More impressively, Fisher and Obama were aware of the knowledge problem (although they did not use Lavoie's neologism). Fisher and Obama (1991b, 5) start with a standard exposition of the price system as "determining not only what is produced, but who, where, how and with what production occurs" so that "a debate about plant closings really translates into a debate about how well prices do their job of coordinating productive activity," but conclude the essay with a nineteen-page argument that leftists should abandon NEPs because the knowledge problem makes NEPs wasteful or infeasible. Fisher and Obama (1991b, 87–88) obliquely refer to Mises ([1920] 1935), writing that "prior to the Soviet Union" economists "declared that a planned economy was an impossibility." Although central planners "can't solve" the computational problems inherent to planning the economy in detail, Fisher and Obama conclude that the Soviet experience showed that large-scale planning was possible though undesirable. In the Soviet context it mostly "failed miserably" outside of a few industries like defense because with "no market and no consumer check on quality," consumers and planners alike had to rely on inefficient gray and "black market" barter to get the goods needed for both consumption and production (88). The market's "peculiar combination of flexibility and efficiency" compared to NEPs arises via its use of price "signals" that "carry information rapidly and efficiently throughout the economy to decentralized decision makers who respond quickly" (84, 91, 95). In an argument clearly borrowed from Hayek (Caldwell 1997), Fisher and Obama conclude that markets "transform society itself into a calculating device" to solve the knowledge problem (Fisher and Obama 1991b, 94–95). Fisher and Obama (1991b, 11) defend "entrepreneurial conjectures . . . tested not by feudal tradition or guild committee but by the demands of the market" with an elaborate analogy to "scientific conjectures . . . tested not by scholastic authority but by immanent reality." The resemblance to Lavoie's ([1985] 2016, 83–84) analogy of the entrepreneur and scientist likely arises from their shared reading of Lakatos (1970) and Popper (1972). Thus, Fisher and Obama recapitulate all three of the problems that Lavoie ([1985] 2016) described with NEP proposals and make the same analogy between the competitive process and scientific discovery.

Origins of Anti-planning Arguments in the HLS Manuscripts

Fisher and Obama (1991b) do a fair job of summarizing the position of the Austrian school in the "socialist calculation debate," but do not cite any of the authors involved in the debate on either side directly (Caldwell 1997, 1858, 1876). Fisher and Obama (1991b, 8) refer to the "Austrian school's leading economist, Joseph Schumpeter" but Schumpeter is not the sole source of their anti-NEP arguments (1991b, c).[18] Although not cited in Fisher (1986) or the HLS manuscripts, Fisher confirmed in a 2021 phone call that he read Hayek ([1944] 2014) closely as an undergraduate at Duke and encountered a variety of anti-NEP arguments, including Hayek's description of the knowledge problem, as a research assistant working on a project studying how the Soviet economy worked. Thus, the resemblance of Fisher and Obama's arguments against NEPs to Lavoie's appears to be a case of parallel evolution based on a shared reading of the same sources, especially Hayek, Lakatos, and Popper. Writing in a similar domestic political context, they came to the same conclusions as Lavoie about the compatibility of leftism and planning: markets are more compatible with social progress because they are not as vulnerable to the totalitarian problem and more efficiently solve the knowledge problem than planning. These criticisms of planning appeared vindicated by the then-collapsing Soviet Union's failure to solve either problem across its 70-year existence.

OBAMA AND THE LIMITED APPEAL OF LAISSEZ-FAIRE FOR POLITICAL ENTREPRENEURS

Fisher and Obama (1991a, b, c) developed a nuanced political program that accepted the logic of Wilson's hidden agenda (in some cases) but remained compatible with what they saw as the requirements of a market society and retaining the benefits generated by creative destruction. As might be surmised from the previous discussion of NEPs, Fisher and Obama's (1991b, 99) different understanding of the market system led them to diverge from Wilson in their policy recommendations. Contrast Wilson's ([1987] 2012, 121) call for a NEP to ensure "wage and price stability" with the following "minimum" requirements of the market system that Fisher and Obama (1991b, 99) list, which include: "free exchange over a large area," "relatively flexible prices, wages, and interest rates," "relative mobility of capital and labor," and "allocative decision-making in highly decentralized profit-seeking units." In general, Fisher and Obama's minimum requirements would lead them to reject legal changes or government interventions prohibiting free exchange, freezing prices or wages, freezing capital or labor, or attempting to eliminate the profit motive. None of the concrete NEP proposals analyzed by Lavoie ([1985] 2016, 99–103, 154–156, 197–198) would satisfy the minimum criterion Fisher and Obama list. In other words, Obama had already adopted ideas that would naturally lead him to skepticism of concrete proposals for government-directed economic transformation and Wilson's NEP proposals in particular by the time he left Harvard.

Neoliberalism, Laissez-faire, and the "Hidden Agenda"

Although they shared Lavoie's skepticism of NEPs, Fisher and Obama also rejected Lavoie's ([1985] 2016, 241) "radical vision of the free market and a free society." Rather than laissez-faire, Fisher and Obama (1991b, 82, emphasis in original) implored the left to consider "possibilities of social control THROUGH the market." They elaborate that leftists should "promote more inclusive and democratic markets" which can then be used "as a weapon to wield in the best interests of the people." An exploration of what Fisher and Obama's brand of market-oriented leftism entailed contributes to our understanding of how elite institutions and networks shaped future policymakers' responses to persistent, racially charged urban social issues without upsetting the then-emerging neoliberal consensus.[19] Here, I use the term "neoliberal" to capture a tendency on the political left characterized by an empirical bent, a commitment to the use of markets as a policy instrument for solving social problems in post-industrial economies, and a recognition that NEPs were infeasible. Boas and Gans-Morse (2009, 145, 157) incisively point out that in its contemporary academic usage, "neoliberalism conveys little common substantive meaning but serves as a clear indicator that one does not evaluate free markets positively." Rather than being a term of abuse, my usage of the term neoliberal is meant to capture its historical usage that "emphasized humanistic values, a preoccupation with social welfare, and moderation vis-à-vis classical liberalism" characterized by "its rejection of laissez-faire policies" (148, 145).

Fisher and Obama (1991b, 99) conclude that even though NEPs are infeasible, and prosperity requires that the "bulk of national production" be allocated through markets, a broad range of interventions are economically feasible, can solve social problems, and reduce racial inequalities. In

Lavoie's ([1985] 2016, 146) telling, "victims of racism and sexism" should prefer laissez-faire over social democracy because they "would like to live unmolested in a prosperous economy, just as much as anyone else." Fisher and Obama (1991c, 3) simply reject this logic as "as an impediment, to genuine equality" because "liberty for the majority has frequently meant black confinement in inferior schools or menial jobs . . . the 'private order' has effectively served to preserve such racial oppression." In other words, leftists might prefer racial (or any identity category) equality as an end in-and-of itself, and this preference immediately leads them away from laissez-faire. If Wilson's ([1987] 2012) specific NEP proposal aimed at redistributing resources to the mostly African-American ghetto poor was rightly regarded as infeasible circa the early 1990s, what alternatives did Fisher and Obama propose to reduce the racial inequalities that they saw at the center of so many social problems?

Rejecting Wilson's means did not entail rejecting his ends. Fisher and Obama (1991c, 85) agreed with Wilson that the "common good—whether expressed in terms of a competitive America or renewed safety in public spaces—requires a large-scale commitment of resources to the black inner city." Nor did Fisher and Obama (1991c, 126) reject Wilson's ([1987] 2012, 121–124) political analysis: they agreed that straightforward redistribution of resources from Whites to Blacks in a time of economic contraction is politically infeasible, writing that, "[W]hites would today be willing to assist in workable programs for bringing blacks into the mainstream, but . . . the real contraction of their own opportunities over the past two decades . . . makes any redistributionist program that would take money from their pockets seem increasingly threatening." Fisher and Obama (1991c, 55) argue that "working class whites who have been most vociferous in their opposition to affirmative action" do so out of "an accurate assessment that they are the most likely to lose in any redistributionist game." On the same page, they summarize more sophisticated critics as worrying about the totalitarian problem because a "program of increased equality" would "manifest itself in a government bureaucracy that really does erode the freedoms of all individuals." Therefore, to achieve the redistribution that they want, Fisher and Obama (1991c, 124) embrace the logic of Wilson's hidden agenda, urging "[B]lacks to use class as a proxy for race in the political arena." On the other hand, Fisher and Obama (1991c, 137) argue that, with an intersectional strategy combining race, sex, and class-anxieties, the left can more successfully agitate for both hidden and not so hidden resource transfers to members of its coalition, "[E]fforts to increase levels of welfare support for poor blacks should continue to be an important civil rights goal in the near future. . . . We should be shifting our programmatic emphasis on those programs that can lead to long-term employment opportunity, and begin the process of meshing black employment concerns with such issues as comparable worth, worker ownership, and industrial restructuring that appeal to the interests of other groups."

Human Capital Policy as Political Economy Panacea

Boas and Gans-Morse (2009, 157) insightfully point out that an alternative usage of the term "neoliberalism" might focus on "the multiple features of today's liberal models that set them apart from their predecessors, including . . . knowledge-based forms of property . . . the emergence of large service sectors in the developed world." Indeed, the latter's "emergence" in America's historical urban cores coincided with a disappearance of manufacturing jobs that left many less-educated men, especially Black men, without work that would allow them to provide for a then-normative two-parent household with children.

Neoliberal commitments rule out NEPs as a redistributionist vehicle to address urban social problems via reindustrialization or a jobs guarantee. As Fisher and Obama (1991c, 54–56) lament, direct resource transfers to client groups can be politically difficult to sustain (Shenk 2022b, chap. 8). Absent NEPs and direct resource transfers, human capital policy emerged as an alternative vehicle for government interventions aimed at equalizing outcomes and solving social problems arising from major socioeconomic transitions (Tyack 1974; Groeger 2021). Thus, Fisher and Obama (1991b, 79) conclude that the "ultimate answer to plant closings . . . lies in making workers more flexible, and their human capital more transferable" so that workers "can move from one employment to another." Commenting on the proposal, Minow (1991, 2) asks whether, "[S]chooling as a set of vouchers that can be used to retool workers throughout their life times?" might prove a worthy addition to the policies they suggest. In this worldview education also holds the key to reducing conflicts and social problems. Fisher and Obama (1991c, 118, emphasis in original) write that "Affirmative action at the university level can only supplement, and not replace, the foundational skills that children receive in earlier years. The more explicitly we focus on those early years, and close the gap in educational achievement between black and white primary and secondary school students, the more we will drain away the bitterness and contentiousness surrounding affirmative action." Fisher and Obama's (1991c, 120–121) plans for achieving this objective is to propose a political strategy that will lead, "African-Americans to reconsider their role in making their schools effective. . . . Black parents will need to ask themselves whether they are willing to forego the hiring of talented and qualified white teachers." From this perspective, Wilson ([1987] 2012), who advocated for pairing education and workforce training with NEPs, looks like a bridge from the earlier writers concerned with deindustrialization (Bluestone and

Harrison 1982; Harrington 1982; Rohatyn 1983) who had remarkably little faith in the power of human capital investments to solve the US's social and political problems to Fisher and Obama (1991a), who apparently wanted to add an additional chapter on public education to the HLS manuscripts.

CONCLUSIONS: LEFTISM AFTER HAYEK

Fisher and Obama were not particularly interested in market organization because of any *a priori* philosophical commitment. Rather, they were persuaded that alternatives like NEPs appeared undemocratic, costly, and possibly infeasible. For the loose network of neoliberals, arguments made by the Austrian school of economics were not persuasive when it came to transfer payments or government interventions generally. The neoliberal policy consensus in the developed world consisted primarily of government taxation to supply individuals with basic needs, limited, rule-of-law based intervention in goods, labor, and financial markets to ameliorate specific harms rather than to achieve a particular pattern of production, and a general commitment to a vision of human emancipation without traditional national, religious, or tribal constraints (Boas and Gans-Morse 2009; Lindsey, Teles, Wilkinson, and Hammond 2018). Starting in the 1960s, politicians and populations often conceptualized their challenges to this consensus as a means to address the social problems induced by the transition to a post-industrial economy. Obama's intellectual journey provides a case study of how rising elite policymakers responded to one set of left-wing anti-liberal criticisms engendered by this economic restructuring. In the case of Obama, by the time he graduated HLS, he had absorbed a powerful set of arguments against specific reindustrialization proposals and NEPs in general.

There are three major takeaways. First, academic networks were key to the spread of neoliberal concepts and contentions. Former President Obama's educational experiences were mostly ignored prior to Garrow (2017). Instead, where scholars broached the subject of Obama's outlook on markets, they often substituted plausible conjectures about the role of Obama's teaching at UCLS in shaping his ideas absent specific evidence. Future research should explore the role of academic experiences in shaping the economic outlook of politicians.

Second, the broader Austrian school of economics gave Obama a set of policy analytics that enabled him to reject NEPs and reindustrialization as wasteful or infeasible. When it came to how policymakers should think about and respond to urban deindustrialization, these arguments proved decisive. Yet, Obama did not embrace laissez-faire. Why? Lavoie's arguments in NEP-WIL essentially argue that deviations from laissez-faire yield outcomes that fall short of a particular notion of economic efficiency. A policymaker with commitments to reducing group (e.g., racial) inequalities or solving a particular social problem (e.g., illiteracy) may simply dislike the laissez-faire equilibrium. On that basis they might attempt to use political power to achieve an outcome (e.g., distribution of resources between groups) that they find more to their liking. Lavoie's arguments for laissez-faire rely on an overriding normative commitment to a specific efficiency criterion not shared by most actual leftists. Specifically, left-wing demands for resource redistribution to specific economic and racial groups, whether in the form of direct transfers or hidden agenda-type policymaking, were interpreted as a means to an end by Lavoie, but in fact constituted an end in search of a means for rising leftist elites like Obama.[20]

Third, Lavoie's observations *were* key to the development of a rising and successful radical left movement. Fisher, Lavoie, and Obama were right: shorn of their commitment to central planning both through understanding the theoretical proofs of why NEPs were infeasible and by its practical failure exemplified by the Soviet collapse, the US left would go on to achieve incredible success in the sociopolitical arena. The combination of markets and regulatory (rather than direct) control, for example, via civil rights law, has proven to be a powerful political formula for sustaining radical social transformations. Since the manuscripts were drafted, the left-of-center party in the United States would win a plurality of the popular vote in all but one presidential election, and would consolidate its advantages in the academy, mainstream and social media, nearly all major public corporations, and the federal government so as to make it nearly impossible for any employee of these organizations to publicly hold once widespread socially conservative views (Gottfried 1999; Kaufmann 2021). An insight that helped contribute to this state of affairs—that substantial levels of resource redistribution, social progress, and social control can be achieved without recourse to central planning—was absorbed by Obama by the time he completed his formal education.

NOTES

1. David Garrow generously shared the HLS manuscripts with me. Comments from N. Finkelstein, who drew my attention to the existence of the manuscripts, A. Hall, C. Coyne, S. Stein, R.M. Fisher, J. Yu, S. Hammond, D. Grazian, E. Norcross, W.J. Wilson, Markets and Society Conference participants, participants in the Race, Ethnicity, and Immigration Workshop, and the Bastiat Fellows are gratefully acknowledged. Errors in this chapter are my own.

2. I will not have much to say about (4). See Garrow (2017) for a description.

3. Learned from phone correspondence with Robert Fisher in 2021.

4. I defined families in the figure as a household including at least one male to reduce confounding by changes to family structure over this time period.

5. In fact, *The Audacity of Hope: Thoughts on Reclaiming the American Dream* has no explicit citations at all. Presidential campaign books are not typically generous in their citations to social scientists. Candidates prefer to avoid the potential controversy of citing authors who may have contentious ideas, even if the particular contentious ideas are not what is being borrowed from the author in question. Furthermore, there are usually only limited sanctions if any for borrowing without attribution in that domain. Thus, discerning academic influences on political campaign proposals is a task typically left to journalists and historians.

6. On the other hand, Obama (1988) favorably cites Wilson ([1987] 2012).

7. Obama's presentation suggests that Reverend Wright took Wilson as endorsing the 1970s transformation of the black community rather than as description of what was happening. This confusion of positive description and normative policy endorsement was apparently typical. Wilson ([1987] 2012, vii–x) *explicitly cited* these confused interpretations of Wilson ([1978] 2012) as a motivation for writing *The Truly Disadvantaged.*

8. A leaked copy of the original typescript of *Dreams from My Father* reveals that Reverend Wright was especially concerned that his secretary's son would be racially isolated and grow up with a lack of racial self-consciousness (Obama 1993).

9. Obama and Wilson had a brief exchange during the question-and-answer session which has not been recorded and which, in a 2020 email exchange, Wilson could not recall.

10. Shenk (2022b, chap. 8) comes to the same conclusion, writing that, "Citing Bayard Rustin, Wilson argued that a program built on 'race-neutral' reforms—including universal health care, full employment, and a system of national economic planning—could draw support from a multiracial coalition while addressing the problems of the ghetto underclass. It might not have been a coincidence, then, that Obama told his boss he was quitting on the same day the two of them attended a conference featuring a lecture from Wilson."

11. In a 2020 email exchange, Wilson maintained that he and Obama "had no direct contact" after 2004.

12. Thus, the meaning of the subtitle "What Is Left?" both refers to the abandonment of the aspirations that originally inspired planning (the subsuming of all individual plans into a single, central plan) from practical experience as well as the argument that, in fact, commitments to planning as an economic organizing principle were incompatible with the broader aims of the left.

13. In fact, Lavoie's ([1985] 2016, Appendix) interpretation of these advances in the philosophy of science is idiosyncratic, emphasizing a subjectivist view of knowledge.

14. Specifically, Lavoie ([1985] 2016, 212–222) claims that Marx and Engels (1848) and the leftist movements of the nineteenth century went wrong in uncritically incorporating the authoritarian ideas of Saint-Simon into their conception of socialism.

15. In NEPWIL (126) I count, Samuel Bowles, David Gordon, Thomas Weisskopf, Ronald Muller, Gar Alperovitz, Jeff Faux, Michael Harrington ([1962] 2012, chap. 2), Barry Bluestone, Robert Reich, Felix Rohatyn, Lane Kirkland, William Winpisinger, and Amitai Etzioni as motivated at least in part by the problems brought on by deindustrialization. Robert Lekachman (1966) expresses ambivalence about "structuralist" accounts emphasizing particular economic sectors, but wrote favorably in 1984 about Gar Alperowitz, and Jeff Faux's attempt to preserve particular manufacturing plants in Youngstown. Martin Carnoy, Derek Shearer, Raford Boddy, James Crotty, John Buell, Tom DeLuca, and Wassily Leontief evinced no opinion I could find on the subject prior to 1985. Tom Hayden (1982) appears skeptical of the value of industrialization and one might speculate was sanguine about deindustrialization.

16. Staley (1989) points out the same debate over what the null hypothesis should be occurs between Murray ([1984] 2008) and Wilson ([1987] 2012).

17. The vast majority of articles and scholarship on UCLS's influence on Obama refers back to precisely two individuals: Cass Sunstein and Austan Goolsbee. Sunstein modestly argues that Obama's experiences at UCLS gave him an "intellectual framework for his instincts . . . and probably made him come to appreciate markets more" (Leonhardt 2008). In the same article, Obama acknowledges an influence from U. Chicago, but does not explain in any detail what that influence was.

18. It is a matter of some controversy as to whether Schumpeter should be considered a member of the Austrian school of economics at all (Simpson 1983). Most importantly for genealogical purposes, Schumpeter disagreed with what would become the canonical Austrian position on the viability of socialist central planning (Lavoie [1985] 2016, 242n1).

19. For a complementary discussion of what this consensus entailed, see Lehto's (2022, 226) discussion of the "post-Hayekian minimal consensus on socialist calculation."

20. The manuscripts being a work in progress ensures that the authors voices occasionally clash. For instance, Fisher and Obama (1991c) self-identify on page 83 as Black and on page 79 as a leftist.

REFERENCES

Bluestone, Barry, and Bennett Harrison. 1982. *The Deindustrialization of America: Plant Closings, Community Abandonment, and the Dismantling of Basic Industry*. New York: Basic Books.

Boas, Taylor C., and Jordan Gans-Morse. 2009. "Neoliberalism: From New Liberal Philosophy to Anti-liberal Slogan." *Studies in Comparative International Development* 44 (2): 137–161.

Bowles, Samuel, David Gordon, and Thomas Weisskopf. 1983. *Beyond the Wasteland: A Democratic Alternative to Economic Decline*. New York: Anchor Books.

Burczak, Theodore. 1996. "Socialism after Hayek." *Rethinking Marxism* 9 (3): 1–18.

Caldwell, Bruce. 1997. "Hayek and Socialism." *Journal of Economic Literature* 35 (4): 1856–1890.

Fisher, Robert M. 1986. *The Logic of Economic Discovery: Neoclassical Economics and the Marginal Revolution*. New York: New York University Press.

Fisher, Robert and Obama, Barack. 1991a. "Outline–Transformative Politics." Unpublished Manuscript, March, PDF file, 1–10.

———. 1991b. "Plant Closings: Creative Destruction and the Viability of the Regulated Market." Unpublished Manuscript, March, PDF file, 1–103.

———. 1991c. "Race and Rights Rhetoric." Unpublished Manuscript, April, PDF file, 1–144.

Flood, Sarah, Miriam King, Renae Rodgers, Steven Ruggles, J. Robert Warren, and Michael Westberry. 2021. Integrated Public Use Microdata Series, Current Population Survey: Version 9.0 [dataset]. Minneapolis, MN: IPUMS.

Garrison, Howard H. 1979. "Gender Differences in the Career Aspirations of Recent Cohorts of High School Seniors." *Social Problems* 27 (2): 170–185.

Garrow, David. 2017. *Rising Star: The Making of Barack Obama*. New York: HarperCollins.

Gates, Henry Louis. 2009. "A Conversation with William Julius Wilson on the Election of Barack Obama." *Du Bois Review: Social Science Research on Race* 6 (1): 15–23.

Goldin, Claudia. 1998. "America's Graduation from High School: The Evolution and Spread of Secondary Schooling in the Twentieth Century." *The Journal of Economic History* 58 (2): 345–374.

Gottfried, Paul Edward. 1999. *After Liberalism*. Princeton, NJ: Princeton University Press.

Groeger, Cristina Viviana. 2021. *The Education Trap: Schools and the Remaking of Inequality in Boston*. Cambridge, MA: Harvard University Press.

Harrington, Michael. [1962] 2012. *The Other America*. New York: Scriber.

———. 1982. "A Path for America: Proposals from the Democratic Left." *Dissent* (Fall).

Hayden, Tom. 1982. *The American Future: New Visions Beyond the Reagan Administration*. New York: Washington Square Press.

Hayek, Friedrich August. 1935. *Collectivist Economic Planning: Critical Studies on the Possibilities of Socialism*. London: Routledge.

———. [1944] 2014. *The Road to Serfdom: Text and Documents: The Definitive Edition*. Chicago, IL: University of Chicago Press.

———. 1945. "The Use of Knowledge in Society." *The American Economic Review* 35(4): 519–530.

———. 1948. *Individualism and Economic Order*. Chicago, IL: University of Chicago Press.

Hurst, Erik., Yona Rubinstein, and Kazuatsu Shimizu. 2021. "Task-Based Discrimination." *NBER* Working Paper 29022.

Jargowsky, Paul A. 1997. *Poverty and Place: Ghettos, Barrios, and the American City*. New York: Russell Sage Foundation.

Kantor, Jodi. 2008. "Teaching Law, Testing Ideas, Obama Stood Slightly Apart." *The New York Times*, July 30.

Kaufmann, Eric. 2021. "Academic Freedom in Crisis: Punishment, Political Discrimination, and Self-Censorship." *Center for the Study of Partisanship and Ideology*. Report No. 2: 1–195.

Lakatos, Imre. 1976. *Proofs and Refutations*. Cambridge: Cambridge University Press.

———. 1970. "Falsification and the Methodology of Scientific Research Programmes." In *Criticism and the Growth of Knowledge*, edited by Lakatos Imre and Alan Musgrave, 91–195. Cambridge: Cambridge University Press.

Latzer, Barry. 2016. *The Rise and Fall of Violent Crime in America*. New York: Encounter Books.

Lavoie, Donald. [1985] 2016. *National Economic Planning: What Is Left?* Arlington, VA: Mercatus Center at George Mason University.

Lehto, Otto. 2022. "Complex Adaptation and Permissionless Innovation: An Evolutionary Approach to Universal Basic Income." PhD diss., King's College London.

Lekachman, R. 1966. "The Automation Report." *Commentary* 41 (5): 65–71.

———. 1984. "Blaming the Corporate Sector." *The New York Times*, May 20.

Leonhardt, D. 2008. "How Obama Reconciles Dueling Views on Economy." *The New York Times Magazine*, August 20.

Lindsey, Brink, Will Wilkinson, Steven Teles, and Samuel Hammond. 2018. "The Center Can Hold: Public Policy for an Age of Extremes." *Policy Essay*. Washington, DC: Niskanen Center.

Jaffé, William. 1976. "Menger, Jevons and Walras De-Homogenized." *Economic Inquiry* 14 (4): 511–524.

Jencks, Christopher. 1992. *Rethinking Social Policy: Race, Poverty, and the Underclass*. New York: HarperCollins.

Marx, Karl, and Friedrich Engels. 1848. *Manifesto of the Communist Party*.

Massey, Douglas and Denton, Nancy. 1993. *American Apartheid: Segregation and the Making of the Underclass*. Cambridge, MA: Harvard University Press.

McClelland, Edward. 2010. *Young Mr. Obama: Chicago and the Making of a Black President*. New York: Bloomsbury Publishing.

Minow, Martha. 1991. "Your Manuscript." Comments on an unpublished manuscript.

Mises, Ludwig von. [1920] 1935. "Economic Calculation in the Socialist Commonwealth." In *Collectivist Economic Planning*, edited by F. A. Hayek, 87–130. London: G. Routledge.

———. [1922] 1981. *Socialism: An Economic and Sociological Analysis*. Auburn, AL: Ludwig von Mises Institute.

———. [1962] 2012. *The Ultimate Foundation of Economic Science*. Carmel, IN: Liberty Fund.

Murray, Charles. [1984] 2008. *Losing Ground: American Social Policy, 1950–1980*. New York: Basic Books.

Obama, Barack. 1988. "Why Organize? Problems and Promise in the Inner City." *Illinois Issues* August/September: 35–40.

———. 2006. *The Audacity of Hope: Thoughts on Reclaiming the American Dream*. Edinburgh: Canongate Books.

———. [1995] 2007. *Dreams From My Father: A Story of Race and Inheritance*. Edinburgh: Canongate Books.
———. 1993. "Claims of Inheritance." Unpublished Manuscript, 1–566. https://aletheianyheter.files.wordpress.com/2016/07/claims-of-inheritance.pdf.
———. 2020. *A Promised Land*. New York: Crown.
Pattillo, Mary. [1999] 2013. *Black Picket Fences: Privilege and Peril Among the Black Middle Class*. Chicago, IL: University of Chicago Press.
Peters, Michael A. 2012. *Obama and the End of the American Dream: Essays in Political and Economic Philosophy*. Berlin: Springer Science & Business Media.
Peterson, P.E. 1991. "The Urban Underclass and the Poverty Paradox." *Political Science Quarterly* 106 (4): 617–638.
Popper, Karl R. 1972. *Objective Knowledge: An Evolutionary Approach*. Oxford: Oxford University Press.
Raymond, B. 2021. "City Uncertain: A Catalytic Vision for Urbanism in Youngstown, Ohio." *PhD diss*., University of Cincinnati.
Reed, Adolph Jr. 2000. "The Curse of Community." *Village Voice*, January 16, 1996, reproduced in Reed, *Class Notes: Posing as Politics and Other Thoughts on the American Scene* New York: New Press.
Rohatyn, Felix. 1983. *The Twenty-Year Century: Essays on Economics and Public Finance*. New York: Random House.
Shenk, Timothy. 2022a. "A Lost Manuscript Shows the Fire Barack Obama Couldn't Reveal on the Campaign Trail." *The New York Times*, October 7.
———. 2022b. *Realigners: Partisan Hacks, Political Visionaries, and the Struggle to Rule American Democracy*. New York: Farrar, Straus and Giroux.
Simpson, David. 1983. "Joseph Schumpeter and the Austrian School of Economics." *Journal of Economic Studies* 10 (4): 18–28.
Sugrue, Thomas J. 2010. *Not Even Past: Barack Obama and the Burden of Race*, Vol. 2. Princeton, NJ: Princeton University Press.
Staley, Sam. 1989. "The Truly Disadvantaged: The Inner City, the Underclass, and Public Policy." *Journal of Urban Affairs* 11 (3): 315–326.
Tyack, David B. 1974. *The One Best System: A History of American Urban Education*. Cambridge, MA: Harvard University Press.
Wacquant, Loïc. 2022. *The Invention of the 'Underclass': A Study in the Politics of Knowledge*. New York: John Wiley & Sons.
Wilson, William Julius. [1978] 2012. *The Declining Significance of Race: Blacks and Changing American Institutions*. Chicago, IL: University of Chicago Press.
———. [1987] 2012. *The Truly Disadvantaged: The Inner City, the Underclass, and Public Policy*. Chicago, IL: University of Chicago Press.
———. [1996] 2011. *When Work Disappears: The World of the New Urban Poor*. New York: Knopf Doubleday Publishing Group.
———. 2011. "Reflections on a Sociological Career that Integrates Social Science with Social Policy." *Annual Review of Sociology* 37(1): 1–18.

Index

About the Editors

Christopher J. Coyne, professor of economics, George Mason University; associate director, F. A. Hayek Program for Advanced Study in Philosophy, Politics, and Economics, Mercatus Center at George Mason University.

Abigail R. Hall, associate professor of economics at the University of Tampa.

Eileen Norcross, vice president of policy research and a senior research fellow at the Mercatus Center at George Mason University.

About the Contributors

Ximena Benavides, lecturer and postdoctoral associate in the Ethics, Politics & Economics Program of the Department of Political Science at Yale University; and fellow of the Information Society Project at Yale Law School.

Olivia Gonzalez, Ph.D. student in economics at George Mason University; economist at U.S. Small Business Administration.

Alexander Köhler, received an MA in international affairs from the Hertie School of Governance; policy advisor at Initiative D21.

Michael Lachanski, Ph.D. student in demography at the University of Pennsylvania.

Christian McGuire, received a J.D. at the University of Chicago.

Carlos Noyola, Ph.D. candidate in romance languages and literatures at the University of Notre Dame; received an MSc in economics from the University of Bristol.

Dallin Overstreet, Ph.D. student in public policy and administration at Arizona State University.

Natalia Pushkareva, Ph.D. student in global studies at the University of Urbino.

Thomas Storrs, Ph.D. student in history at the University of Virginia.

Arthur R. Wardle, Ph.D. student in agricultural and resource economics at the University of California, Berkeley.

www.ingramcontent.com/pod-product-compliance
Ingram Content Group UK Ltd.
Pitfield, Milton Keynes, MK11 3LW, UK
UKHW040858081026
15587UKWH00016B/756

9 781666 934137